T0214184

Lecture Notes in Computer Science   11761

More information about this series at http://www.springer.com/series/7408

Hossein Hojjat · Mieke Massink (Eds.)

Fundamentals of Software Engineering

8th International Conference, FSEN 2019
Tehran, Iran, May 1–3, 2019
Revised Selected Papers

 Springer

Editors
Hossein Hojjat ⓘ
Rochester Institute of Technology
Rochester, NY, USA

Mieke Massink ⓘ
CNR-ISTI
Pisa, Italy

ISSN 0302-9743   ISSN 1611-3349   (electronic)
Lecture Notes in Computer Science
ISBN 978-3-030-31516-0   ISBN 978-3-030-31517-7   (eBook)
https://doi.org/10.1007/978-3-030-31517-7

LNCS Sublibrary: SL2 – Programming and Software Engineering

This Springer imprint is published by the registered company Springer Nature Switzerland AG
The registered company address is: Gewerbestrasse 11, 6330 Cham, Switzerland

Preface

The increasing complexity of software and hardware systems and their ever more central role in society poses many challenges concerning their reliability, safety, correctness, and robustness. Based on a variety of fundamental concepts from theoretical computer science to formal methods techniques aimed at making a significant contribution to better quality systems. The development and use of formal methods aspire to mathematically sound methods and tools for system analysis and verification.

The present volume contains the post-proceedings of the 8th IPM International Conference on Fundamentals of Software Engineering (FSEN 2019), which was held in Tehran, Iran, during May 1–3, 2019. This two-yearly event is organized by the School of Computer Science at the Institute for Research in Fundamental Sciences (IPM) in Iran. The topics of interest in FSEN span over all aspects of formal methods, especially those related to advancing the application of formal methods in the software industry and promoting their integration with practical engineering techniques.

The Program Committee of FSEN 2019 consisted of 44 top researchers from 17 countries. In this edition of FSEN, 47 submissions were received from 19 countries. Each submission was reviewed by at least three independent referees, for its quality, originality, contribution, clarity of presentation, and its relevance to the conference topics. After thorough discussions on each individual paper, the referees selected 14 full papers and 3 short papers for inclusion in the present post-proceedings after a further review of their revised versions.

Many people contributed to making FSEN 2019 a success. First of all, we would like to thank all authors that submitted high-quality papers. Special thanks also go to the Institute for Research in Fundamental Sciences (IPM) in Tehran, Iran, for their financial support and for hosting FSEN 2019. We thank the distinguished keynote speakers for their excellent presentations: Rocco De Nicola, Giovanna Di Marzo Serugendo, and Martin Wirsing. We also thank the members of the Program Committee for their excellent contributions, making FSEN a high-quality international conference. Special thanks also go to the general chairs, Farhad Arbab and Hamid Sarbaziazad, and to the Steering Committee, in particular Marjan Sirjani, for their valuable support during all phases of the organization. We also thank the publicity chair Maurice ter Beek for the efficient publicity, the local organization chair Hamidreza Shahrabi and his wonderful team for their fantastic hospitality, as well as EasyChair and Springer for their facilities that greatly helped us run the review process and prepare the proceedings. Finally, we are indebted to all conference attendees for their active and lively participation, also through the presentation of more than 15 posters, ultimately contributing to the success of this special conference series.

July 2019

Hossein Hojjat
Mieke Massink

Organization

Conference Chairs

Hossein Hojjat   Rochester Institute of Technology, USA
Mieke Massink   CNR-ISTI, Italy

Publicity Chair

Maurice H. ter Beek   CNR-ISTI, Italy

Program Committee

Mohammad Abdollahi Azgomi	Iran University of Science and Technology, Iran
Erika Abraham	RWTH Aachen University, Germany
Gul Agha	University of Illinois at Urbana-Champaign, USA
Christel Baier	Technical University Dresden, Germany
Ezio Bartocci	Vienna University of Technology, Austria
Marcello Bonsangue	University of Leiden, The Netherlands
Mario Bravetti	University of Bologna, Italy
Michael Butler	University of Southampton, UK
Alessandra Di Pierro	University of Verona, Italy
Ali Ebnenasir	Michigan Technological University, USA
Wan Fokkink	Vrije Universiteit Amsterdam, The Netherlands
Adrian Francalanza	University of Malta, Malta
Masahiro Fujita	University of Tokyo, Japan
Maurizio Gabbrielli	University of Bologna, Italy
Fatemeh Ghassemi	University of Tehran, Iran
Jan Friso Groote	Eindhoven University of Technology, The Netherlands
Hassan Haghighi	Shahid Beheshti University, Iran
Philipp Haller	KTH Royal Institute of Technology, Sweden
Hossein Hojjat	Rochester Institute of Technology, USA
Mohammad Izadi	Sharif University of Technology, Iran
Narges Khakpour	Linnaeus University, Sweden
Ramtin Khosravi	University of Tehran, Iran
Natallia Kokash	IT Consultant NK Research, The Netherlands
Eva Kühn	Vienna University of Technology, Austria
Kim Gulstrand Larsen	Aalborg University, Denmark
Zhiming Liu	Southwest University, China
Mieke Massink	CNR-ISTI, Italy
Emanuela Merelli	University of Camerino, Italy

Hassan Mirian-Hosseinabadi	Sharif University of Technology, Iran
Ugo Montanari	University of Pisa, Italy
Peter Mosses	Swansea University, UK
Mohammadreza Mousavi	University of Leicester, UK
Ali Movaghar	Sharif University of Technology, Iran
Magnus O. Myreen	Chalmers University of Technology, Sweden
Shiva Nejati	University of Luxemburg, Luxemburg
Jose Proença	CISTER-ISEP and HASLab-INESC TEC, Portugal
Wolfgang Reisig	Humboldt-Universitaet zu Berlin, Germany
Philipp Rümmer	Uppsala University, Sweden
Gwen Salaün	University of Grenoble Alpes, France
Cristina Seceleanu	Mälardalen University, Sweden
Marjan Sirjani	Mälardalen University, Sweden, and Reykjavík University, Iceland
Marielle Stoelinga	University of Twente, The Netherlands
Meng Sun	Peking University, China
Carolyn Talcott	SRI International, USA
Erik de Vink	Eindhoven University of Technology, The Netherlands
Peter Ölveczky	University of Oslo, Norway

Steering Committee

Farhad Arbab	CWI and Leiden University, The Netherlands
Christel Baier	Technical University Dresden, Germany
Frank de Boer	CWI and Leiden University, The Netherlands
Ali Movaghar	Sharif University of Technology, Iran
Hamid Sarbazi-azad	IPM and Sharif University of Technology, Iran
Marjan Sirjani (Chair)	Mälardalen University, Sweden, and Reykjavík University, Iceland
Jan Rutten	CWI and Free University Amsterdam, The Netherlands

Additional Reviewers

Hugo Araujo
Giovanni Bacci
Maryam Bagheri
Shirin Baghoolizadeh
Paolo Baldan
Frederik M. Bønneland
Mohammadsadegh Dalvandi
Carlos Diego Damasceno
Eduard Enoiu
Predrag Filipovikj
Herman Geuvers
Stefania Gnesi

Ali Jafari
Sung-Shik Jongmans
Sebastian Junges
Saeed Khalafinejad
Ajay Krishna
Alfons Laarman
Ivan Lanese
Tong Liu
Alberto Lluch Lafuente
Florian Lorber
Raluca Marinescu
Chiara Muzi
Muhammad Nakhaee

Thomas Neele
Ali Nosrati
Tope Omitola
Marco Piangerelli
Elisa Quintarelli
Mehran Rivadeh
Ali Sedaghatbaf
Mahsa Varshosaz
Kim Völlinger
Stefano Pio Zingaro
Johannes Åman Pohjola

Contents

Agent Based Systems

A Formal Model to Integrate Behavioral and Structural Adaptations in Self-adaptive Systems

Narges Khakpour[1(✉)], Jetty Kleijn[2], and Marjan Sirjani[3]

[1] Linnaeus University, Växjö, Sweden
narges.khakpour@lnu.se
[2] LIACS, Leiden University, Leiden, The Netherlands
[3] Mälardalens Högskola, Sweden and Reykjavik University, Västerås, Sweden

Abstract. An approach for modelling adaptive complex systems should be flexible and scalable to allow a system to grow easily, and should have a formal foundation to guarantee the correctness of the system behavior. In this paper, we present the architecture, and formal syntax and semantics of HPobSAM which is a model for specifying behavioral and structural adaptations to model large-scale systems and address reusability concerns. Self-adaptive modules are used as the building blocks to structure a system, and policies are used as the mechanism to perform both behavioral and structural adaptations. While a self-adaptive module is autonomous to achieve its local goals by collaborating with other self-adaptive modules, it is controlled by a higher-level entity to prevent undesirable behavior. HPobSAM is formalized using a combination of algebraic, graph transformation-based and actor-based formalisms.

1 Introduction

The growth and adaptation of a system is realized by behavioral adaptation and/or structural adaptation. While structural adaptation aims to adapt the system behavior by changing its architecture, behavioral adaptation focuses on modifying the functionalities of computational entities. Behavioral adaptation is usually suitable for the cases that minor changes are required to adapt the system. Structural adaptation is more scalable and suitable for large-scale and distributed adaptations. Yet changing the system structure to achieve minor changes is rather expensive. Hence, both behavioral and structural adaptations are often required to design complex adaptive systems.

A system must be able to evolve and grow continually even in unforeseen situations. Since an adaptation requirement might be unknown at design time, adaptive behavior must be built in a way that is *flexible* and *modifiable* at runtime. Furthermore, to guarantee the functionality of a complex software system, we have to provide mechanisms to ensure that the system is operating correctly. Here formal methods can play a key role.

© IFIP International Federation for Information Processing 2019
Published by Springer Nature Switzerland AG 2019
H. Hojjat and M. Massink (Eds.): FSEN 2019, LNCS 11761, pp. 3–19, 2019.
https://doi.org/10.1007/978-3-030-31517-7_1

Several frameworks and models have been inspired by natural systems to design large-scale adaptive systems [5,22,26,27]. Although, they support self-organization, self-adaptability and long-lasting evolvability, they are not provided with a formal foundation. Moreover, specification and analysis of dynamic adaptation have been given lots of attention in the last decade [1,2,8,14,19,20,25] where most of the approaches deal with either behavioral adaptation or structural adaptation [6,7]. However, dynamic adaptation and self-* properties are restricted to responding to short-term changes, while systems must be additionally able to evolve and grow to cover the long-term evolution of systems [9]. Therefore, we need an approach to design complex software systems which supports behavioral and structural adaptations to tackle the long-term evolution, flexibility, complexity, scalability and assurance problems.

The use of policies has been given attention as a powerful mechanism to achieve flexibility in adaptive and autonomous systems which allows one to "*dynamically*" specify the requirements in terms of high level goals. A policy is a rule describing under which conditions a specified subject must (can or cannot) perform an action on a specific object [15]. PobSAM (Policy-based Self-Adaptive Model) is a policy-based model with formal foundation for developing and modeling self-adaptive systems that supports *behavioral adaptation*. A PobSAM model consists of a set of managers and actors. Managers control the behavior of actors by enforcing policies. This model provides a high degree of flexibility at the behavioral level by allowing one to change policies dynamically. However, it only supports behavioral adaptation.

In this paper, we consider an extension of PobSAM [14,15], called HPobSAM (Hierarchical PobSAM) to support modeling large-scale adaptive systems. In HPobSAM, *self-adaptive modules* have been added to PobSAM as a structuring feature. A self-adaptive module consists of managers, actors and possibly other self-adaptive modules. The notion of a *role* is introduced to specify structure-independent adaptations. Roles are dynamically assigned to self-adaptive modules and actors. Structural adaptation occurs by changing the roles of entities which leads to creation, removal or changing the interactions of entities. The managers are responsible to perform structural adaptations using *structural adaptation policies* that are defined in terms of roles.

HPobSAM is used in [13] to model a case study in the area of smart airports. In [13], we refer to an unpublished technical report for a complete description of HPobSAM. Here we present the description, architecture, and formal syntax and semantics of HPobSAM. We use prioritized hierarchical hypergraph (hh-graph) transition systems to specify the operational semantics of HPobSAM. Prioritized hh-graph transition systems are essentially classical prioritized state transition systems augmented with a function mapping states into hh-graphs and transitions into partial morphisms, i.e. a state is provided with a hh-graph indicating the current system structure.

Formal methods have been proposed for the modeling and analysis of adaptive software systems, but they are not always suitable for designing large-scale software systems. We propose a flexible policy-based approach with formal foundation to design large-scale software systems. Compared to existing work, our approach has the following novel features:

1. We present a formal extension of PobSAM to model large-scale systems that is flexible and supports both structural and behavioral adaptations. We use structural adaptation policies as a mechanism for performing structural adaptation that can be modified at runtime, without the need to change the low-level programs.
2. We present an operational semantics for HPobSAM whose semantics rules allow us to transform a substructure that is specified only partially, i.e. we can add or remove a self-adaptive module whose internal structure is not known completely. This feature is an advantage in open systems where limited knowledge is available about the entities.

2 Case Study

Here, we introduce the running example of the paper shown in Fig. 1. Consider a service-based system that dynamically adapts its behavior to provide an appropriate quality of service to clients. The system includes several clusters of application servers that require data provided by the data servers. The *cache handler* is used to determine the best cluster for handling a request considering the quality of service constraints, and the *logger* monitors the incoming requests. The *request receiver* analyzes the requests and transmits them to the *request dispatcher* of the proper cluster. The latter forwards the request to an application server in the cluster. When a request is processed, the result is sent back to the *request receiver* component. This component sends the result back to the requester and/or to the *cache handler*.

The system should be able to adapt its behavior to provide the requested service properly. The behavioral adaptation is done by dynamically balancing the load of clusters/servers and can be effective to some extent. However, if the load of system becomes high enough such that the current number of servers cannot handle the requests, structural adaptations come into play. We need to adapt the system structure by adding or replacing the clusters to improve the system throughput.

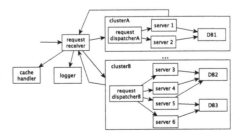

Fig. 1. The architecture of server clusters.

3   Overview of PobSAM

A PobSAM model is composed of three layers [14, 15]:

- The functional behavior of the system is implemented by the *actor layer* and contains computational entities, i.e., the actors.
- The *view layer* consists of view variables that provide an abstraction of the actors' states for the managers. A view variable is an actual state variable, or a function applied to state variables of actors.
- The main layer of PobSAM is the *manager layer* containing the autonomous managers. Managers control the behavior of actors according to predefined policies. A manager may have different configurations of which one is active at a time. Behavioral adaptation is performed by switching among those configurations. A configuration contains two classes of policies: governing policies and behavioral adaptation policies. A manager directs the actors' behavior by sending messages to them according to the governing policies. A governing policy is of the form $\langle o, e, \psi \rangle \bullet a$ where $o \in \mathbb{N}$ is the policy priority, $e \in \mathcal{E}$ is an event, ψ is the policy condition defined over views, and a is the policy action. Whenever a manager receives an event e it identifies all the governing policies that are triggered by that event. For each of the triggered policies, if the policy condition evaluates to true and there is no other triggered governing policy with priority higher than o, action a is requested to be executed by instructing the relevant actors to do so (by sending them asynchronous messages). The behavioral adaptation policies are used to perform behavioral adaptations by switching among different configurations.

Example 1. We model the request dispatcher of a cluster as a manager that is responsible to manage and control the behavior of the cluster. This manager has two configurations `lowConf` and `highConf` to control the cluster behavior respectively, in low-loaded and high-loaded conditions. The servers are modeled as the actors responsible for handling incoming requests. The view layer provides some information about the processing power of each server, their current loads, the whole throughput of the cluster, and the average number of handled requests by each server. The following governing policy of `lowConf` with priority n defined for the request dispatcher of the cluster A states that when a new request x is received and the load of `server1` is less than l, ask `server1` to handle the request: $g = \langle n, \mathsf{newreq}(x), \mathsf{load1} < l \rangle \bullet (\mathsf{server1.handle}(x))$.

4   The Architecture of HPobSAM

The components of a HPobSAM model are (i) self-adaptive modules, (ii) actors, (iii) the multi-level view layer, (iv) managers, and (v) roles. A system at the highest level is defined as a self-adaptive module. Figure 2 gives a schematic view of the HPobSAM architecture.

The concept of self-adaptive modules is inspired by SMC (Self-Managed Cells) [24] for structuring complex adaptive systems. A Self-Adaptive Module

(SAM) is a policy-based building block which is able to automatically adapt its behavior in a complex dynamic environment. A self-adaptive module contains (i) possibly other lower-level self-adaptive modules, (ii) the actors, (iii) a view layer, and (iv) a manager. To cater for large-scale systems, multiple self-adaptive modules are composed and aggregated hierarchically into a single larger self-adaptive module. A self-adaptive module may provide services to other self-adaptive modules. Note that the services are provided and used by the manager of a self-adaptive module.

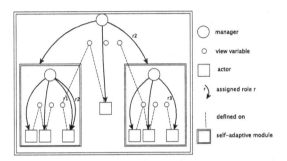

Fig. 2. A typical self-adaptive module.

A manager is aware of its substructure and is responsible for performing structural and behavioral adaptations of its module. The managers are provided with a new type of policies, so-called structural adaptation policies to perform structural adaptation. When the system requires adaptation, different managers are informed and they plan various adaptations to adapt the system behavior to the current context. Hence, adaptation is performed in a *distributed* manner in the system and not a single entity is responsible for performing an adaptation.

In PobSAM, the view layer provides information about the actor layer to the managers. In HPobSAM, a view layer exists at multiple levels. Each self-adaptive module has a view layer defined based on the view layers of its self-adaptive modules in addition to the actors' state variables of that module. The view layer acts as a tuple space to coordinate interactions of self-adaptive modules and a self-adaptive module can have controlled access to the view layer of other self-adaptive modules.

The structure of a system can change due to adding or removing an actor or a self-adaptive module, and modifying the actors and/or the self-adaptive modules interconnections. If the policies of a manager are described in terms of individual actors or self-adaptive modules, any modification of the manager's underlying substructure (i.e. by joining or deleting actors or self-adaptive modules) influences the specification of its policies and the view layer, and subsequently, policies and view variables have to be redefined to become consistent with the new structure. To tackle this problem of structure-dependent policies, we use the notion of *roles* to refer to the agents with the same functionality. The roles are assigned by a manager to the actors and the self-adaptive modules that it controls, and managers' policies as well as view variables are described in terms of roles. A structural reconfiguration is realized by changing the roles assigned to the entities, and hence, the managers' policies become structure-independent and do not have to be modified after a structural reconfiguration.

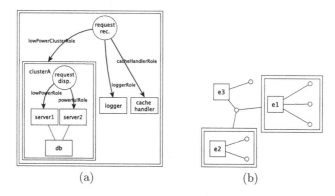

(a)   (b)

Fig. 3. (a) HPobSAM architecture of running example; (b) a hierarchical hypergraph.

Example 2. Figure 3(a) partially shows the HPobSAM architecture of our example. The whole system is a self-adaptive module that contains (i) several lower-level self-adaptive modules each corresponding to a cluster, (ii) a manager modeling the request receiver, and (iii) two actors for the cache handler and the logger. The roles lowPowerClusterRole, loggerR, and cacheHandlerRole are assigned by the request receiver to the cluster A (as a low-power cluster), the logger, and the cache handler, respectively.

5   The Syntax of HPobSAM

In this section, we first briefly introduce hierarchical hypergraphs that are used to model the system structure; then we specify the structural modeling of HPob-SAM; and,finally, we give the syntax of HPobSAM.

5.1   Hierarchical Hypergraphs Overview

A hypergraph is a generalization of a graph, where an edge can connect any number of nodes.

Definition 1 (Hypergraph). *A hypergraph is a tuple $G = (N, E, \theta)$, where N is the set of nodes, E is the set of hyperedges, $\theta : E \to N^*$ is the tentacle function mapping each hyperedge to a unique finite non-empty multiset of nodes.*[1]

Given two hypergraphs G_1 and G_2 with $G_i = (N_i, E_i, \theta_i)$ for $i = 1, 2$, a hypergraph morphism $m : G_1 \to G_2$ is a pair of mappings $m = (m_N, m_E)$ with $m_N : N_1 \to N_2$ and $m_E : E_1 \to E_2$, such that for all $e \in E_1$, the multiset defined by $\theta_2(m_E(e))$ is the multiset defined by $m_N(\theta_1(e))$.[2]

Such a morphism is injective (surjective, bijective) if both m_N and m_E are injective (respectively surjective, bijective, partial or total). If there is a bijective morphism $m : G_2 \to G_1$, then G_1 and G_2 are isomorphic.

Hierarchical hypergraphs [10] are hypergraphs in which some hyperedges, called *frames*, may refer to hypergraphs that can be hierarchical again, with an arbitrary but finite depth of nesting.

Definition 2 (Hierarchical Hypergraph). *Let $\mathcal{X}$ be a set of symbols called variables. Let $\mathcal{H} = \mathcal{H}_0(\mathcal{X})$ be a set of triples $H = \langle G, F, cts \rangle$ where G is a hypergraph, $F = \emptyset$, and cts the trivial function from F to $\mathcal{X}$.*

For $i > 0$, $\mathcal{H}_i(\mathcal{X})$ consists of all triples $H = \langle G, F, cts \rangle$ where $G = (N, E, \theta)$ is a hypergraph, $F \subseteq E$ is the set of frame hyperedges of G, and $cts : F \to \mathcal{H}_{i-1}(\mathcal{X}) \cup \mathcal{X}$ assigns to each frame its content.

The class $\mathcal{H}(\mathcal{X}) = \bigcup_{i \geq 0} \mathcal{H}_i(\mathcal{X})$ is the set of hierarchical hypergraphs (hhgraphs) derived from $\mathcal{H}$ with variables in $\mathcal{X}$.

Example 3. Figure 3(b) shows a hh-graph which has hyperedges $\{e_1, e_2, e_3\}$, seven nodes depicted by circles, and two frames depicted using double-lined rectangles.

The concept of a graph morphism can be generalized to the hierarchical case [10]. Let $\mathcal{X}$ be a set of variables. For $i = \{1, 2\}$, let $H_i = \langle G_i, F_i, cts_i \rangle$ be two hypergraphs with variables in $\mathcal{X}$, and let X_i denote the set $\{f \in F_i \mid cts_i(f) \in \mathcal{X}\}$ of *variable (or primitive) frames* of H_i.

Definition 3 (Hierarchical Morphism). *A hierarchical morphism m from H_1 to H_2 is a pair $m = (\bar{m}, m^f)$ where $f \in F_1 \backslash X_1$ and*
(i) $\bar{m} : G_1 \to G_2$ is a graph morphism;
(ii) for all frames $f \in F_1$, $\bar{m}_E(f) \in F_2$, and if $\bar{m}_E(f) \in X_2$ then $f \in X_1$;
(iii) $m^f : cts_1(f) \to cts_2(\bar{m}_E(f))$ is a hierarchical morphism for all $f \in F_1 \backslash X_1$.

A hierarchical morphism is injective (surjective, bijective, partial or total) if both $\bar{m}$ and m^f are injective (respectively surjective, bijective, partial or total).

---

[1] Note that we choose to represent multisets as elements of N^*, i.e. strings of occurrences of elements from N. Thus, e.g., the string *bab* represents the multiset $\{a, b, b\}$ as do *abb* and *bba*. Moreover, for every hyperedge e the string $\theta(e)$ is not empty; and for every hyperedge $e' \neq e$, the multisets represented by $\theta(e)$ and $\theta(e')$ are not the same.

[2] Note that the application of m_N to the string $\theta_1(e)$ yields a string in N_2^*.

With graph constraints, certain graph properties can be expressed. In particular, it can be formulated that a graph G must (or must not) contain a certain subgraph G'. An atomic graph constraint ($\mathsf{gcons}(C, C')$) informally states that if a graph G contains the sub-graph C (premise), then it contains the sub-graph C' (conclusion) too [11].

Definition 4 (Atomic Graph Constraint). *Let C and C' be two graphs. An atomic graph constraint is specified as a graph morphism $k : C \to C'$.*

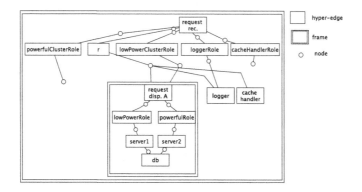

Fig. 4. Part of the hierarchical hypergraph model of our example.

A graph G satisfies atomic graph constraint $\mathsf{gcons}(C, C')$ specified by the graph morphism $k : C \to C'$. if, for every injective graph morphism $p : C \to G$, there exists an injective graph morphism $q : C' \to G$ with $q \circ k = p$. A graph constraint is a boolean formula over atomic graph constraints: (i) True and every atomic graph constraint are graph constraints, and (ii) if c and c' are two graph constraints, then $c \vee c'$, $c \wedge c'$ and $\neg c$ are graph constraints.

5.2   HPobSAM Syntax

Structural Modeling. The system structure is modeled as a hh-graph. We model role assignments as nodes, self-adaptive modules as frames, and managers, actors and roles as hyperedges. The hh-graph $H = (G, \mathcal{K}, cts)$ describes how several elements of a self-adaptive module κ are connected together logically. The set of self-adaptive modules of κ is given by $\mathcal{K}$, and cts gives their internal structure. The hypergraph G shows the first-level internal structure of κ defined as follows:

$$G = (N, E, \theta) \,, \; E = \{m\} \cup A \cup R \cup \mathcal{K}$$

where m is the manager of κ, A indicates the set of κ's actors, and R indicates the set of roles assigned by m.

Example 4. Figure 4 partially depicts the hh-graph of our example.

Views. A self-adaptive module κ has its own view layer V consisting of view variables defined over the state variables of its (immediate) actors (A) and the view variables of its (immediate) self-adaptive modules ($\mathcal{K}$), i.e., a view variable $v \in V$ is a function over V, $\mathcal{K}$, and the state variables of the actors in A.

Managers. A manager m is defined as a tuple $m = \langle C, c_0, \kappa, V, H \rangle$, with C the (finite) set of configurations of m, $c_0 \in C$ its initial configuration, κ the self-adaptive module of which m is the manager, V the (finite) set of view variables of κ, and the hierarchical hypergraph $H = (G, \mathcal{K}, cts)$ describes how m is logically connected to other agents.

A configuration $c \in C$ is defined as $c = \langle P_G, P_B, P_S \rangle$, where P_G, P_B and P_S indicate the governing policy set, the behavioral adaptation policies set, and the structural adaptation policy set of c, respectively. A primitive action of a governing policy is of the form r.msg and is intended to send the message msg to some actors/self-adaptive modules with role r. The behavioral adaptation policies are not influenced by this extension (See Sect. 3).

A structural adaptation policy $sp \in P_S$ is defined as $sp = \langle o, e, \psi_H \rangle \bullet a_H$ consists of priority $o \in \mathbb{N}$, event e, condition ψ_H and an action a_H. The condition ψ_H can be defined as a combination of ordinary boolean expressions defined over the view layer and graph constraints defined over H, the internal structure of κ. Let as be an actor or a self-adaptive module. The action a_H is a strategy to apply a dynamic reconfiguration with the primitive actions of the forms

- r.msg to send the message msg to the agents with role $r \in R$,
- join(r, as) for assigning role r to as,
- quit(r, as) for releasing as from role r,
- add(as) for adding as to the substructure of m, and
- remove(as) for removing as from the substructure of m.

The condition ψ_H of a structural adaptation policy is defined as follows where gcons(Y, Y') is an atomic graph constraint:

$$\psi_H = (\exists r \in R).\psi_H \mid (\forall r \in R).\psi_H \mid \psi_H \wedge \psi_H' \mid \neg\psi_H \mid \mathsf{gcons}(Y, Y')$$

Example 5. The policy PolicyA states that when the request load is high, the cache handler is activated, i.e. the role cacheHandlerRole is assigned to the cache handler by executing the action join(cacheHandlerRole, cachehandler). Then, the logger is deactivated (quit(loggerRole, logger)) and a new cluster with powerful servers (clusterD) is added to the system. The operators ; and || are resp. the sequential and parallel composition of the algebra CA^a that is used to specify policy actions (See [15]):

PolicyA = $\langle 1,$ onhighload, $\top \rangle \bullet$ (join(cacheHandlerRole, cachehandler);
  quit(loggerRole, logger))||(add(clusterD) ; join(powerfuleClusterRole, clusterD))

Self-adaptive Modules. A self-adaptive module κ is formally defined as $\kappa = \langle V, H_\kappa \rangle$ where V and H_κ respectively represent the view layer and the hh-graph of κ. Observe that H_κ is a hyperedge with the content H as defined above.

6   Structural Operational Semantics

We present prioritized hh-graph transition systems to define the operational semantics of HPobSAM models. Prioritized hh-graph transition systems are essentially prioritized state transition systems [15] augmented with a function mapping states into hierarchical hypergraphs and transitions into partial hierarchical morphisms. Thus every state is provided with a graph indicating the current system structure.

Definition 5. (Prioritized State Transition System). *A prioritized state transition system is a tuple $T = \langle S, \delta, L, s_0 \rangle$ where S is a set of states, $s_0 \in S$ is the initial state, L is a set of labels, and $\delta \subseteq S \times L \times S$ is a set of transitions.*

Labels $l \in L$ are of the form (ϕ, α, n) and a transition $s \xrightarrow{(\phi, \alpha, n)} s'$ means that it is possible to perform action α under condition ϕ in state s when there is no enabled transition with higher priority than n in state s, and then make a transition to s'.

Definition 6. (Prioritized hh-Graph Transition System). *A prioritized hh-graph transition system is given by a pair $\langle T, g \rangle$, where T is a prioritized state transition system and g is a pair $g = \langle g_1, g_2 \rangle$ of mappings such that $g_1(s)$ is a hh-graph for each state $s \in S$, and $g_2(t) : g_1(s) \rightarrow g_1(s')$ is an injective partial hierarchical morphism for each transition $t : s \xrightarrow{l} s' \in \delta$.*

The conditions of a transition $t : s \xrightarrow{l} s' \in \delta$ can contain graph constraints that are to be evaluated over $g_1(s)$. The semantics of the actor layer remains unchanged by this extension. The semantics of the view layer is similarly defined as that of PobSAM [14,15]. In this paper, we restrict ourselves to introduce the semantics of managers as the core part of HPobSAM.

Overview of a Manager's Semantics. We use the notation $[M]^c \langle b, p, a, q, H \rangle$ to describe a manager M where $c = \langle P_G, P_B, P_S \rangle$ is its current configuration, $b \in P_B$ is its triggered behavioral adaptation policy, $p \subseteq P_G \cup P_S$ is its set of triggered governing/structural adaptation policies, a is its current executing action (that can belong to a governing policy or a structural adaptation), q is its input message queue, and H is a hh-graph denoting the substructure of M. The semantics of triggering structural policies is identical to that of governing policies presented in [15]. Hence, we focus on their enforcement and use the notation $M \langle p, a, q, H \rangle$ for the sake of simplicity. The notation $\sqrt{}$ is used to show an empty action. The operational semantics of managers in HPobSAM is described by the transition rules for PobSAM proposed in [15] and the transition rules given in Figs. 5 and 7 which we explain later. The conditions of transitions specifying managers' semantics (e.g. ϕ in Fig. 5) are evaluated on M's view and its substructure.

The Semantics of a Manager's Interactions is presented in Fig. 5 that contains graph constraints presented in Fig. 6. The rules description and the definition of symbols are described in the following. A primitive action of a PobSAM manager is sending an asynchronous message msg to an actor a that results in putting the message msg in a's queue. In HPobSAM, there are three types of interactions that a manager may initiate: (i) sending a message to an actor with the role r, (ii) sending a message to a lower-level self-adaptive module with the role r, and (iii) sending a message to the sibling self-adaptive modules with the role r. The operational semantics of case (i) is expressed using the rule MSR1 where G_1 is a graph depicted in Fig. 6(a), $\mathsf{gcons}(\emptyset, G_1)$ is a graph constraint that holds if the actor a has the role r, and s_a and s_a' indicate the local states of a before and after receiving the message msg. The rule MSR2 expresses the semantics of case (ii). In this rule, a message is sent to a lower-level self-adaptive module κ' with the role r that contains a manager M_2. The graph G_2 is defined in Fig. 6(b). The manager M_1 in the self-adaptive module κ has assigned the role r to its sibling self-adaptive module κ' that contains the manager M_2. The manager M_1 uses the rule MSR3 to send a message to M_2 (case (iii)) where $\mathsf{gcons}(\emptyset, G_3)$ is a graph constraint with graph G_3 as defined in Fig. 6(c) and $H_{\kappa'} \cup H_\kappa$ is the union of $H_{\kappa'}$ and H_κ.

$$\text{MSR1} \quad \frac{M\langle p, \mathsf{r.msg}, q, H\rangle \xrightarrow{(\top, r.\mathsf{msg}, n)} M\langle p, \sqrt{}, q, H\rangle \qquad H \vDash \mathsf{gcons}(\emptyset, G_1)}{s_a \xrightarrow{(\top, r.\mathsf{msg}, n)} s_a'}$$

$$\text{MSR2} \quad \frac{M_1\langle p, \mathsf{r.msg}, q, H\rangle \xrightarrow{(\top, r.\mathsf{msg}, n)} M_1\langle p, \sqrt{}, q, H\rangle \qquad H \vDash \mathsf{gcons}(\emptyset, G_2)}{M_2\langle p', a', q', H'\rangle \xrightarrow{(\top, \ r.\mathsf{msg} \ , \ n)} M_2\langle p', a', q' : \mathsf{msg}, H'\rangle}$$

$$\text{MSR3} \quad \frac{M_1\langle p, \mathsf{r.msg}, q, H\rangle \xrightarrow{(\top, r.\mathsf{msg}, n)} M_1\langle p, \sqrt{}, q, H\rangle \qquad H_{\kappa'} \cup H_\kappa \vDash \mathsf{gcons}(\emptyset, G_3)}{M_2\langle p', a', q', H'\rangle \xrightarrow{(\top, \ r.\mathsf{msg} \ , \ n)} M_2\langle p', a', q' : \mathsf{msg}, H'\rangle}$$

Fig. 5. The rules for managers' interactions.

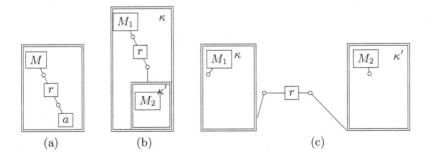

(a)   (b)   (c)

Fig. 6. The graph constraints of interactions semantics.

The Semantics of Structural Adaptation is presented in Fig. 7. In this figure, a function $f' = f|\{(e_1, v_1), \ldots, (e_2, v_n)\}$ is defined as $f'(x) = \begin{cases} v_k & x = e_k \\ f(x) & - \end{cases}$. The predicate $\mathsf{conn}(e, n, e') = n \in \theta(e) \cap \theta(e')$ informally states that the hyperedges e and e' are connected through the node n in a hypergraph G. The underlying substructure of M before and after a reconfiguration is respectively H and H' where $H = \langle G, F, cts \rangle$, $G = (N, E, \theta)$, and $H' = \langle G', F', cts' \rangle$, $G' = (N', E', \theta')$. Note that for the sake of readability, only updated components of H are given in the rules.

$$(\text{AAR}) \quad \frac{\mathsf{conn}(M, n_1, \iota), n_2 \in \theta(\iota)\backslash\{n_1\}, \theta' = \theta|\{(as, \{n_2\})\}, as \notin E, E' = E \cup \{as\}}{M\langle p, \mathsf{add}(as), q, H\rangle \xrightarrow{(\top, \mathsf{add}(as), 1)} M\langle p, \sqrt{}, q, H'\rangle}$$

$$(\text{RAR}) \quad \frac{\mathsf{conn}(M, n_1, r), \mathsf{conn}(r, n_2, as), E' = E\backslash\{as\}, E' \neq \emptyset}{M\langle p, \mathsf{remove}(as), q, H\rangle \xrightarrow{(\top, \mathsf{remove}(as), 1)} M\langle p, \sqrt{}, q, H'\rangle}$$

$$(\text{JAR}) \quad \frac{\mathsf{conn}(M, n_1, r), as \in E, n_2 \in \theta(r)\backslash n_1, \theta' = \theta|\{(as, \theta(as) \cup \{n_2\})\}}{M\langle p, \mathsf{join}(r, as), q, H\rangle \xrightarrow{(\top, \mathsf{join}(r, as), 1)} M\langle p, \sqrt{}, q, H'\rangle}$$

$$(\text{QAR}) \quad \frac{\mathsf{conn}(M, n_1, r), \mathsf{conn}(r, n_2, as), r \neq \iota, \theta' = \theta|\{(as, \theta(as)\backslash\{n_2\})\}}{M\langle p, \mathsf{quit}(r, as), q, H\rangle \xrightarrow{(\top, \mathsf{quit}(r, as), 1)} M\langle p, \sqrt{}, q, H'\rangle}$$

Fig. 7. The rules for structural adaptation.

When the action $\mathsf{add}(as)$ is executed by the manager M, the actor or the self-adaptive module as is added to its underlying structure (Rule AAR). The hyperedge as is added to the hyperedge set ($E' = E \cup \{as\}$), and it becomes connected to the predefined role ι through the node n_2. If as is associated to a hh-graph with the content G_{as} ($\mathsf{hhyper}(as, G_{as})$), it is added to the frame set ($F' = F \cup \{as\}$) and cts is updated to reflect the content of as. The rule RAR is used to remove an actor or a self-adaptive module as ($E' = E\backslash\{as\}$). If as is a self-adaptive module, it is removed from the frame set ($F' = F\backslash\{as\}$) and cts is updated correspondingly.

The rule JAR is used to assign the role r to as. This rule adds the node n_2 to the set of nodes connecting by the hyperedge as ($\theta' = \theta|\{(as, \theta(as) \cup \{n_2\})\}$). Similarly, execution of the primitive action $\mathsf{quit}(r, as)$ results in quitting as from the role r using the rule QAR. In this rule, as is connected to r through the node n_2 and this connection is removed by eliminating n_2 from the nodes connected by as, i.e., ($\theta'(as) = \theta(as)\backslash\{n_2\}$). If an actor or a self-adaptive module quits from all of its roles, since it has the predefined role ι, will remain as an underlying actor of the manager m.

Example 6. Let Fig. 4 show the current structure of our example. Figure 8(a) illustrates the structure after the execution of $\mathsf{add}(\mathsf{clusterD})$ in Example 5 that assigns the default role r to the self-adaptive module clusterD. Then, execution of the action join(powerfuleClusterRole, clusterD) leads to the system structure shown in Fig. 8(b). To remove or add a cluster, the request receiver does not need to know the internal structure of the cluster which is an advantage of our model.

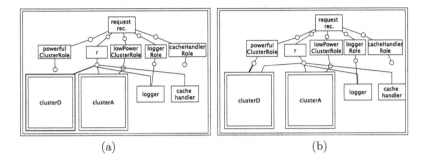

(a)   (b)

Fig. 8. The graph transformations of Example 6.

The set of nodes connected by a set X is defined as $\theta(X) = \bigcup_{e \in X} \theta(e)$. Let a self-adaptive module κ contain a manager M, the set of actors A, the set of self-adaptive modules $\mathcal{K}$ and the set of roles R assigned by M. We define the well-formedness of κ's structure as follows:

Definition 7. Well-formed structure. *The hh-graph $H = (G, \mathcal{K}, cts)$ describing κ's internal architecture, is well-structured if (1) H has at least a managed element, i.e. $A \cup \mathcal{K} \neq \emptyset$, (2) the manager M is only connected to the roles, i.e. $\theta(M) \subseteq \theta(R)$, (3) every role $r \in R$ is connected to M (i.e. $\exists n. \theta(M) \cap \theta(r) = \{n\}$) in addition to the actors and the self-adaptive modules (i.e. $\theta(r) \subseteq \theta(\mathcal{K}) \cup \theta(A)$), (4) every actor $a \in A$ is only connected to other actors or roles, i.e. $\theta(a) \subseteq \theta(R) \cup \theta(A \backslash \{a\})$, (5) every self-adaptive module $\kappa \in \mathcal{K}$ is connected to the role hyperedges, i.e. $\theta(\kappa) \subseteq \theta(R)$, and (6) every self-adaptive module $\kappa \in \mathcal{K}$ is well-formed.*

The following lemma states that the transformation rules used to specify the reconfiguration semantics are sound:

Lemma 1. *If H is a well-formed hh-graph showing the underlying structure of M, then H' obtained after some structural adaptations by M is also a well-formed hh-graph.*

Proof. We prove this by induction on the number of performed structural adaptations. We show the structure after n structural adaptations by H_n.

Base Case. *If there is no structural adaptation, $H' = H = H_0$ and the conclusion is obvious.*

Inductive Step. Assume it holds for n adaptations, i.e. H_n is well-formed. We should prove that H_{n+1} is well-formed. To prove this, we should prove that all six conditions are preserved by each of the rules in Fig. 7.

None of the rules changes the manager M, the roles and the nodes connected by M, i.e. $\theta'(M) = \theta(M)$ and $\theta'(R) = \theta(R)$, therefore, (1), (2) and the first part of (3) are preserved by all the rules. In the first rule, two cases can happen:

- if as isn't aframe, this rule adds a new edge as that connects only the node n_2 where n_2 belongs to $\theta(\iota)$, i.e. $n_2 \in \theta(\iota)$. The updates performed by this rule include adding the new hyperedge as and setting $\theta'(as)$ to $\{n_2\}$, i.e. $\theta'(as) = \{n_2\}$. From, $n_2 \in \theta(\iota)$ and $\iota \in R$, we can conclude $\theta'(as) \subseteq \theta'(R)$ and subsequently the item (4) holds. The self-adaptive modules do not change, i.e. $\theta'(\mathcal{K}) = \theta(\mathcal{K})$, hence (5) and (6) are followed from the inductive step hypothesis and the fact that $\theta'(\kappa) = \theta(\kappa)$ for all $\kappa \in \mathcal{K}$.
- if as is a frame, the proof of (5) will be similar to that of (4) in the previous case. This rule also adds as to the frames and (6) is trivially followed from the side-conditions of this rule (i.e. wellFormed(G_{as})) and the inductive step hypothesis.

The proof for the rule RAR is similar to that of AAR. The rule JAR only updates the graph by adding n_2 to the nodes connected by as, i.e. $\theta'(as) = \theta(as) \cup \{n_2\}$. If as is a self-adaptive module, from $n_2 \in \theta'(r)$ and the assumption that $\theta(as) \subseteq \theta(R)$, it follows $\theta'(as) \subseteq \theta'(R)$ (i.e. (5) holds). The conditions (4) and (6) are respectively followed from the facts that this rule does not change nodes connected by the actors (i.e. $\theta'(A) = \theta(A)$) and no frame is added or modified by this rule (i.e. $\theta'(R) = \theta(R)$). Similarly, we can prove QAR.

7   Discussion and Related Work

In [13], the suitability of HPobSAM for modeling large-scale self-adaptive systems has been discussed, particularly, it was discussed how the hierarchical structure of this model to support centralized and decentralized adaptations, improves scalability. In [17], the authors refer to [13] and mention that how the hierarchical structure offers a form of controlled autonomy and balances agent autonomy and system controllability, for example to prevent unsafe situations caused by a selfish acting ATV. Since we use hierarchical hypergraphs and a type of graph transformation rules which allows us to add or remove components with no need to be aware of their internal structure, this feature enables us to model open evolving systems where components enter or leave at any time, while their internal structure is unknown. Moreover, we use roles to specify structure-independent adaptation logic which allows us to adapt the system without changing the adaptation logic.

Three different features - separation of concerns, computational reflection and component-based design - guarantee th flexibility of the apporach to develop self-adaptive systems. Policies are used to adapt the system behavior and the system structure which can be changed and loaded dynamically. This feature provides a high-degree of flexibility and makes HPobSAM a suitable model to model evolving software systems. We believe this work is original in using both structural and behavioral adaptations which are directed by an identical flexible mechanism. The applicability of this model has been shown by applying it on two case studies in the areas of server clusters and an autonomous transportation system in a smart airport [13].

In [14,15], we have compared PobSAM with existing approaches for modeling behavioral adaptation in terms of flexibility, separation of concerns and formal foundation. The main aim of the research presented here is to extend our formal approach for architectural modeling and structural adaptation of software intensive systems. Hence we focus here on related work concerned with the design of software-intensive systems and formal modeling of structural adaptation.

Another related area of research is structural adaptation which has been given strong attention. Formal techniques have been extensively used to model and analyze dynamic structural adaptation (see [7]). Structural adaptation (or dynamic reconfiguration) is usually modeled using graph-based approaches (e.g. [8,25]) or ADL-based approaches (e.g. [18,21]). Compared to the proposed approaches based on graph transformation, we use hierarchical hypergraphs and a type of graph transformation rule which allows us to add or remove components without need to be aware of their internal structure. Moreover, most existing work concentrates on modeling structural changes [6,7], while we have integrated both behavior and architecture in our model. The authors in [6] model the system as graphs and use graph transformation to model the system behavior. In this work, both behavior and structure are modeled with the same formalism, however handling large and complex graphs would be difficult for large-scale systems. We take the benefit of both an ordinary state-based formalism for specifying behavioral information in addition to graphs as a natural model to express the system structure.

In [3,4], a coordinated actor model for self-adaptive track-based traffic control systems is introduced which is inspired from PobSAM and Rebeca language [23]. In coordinated actor model, unlike HPobSAM we have a centralised coordinator. Creol is a formal object-oriented language to develop open distributed systems that supports dynamic upgrading of classes [28]. While this language supports some limited levels of dynamism that can be used for behavioural adaptations (e.g. by upgrading a method) or structural adaptations (e.g. by defining new interfaces), however, (i) it is not flexible as HPobSAM is, and (ii) its supported adaptations are limited and fine-grained, e.g. one cannot remove a whole subsystem. DR-BIP [12] is a component framework for programming reconfigurable systems that supports structural adaptations. In contrast to HPobSAM, this framework does not support behavioural adaptation and is not flexible.

8 Conclusion

We provided a formal semantics for HPobSAM which is a formal model to specify structural and behavioral adaptations in large-scale systems. In this model, self-adaptive modules are used as autonomous building blocks to structure a system.

We used hierarchical hypergraphs to model the system structure. The proposed semantics rules enable us to add or remove a component of which the internal structure is not given. To support reasoning about systems designed using HPob-SAM, we plan to extend a tool developed in [13] to generate Maude specifications from HPobSAM models which will allow us to use the reasoning techniques provided by Maude (e.g. model checking). Furthermore, the behavioural equivalence theory proposed for PobSAM [15,16] can be slightly extended to support graph morphisms and reason about behavioural/structural equivalence.

Acknowledgment. We thank the anonymous reviewers for their helpful comments that improved the paper.

References

1. Arcaini, P., Riccobene, E., Scandurra, P.: Modeling and analyzing MAPE-K feedback loops for self-adaptation. In: 10th IEEE/ACM International Symposium on Software Engineering for Adaptive and Self-Managing Systems, SEAMS 2015, Florence, Italy, May 18–19, 2015, pp. 13–23 (2015)
2. Arcaini, P., Riccobene, E., Scandurra, P.: Formal design and verification of self-adaptive systems with decentralized control. TAAS **11**(4), 25:1–25:35 (2017)
3. Bagheri, M., et al.: Coordinated actors for reliable self-adaptive systems. In: Kouchnarenko, O., Khosravi, R. (eds.) FACS 2016. LNCS, vol. 10231, pp. 241–259. Springer, Cham (2017). https://doi.org/10.1007/978-3-319-57666-4_15
4. Bagheri, M., et al.: Coordinated actor model of self-adaptive track-based traffic control systems. J. Syst. Softw. **143**, 116–139 (2018)
5. Beal, J., Bachrach, J.: Infrastructure for engineered emergence on sensor/actuator networks. IEEE Intell. Syst. **21**(2), 10–19 (2006)
6. Becker, B., Giese, H.: Modeling of correct self-adaptive systems: a graph transformation system based approach. In: Proceedings of the 5th International Conference on Soft Computing as Trans Disciplinary Science and Technology, pp. 508–516 (2008)
7. Bradbury, J.S., Cordy, J.R., Dingel, J., Wermelinger, M.: A survey of self-management in dynamic software architecture specifications. In: Proceedings of 1st ACM SIGSOFT Workshop on Self-managed Systems, pp. 28–33. ACM (2004)
8. Cansado, A., Canal, C., Salaün, G., Cubo, J.: A formal framework for structural reconfiguration of components under behavioural adaptation. Electr. Notes Theor. Comput. Sci. **263**, 95–110 (2010)
9. Deiters, C., et al.: Demsy - a scenario for an integrated demonstrator in a smart city. Technical report, NTH - Niedersachsische Technische Hochschule (2010)
10. Drewes, F., Hoffmann, B., Plump, D.: Hierarchical graph transformation. J. Comput. Syst. Sci. **64**(2), 249–283 (2002)
11. Ehrig, H., Ehrig, K., Prange, U., Taentzer, G.: Fundamentals of Algebraic Graph Transformation. MTCSAES. Springer, Heidelberg (2006). https://doi.org/10.1007/3-540-31188-2
12. El Ballouli, R., Bensalem, S., Bozga, M., Sifakis, J.: Programming dynamic reconfigurable systems. In: Bae, K., Ölveczky, P.C. (eds.) FACS 2018. LNCS, vol. 11222, pp. 118–136. Springer, Cham (2018). https://doi.org/10.1007/978-3-030-02146-7_6

13. Khakpour, N., Jalili, S., Sirjani, M., Goltz, U., Abolhasanzadeh, B.: Hpobsam for modeling and analyzing it ecosystems - through a case study. J. Syst. Softw. **85**(12), 2770–2784 (2012)
14. Khakpour, N., Jalili, S., Talcott, C., Sirjani, M., Mousavi, M.R.: Pobsam: policy-based managing of actors in self-adaptive systems. Electr. Notes Theor. Comput. Sci. **263**, 129–143 (2010)
15. Khakpour, N., Jalili, S., Talcott, C.L., Sirjani, M., Mousavi, M.R.: Formal modeling of evolving adaptive systems. Sci. Comput. Program. **78**, 3–26 (2012)
16. Khakpour, N., Sirjani, M., Goltz, U.: Context-based behavioral equivalence of components in self-adaptive systems. In: Qin, S., Qiu, Z. (eds.) ICFEM 2011. LNCS, vol. 6991, pp. 16–32. Springer, Heidelberg (2011). https://doi.org/10.1007/978-3-642-24559-6_4
17. Lee, E.A., Sirjani, M.: What good are models? In: Bae, K., Ölveczky, P.C. (eds.) FACS 2018. LNCS, vol. 11222, pp. 3–31. Springer, Cham (2018). https://doi.org/10.1007/978-3-030-02146-7_1
18. J. Magee, J. Kramer: Dynamic structure in software architectures. In: Proceedings of the Fourth ACM SIGSOFT Symposium on the Foundations of Software Engineering (1996)
19. Merelli, E., Paoletti, N., Tesei, L.: Adaptability checking in complex systems. Sci. Comput. Program. **115–116**, 23–46 (2016)
20. Moreno, G.A., Cámara, J., Garlan, D., Schmerl, B.R.: Proactive self-adaptation under uncertainty: a probabilistic model checking approach. In: Proceedings of the 2015 10th Joint Meeting on Foundations of Software Engineering, ESEC/FSE 2015, Bergamo, Italy, August 30 - September 4, 2015, pp. 1–12 (2015)
21. Oreizy, P., Medvidovic, N., Taylor, R.N.: Architecture-based runtime software evolution. In Proceedings of the 20th International Conference on Software Engineering, ICSE 1998, pp. 177–186. IEEE Computer Society, Washington, DC (1998)
22. Shen, W.-M., Will, P.M., Galstyan, A., Chuong, C.-M.: Hormone-inspired self-organization and distributed control of robotic swarms. Auton. Robots **17**(1), 93–105 (2004)
23. Sirjani, M., Movaghar, A., Shali, A., de Boer, F.S.: Modeling and verification of reactive systems using rebeca. Fundam. Inform. **63**(4), 385–410 (2004)
24. Sloman, M., Lupu, E.C.: Engineering policy-based ubiquitous systems. Comput. J. **53**(7), 1113–1127 (2010)
25. Taentzer, G., Goedicke, M., Meyer, T.: Dynamic change management by distributed graph transformation: towards configurable distributed systems. In: Ehrig, H., Engels, G., Kreowski, H.-J., Rozenberg, G. (eds.) TAGT 1998. LNCS, vol. 1764, pp. 179–193. Springer, Heidelberg (2000). https://doi.org/10.1007/978-3-540-46464-8_13
26. Villalbaa, C., Zambonelli, F.: Towards nature-inspired pervasive service ecosystems: concepts and simulation experiences. J. Network Comput. Appl. **34**(2), 589–602 (2011)
27. Viroli, M., Casadei, M., Nardini, E., Omicini, A.: Towards a pervasive infrastructure for chemical-inspired self-organising services. In: Weyns, D., Malek, S., de Lemos, R., Andersson, J. (eds.) SOAR 2009. LNCS, vol. 6090, pp. 152–176. Springer, Heidelberg (2010). https://doi.org/10.1007/978-3-642-14412-7_8
28. Yu, I.C., Johnsen, E.B., Owe, O.: Type-safe runtime class upgrades in creol. In: Gorrieri, R., Wehrheim, H. (eds.) FMOODS 2006. LNCS, vol. 4037, pp. 202–217. Springer, Heidelberg (2006). https://doi.org/10.1007/11768869_16

A Two-Dimensional Self-coordination Mechanism of Agents in a Minority Game

Sanaz Hasanzadeh Fard and Hadi Tabatabaee Malazi[✉]

Faculty of Computer Science and Engineering,
Shahid Beheshti University, G.C., Tehran, Iran
s.hasanzadehfard@gmail.com, h_tabatabaee@sbu.ac.ir

Abstract. Coordination of several agents in accessing a limited resource is a common problem among various systems. In the absence of a central coordinator, the primary challenge of the problem is to bring equilibrium among agents in accessing a limited shared resource. The *El Farol Bar Problem* is the generic description of this problem. In this paper, we devised a new two-dimensional approach called Social Coordination (*SoCo*). In the first dimension, we define a new function, called *Effect()*, that plays a determinative role in choosing the strategy for the current action. In the second dimension, we define a new social coordination constraint that boosts the system to achieve the entire equilibrium, in which near optimum status in social and individual utilities are reached without any starvation cases. *SoCo* not only attempts to improve the social utility but also considers the individual utility and starvation as the optimization goals. The simulation results show that *SoCo* improves social utility by 57.61% compared to similar approaches. The simulations demonstrate that the maximum starvation length of agents in *SoCo* is 7.93 times less than similar methods.

Keywords: Distributed systems · Self-coordination ·
El farol bar problem · Social utility · Individual utility ·
Resource starvation

1 Introduction

One of the common problems in distributed systems is to establish a kind of distributed coordination among competing players in accessing a limited resource [1,2]. In absence of a central coordinator, different players have to establish a coordination mechanism to optimize resource usage by avoiding excessive accesses or leaving the resource underused. In systems with unknown players or in cases where the players do not know each other, the coordination problem has to be addressed without communication among the participants. That is, the players are not able to communicate with each other to share their previous history of accessing the resource or their intentions. The El Farol Bar [3] and

© IFIP International Federation for Information Processing 2019
Published by Springer Nature Switzerland AG 2019
H. Hojjat and M. Massink (Eds.): FSEN 2019, LNCS 11761, pp. 20–36, 2019.
https://doi.org/10.1007/978-3-030-31517-7_2

minority games [4] (which are inspired by El Farol Bar Problem) are the games that try to address the problem of coordinating a set of selfish players to regulate cooperation in accessing a resource in the absence of communications. The lack of a suitable coordination mechanism may result in congestion, starvation, or degradation in social and individual utilities of the players.

The classic El Farol Bar Problem [3] happens in Santa Fe city, where every Thursday one hundred citizens (agents) have to decide whether to attend the city bar or not. The bar has a limited capacity (60 seats). If the attendees are more than the capacity, no one will have a pleasant time. Therefore, each agent thinks of the bar situation before making a decision. He will go to the bar if he thinks that the bar is not crowded. Otherwise, he would prefer to stay at home. The individual utility of an agent for each iteration (week) is the result of his decision. If he stays at home, the value of his individual utility is equal to zero. If he decides to go to the bar and the bar was over-crowded, he will receive -1. Otherwise, he will get $+1$ for his individual utility in that iteration. The social utility of the city for an iteration is the sum of the individual utilities of all agents. The challenging issue is that agents cannot communicate before making their decisions. In other words, no one is aware of the bar's condition before going to the bar. Moreover, there is no central coordination controller.

The main objective of any candidate solution is to converge the number of attendees to the bar capacity. Consequently, the system will achieve the highest social utility. An alternative goal is to decrease the convergence time, which yields the maximization of the total social utility (sum of social utilities for all of the iterations). Another important factor is to increase individual utility, which implies that all agents benefit from the resource fairly. Finally, the starvation of agents is the last evaluation metric that illustrates the fairness level in smaller time units for the resource distribution among agents. For instance, it is possible to have a high individual utility for most agents, but a minority of them do not have any access to the resource for a long period of time. To analyze the metric, the maximum starvation length of agents has to be monitored.

Some research concentrates on providing solutions for the generic El Farol problem. They can be classified into several categories [5]. One category of researches is named predictor based [3,6,7]. These solutions have a top-down view, and the decision-making process is performed by predicting the aggregated system behavior. In another category of the solutions [8–11], the agent's individual information is in the center of attention. These solutions have a bottom-up view of the problem. The analyses reveal several drawbacks. Firstly, the level of being over-crowded does not have a significant effect on the decision-making process. For instance, in iteration x, twenty persons above the bar capacity wanted to attend, and in iteration y only one extra attendee intended to join the bar. The level of being over-crowded in iteration x is different from iteration y, but both cases are treated the same. Secondly, studies such as [3] are that the optimization of individual utility is not considered as the objectives. Similarly, minimizing the starvation length is not addressed in [3,6–9]. Finally, in some of the methods such as [10,11], the scalability in terms of the number of agents is an issue.

In this paper, we devise a new approach, called Social Coordination (*SoCo*) that uses a bottom-up view. To differentiate the impact of the previous iterations in terms of the level of being over-crowded, it uses a second dimension and defines a new function called *Effect*(t). The function returns the coefficient (impact) of iteration t that discriminates the over-crowded situations from each other as well as the under-crowded ones. We also define a new coordination factor that defines the optimum limit of attendance for an agent according to the bar's condition and its capacity. The factor is called C_a and defines the social coordination among agents to maintain the optimum number of attendance and it is calculated according to the history of agent's experiences. It leads to the distribution of resource among agents in a balanced manner. Finally, in *SoCo*, the decision strategies are designed in a way that hinders the starvation.

The rest of the paper is organized as follows: In Sect. 2, we review some of the outstanding work. Section 3 is dedicated to the problem definition. Then, the details of *SoCo* are explained, and the performance is analyzed in Sects. 4 and 5, respectively. Finally, Sect. 6 concludes the paper.

2   Related Work

Several researchers studied the El Farol Bar Problem due to its capabilities in modeling real-world applications. Some of the studies concentrated on addressing the classic problem, while others employ it in applications. This section briefly reviews some of the distinguished researches.

The El Farol Bar Problem was introduced by Arthur et al. in [3] for the first time. In his paper, the behavior of agents is considered in a complex system with limited decision-making information. It is explained that deductive reasoning is not sufficient, and inductive reasoning can be used in such an environment. The decision-making is performed using predictors such as *"same as last week"* and *"an average of four recent weeks"*. Then, the system uses the predictors for inductive reasoning and estimates the number of agents, which go to the bar. The goal is to converge the number of attendees to the bar capacity. The shortcomings of the solution are that it does not consider minimizing agent starvation and maximizing individual utility.

The agent starvation is investigated in the *Adaptive Parasitized* approach [9]. The idea is to add *behaviosit* to alter the behavior of the agent. The main objective of the *behaviosit* is to decrease the attending period of an agent, which intends to go to the bar in the far future. That is if the attending period of an agent is above a predefined threshold, the *behaviosit* is added, and consequently, the attending period starts to decrease. This leads to the mitigation of the starvation problem in accessing the bar. Similar to the Adaptive method [8], the *Adaptive Parasitized* does not exploit complex predictors.

The researchers in [7] applied cognitive modeling to equip agents with human-inspired ability. The authors used the cognitive emotion theory [12,13], which is relied on *belief* and *desire* concepts. The *belief* shows the level of confidence to the reliability of the strategy, and the desire represents the agent's tendency for maintaining and operating the current strategy. In the beginning, each agent chooses a strategy randomly among the same set of strategies. The agent predicts the system situation according to the selected strategy and performs the specified action. If the action is correct, the *belief* will increase accordingly, and the agent keeps repeating the current strategy. Otherwise, it will decrease. If the decreased belief falls below the threshold, the agent will decide to change the current strategy. One of the interesting features of the approach is supporting the heterogeneity of agents. The authors in their next work in [14] analyze the effect of extending the memory size and did not find any clue for improvement of system performance.

Szilagyi in [15] solved the El Farol Bar Problem as a special case of the N-person battle of sexes. He modeled agents as stochastic learning cellular automata. The interacting environment of the agents is described with cellular automata, and stochastic learning rules are used for the agents' behavior. In the described model a range of different personality profiles can be used, such as Pavlovian, stochastically predictable (angry, benevolent, and unpredictable), accountant, conformist, and greedy.

Shu-Heng et al. in [10] defined a *good society* equilibrium with economic efficiency and economic equality characteristics. The authors propose the probability of achieving this equilibrium by a suitable topological network and agents with social preferences. The network of agents is established using the Von Neumann Network. Additionally, agents have extrinsic or intrinsic preferences. In the first one, agents are described by the minimum attendance threshold, while in the second one the awareness of inequity is formed through interactions with neighbors by averaging the attendance frequencies of the neighbors. That is, the original El Farol Bar Problem model is changed to the bi-dimensional one, which will boost the emergence of the good society. The authors performed a sensitivity analysis of the approach in [11], and study the effects of size-related parameters such as network size (number of agents), number of each agent's neighbors, and agent's memory size on the equilibrium. The main drawback is that, for large networks, the chance of reaching equilibrium is low compared to small networks. For very large networks, this chance is almost zero. Moreover, the other size related parameters do not have a considerable effect on achieving the equilibrium.

Overall, the main objective in most of the studies is the optimization of resource efficiency, while the individual utility and starvation are not in the center of attention.

3   Problem Definition

In the original El Farol Bar Problem [3], a set of n agents is considered. Let A denote the set of agents and a_i be a sample one. Each agent (a_i) may tend to go to the bar every Thursday. Each week is defined by an iteration (E^t), where $1 \leq t \leq T$, and T is the total number iterations. Each agent has a memory that remembers his last h iterations (history). The decision of agent i at iteration

t is denoted as d_i^t. If the agent decides to attend the bar, the value of d_i^t is 1, otherwise, the value is 0. The bar has a limited capacity (C), and if the number of attendees at the iteration t (att^t) exceeds more than C, the bar will be over-crowded $(att^t = \sum_{i=1}^{n}(d_i^t) > C)$. Hence, all the attending agents will have an unpleasant time and will receive a negative utility. On the other hand, when the bar is under-crowded $(att^t = \sum_{i=1}^{n}(d_i^t) \leq C)$, the visiting agent will have a pleasant time.

Definition 1: The individual utility of an agent (a_i) at iteration t is denoted by r_i^t and is calculated according to Eq. 1.

$$r_i^t = \begin{cases} +1 & att^t \leq C, d_i^t = 1 \\ 0 & d_i^t = 0 \\ -1 & att^t > C, d_i^t = 1 \end{cases} \tag{1}$$

Definition 2: The total individual utility (tiu) of an agent a_i is the sum of his individual utilities in every iteration (Eq. 2).

$$tiu_i = \sum_{t=1}^{T} r_i^t \tag{2}$$

Definition 3: The social utility (su^t) of the system at iteration t is the sum of all agents' individual utility at that iteration (Eq. 3). The upper bound of su^t is C and the lower bound is $-n$ $(-n \leq su^t \leq C)$.

$$su^t = \sum_{i=1}^{n} r_i^t \tag{3}$$

Definition 4: The total social utility (tsu) is defined as the summation of the social utilities in all iterations (Eq. 4).

$$tsu = \sum_{t=1}^{T} su^t \tag{4}$$

Definition 5: The starvation length of an agent a_i is the maximum number of consecutive iterations in which the agent does not get any positive individual utility, and it is denoted by x_i (Eq. 5). This definition is more rigorous compared to the definition provided in [9].

$$\forall p, q : p \leq t \leq q, r_i^t \leq 0; \exists m, n : m \leq t \leq n, r_i^t \leq 0; \mid n - m \geq q - p \Rightarrow x_i = n - m \tag{5}$$

The maximum starvation length (X) of the system is the maximum of x_i for all agents.

$$X = Max_{i=1}^{n}(x_i) \tag{6}$$

The main constraint of the problem is that agents do not know what the other agents' actions are for the current iteration, and the situation of the bar is not revealed before attending. Furthermore, the system does not have any central coordinating entity.

The main goal of a candidate solution is to establish a self-coordination mechanism that:

1. Leads the system to converge the number of attendees (att^t) to the bar capacity (C): Fast convergence toward the bar capacity results in a higher total social utility.
2. Maximizes the total individual utility: It is expected that the total individual utility of an agent a_i reaches a floor threshold (a specific portion of the summation of the bar capacity in all iterations). This objective is to ensure that each agent gets a fair share of the bar. The ideal value of the threshold is $\frac{tsu}{n}$. But, practically the total individual utility is bounded by $\frac{tsu}{n} \pm \varepsilon$ (Eq. 7). A fair approach has an ε value close to zero.

$$\frac{tsu}{n} - \varepsilon \leq tiu_i \leq \frac{tsu}{n} + \varepsilon \tag{7}$$

3. Minimizes the maximum starvation length of agents: It is worth pointing out that a low starvation length will not necessarily lead to a high total individual utility. On the other hand, an agent may not attend the bar in half of the consecutive iterations but joins the bar for all the iterations of the second half. Therefore, the maximum starvation length is $x_i = T/2$, but the total individual utility may reach above the floor threshold.

4   The Devised Social Coordination Method

We devised a two-dimensional method that uses agents' previous experiences to make a decision about the next action. The objective of the first dimension is to differentiate the over-crowded situations from each other along with the under-crowded ones. We define the *Effect*() function that considers the number of attendees for each iteration. The second dimension examines the experiences of an agent independently from other agents. We define a new parameter called *social coordination constraint* (C_a), which is the optimum times that an agent attends the bar in his last h iterations. In the rest of this section, the *Effect*() function is introduced, then the social coordination constraint is described. Finally, the decision-making process is explained in detail.

4.1   The *Effect*() Function

The effect of iteration t is defined as the subtraction of the number of attendees (att^t) from the bar capacity $(Effect(t) = C - att^t)$. The function is used for the last h iteration to calculate the impact of previous experiences of the agent. The *Effect*() value can be positive, zero, or negative for each iteration according to the following situations:

- **Under-crowded case** ($att^t < C \Rightarrow Effect(t) > 0$): The positive value indicates that the previous decision was right, and the agent tends to continue this trend. The value also indicates the number of free seats in the bar. The closer the value is to the zero, the closer the system is to the equilibrium.
- **The same number of attendees as the bar capacity** ($att^t = C \Rightarrow Effect(t) = 0$): The value of the function at iteration t is equal to zero. That is, the number of attending agents is the same as the bar capacity. This is the ideal case where the participating agents made the right decision, as they get positive individual utilities. Moreover, agents who choose to stay at home have also made a correct decision, since the bar was not under-crowded, and in case they decided to participate, the bar would be over-crowded. The value of the *Effect*() function for both types of agents must be equally the same for their right decision.
- **Over-crowded case** ($att^t > C \Rightarrow Effect(t) < 0$): In the last case, the negative value implies the over-crowded situation of the bar, and shows the incorrect decision. The value presents the number of extra attendees that made the bar crowded. Hence, the agent is willing to change the decision in future iterations.

The *Effect* value of the agent who did not attend the bar is considered zero, regardless of the status of the bar. The main reason is to preserve the condition that an agent that stayed at home should not have any information about the over-crowded or under-crowded situation of the bar.

To show how the *Effect*() function discriminates over-crowded cases as well as under-crowded ones, consider an agent a_i's experiences in two different iterations of t_1 and t_2. The $Effect(t_1)$ and $Effect(t_2)$ have the same sign. If they both are positive ($0 < Effect(t_1) < Effect(t_2)$), the one with lower value (t_1) will be close to equilibrium. The value of the *Effect*() function illustrates the number of needed agents to complete the bar capacity. Besides, the social utility of t_1 is higher, since the number of free seats is less. In the second case, if they both are negative ($Effect(t_2) < Effect(t_1) < 0$), the one with higher value (t_1) is favored. The reason is that the *Effect*() function represents the number of extra attendance. To conclude, the distance of the value from zero shows how far the system is to the equilibrium.

4.2   The Social Coordination Constraint

Potentially, the *Effect*() function can be used to lead the system to equilibrium, but it does not inhibit the starvation problem. Assuming a case in which a group of agents always attend the bar and the rest of them do not try it at all is a good example. To cope with this issue, a new constraint is defined, which is called *social coordination* (C_a). Agents that reach C_a accesses to the bar, will abstain themselves for new access attempts to prevent possible congestions. It defines an optimum limit and a fair quota for an agent in attending the bar without facing any congestion.

The C_a is computed according to the bar capacity (C), the population of agents (n), and the history length (h). In Eq. 9, C_a is the total bar capacity during the h iterations (Eq. 8) divided by the number of agents.

$$C_h = h \times C \tag{8}$$

$$C_a = \frac{C_h}{n} = \frac{h \times C}{n} \tag{9}$$

4.3   Decision-Making Process

In the devised method, the decision process of an agent has a two-dimensional approach. The first dimension is the *Effect* value of each iteration. The second dimension is the history of an agent during the past h iterations. To combine these factors, we define a pre-decision parameter pd_i^t that denotes the pre-decision of agent a_i at iteration t. It is computed according to Eq. 10. It is worth mentioning that if an agent does not attend the bar in an iteration $(d_i^\tau = 0)$, it will not have any effect on the pre-decision parameter.

$$pd_i^t = \sum_{\tau=t-h}^{t-1} (Effect(\tau) \times d_i^\tau) \tag{10}$$

In the first h iterations, agents randomly choose to join the bar or stay at home. After these setup iterations, agents select a proper strategy according to their pre-decision value. In the following, these cases are introduced.

The Negative Value of Pre-decision: The negative value of pd_i^t indicates that the over-crowded experiences dominate the pleasant ones. Thus, a_i decides to stay at home to prevent the continuity of this situation (Eq. 11).

$$\textbf{Strategy 1:} \quad pd_i^t < 0 \Rightarrow d_i^t = 0 \tag{11}$$

The Zero Value of Pre-decision: There are two cases in which the zero value for the pre-decision parameter can be obtained. In the first case, the summation of the positive *Effect* values and the negative ones is zero. The case implies that neither the positive *Effect* values are encouraging enough to attend the bar, nor the negative *Effect* values are strong enough to stay at home. Therefore, a_i will decide to stay at home (Eq. 12).

$$\textbf{Strategy 2:} \quad (pd_i^t = 0) \;\; and \;\; (\exists \tau : t-h \leq \tau < t, Effect(\tau) < 0) \Rightarrow d_i^t = 0 \tag{12}$$

In the second case, all the *Effect*() values of the past h iterations are zero. This is due to the prevention of the agent from going to the bar, or the equilibrium state of the bar is reached. Therefore, the agent considers the number of times that he/she attends the bar, and compares it with the social coordination constraint. If the value is below the C_a threshold, it has not benefited enough from the bar. So, he will decide to go to the bar (Eq. 13). On the other hand, if he has attended equal to or more than the C_a threshold, he will decide to stay at home to prevent further congestion (Eq. 14). In this case, C_a constraint plays a social coordination role among agents.

Strategy 3: $(pd_i^t = 0)$ and $(\forall \tau : t - h \leq \tau < t, Effect(\tau) = 0)$

$$and \ (\sum_{\tau=t-h}^{t} d_i^\tau \geq C_a) \Rightarrow d_i^t = 0 \tag{13}$$

Strategy 4: $(pd_i^t = 0)$ and $(\forall \tau : t - h \leq \tau < t, Effect(\tau) = 0)$

$$and \ (\sum_{\tau=t-h}^{t} d_i^\tau < C_a) \Rightarrow d_i^t = 1 \tag{14}$$

The Positive Value of Pre-decision: In the last case, the value of pd_i^t is positive. It indicates that the overall effects of the previous experiences are positive and the agent is encouraged to continue this trend. The main obstacle is the starvation of the other agents. To avoid the problem, the agent counts the number of times he attended the bar. If the number is below the C_a, he will attend the bar (Eq. 15), otherwise, he will choose to stay at home (Eq. 16).

Strategy 5: $(pd_i^t > 0)$ and $(\sum_{\tau=t-h}^{t} d_i^\tau \geq C_a) \Rightarrow d_i^t = 0$ $\qquad$ (15)

Strategy 6: $(pd_i^t > 0)$ and $(\sum_{\tau=t-h}^{t} d_i^\tau < C_a) \Rightarrow d_i^t = 1$ $\qquad$ (16)

4.4   Discussion on the Convergence Stability

The stability of El Farol after reaching equilibrium is analyzed with an example. Table 1 exhibits five consecutive sample iterations that the system converges to an equilibrium, where each row of the table presents ten agents. Let the bar capacity be sixty, and the number of agents is one hundred, where each agent remembers his last five iterations. The number of attendees in each iteration is sixty. The optimum number of participation for each agent in five iterations is three (according to Eq. 9). It is expected for each agent to go to the bar three times during every five consecutive iterations in an equilibrium state (Eq. 17).

$$\frac{h \times C}{n} = \frac{5 \times 60}{100} = 3 \tag{17}$$

Considering that the system is in the optimum state, we analyze the situation of agents in iteration E^{t6}. To make a decision for the next iteration (E^{t6}), each agent checks its last four iterations (E^{t2} to E^{t5}). If he went to the bar three

Table 1. The bar condition in a five sample consecutive iterations

Agents	E^{t1}	E^{t2}	E^{t3}	E^{t4}	E^{t5}	E^{t6}	E^{t7}
$a_{i:i=1,2,\dots,10}$	×		×		×		
$a_{i:i=11,12,\dots,20}$		×	×		×		
$a_{i:i=21,22,\dots,30}$	×	×			×		
$a_{i:i=31,32,\dots,40}$	×	×			×		
$a_{i:i=41,42,\dots,50}$		×		×	×		
$a_{i:i=51,52,\dots,60}$	×		×	×			
$a_{i:i=61,62,\dots,70}$		×	×	×			
$a_{i:i=71,72,\dots,80}$	×			×	×		
$a_{i:i=81,82,\dots,90}$	×		×	×			
$a_{i:i=91,92,\dots,100}$		×	×	×			

times during the last four iterations, he would not attend the bar for the current one to protect his individual utility as well as the social utility. Consequently, there will be no congestion. According to Table 1, sixty agents attend the bar in the first iteration. These are agents that join the bar only two times from E^{t2} to E^{t5}, and will decide to go to the bar again. On the other hand, the rest of agents that do not join the bar in the first iteration, have already gone to the bar for three times from E^{t2} to E^{t5}, and will decide to stay at home.

It has to be mentioned that we used five setup iterations with an equilibrium status, but in the real world, these iterations happen randomly. That is the reason for the distinction between this example and our simulations in the next section.

5   Evaluation and Discussion

Before analyzing the performance of *SoCo*, we first present the simulation environment and its configuration. Then, the evaluation parameters and the comparing approaches are introduced. Finally, we present the simulation scenarios and discuss the results.

5.1   The Simulation Environment

We use Matlab R2012b to simulate the El Farol Bar Problem environment. It is a discrete time simulator that fits well with the problem. The main reason is its capabilities in modeling the problem as a set of matrices, and its speed in running thousands of iterations. Similar to the original definition of the El Farol Bar Problem [3], the number of agents is set to one hundred. But to analyze the scalability, we also use 200, 300, and 400 agents as well. The initial value of the bar capacity is sixty, and for the scalability scenarios, we apply 120, 180, and 240 seats. The applied values for agents' memory size (history) are 3, 5, 7, 9, 11,

Table 2. The simulation configuration

Parameter	Value(s)
Number of agents (n)	100, 200, 300, 400
Bar capacity (C)	60, 120, 180, 240
Total number of iterations (T)	2000
History size (h)	3, 5, 7, 9, 11, 13, 15

13, and 15. Finally, the total number of iterations for each experiment is 2000 to reflect the behavior of the methods during the time. To reduce the effect of randomness, we repeated each experiment one hundred times, and present the mean values. The simulation configuration is presented in Table 2.

The evaluation parameters are social utility (which is the average over all iterations) (Eq. 4), total individual utility (Eq. 2), maximum starvation length (Eq. 6), and the scalability in the number of agents. We compare the performance of our approach with the researches presented in [9, 10]. The study presented in [10] is one of the latest work on the El Farol Bar Problem that studied the effect of network topology (Von Neumann network) in social networks. Also, the work [9] is selected due to its emphasis on the starvation issue.

5.2 The Effect of History Size

Table 3 demonstrates the effect of history size on the individual and social utilities as well as the maximum starvation length in seven different history sizes. We repeated the simulations for one hundred times for each case and averaged the results. The results show that larger history sizes lead to longer starvation. The history length of five performs the best individual and social utilities. Besides, it has a comparatively low starvation length. Due to this, we used $h = 5$ in the rest of the simulations.

Table 3. The effect of history size

History size	Total individual (mean)	Social utility (mean)	Max starvation length (mean)
3	481.93	24.10	2.94
5	873.72	43.69	2.66
7	824.48	41.22	3.5463
9	864.08	43.20	4.01
11	778.24	38.91	6.79
13	833.30	41.67	6.50
15	331.17	16.56	18.19

5.3   The Analysis of Social Utility

The main objective of the El Farol Bar Problem is to maximize social utility. Figures 1, 2, and 3 demonstrate the overall performance of the methods according to this metric. The X axis shows the iterations (weeks), and the Y axis is the social utility of the iterations. The social utility of agents in each iteration for *Adaptive Parasitized* method is presented in Fig. 1. The figure shows that it is relatively low in the starting iterations and slowly rises until it reaches near the optimum point. The main reason for the low social utility at early iterations is the randomly chosen parameters of C_i (frequency of attendance for agent a_i) and P_i (time step until the next attendance of agent a_i). The average social utility of the system during the 2000 iteration is 19.09. Its minimum number is 5.24, and the maximum is 49.12.

Figure 2 demonstrates the social utility of the *Good Society* method for each iteration. The utility fluctuates between positive and negative values. The main reason is that the numbers of attendees oscillate around the bar capacity. Although in some iterations the number of attendees is near the optimum, in some others the over-crowded case happens. Therefore, all agents get negative

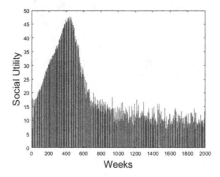

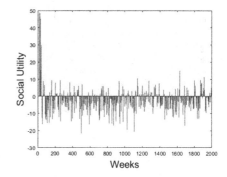

Fig. 1. The social utility of *Adaptive Parasitized* [9].

Fig. 2. The social utility of *Good Society* [10].

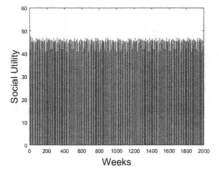

Fig. 3. The social utility of *SoCo*.

points, and it results in the poor social utility of the system. The average social utility of the method is −5.74, and the values are bounded to −28.54 and 48.40.

Figure 3 shows the results for *SoCo*, which is closer to the optimum point compared to the other two methods. The social coordination mechanism (C_a) suppresses the participants that cause congestion. Besides, the *Effect* function persuades agents to attend the bar based on the previous iterations. The mean social utility of the system in this method is 46.56. The minimum and maximum values of the gained social utility are 42.71 and 50.11.

5.4   The Analysis of Total Individual Utility

In this simulation, we analyze the performance of the methods from the total individual utility point of view. Figures 4, 5, and 6 depict the achieved results for *Adaptive Parasitized*, *Good Society*, and *SoCo* methods in 2000 iterations (weeks), respectively. The horizontal axis shows agents, and the vertical one is

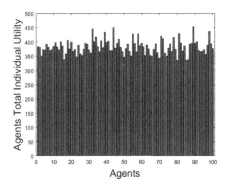

Fig. 4. The total individual utility of agents in *Adaptive Parasitized* [9].

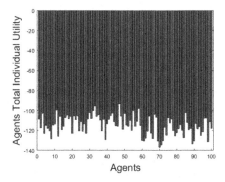

Fig. 5. The total individual utility of agents *Good Society* [10].

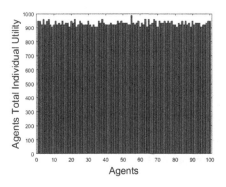

Fig. 6. The total individual utility of agents in *SoCo*.

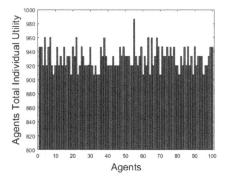

Fig. 7. The total individual utility of agents in *SoCo* (magnified).

the gained total individual utility of agents. Due to small fluctuations of *SoCo* method in Fig. 6, we heightened the chart in Fig. 7.

According to the achieved results, the individual utilities of agents in *Adaptive Parasitized* are bounded to 334.30 and 452.62 with the average value of 381.83. The *Good Society* method does not provide promising results. The best value gained by an agent is −93.23, and worst value is −136.73. Considering that the bar has sixty seats, in the best case, each agent may receive total individual utility of 1200 in 2000 iterations. In the proposed method, the total individual utilities of agents are between 906.74 and 986.40 with the mean value of 931.29. The distance between the highest and the lowest achieved values are 30.07% in *Adaptive Parasitized* and 8.41% in *SoCo*.

5.5   The Maximum Starvation Length

One of the secondary goals of the devised method is to minimize the starvation length of agents in accessing the bar. Figures 8, 9, and 10 present the results for *Adaptive Parasitized* [9], *Good Society* [10], and *SoCo*, respectively. The horizontal axis represents agents, and the vertical one shows the maximum starvation length of the agent during the 2000 iterations.

In the *Adaptive Parasitized* method, a less rigorous definition of maximum starvation length is provided, which indicates the maximum consecutive times that an agent does not intend to join the bar. The definition does not consider the cases in which an agent attends the over-crowded bar. The maximum starvation length of the method, according to the above definition, is equal to the threshold, which is set to 15 to achieve the best social utility. We rigorously redefine the maximum starvation length. Based on the new definition, the maximum starvation length of agents in *Adaptive Parasitized* method is bounded to 19.87 and 22.52 with the mean value of 21.10. Figure 8 reveals the results.

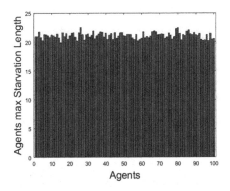 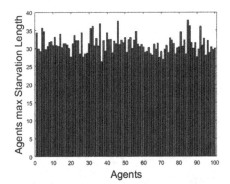

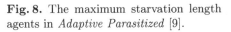

Fig. 8. The maximum starvation length agents in *Adaptive Parasitized* [9].

Fig. 9. The maximum starvation length of agents in *Good Society* [10].

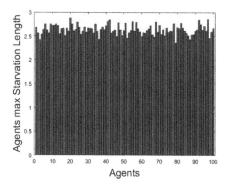

Fig. 10. The maximum starvation length of agents in *SoCo*.

Figure 9 depicts the outcome of the *Good Society* method. The mean value of maximum starvation of agents is 31.23. The highest value is 37.82, and the lower one is 26.26.

The *SoCo* achieves the best results. They are bounded to 2.36 and 2.88 with an average of 2.63. It is almost eight times less than *Adaptive Parasitized* method, and about eleven times less than *Good Society* method. Moreover, *Adaptive Parasitized* method needs to divide the agents into casual and regular classes, whereas *SoCo* method does not require any classification of agents. The winning point of our devised approach is the social coordination factor (C_a), which brings equilibrium in accessing the bar.

5.6   Scalability

The last evaluation scenario is the scalability of the devised method. Figures 11, 12, 13, and 14 show the results for 100, 200, 300, and 400 agents, respectively. We used the total individual utility metric to compare these cases since its range

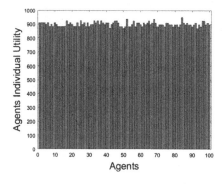

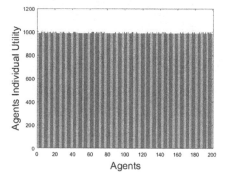

Fig. 11. The individual utility of agents for n = 100.

Fig. 12. The individual utility of agents for n = 200.

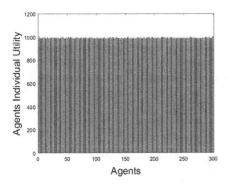

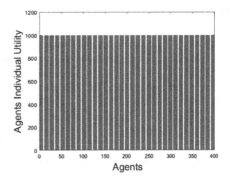

Fig. 13. The individual utility of agents for n = 300.

Fig. 14. The individual utility of agents for n = 400.

does not change with the number of agents. In Fig. 11, one hundred agents are competing for seats of the bar. The total individual utility of agents are in the range of 866.60 and 1000.30. Figure 12 shows a similar experiment for 200 agents in which their gained total individual utility is between 999.20 and 1000.5. The results for 300 and 400 agents are similar to the previous ones. The simulation outcome demonstrates that the devised approach is scalable in terms of the number of participating agents. This is in contrast to *good society* method, where the performance degrades by surging the number of agents.

6   Conclusion

In the lack of a central coordinator, the establishment of a self-coordination mechanism for accessing a limited resource is a common problem that a variety of systems are facing. The classic El Farol Bar Problem models the situation, where a number of citizens may decide to go to the bar with a limited capacity. According to the number of attendees, they may receive a negative utility if the bar is over-crowded, positive utility if it is not over-crowded, or zero utility if they do not attend the bar. Agents' decision is only based on their previous experiments. In this paper, we introduced a new method that applied a two-dimensional approach. The main idea was to use some details of each iteration as well as the agents' past experiences. For the first case, we defined a new function called *Effect*() that discriminates over-crowded cases from each other, as well as under-crowded ones. For the second case, we introduced a new *social coordination* parameter that hindered agents from overusing the resource. The simulation results showed the performance of the devised approach in terms of convergence speed, social utility, total individual utility, starvation length.

As future work, we are going to apply this method to various applications such as energy consumption in smart homes, public transportation, and network traffic.

References

1. Franks, H., Griffiths, N., Jhumka, A.: Manipulating convention emergence using influencer agents. Auton. Agent. Multi-Agent Syst. **26**(3), 315–353 (2013)
2. Tuyls, K., Hoen, P.J.T., Vanschoenwinkel, B.: An evolutionary dynamical analysis of multi-agent learning in iterated games. Auton. Agents Multi-Agent Syst. **12**(1), 115–153 (2006)
3. Arthur, W.B.: Inductive reasoning and bounded rationality. Am. Econ. Rev. **84**(2), 406–411 (1994)
4. Challet, D., Zhang, Y.C.: On the minority game: analytical and numerical studies. Phys. A: Stat. Mech. Appl. **256**(3), 514–532 (1998)
5. Tumer, K., Proper, S.: Coordinating actions in congestion games: impact of top-down and bottom-up utilities. Auton. Agent. Multi-Agent Syst. **27**(3), 419–443 (2013)
6. Baccan, D.D., Macedo, L.: Are markets more efficient when cognitive agents act rationally? evidence from the El Farol. In: 16th Portuguese Conference on Artificial Intelligence, pp. 438–449 (2013)
7. Baccan, D.D.A., Macedo, L.: Revisiting the el farol problem: a cognitive modeling approach. In: Giardini, F., Amblard, F. (eds.) MABS 2012. LNCS (LNAI), vol. 7838, pp. 56–68. Springer, Heidelberg (2013). https://doi.org/10.1007/978-3-642-38859-0_5
8. Bell, A.N., Sethares, W.A.: The El Farol problem and the internet: congestion and coordination failure. In: Fifth International Conference of the Society for Computational Economics, Boston, MA (1999)
9. Sheikhha, F., Tabatabaee Malazi, H., Amjadifard, R.: Adaptive parasitized El Farol bar problem. In: WRI World Congress on Computer Science and Information Engineering, vol. 7, pp. 422–426. IEEE (2009)
10. Chen, S.H., Gostoli, U.: Coordination in the El Farol bar problem: the role of social preferences and social networks. J. Econ. Interact. Coord. **12**(1), 59–93 (2017)
11. Chen, S.H., Gostoli, U.: On the complexity of the El Farol bar game: a sensitivity analysis. Evol. Intell. **9**(4), 113–123 (2016)
12. Lazarus, R.S.: Emotion and Adaptation. Oxford University Press on Demand, New York (1991)
13. Reisenzein, R.: Emotions as meta representational states of mind: naturalizing the belief-desire theory of emotion. Cogn. Syst. Res. **10**(1), 6–20 (2009)
14. Baccan, D., Macedo, L., Sbruzzi, E.: Is the El Farol more efficient when cognitive rational agents have a larger memory size? In: 2014 IEEE International Conference on Systems, Man, and Cybernetics, pp. 39–44. IEEE (2014)
15. Szilagyi, M.N.: The El Farol bar problem as an iterated n-person game. Complex Syst. **21**(2), 153 (2012)

A Persistent Entropy Automaton for the Dow Jones Stock Market

Marco Piangerelli$^{(\boxtimes)}$ ⓘ, Luca Tesei ⓘ, and Emanuela Merelli ⓘ

School of Sciences and Technology, University of Camerino,
Via Madonna delle Carceri 9, 62032 Camerino, MC, Italy
{marco.piangerelli,luca.tesei,emanuela.merelli}@unicam.it

Abstract. Complex systems are ubiquitous. Their components, agents, live in an environment perceiving its changes and reacting with appropriate actions; they also interact with each other causing changes in the environment itself. Modelling an environment that shows this feedback loop with agents is still a big issue because the model must take into account the emerging behaviour of the whole system. In this paper, following the S[B] paradigm, we exploit topological data analysis and the information power of persistent entropy for deriving a persistent entropy automaton to model a global emerging behaviour of the Dow Jones stock market index. We devise early warning states of the automaton that signal a possible evolution of the system towards a financial crisis.

Keywords: Complex systems · S[B] paradigm · Emerging behavior · Topological data analysis · Stock market

1 Introduction

A complex system is any system consisting of a great number of heterogeneous entities interacting with each other within an environment to shape an emerging behavior. Such emerging behaviour depends on a non-trivial space of correlations that derive from the interplay of agents *entangled in loops of non-linear interactions*. In the metaphor of the flock of starlings, any environmental change perceived by the starlings during their flight is visible in the formation of the flock shape due to their reaction. This implies that there is an underlying feedback loop between the agents and the global system.

Mastering the complexity of these systems has always been a challenge in almost every branch of science. In computer science, process-, actor- and agent-based models and languages have been developed for describing the behaviour of complex software systems [1,2,6,11]. All these approaches require an *a priori* knowledge of the basic rules governing the dynamic of the system in order to define the behaviour of the components and of the environment. Unfortunately, for natural or social phenomena, it is quite impossible to have enough knowledge about the real interaction rules. However, global information about the system

© IFIP International Federation for Information Processing 2019
Published by Springer Nature Switzerland AG 2019
H. Hojjat and M. Massink (Eds.): FSEN 2019, LNCS 11761, pp. 37–42, 2019.
https://doi.org/10.1007/978-3-030-31517-7_3

is hidden inside phenomenological data produced by the individual components. Thus, we need suitable methods to extract a specific model of interest.

Topological Data Analysis (TDA) is a relatively new field of study in which topology driven methods are used to analyse big collections of data [4,5,8]. The $S[B]$ paradigm is a general framework of modelling in which a complex system is described as a pair of entangled systems: S, the global environment, and B, a set of interactive agents [13,14]. Persistent Entropy (PE) is a Shannon-like entropic measure able to describe the global dynamics of a complex system [16]. PE has been used for studying complex phenomena in different fields [15–17]. As shown in [16], by analysing the trajectories of PE and its derived quantities, an automaton, called Persistent Entropy Automaton (PEA), which models the global dynamics of the system under study, can be manually devised.

The global financial system is one of the most important, human-made, complex systems. This system is composed of multiple interacting autonomous components or "selfish" agents, who - very often - act for their own benefit, and of complex interactions among those components. Each component behaves according to his/its own strategies, under the influence of the environment and interacting with other heterogeneous components. Classical tools for analysing and modelling such systems operate under a range of rather unrealistic assumptions. For example, interactions are normally abstracted with equations: this implies that the system reaches the equilibrium through non-linear optimisation methods rather than emerging from the agents interactions [12].

In this paper we use TDA to construct a data space from the components of the Dow Jones stock market index. The considered data set is the time series of the daily log-returns of Dow Jones' components from 1987 to 2017. From the data space, we calculate the PE and we devise a PEA whose locations model global states of the stock market. We show that early warnings about the emergence of the already occurred financial crisis can be identified by the PEA.

2   Methods

TDA employs concepts and principles of the field of computational topology to reveal higher dimensional patterns hidden in big data sets [5,8]. Computational topology studies invariants of shapes among which the so called Betti numbers, or barcodes, that characterise the existence of n-dimensional holes in the topological data space. TDA builds a discrete topological space, a simplicial complex, following a filtration procedure. In this work we use the Vietoris-Rips complex filtration that works on point clouds [8]. At each step of the filtration the persistent homology is computed yielding a collection of barcodes that indicate the life span of the topological invariants. PE is then computed from the barcodes [15].

The 24 time series of the considered Dow Jones components were mapped into a point cloud using a sliding window of 50 days and scrolling one point at a time with superposition of 49 points. Each window then produced 50 points in $\mathbb{R}^{24}$. This technique has been demonstrate suitable for studying the time-varying properties of systems similar to the one we are studying [9,15].

The mechanism driving critical transitions in complex systems is called *tipping point*, which is an abrupt qualitative change in the behaviour of a dynamical system when one or more control parameters change. In approaching a tipping point, a complex system shows a phenomenon called Critical Slowing Down (CSD), which can be considered an Early Warnings Signal (EWS) for the critical transition [3,18]. Since PE describes a system globally, it contains a summary of the knowledge about the system. Moreover, it can be considered a time series itself and can be calculated for all the dimensions. Thus, we study the *total* PE time series (PE_{tot}) - calculated as the sum of PEs for all the dimensions - with an analytical approach. The goal is to identify EWSs about a crisis by detecting the occurrence of tipping points. The obtained PE_{tot} is shown in Fig. 1.

To delimit the CSD areas we used an adaptation of the W_2 index, i.e. a combination of statistical indices (coefficient of variation, 1-lag autocorrelation, and kurtosis), described in [7]. W_2 is computed from PE_{tot} with the R package "earlywarnings" using another sliding window of size 450. Thus, W_2 is another time series and it is plotted along with its running average and 2σ confidence bands in Fig. 1. Potential areas of CSD are identified by finding points where $W_2 > \overline{W_2} + 2\sigma$ [7]. These areas are shown in Fig. 1 with black bands and represent the EWSs in our system.

Identified CSD areas can be used to define PEA states. A PEA *monitors* the PE and derived functions w. r. t. equilibrium conditions that define its states [16]. It remains in a state s as long as the associated equilibrium condition $ec(s)$ is satisfied. When it is violated, the PEA exits s and starts a non-instantaneous transition, which can be seen as an adaptation phase. This adaptation may end into an adjacent PEA state s' as soon as $ec(s')$ is satisfied or may not terminate. This definition is based on the fact that PEA states are devised from the observed trajectories of PE and derived functions. Indeed, it may happen that the monitored functions exhibit evolutions that were not identified as equilibrium conditions. This is expected for natural complex systems for which "complete" models can not be established. The main difference between a PEA and a hybrid automaton, which is a top-down defined model not considering unknown evolutions [10], is essentially in this different perspective.

3   Persistent Entropy Automaton of Dow Jones

In the $S[B]$ paradigm the structural level S is a model of the global dynamics of the system and the behavioural level B is a model of the local interactions among the entities of the system [13]. In this study, the behavioural level B is represented by real human agents that produced the data that we use. The structural level S is defined as a PEA in the following.

We consider two financial crises, dot-Com and Lehman Brothers Crash, both represented with coloured bands in Fig. 1. We devise the PEA by monitoring the functions $PE_{tot}(t)$, $W_2(t)$, their running average $\overline{PE_{tot}}(t)$, $\overline{W_2}(t)$ together with their derivatives indicated with a dot over the symbol. Each discrete instant t corresponds to one day observation. The derived PEA is called PEA_{W_2}, is

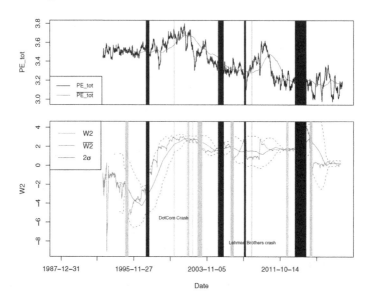

Fig. 1. Plot of PE_{tot} and its running average (above). Plot of W_2 and its running average with confidence bands (below). The grey and black vertical bands correspond to the relative states of the automaton in Fig. 2. The thin coloured vertical bands correspond to financial crises. (Color figure online)

depicted in Fig. 2 and its states are described in the following. A *stable* state is characterised by the equilibrium condition $|W_2 - \overline{W_2}| < 2\sigma$, that is W_2 does not exceed the confidence bands. The state called Stable is the initial one and holds this condition. As soon as the functions violate the stable condition, PEA_{W_2} exits state Stable and starts an adaptation. The only state in which the adaptation can end is the one called Grey, a state indicating that there was in the past at least one violation of the stable state condition. The equilibrium condition of Grey is $\dot{\overline{W_2}} \approx 0 \wedge \dot{\overline{PE_{tot}}} < 0 \wedge W_2 < \overline{W_2} - 2\sigma$, which means that the running average of W_2 has minimal oscillations, the running average of the total PE is decreasing and W_2 exits the confidence band -2σ. Visually, the periods in which PEA_{W_2} stays in this state are represented by the grey bands in Fig. 1. State White corresponds visually to the period after a grey band, it has the stable equilibrium condition and records the fact that the system entered at least once state Grey. After White, another grey band can occur (in this case the PEA goes back to Grey) or a black band occurs. A black band corresponds to state Black. This is the early warning state because from Black the system can only evolve to state Tipping that represents a tipping point. In Tipping a crisis, represented by the dashed transition towards state Stable, can occur or the system can return to state Grey. The dashed transition can be interpreted as the occurrence of a phase transition of the system.

PEA_{W_2} is then able to give a warning, in state Black, that a crisis may occur, without giving a prediction. However, if the current state is different from Black, the model says that a crisis cannot occur immediately: there must be at least one (or more) adaptations before the tipping point state is reached.

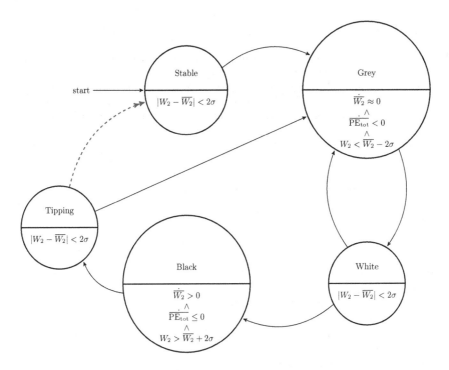

Fig. 2. PEA$_{W_2}$, describing the transitions among the global states of the system.

4   Conclusions

In this work we have modelled the global dynamics of a complex system by manually devising a PEA. TDA has been used for analysing the phenomenological data of the system and PE has been calculated from a topological space derived from a data set. The application domain is the Dow Jones stock market. The derived automaton models the global behaviour of the market and is able to recognise a tipping point state in which a financial crisis may occur and previous states in which there is some degree of warning but there is not an immediate alarm because some other adaptations are required to reach the tipping point state. The transition that goes from the tipping point state to the stable state can be interpreted as a phase transition of the system.

Despite the encouraging result we are aware that the proposed analysis presents some limitations: one is about the peculiarity of the data set that does not allow one to set up a statistical validation of the results because of the unicity of the phenomenon under study, for which other instances do not exist.

Another regards the computation of the indices for deriving the W_2, for which it is necessary to try different lengths of the sliding windows.

References

1. Arbab, F.: Reo: a channel-based coordination model for component composition. Math. Struct. Comput. Sci. **14**(3), 329–366 (2004)
2. Baier, C., Sirjani, M., Arbab, F., Rutten, J.: Modeling component connectors in Reo by constraint automata. Sci. Comput. Program. **61**(2), 75–113 (2006)
3. Battiston, S., et al.: Complexity theory and financial regulation. Science **351**(6275), 818–819 (2016)
4. Binchi, J., Merelli, E., Rucco, M., Petri, G., Vaccarino, F.: jHoles: a tool for understanding biological complex networks via clique weight rank persistent homology. Electron. Not. Theor. Comput. Sci. **306**, 5–18 (2014)
5. Carlsson, G.: Topology and data. Bull. AMS **46**(2), 255–308 (2009)
6. De Nicola, R., Ferrari, G.L., Pugliese, R.: KLAIM: a kernel language for agents interaction and mobility. IEEE Trans. Softw. Eng. **24**, 315–330 (1998)
7. Drake, J.M., Griffen, B.D.: Early warning signals of extinction in deteriorating environments. Nature **467**(7314), 456 EP - (2010)
8. Edelsbrunner, H., Harer, J.: Computational Topology: An Introduction. AMS, Providence (2010)
9. Gidea, M., Katz, Y.: Topological data analysis of financial time series: landscapes of crashes. Phys. A **491**, 820–834 (2018)
10. Henzinger, T.: The theory of hybrid automata. In: Inan, M., Kurshan, R. (eds.) Verification of Digital and Hybrid Systems, NATO ASI Series (Series F: Computer and Systems Sciences), vol. 170, pp. 265–292. Springer, Heidelberg (2000). https://doi.org/10.1007/978-3-642-59615-5_13
11. Jennings, N.R.: An agent-based approach for building complex software systems. Commun. ACM **44**(4), 35–41 (2001)
12. Landini, S., Gallegati, M., Rosser, J.B.: Consistency and incompleteness in general equilibrium theory. J. Evol. Econ. (2018). https://doi.org/10.1007/s00191-018-0580-6
13. Merelli, E., Paoletti, N., Tesei, L.: Adaptability checking in complex systems. Sci. Comput. Program. **115–116**, 23–46 (2016)
14. Merelli, E., Pettini, M., Rasetti, M.: Topology driven modeling: the IS metaphor. Nat. Comput. **14**(3), 421–430 (2015)
15. Merelli, E., Piangerelli, M., Rucco, M., Toller, D.: A topological approach for multivariate time series characterization: the epileptic brain. In: EAI Endorsed Transactions on Self-Adaptive Systems (2016). https://doi.org/10.4108/eai.3-12-2015.2262525
16. Merelli, E., Rucco, M., Sloot, P., Tesei, L.: Topological characterization of complex systems: using persistent entropy. Entropy **17**(10), 6872–6892 (2015)
17. Piangerelli, M., Rucco, M., Tesei, L., Merelli, E.: Topological classifier for detecting the emergence of epileptic seizures. BMC Res. Not. **11**, 392 (2018)
18. Scheffer, M.: Complex systems: foreseeing tipping points. Nature **467**, 411 EP (2010)

Theorem Proving

Proof Guidance in PVS with Sequential Pattern Mining

M. Saqib Nawaz[1]([✉]), Meng Sun[1], and Philippe Fournier-Viger[2]

[1] LMAM and Department of Informatics, School of Mathematical Sciences,
Peking University, Beijing, China
`{msaqibnawaz,sunm}@pku.edu.cn`
[2] School of Humanities and Social Sciences,
Harbin Institute of Technology (Shenzhen), Shenzhen, China
`philfv8@yahoo.com`

Abstract. The recent introduction of the big data paradigm and advancements in machine learning and deep mining techniques have made proof guidance and automation in interactive theorem provers (ITPs) an important research topic. In this paper, we provide a learning approach based on sequential pattern mining (SPM) for proof guidance in the PVS proof assistant. Proofs in a PVS theory are first abstracted to a computer-processable corpus. SPM techniques are then used on the corpus to discover frequent proof steps and proof patterns, relationships of proof steps / patterns with each other, dependency of new conjectures on already proved facts and to predict the next proof step(s). Obtained results suggest that the integration of SPM in proof assistants can be used to guide the proof process and in the development of proof tactics/strategies.

Keywords: PVS · Proof development process · Proof corpus ·
Frequent patterns · Sequential pattern mining

1 Introduction

Theorem provers allow the formal development and verification of system properties that can be defined in appropriate logical formalisms. Automated (first-order) theorem provers (ATPs) deal with the development of computer programs that can automatically perform logical reasoning. However, first-order logic (FOL) lacks the expressibility power that is required to define complex systems with an infinite domain. On the other hand, higher-order logic (HOL) allows quantification over predicates and functions. HOL based theorem provers, also known as interactive theorem provers (ITPs), offer support for rich logical formalisms such as dependent and (co)inductive types as well as recursive functions, which enable ITPs to model complex systems. Today, these mechanical reasoning systems are used in verification projects that range from operating

ⓒ IFIP International Federation for Information Processing 2019
Published by Springer Nature Switzerland AG 2019
H. Hojjat and M. Massink (Eds.): FSEN 2019, LNCS 11761, pp. 45–60, 2019.
https://doi.org/10.1007/978-3-030-31517-7_4

systems, compilers and hardware components to prove the correctness of large mathematical proofs such as the Feit-Thomson Theorem and the Kepler conjecture [22]. However, automatic reasoning in ITPs is still a hard problem due to undecidable algorithms and proof methods [20].

Unlike ATPs where the proof process is generally automatic, ITPs follow the user driven proof development process. The user guides the proof process by providing the proof goal and by applying proof commands and tactics to prove the goal. Generally, the user does lots of repetitive work to prove a non-trivial theorem (goal), which is laborious and consumes a large amount of time. Proof guidance and proof automation in ITPs are two extremely desirable features. ITPs now do have a large corpora of computer-understandable formalized knowledge [5,19] in the form of proof libraries. In PVS, proof scripts for a particular theory are stored separately in a file that can also be considered as a proof corpus for the theorems and lemmas in that theory. Proof scripts of different theories can be combined together to develop a more complex corpora. These corpora play an important role in artificial intelligence based methods, such as concept matching, structure formation and theory exploration. The ongoing fast progress in machine learning and data mining made it possible to use these learning techniques on such corpora in guiding the proof search process, in proof automation and in developing proof tactics/strategies, as indicated in recent works [8,9,15–17,21,26].

In this paper, the focus is on proof guidance and premise selection in ITPs from the perspective of sequential pattern mining (SPM) techniques. SPM techniques are used in data mining to find interesting and useful patterns (information) that are hidden in large corpora of sequential data [14]. A particular proof goal in PVS depends on the specifications inside the theory and it can be completed with different combinations of proof commands, inference rules and decision procedures [30]. This makes it difficult to infer useful proof tactics and strategies from specific examples that can be applied more generally. Moreover, a proof corpus contains too much information, which makes it hard to carry out the brute force approach for proof search. However, there is the potential to identify useful and interesting hidden proof patterns in these corpora and relationships of such proof patterns with each other. With such information, SPM techniques can be used to investigate the dependency of new conjectures on already proved facts and to predict the next proof step(s) or pattern(s) for guiding the proof of a novel non-trivial theorem/lemma.

We present an SPM-based proof process learning approach for the PVS proof assistant. The basic idea is to convert the PVS proofs for a theory into a proof corpus that is suitable for learning. SPM techniques are applied on the corpus to find frequent proof steps and patterns that are used in the proofs. Moreover, relationships of a proof steps/patterns with each other are discovered through sequential rule mining. The learning approach is also used to find the relevance of the new conjectures with the proofs and the performance of some state-of-the-art prediction models are examined by training and testing them on the corpus to predict the next proof step(s). Besides PVS, the proposed approach can also be used to guide the proof process in other proof assistants. The ultimate goal is to develop proof tactics/strategies with useful patterns that can be invoked directly by the user in the proof development process.

The rest of this paper is organized as follows: Sect. 2 elaborates the SPM-based learning approach that is used to discover useful proof steps/patterns in the proof corpus, their relationship and prediction of next proof step(s). Evaluation of the proposed approach on a case study and obtained results are discussed in Sect. 3. Related work on using the machine learning and data mining techniques for automated reasoning in ATPs and ITPs is presented in Sect. 4. Finally, the paper is concluded with some future directions in Sect. 5. PVS dump files and SPM related data for this work can be found at [31].

2   Proof Corpus Mining with SPM

The structure of the SPM-based learning approach is shown in Fig. 1. It consists of two main parts:

1. Development of proof corpus: PVS proof steps for theorems and lemmas in a theory are converted to a proof corpus, where each complete proof is abstracted to sequences of proof commands.
2. Learning through SPM: SPM algorithms are used on the corpus to discover the common proof steps and patterns, relationships of proof steps/patterns with each other, dependency of new conjectures on already proved facts and prediction of next proof step(s). Each part is further elaborated next.

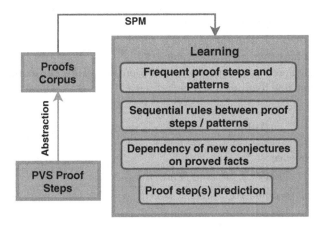

Fig. 1. SPM-based approach to learn the proof process

In general, data is assembled first, so that data mining algorithms can be used. To make the proof corpus suitable for learning, it should satisfy certain minimum requirements, such as:
− It is stored in a computational and electronic form.

- It contains many examples of proofs that offer diversity in kinds of proof steps. The corpus should have different proof steps so that useful proof patterns as well as the dependency of proof steps and prediction of next proof steps can be discovered.
- It is transformed in a suitable abstraction, so that no meaningful information from the proofs is left out. For this, we use the "*proof sequences to integers*" abstraction, where each proof command is converted to a distinct positive integer. Such abstraction allows wide diversity and makes the approach more general in nature.

Besides the dump file that contains the specifications for a particular theory with imported libraries and proof scripts (collection of proof steps) for theorems/lemmas, PVS also saves the proof scripts for a theory in a separate proof file. These files contain proof commands with some other information related to PVS. After removing the redundant information from the proof files, the complete proof is a sequence of proof steps. In the following we present some concepts related to sequences in the context of this work.

Let $PS = \{ps_1, ps_2, ..., ps_m\}$ represent the set of proof commands. A *proof steps set PSS* is a set of proof commands, that is $PSS \subseteq PS$. $|PSS|$ denotes the set cardinality. PSS has a length k (called k-PSS) if it contains k proof commands, i.e., $|PSS| = k$. For example, consider the set of PVS proof commands $PS = \{skolem, flatten, inst?, split, beta, iff, assert\}$. The set $\{skolem, flatten, assert\}$ is a proof steps set that contains three proof commands. For the purpose of processing commands in some order, a total order relation on proof commands is assumed to exist (e.g. the lexicographical order), denoted as $\prec$.

A proof sequence is a list of proof steps sets $S = \langle PSS_1, PSS_2, ..., PSS_n \rangle$, such that $PSS_i \subseteq PSS$ $(1 \leq i \leq n)$. For example, $\langle \{skolem, flatten\}, \{inst?\}, \{beta, iff\}, \{assert\} \rangle$ is a proof sequence which has four proof steps sets being used to prove a theorem. A *proof corpus PC* is a list of proof sequences $PC = \langle S_1, S_2, ..., S_p \rangle$, where each sequence has an identifier (ID). For example, Table 1 shows a PC that has five proof sequences with IDs 1, 2, 3, 4 and 5.

Table 1. A sample of a proof corpus

ID	Proof sequence
1	$\langle\{$*inst 1 "lambda (x,y: sequence[Time]): false", grind*$\}\rangle$
2	$\langle\{$*skosimp, expand "Teq", flatten, assert*$\}\rangle$
3	$\langle\{$*skosimp, expand "Fifon", propax*$\}\rangle$
4	$\langle\{$*skeep, expand "Tle", typepred "<", expand "strict_order?", flatten, expand "transitive?", inst -2 "T(s1)" "T(s2)" "T(s3)", assert* $\}\rangle$
5	$\langle\{$*induct n*$\},\{$*expand "sum", propax*$\},\{$*skosimp, expand "sum" +, assert*$\}\rangle$

The final step is to convert the proof sequences into sequences of integers to bring the corpus in a more suitable format for SPM techniques. In the final corpus, each line represents a proof sequence that was used for the proof of a theorem/lemma. Each proof command in the sequence is replaced by a positive integer. For example, the proof command *skosimp* is replaced by 1. Moreover, proof commands are separated with a single space followed by a negative integer -1. The negative integer -2 appears at the end of each line to indicate the end of a proof sequence. It is to note that the same integers are used for similar proof commands such as *(inst?())* and *(inst fnum constants)*, and *(skosimp)* and *(skosimp*)*. This makes the learning process more general in nature and can be used for other PVS theories, in particular for the PVS library.

A proof sequence $S_\alpha = \langle \alpha_1, \alpha_2, ..., \alpha_n \rangle$ is present or contained in another proof sequence $S_\beta = \langle \beta_1, \beta_1, ..., \beta_m \rangle$ iff there exist integers $1 \leq i_1 < i_2 < ... < i_n \leq m$, such that $\alpha_1 \subseteq \beta_{i1}, \alpha_2 \subseteq \beta_{i2}, ..., \alpha_n \subseteq \beta_{im}$ (denoted as $S_\alpha \sqsubseteq S_\beta$). If S_α is present in S_β, then S_α is a *subsequence* of S_β. In SPM, various measures are used to evaluate the importance and interestingness of a subsequence. The *support* measure is used by most SPM techniques. The *support* of S_α in PC is the total number of sequences (S) that contain S_α, and is represented by $sup(S_\alpha)$:

$$sup(S_\alpha) = |\{S | S_\alpha \sqsubseteq S \wedge S \in PC\}|$$

SPM is an enumeration problem that aims to find all the *frequent subsequences* in a sequential dataset. A sequence S is a *frequent sequence* (also called *sequential pattern*) iff $sup(S) \geq minsup$, where $minsup$ (minimum support) is the threshold being determined by the user. A sequence containing n items (proof commands in this work) in a corpus can have up to $2^n - 1$ distinct subsequences. This makes the naive approach to calculate the support of all possible subsequences infeasible for most corpora. Several efficient algorithms have been developed in recent years that do not explore all the search space for all possible subsequences.

All SPM algorithms investigate the patterns search space with two operations: *s-extensions* and *i-extensions*. A sequence $S_\alpha = \langle \alpha_1, \alpha_2, ..., \alpha_n \rangle$ is a *prefix* of another sequence $S_\beta = \langle \beta_1, \beta_1, ..., \beta_m \rangle$, if $n < m$, $\alpha_1 = \beta_1$, $\alpha_2 = \beta_2$, ..., $\alpha_{n-1} = \beta_{n-1}$, where α_n is equal to the first $|\alpha_n|$ items of β_n according to the $\prec$ order. Note that SPM algorithms follow a specific order $\prec$ so that the same potential patterns are not considered twice and the choice of the order $\prec$ does not affect the final result produced by SPM algorithms. A sequence S_β is an *s-extension* of a sequence S_α for an item x if $S_\beta = \langle \alpha_1, \alpha_2, ..., \alpha_n, \{x\} \rangle$. Similarly, for an item x, a sequence S_γ is an *i-extension* of S_α if $S_\gamma = \langle \alpha_1, \alpha_2, ..., \alpha_n \cup \{x\} \rangle$. SPM algorithms either employ a breadth-first search or a depth-first search. In the following, a brief description of state-of-the-art SPM algorithms is presented.

The TKS (Top-k Sequential) algorithm finds the top-k sequential patterns in a corpus, where k is set by the user and it represents the number of sequential patterns to be discovered by the algorithm. TKS employs the basic candidate generation procedure of SPAM and vertical database representation. With vertical representation, support for patterns can be calculated without performing costly database scans. This makes vertical algorithms to perform better on dense or long sequences. TKS also uses several strategies for search space pruning and depends on the PMAP (Precedence Map) data structure to avoid costly operations of bit vector intersection. Another SPM algorithm is the CM-SPAM algorithm that performs a depth-first search to discover frequent sequential patterns in a corpus. The CMAP (Co-occurrence MAP) data structure is used in CM-SPAM to store co-occurrence of item information. A generic pruning mechanism that is based on CMAP is used for pruning the search space with vertical database representation, to efficiently discover sequential patterns. More detail on TKS and CM-SPAM can be found in [10,11] respectively.

Sequential patterns that appear frequently in a corpus with low confidence are worthless for decision making or prediction. Sequential rules discover patterns by considering not only their support but also their confidence. A sequential rule $X \rightarrow Y$ is a relationship between two PSSs $X, Y \subseteq PS$, such that $X \cap Y = \emptyset$ and $X, Y \neq \emptyset$. The rule $r : X \rightarrow Y$ means that if items of X occur in a sequence, items of Y will occur afterward in the same sequence. X is contained in S_α (written as $X \sqsubseteq S_\alpha$) iff $X \subseteq \bigcup_{i=1}^n \alpha_i$. A rule $r : X \rightarrow Y$ is contained in S_α ($r \sqsubseteq S_\alpha$) iff there exists an integer k such that $1 \leq k < n$, $X \subseteq \bigcup_{i=1}^k \alpha_i$ and $Y \subseteq \bigcup_{i=k+1}^n \alpha_i$. The confidence of r in PC is defined as:

$$conf_{PC}(r) = \frac{|\{S|r \sqsubseteq S \wedge S \in PC\}|}{|\{S|X \sqsubseteq S \wedge S \in PC\}|}$$

The support of r in PC is defined as:

$$sup_{PC}(r) = \frac{|\{S|r \sqsubseteq S \wedge S \in PC\}|}{|PC|}$$

A rule r is a *frequent sequential rule* iff $sup_{PC}(r) \geq minsup$ and r is a *valid sequential rule* iff it is frequent and $conf_{PC}(r) \geq minconf$, where the thresholds $minsup, minconf \in [0, 1]$ are set by the user. Mining sequential rules in a corpus deals with finding all the valid sequential rules. For this, the ERMiner (Equivalence class based sequential Rule Miner) algorithm [12] is used. It relies on a vertical database representation and represents the search space of rules using equivalence classes of rules having the same antecedent or consequent. It employs two operations (left and right merges) to explore the search space of frequent sequential rules, where the search space is pruned with the Sparse Count Matrix (SCM) technique, which makes ERMiner more efficient than other sequential rule finding algorithms.

The statistical Naive Bayes (NB) classifier [32] is based on Bayes' theorem and is used to compute the probability of using the proof p in the corpus to prove a new conjecture c. A conjecture is a proposition or statement that has not been proved yet, but is thought to be true. The probability is based on the fact that some p are already used before in the proof of conjectures similar to c. As each p contains a set of proof steps, the conditional probability $P(PSS|c)$ estimates the relevance of PSS for c. The conditional probability is computed and multiplied to get the overall probability for c.

The Compact Prediction Tree+ (CPT+) model is used to predict the next proof step(s) [18]. CPT+ implements two strategies for compression to reduce the CPT size and one strategy for the reduction of prediction time. In the training phase, CPT+ takes a set of training sequences as input and generates three data structures: a prediction tree, a lookup table and an inverted index. These three structures are built incrementally by considering the sequence one by one during training. For a proof sequence S_α of n elements, the suffix of S_α of size y where $1 \le y \le n$ is defined as $P_y(S_\alpha) = \langle \alpha_{n-y+1}, \alpha_{n-y+2}, ..., \alpha_n \rangle$. Predicting the next proof steps of S_α is done by finding those sequences that are similar to $P_y(S_\alpha)$ in any order. For prediction, CPT+ uses the *consequent* of each sequence that is similar to S_α. Let S_β be another proof sequence similar to S_α. The consequent of S_β with respect to S_α is the longest subsequence $\langle \beta_v, \beta_{v+1}, ..., \beta_m \rangle$ of S_β such that $\bigcup_{k=1}^{v-1} \{\beta_k\} \subseteq P_y(S_\alpha)$ and $1 \le v \le m$. Each proof command discovered in the consequent of a similar proof sequence of S_α is stored in the count table (CT) data structure. CPT+ in last returns the most supported proof step(s) in the CT as prediction(s).

3 Experiments

All the following experiments are performed on an HP laptop with a fifth generation Core i5 processor and 8 GB RAM. For the case study, we select our previous work [29], where PVS is used for the analysis and verification of Reo connectors composed of untimed and timed channels. The main reason to select the proofs in [29] is that we are extending the formalization framework to cover the probabilistic [3] and stochastic [4] behavior of Reo connectors. The approach not only enabled us to comprehend the proof process for probabilistic connectors but also can be considered far effective in providing the necessary guidance to attain the proofs of such connectors.

SPMF data mining library, developed in JAVA, is used to analyze the proof corpus. It is an open-source and cross-platform framework that is specialized in pattern mining tasks. SPMF offers implementations for more than 150 data mining algorithms. More detail on SPMF can be found in [13].

3.1 Case Study

Reo [2] is a channel-based exogenous coordination language that allows the construction of complex *connectors* from primitive *channels* through compositional operators. Connectors in Reo provide the protocol for controlling and organizing the communication, synchronization and cooperation between components. Each channel in Reo has two channel ends type *source* or *sink*. The connector behavior in PVS is formalized by means of data-flows on its sink and source nodes, which are essentially infinite sequences. In PVS, record structure named *TD* is used to represent the *timed-data* sequences on sink and source nodes, where *time* is defined as a *positive real number* ($\mathbb{R}^+$) and *data* is defined as a *positive* type. Three main composition operators (flow through, replicate and merge) are used in Reo for connector construction. Flow through and replicate operators can be achieved explicitly in PVS, whereas merge operator is defined inductively.

We omit the details of Reo connector modeling in PVS due to the length limitation. Interested readers can find more details in [29,31]. Here, one example is provided to show how connectors are modeled and how properties for connectors are proved in PVS.

Example 1. Figure 2 shows a connector which consists of one *Synchronous (Sync)* channel (AB) and one *FIFO1* channel (BC), that accepts data items at source node A and stores the data items in the buffer, before dispensing them through the sink node C. The mixed node B allows the data items to move from the *Sync* channel to *FIFO1* channel without any change.

Fig. 2. A connector composed of a Sync and a FIFO1 channel

Let a, b, c denote the time sequences when the corresponding data sequence flows through nodes A, B and C respectively. According to the semantics of *Sync* and *FIFO1* channels, $a = b < c$. Let α, γ represent the data sequences being observed at nodes A and C respectively, and $\alpha = \gamma$. In PVS, these results are proved with the following theorem.

Theorem 1. *Sync(A,B)* $\wedge$ *Fifo1(B,C)* $\Rightarrow$ *Tle(A,C)* $\wedge$ *Teq(A,B)* $\wedge$ *Deq(A,C)*

Proof. PVS prover is based on *sequent calculus* and it can build a graphical proof tree for a proof goal. The nodes in the proof tree are sequents. PVS proof commands may divide the main goal into sub-goals (tree leaves). The proof is completed when all the sub-goals are proved. The proof steps for Theorem 1 are shown in Fig. 3.

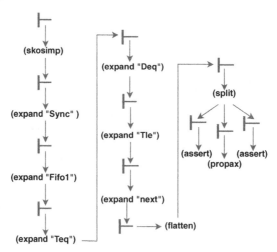

Fig. 3. PVS proof tree for Theorem 1

3.2   Results and Discussion

Results obtained by applying SPM algorithms on the proof corpus are discussed in this section.

The TKS algorithm is first applied on the corpus to find hidden proof steps and patterns. TKS takes a corpus and a user specified parameter k as input and returns the top-k most frequent patterns as output. The parameter k is used in place of *minusp* threshold due to the following two reasons:

1. Selection of a proper minimum support to discover the desired amount of useful patterns has an effect on the performance of SPM algorithms.
2. The minimum support fine-tuning process is hard and time consuming.

To overcome these drawbacks, the parameter k puts a bound on the total number of patterns to be discovered by the algorithm. Some proof patterns discovered by the TKS algorithm with varying length are shown in Table 2. The column **Sup** indicates the occurrence count of each pattern in the corpus. Table 3 provides some useful information related to frequent occurrence of proof steps and patterns that are used in the verification of Reo channels and connectors.

Table 2. Extracted proof steps/patterns with TKS algorithm

Pattern (length = 1)	Sup	Pattern (length = 2)	Sup
expand	40	expand, expand	34
skosimp	39	skosimp, expand	31
assert	33	skosimp, assert	25
inst	24	flatten, assert	19
flatten	20	expand, inst and skosimp, inst	14
typepred	11	typepred, expand	10
grind and propax	10	flatten, split	9
Pattern (length = 3)	Sup	Pattern (length = 4)	Sup
expand, expand, expand	25	expand, expand, expand, expand	22
typepred, expand, assert	9	expand, expand, flatten, assert	14
expand, expand, flatten	15	expand, expand, expand, assert	20
skosimp, expand, expand	26	skosimp, expand, expand, expand	19
skosimp, expand, assert	20	induct, skosimp, expand, assert	5
skosimp, expand, inst	10	skosimp, flatten, split, assert	7
expand, flatten, split	9	typepred, expand, expand, inst	5

Pattern (length $\geq$ 5)	Sup
expand, expand, expand, expand, assert	17
skosimp, expand, expand, expand, expand	19
skosimp, expand, expand, expand, assert	15
skosimp, expand, expand, flatten, assert	13
skosimp, expand, flatten, split, assert	7
typepred, expand, flatten, expand, inst, assert	4
skosimp, expand, expand, expand, assert, split	6
induct, skosimp, expand, expand, assert	5
skosimp, expand, expand, expand, assert, split	5

Unlike TKS, the CM-SPAM algorithm offers the *minsup* threshold. Table 3 lists some of the most useful frequent proof patterns in the corpus which are extracted with the CM-SPAM algorithm. The first six proof patterns appear in at least 50% of the sequences in the corpus. The next six patterns appear in at least 40% of the sequences and last two patterns appear in at least 10% of the sequences. Discovered patterns with the CM-SPAM algorithm are almost similar to the results obtained with the TKS algorithm. As the outputs of TKS and CM-SPAM are very similar, the performance of TKS with CM-SPAM is compared in terms of execution time and memory used. The CM-SPAM is fine tuned with the *minsup* threshold to generate the k proof patterns. For optimal support, TKS execution time is very similar to CM-SPAM. Similarly, TKS showed excellent scalability. These results, which are consistent with [11], are important because finding the top-k sequential proof patterns is a harder problem than mining all proof patterns, as the *minsup* requires dynamic raising that starts from 0.

Table 3. Frequent proof patterns extracted with CM-SPAM

Pattern	Sup	Min. Sup
expand	40	0.5
assert	33	0.5
skosimp	39	0.5
expand, expand	34	0.5
expand, assert	28	0.5
skosimp, expand	31	0.5
inst	24	0.4
expand, expand, expand	25	0.4
expand, expand, expand, expand	22	0.4
expand, expand, assert	25	0.4
skosimp, expand, expand	26	0.4
skosimp, assert	25	0.4
inst, assert	6	0.1
expand, typepred, inst	6	0.1

Figure 4 shows the relationships between proof steps/patterns that are discovered through sequential rule mining with the ERMiner algorithm. The confidence (*misconf*) threshold is set to 70%, which means that rules have a confidence of at least 70% (a rule $X \rightarrow Y$ has a confidence of 70% if the set of proof commands in X is followed by the set of proof commands in Y at least 70% of the times when X appears in a proof sequence). The value above the arrow is for the support and the value below the arrow indicates the confidence (probability). For example, the first rule in Fig. 4 indicates that 94.7% of the time, the *assert* command is followed after the *expand* command. With the ERMiner algorithm, we found some interesting relationship and dependency of proof steps/patterns with each other. Results obtained so far indicate that the total number of proof steps in each proof (abstraction simplicity) has a direct correlation on the efficiency of SPM algorithms.

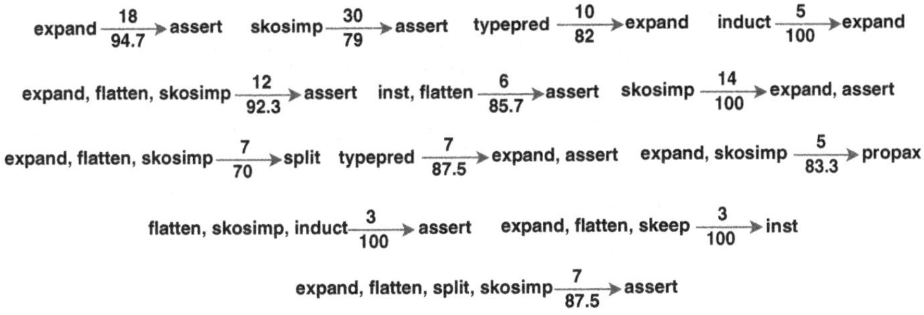

expand $\xrightarrow[94.7]{18}$ assert   skosimp $\xrightarrow[79]{30}$ assert   typepred $\xrightarrow[82]{10}$ expand   induct $\xrightarrow[100]{5}$ expand

expand, flatten, skosimp $\xrightarrow[92.3]{12}$ assert   inst, flatten $\xrightarrow[85.7]{6}$ assert   skosimp $\xrightarrow[100]{14}$ expand, assert

expand, flatten, skosimp $\xrightarrow[70]{7}$ split   typepred $\xrightarrow[87.5]{7}$ expand, assert   expand, skosimp $\xrightarrow[83.3]{5}$ propax

flatten, skosimp, induct $\xrightarrow[100]{3}$ assert   expand, flatten, skeep $\xrightarrow[100]{3}$ inst

expand, flatten, split, skosimp $\xrightarrow[87.5]{7}$ assert

Fig. 4. Sequential rules discovered in corpus

In [7], common proof patterns are found in the Isabelle proofs with a variable length Markov Chain. Proofs are represented in a tree structure format, which are linearized, such as the proofs are split into separate sequences and given weights accordingly. However, linearization means losing any important connections (information) between different branches in the proofs due to which interesting patterns may well be lost. In this work, the proof corpus contains all the necessary important information for pattern discovery and SPM algorithms, which are more user-friendly and work efficiently on the corpus.

The NB classifier implemented in SPMF is used to check the dependency of new conjectures on already proved proofs. For that, the classifier is trained on the proofs presented in the corpus. We then provide new conjectures from our ongoing work on probabilistic Reo connectors. In the output, the classifier successfully classified the new conjectures, which shows that the proofs can be used in guiding the proof process of new conjectures. Moreover, for conjectures taken from PVS libraries, the classifier was unable to classify, which means that their proofs are not dependent on the facts present in the corpus. NB classifiers are also used in [23] for computing the proof dependencies for new conjectures from the theorems taken from the Coq repository. Obtained results are presented with measures such as precision, recall and rank. In SPMF, the NB implementation only provides the binary type output for classification and does not provide information for the measures. In future, we would like to enhance the implementation of NB to provide statistics about the measures.

Predicting the next proof steps for the new conjecture or unproved theorem/lemma has gained increased importance in last few years. The CPT+ model is used for predicting the next proof steps. The model is first trained on the proof sequences in the corpus. The prediction model is then used to predict the next proof step for a new proof sequence. Prediction of the next proof step is based on the scores calculated by the model for each proof command. For example,

CPT+ predicted *assert* for the proof sequence <*flatten, split*>. The statistics and scores assigned by the model to each proof step for the previous example are listed in Table 4. It is to note here that a higher score is considered better for CPT+.

Table 4. Results for TPC+ prediction model

Statistics	Value	Proof step	Score
Number of distinct items	13	*skosimp*	2.018
Itemsets per sequence	12.342	*expand*	20.244
Distinct item per sequence	5.142	*assert*	**26.297**
Occurrence for each item	2.4	*inst*	2.778
Corpus size in MB	124.001	*grind*	2.636

To check the efficiency of CPT+, we compared its performance with various other state-of-the-art prediction models such as Dependency Graph (DG), Transition Directed Acyclic Graph (TDAG), CPT (the predecessor of CPT+), AKOM (All-K-Order-Markov) and LZ78. Each model is trained and tested with 10-fold cross-validation. The cross-validation technique characterizes the performance of each model by evaluating the generalization of independent set over statistical results provided by the model. In k-fold cross-validation, the dataset is randomly partitioned into k sub-datasets. One sub-dataset is then selected as validation set for model testing and the remaining $k-1$ sub-datasets are used for model training. This process is continued for k times and each sub-dataset is used exactly once as the validation set. Single estimation of the result is obtained by taking the average of k results. The main reason to use 10-fold cross-validation is to achieve low variance in each run. Obtained results for various prediction models are shown in Table 5.

Table 5. Accuracy of prediction models

Models	DG	TDAG	CPT+	CPT	AKOM	LZ78
Success	41.176	73.529	79.412	**85.714**	73.529	50
Failure	**58.824**	26.471	20.588	14.286	26.471	50
No Match	0.00	0.00	0.00	**17.647**	0.00	0.00
Overall	41.176	73.529	**79.412**	70.588	73.529	50

For evaluation of prediction models, three measures are used. The result of a prediction can be:
- a *success* if the model predicts accurately,
- a *failure* if the model predicts inaccurately and
- *no match* if the model cannot perform the prediction.

The overall performance of each model is measured through its *accuracy*, which is the total number of successful predictions performed by the model against the total number of test sequences. Two other measures *training time* and *testing time* are not included in the results here as all the models take almost the same time for training and testing. CPT+ achieved higher accuracy (79.412) as compared to other prediction models. CPT has a higher *success rate* than CPT+, but the higher *no match rate* makes its accuracy lower than CPT+. Markov based prediction models DG achieved the lowest *success rate* and highest *failure rate*, while TDAG and AKOM have the same results for all four parameters.

4   Related Work

Using machine learning and data mining in theorem provers is not a new idea and they are used mainly for three tasks: premise selection, strategy selection and internal guidance. Support vector machines (SVMs) and Gaussian processes (GPs) were used in [6] for selection of a good heuristics in the E theorem prover. In [27], kernel methods were applied for strategy scheduling and strategy finding problems in three ATPs: E, Satallax and LEO-II. Deep networks have been used in [28] for internal guidance in E, where deep learning based proof guidance increases the total number of theorems proved while reducing the average number of proof search steps. Moreover, internal proof guidance methods based on the *watchlist* technique were developed in [17] for E prover. A proof search guidance technique based on leanCoP was presented in [24] to guide the tableaux proof search. In [33], GRU networks were used in MetaMath for guiding the proof search of a tableau style proof process. Monte-Carlo tree search methods added with a connection tableau were studied and implemented in leanCoP in [9] for guiding the proof search. A new theorem proving algorithm (implemented in *rlCoP*) was recently presented in [26] for proof guidance that uses Monte-Carlo simulations with reinforcement iterations. *rlCoP* showed better performance than *leanCoP* in solving unseen problems when trained on a large corpus.

For HOL based theorem provers, variable length Markov models (VLMM) technique has been applied in [7] on a proof corpus of the Isabelle prover to identify sequences of proof steps and these sequences were used to form tactics. Particle swarm optimization and NB based techniques were proposed in [8] to internally guide the given-clause algorithm in the Satallax prover. Premise selection techniques were developed in [23] for the Coq system, where machine learning methods are compared on Coq proofs taken from the CoRN repository. Recurrent and convolutional neural networks were used in [21] for premise selection in the Mizar prover. A corpus of proofs was constructed in [1] for training a kernalized classifier with bag-of-word features that show the term occurrences in a vocabulary. Premise selection based on machine learning and automated reasoning for the HOL4 is provided in [15] by adapting HOL(y)Hammer [25]. A learning based automation technique was recently developed in [16] called

TacticToe on top of the HOL4 for automation of theorems proofs. The *HolStep* dataset, introduced in [22], consists of 10 K conjectures and 2M statements to develop new machine learning based proof strategies.

5   Conclusion

The proof development process in ITPs requires heavy interactions between users and the proof assistants, where users are forced to do lots of repetitive work which makes the proving process a more time consuming activity. To make the proof process simpler and for proof guidance, the SPM-based learning approach is adopted in this work to find the frequent proof steps/patterns and their relationship in a PVS theory. NB classifier is used to check the dependency of new conjectures on the already proved proofs. Moreover, the performance of some models for the prediction of next proof step(s) is compared, where CPT+ performs better than other models. Some interesting proof patterns are found with SPM and obtained results show that the number of proof steps in each proof has a direct correlation on the efficiency of SPM algorithms.

There are several directions of future work. First, we would like to use the SPM algorithms on the corpora of proof steps for theories included in PVS library, which contains thousands of theorems. This will enable us to develop a more general learning approach for the proofs of new conjunctures. Another direction is to use evolutionary and heuristics techniques such as genetic programming and particle swarm optimization for the development of PVS strategies from frequently occurring proof patterns. Some other future work includes the implementation of some famous classifiers such as k-nearest neighbor in SPMF and enhancing the implementation of NB to provide statistics about common measures such as precision, recall and f-measure. Last but not the least, using SPM algorithms on the dataset provided by [22] is in our future plan as well.

Acknowledgement. The work has been supported by the National Natural Science Foundation of China under grant no. 61772038, 61532019 and 61272160, and the Guandong Science and Technology Department (Grant no. 2018B010107004).

References

1. Alama, J., Heskes, T., Kühlwein, D., Tsivtsivadze, E., Urban, J.: Premise selection for mathematics by corpus analysis and kernel methods. J. Autom. Reasoning **52**(2), 191–213 (2014)
2. Arbab, F.: Reo: a channel-based coordination model for component composition. Math. Struct.Comput. Sci. **14**(3), 329–366 (2004)
3. Baier, C.: Probabilistic models for Reo connector circuits. J. Univ. Comput. Sci. **11**(10), 1718–1748 (2005)
4. Baier, C., Wolf, V.: Stochastic reasoning about channel-based component connectors. In: Ciancarini, P., Wiklicky, H. (eds.) COORDINATION 2006. LNCS, vol. 4038, pp. 1–15. Springer, Heidelberg (2006). https://doi.org/10.1007/11767954_1

5. Blanchette, J.C., Haslbeck, M., Matichuk, D., Nipkow, T.: Mining the archive of formal proofs. In: Kerber, M., Carette, J., Kaliszyk, C., Rabe, F., Sorge, V. (eds.) CICM 2015. LNCS (LNAI), vol. 9150, pp. 3–17. Springer, Cham (2015). https://doi.org/10.1007/978-3-319-20615-8_1

6. Bridge, J.P., Holden, S.B., Paulson, L.C.: Machine learning for first-order theorem proving - learning to select a good heuristic. J. Autom. Reasoning **53**(2), 141–172 (2014)

7. Duncan, H.: The use of data-mining for the automatic formation of tactics. Ph.D. thesis, University of Edinburgh, UK (2007)

8. Färber, M., Brown, C.: Internal guidance for satallax. In: Olivetti, N., Tiwari, A. (eds.) IJCAR 2016. LNCS (LNAI), vol. 9706, pp. 349–361. Springer, Cham (2016). https://doi.org/10.1007/978-3-319-40229-1_24

9. Färber, M., Kaliszyk, C., Urban, J.: Monte carlo tableau proof search. In: de Moura, L. (ed.) CADE 2017. LNCS (LNAI), vol. 10395, pp. 563–579. Springer, Cham (2017). https://doi.org/10.1007/978-3-319-63046-5_34

10. Fournier-Viger, P., Gomariz, A., Campos, M., Thomas, R.: Fast vertical mining of sequential patterns using co-occurrence information. In: Tseng, V.S., Ho, T.B., Zhou, Z.-H., Chen, A.L.P., Kao, H.-Y. (eds.) PAKDD 2014. LNCS (LNAI), vol. 8443, pp. 40–52. Springer, Cham (2014). https://doi.org/10.1007/978-3-319-06608-0_4

11. Fournier-Viger, P., Gomariz, A., Gueniche, T., Mwamikazi, E., Thomas, R.: TKS: efficient mining of top-k sequential patterns. In: Motoda, H., Wu, Z., Cao, L., Zaiane, O., Yao, M., Wang, W. (eds.) ADMA 2013. LNCS (LNAI), vol. 8346, pp. 109–120. Springer, Heidelberg (2013). https://doi.org/10.1007/978-3-642-53914-5_10

12. Fournier-Viger, P., Gueniche, T., Zida, S., Tseng, V.S.: ERMiner: sequential rule mining using equivalence classes. In: Blockeel, H., van Leeuwen, M., Vinciotti, V. (eds.) IDA 2014. LNCS, vol. 8819, pp. 108–119. Springer, Cham (2014). https://doi.org/10.1007/978-3-319-12571-8_10

13. Fournier-Viger, P., et al.: The SPMF open-source data mining library version 2. In: Berendt, B., et al. (eds.) ECML PKDD 2016. LNCS (LNAI), vol. 9853, pp. 36–40. Springer, Cham (2016). https://doi.org/10.1007/978-3-319-46131-1_8

14. Fournier-Viger, P., Lin, J.C.W., Kiran, R.U., Koh, Y.S., Thomas, R.: A survey of sequential pattern mining. Data Sci. Pattern Recogn. **1**(1), 54–77 (2017)

15. Gauthier, T., Kaliszyk, C.: Premise selection and external provers for HOL4. In: Proceedings of CPP 2015, pp. 48–57. ACM (2015)

16. Gauthier, T., Kaliszyk, C., Urban, J.: TacticToe: learning to reason with HOL4 tactics. In: Proceedings of LPAR 2017. EPiC Series in Computing, vol. 46, pp. 125–143 (2017)

17. Goertzel, Z., Jakubův, J., Schulz, S., Urban, J.: ProofWatch: watchlist guidance for large theories in E. In: Avigad, J., Mahboubi, A. (eds.) ITP 2018. LNCS, vol. 10895, pp. 270–288. Springer, Cham (2018). https://doi.org/10.1007/978-3-319-94821-8_16

18. Gueniche, T., Fournier-Viger, P., Raman, R., Tseng, V.S.: CPT+: decreasing the time/space complexity of the compact prediction tree. In: Cao, T., Lim, E.-P., Zhou, Z.-H., Ho, T.-B., Cheung, D., Motoda, H. (eds.) PAKDD 2015. LNCS (LNAI), vol. 9078, pp. 625–636. Springer, Cham (2015). https://doi.org/10.1007/978-3-319-18032-8_49

19. Harrison, J., Urban, J., Wiedijk, F.: History of interactive theorem proving. In: Computational Logic. Handbook of the History of Logic, vol. 9, pp. 135–214. Elsevier (2014)

20. Hasan, O., Tahar, S.: Formal verification methods. In: Encyclopedia of Information Science and Technology, 3rd edn, pp. 7162–7170. IGI Global (2015)
21. Irving, G., Szegedy, C., Alemi, A.A., Eén, N., Chollet, F., Urban, J.: Deepmath - Deep sequence models for premise selection. In: Proceedings of NIPS 2016, pp. 2243–2251. ACM (2016)
22. Kaliszyk, C., Chollet, F., Szegedy, C.: Holstep: a machine learning dataset for higher-order logic theorem proving. Proc. ICLR **2017**, 1–12 (2017)
23. Kaliszyk, C., Mamane, L., Urban, J.: Machine learning of Coq proof guidance: first experiments. In: Proceedings of SCSS 2014. EPiC Series in Computing, vol. 30, pp. 27–34 (2014)
24. Kaliszyk, C., Urban, J.: FEMaLeCoP: fairly efficient machine learning connection prover. In: Davis, M., Fehnker, A., McIver, A., Voronkov, A. (eds.) LPAR 2015. LNCS, vol. 9450, pp. 88–96. Springer, Heidelberg (2015). https://doi.org/10.1007/978-3-662-48899-7_7
25. Kaliszyk, C., Urban, J.: Hol(y)Hammer: Online ATP service for HOL light. Math. Comput. Sci. **9**(1), 5–22 (2015)
26. Kaliszyk, C., Urban, J., Michalewski, H., Olsák, M.: Reinforcement learning of theorem proving. Proc. NeurIPS **2018**, 8836–8847 (2018)
27. Kühlwein, D., Urban, J.: MaLeS: a framework for automatic tuning of automated theorem provers. J. Autom. Reasoning **55**(2), 91–116 (2015)
28. Loos, S.M., Irving, G., Szegedy, C., Kaliszyk, C.: Deep network guided proof search. In: Proceedings of LPAR 2017. EPiC Series in Computing, vol. 46, pp. 85–105 (2017)
29. Nawaz, M.S., Sun, M.: Reo2PVS: formal specification and verification of component connectors. In: Proceedings of SEKE 2018, pp. 391–396. KSI Research Inc. (2018)
30. Owre, S., Shankar, N., Rushby, J.M., Stringer-Calvert, D.W.J.: PVS system Guide, PVS prover Guide. PVS language reference. Technical report, SRI International, November 2001
31. PVS and SPM data. https://github.com/saqibdola/SPM-in-PVS
32. Russell, S.J., Norvig, P.: Artificial Intelligence - A Modern Approach, 3rd edn. Pearson Education, Upper Saddle River (2010)
33. Whalen, D.. Holophrasm: a neural automated theorem prover for higher-order logic. CoRR, abs/1608.02644 2016

Using PVS for Modeling and Verification of Probabilistic Connectors

M. Saqib Nawaz$^{(\boxtimes)}$ and Meng Sun

LMAM and Department of Informatics, School of Mathematical Sciences,
Peking University, Beijing, China
{msaqibnawaz,sunm}@pku.edu.cn

Abstract. Reo is a channel-based coordination language that allows the construction of connectors to coordinate behavior among different components in distributed systems. Probabilistic connectors in Reo capture the random and probabilistic behavior to deal with the uncertainty of the real world. In this paper we use PVS to provide a mechanical formalization for probabilistic connectors. We first present the formalization of random/probabilistic channels and the composition operators in PVS. Random and probabilistic channels are modeled as relations on timed data distribution sequences that are observed at the source and sink ends of these channels. Composition operators are used to combine random/probabilistic channels together with primitive channels to construct complex component connectors. The approach can be used to naturally specify complex connectors and prove important properties for probabilistic connectors as well as the refinement/equivalence relations between them with the PVS proof assistant.

Keywords: Reo · PVS · Random/probabilistic connectors · Specification · Verification

1 Introduction

Large-scale distributed systems, that are generally transparent and heterogeneous in nature, are built from components that interact with each other to perform some specific tasks. Coordination languages offer possible binding for components in a distributed environment to make the interactions possible. Reo [2,8] is a popular exogenous coordination language where exogenous coordination [1] means that the primitives that support the coordination of an entity with others reside outside of that entity. Reo allows the orchestration of complex connectors from simple ones (called channels) through composition operators.

Connectors in Reo provide the protocols for controlling and organizing the communication, synchronization and cooperation among the components that they interconnect. Formal analysis and verification of connectors have gained much interest in the past decade for component-based software engineering due

© IFIP International Federation for Information Processing 2019
Published by Springer Nature Switzerland AG 2019
H. Hojjat and M. Massink (Eds.): FSEN 2019, LNCS 11761, pp. 61–76, 2019.
https://doi.org/10.1007/978-3-030-31517-7_5

to the recent evolution of software systems and advancements in cloud and grid technologies. It is also important to certify the correctness of connectors, which makes large-scale distributed systems more reliable. Some works have been done in this regard in the past years. For example, a modeling approach based on first-order relational logic in *Alloy* modeling language was provided in [14] for Reo connectors. The symbolic model checker "*Vereofy*" has been developed in [6] to verify CTL-like properties for connectors. Moreover, a formal transformation from Reo to the specification language *mCRL2* that is based on process algebra was presented in [15]. The models were then verified conveniently with the *mCRL2* model checker.

Complex distributed systems need to incorporate many aspects of the communication and coordination between components, such as nondeterminism, probabilistic and stochastic interactions, real-time information and resource consumption, etc. The works reported in [3–5,9,12,17,22] extend classical Reo from different perspective to deal with such requirements. The Unifying Theories of Programming (UTP) semantic framework was used in [21,23] to formalize connectors by providing design models for untimed and timed Reo connectors respectively, and recently extended in [24] to cover connectors that are composed from channels with random and probabilistic behavior. The theorem proving technique has been used in [18] to encode and reason about the design models for untimed/timed Reo connectors in PVS [19]. In this paper, we extend the approach to cover the formalization for Reo connectors with random and probabilistic behavior. The basic idea is to model the observable behavior of a probabilistic connector as a relation on the timed data distribution sequences being observed at the source (input) and sink (output) ends of the connector. The extended approach covers the scenarios for unpredictable, uncertain behavior. Furthermore, the refinement/equivalence relations between probabilistic connectors can be formalized and verified in PVS easily.

Our mechanized verification for probabilistic analysis of connectors is certainly not the first one. A variant of constraint automata called probabilistic constraint automata (PCA) has been developed in [5] to provide the operational semantics for probabilistic Reo connectors. Stochastic Reo automata was proposed in [17] to compositionally derive a QoS-aware semantics for Reo. The automata model was translated to Continuous-Time Markov Chains (CTMCs) so that third-party verification tools can be used for stochastic analysis. Similarly, priced probabilistic timed constraint automata (pPTCA) was used in [12] for the reasoning about nondeterministic, probabilistic and timed behavior with aspects of energy consumption. Reo was also used in [7] to coordinate modules in the PRISM model checker. Although such formalisms scale up quite well, they suffer from the state space explosion problem as Reo connectors generally describe the manifold interactions among components that they interconnect, rather than simple input-output behavior on one individual interface. Moreover, the modeling and verification of unbounded primitives or even bounded primitives with unbounded data domains always lead to the state space explosion problem, which cannot be solved with such finite automata models. However, such behavior can be specified and verified efficiently in theorem provers as shown in our previous works [13,18,25,26].

The remainder of the paper is organized as follows: The coordination language Reo is briefly introduced in Sect. 2. In Sect. 3, we present the specifications in PVS for some basic definitions that are used later to model random/probabilistic channels. Section 4 presents the formal modeling of random/probabilistic channels and composition operators in PVS. Section 5 shows how to reason about properties of probabilistic connectors in PVS and refinement/equivalence relations between them. Finally, Sect. 6 concludes the paper with some future work. The PVS dump file for this work can be found at [20].

2 Preliminaries

Reo offers a compositional framework where component *connectors* can be constructed from primitive *channels* of arbitrary types through composition operators. Connectors provide the protocol for controlling and organizing the communication, synchronization and cooperation between components. Each channel has two channel ends, with one of two types: *source* and *sink*. A source end provides input values to the channel via write actions and a sink end dispenses data out of the channel with read actions. A channel's ends can also be both sinks or both sources. Figure 1 shows few primitive channel types in Reo.

| Sync | LossySync | FIFO1 | SyncDrain | t-Timer |
| Channel | Channel | Channel | Channel | Channel |

Fig. 1. Some primitive channels in Reo

A *synchronous (Sync) channel* has one source and one sink end. Input/Output (I/O) operations can succeed only if the writing and reading operation is synchronized at source and sink end respectively. A *lossy synchronous (LossySync) channel* is a variant of the *Sync* channel. Data items in *LossySync* are transferred successfully if the write operation on the source end and the read operation on the sink end occur simultaneously, otherwise the data items are lost. A *FIFO1 channel* has one buffer cell of capacity 1, one source end and one sink end. *FIFO1* accepts a data item whenever the buffer is empty. After accepting a data item from the source end, it is first stored in the buffer and dispensed out of the channel through the sink end later in the FIFO order. The *synchronous Drain (SyncDrain) channel* is used for synchronizing the writing operations at its two source ends. It has no sink end and all written data items are lost. A *t-timer channel* accepts any data item at its source end and produces a *timeout* signal on its sink end after a delay of t time units. Further details on Reo and primitive untimed/timed channels can be found in [2, 3, 21, 23]. Furthermore, users can specify new channel types with their own requirements and interaction policies in Reo. For example, several probabilistic and stochastic extensions of Reo have been proposed in [5, 9, 16].

A connector can be depicted visually as a graph with some additional information. The nodes represent sets of the channel ends and the edges represent the established channels between the nodes. Nodes can be categorized into source, sink or mixed nodes, depending on whether the node contains only source channel ends, sink channel ends, or both. Therefore, source nodes are analogous to input ports and sink nodes to output ports. Data that flow through source and sink nodes depends on the pending write and read operations of the environment. For channel composition, three types of operators are used, which are (1) *flow-through*, (2) *replicate* and (3) *merge*, as shown in Fig. 2.

Fig. 2. Operators for channel composition

3   Basic Definitions in PVS

The behavior of untimed and timed connectors are formalized by modeling their observable behavior as relations on the timed data sequences at their sink and source nodes. For random and probabilistic behavior, sequences of data distributions where the data passes through connector nodes together with the time moments for data items observation emerges as the key building block to properly describe the connectors. Therefore, the observation on nodes can be specified naturally as *timed data distribution* (TDD) sequences for connectors that behaves probabilistically or randomly.

The PVS library for *probability* [10] and some pre-defined functions from PVS prelude are used in the modeling of random and probabilistic channels. The probability library is built on the firm foundations for probability theory [11]. Based on a σ-algebra, probability measure and probability space, the distribution function (df) for a real-valued random variable X is defined in PVS. We are interested in the cumulative distribution function (CDF) of a random variable. To deal with continuous random variable, we would partially instantiate the sample space T with *real*, σ-algebra with *borel_set* (borel sets) and specify the probability measure to describe the distributions for random variable.

A record structure in PVS is used to represent the *TDD* sequences on the sink and source nodes, where *time* is defined as a *positive real number* ($\mathbb{R}^+$), which is natural and expressive enough for the modeling of connector behavior. For untimed/timed channels, *data* is defined as a *positive type*. To capture the probabilistic behavior, *data* is defined as a function of type $[T \rightarrow real]$ (where T is a positive (non-empty) type). With such a kind of functions, other abstract sets of data can be processed first by mapping them to a set of real numbers in an appropriate way. Moreover, such mapping for data can be expanded easily in accordance with different application domains. The data distribution DD is defined as a Cartesian product with square brackets $[\_, \_]$ in PVS.

```
Time: Type = posreal
Data: TYPE [T -> real]

dfs?(F:[real->probability]):bool = EXISTS X: FORALL x: F(x) = P(X <= x)
df: TYPE+ = (dfs?) CONTAINING (LAMBDA x: IF x < 0 THEN 0 ELSE 1 ENDIF)

DD: TYPE = [Data, df]

TDD: TYPE = [# T: sequence[Time],
               D: sequence[DD] #]
```

Input, Output: VAR TDD

A *TDD* is a record structure type that has two components: *T* and *D*. The *T* component is a sequence of *time points* being used to represent the *time* when the data in the *D* component is observed. The *D* component is a sequence of *data distributions*. The *Input* and *Output* are declared as variables of type *TDD*. The components of a record type can be accessed through the corresponding field name. For example in our case, the *T* component of *Input* is accessed by *Input'T*.

Since the type of component *T* in *TDD* is defined as *sequence[Time]*, we have to define the operators "$<$" and "$>$" for sequences of times. A strict order (that is both transitive and irreflexive) is assumed for "$<$" and "$>$". The type system of PVS is not algorithmically decidable and may lead to proof obligations called type correctness conditions (TCCs). Defining "$<,>$" for sequence of time generated two TCCs. Proof steps for these two TCCs can be found at [20].

```
<: (strict_order?[sequence[Time]])
>: (strict_order?[sequence[Time]]) =
   LAMBDA (s1, s2: sequence[Time]): s2 < s1
```

Some more functions and predicates are used in PVS for concise modeling of probabilistic channels and composition operators. For example, *Teq* returns *true* if the time of two sequences are exactly equal to each other. *Tle* (*Tgt*) represents that time of the first sequence is strictly less (greater) than the second sequence. *Deq* (*Dneq*) shows the equality of data: data sequence at one end is equal (not equal) to data sequence at the other end. For primitive (untimed) channels, the time of input sequence is a simulation of real time which means that time sequence is increasing as time passes by. For probabilistic connectors including timed channels, some more predicate formulas are defined in a similar way. For example, *Tltt* (*Tgtt*) represents that the time of the first sequence with a delay *t* is less (greater) than the second sequence. And the *next* function takes a *TDD* and returns the derivative of the sequence. Suffix function that is used in the *next* function is used to return a suffix sequence and its definition can be found in the prelude library of PVS.

```
next(T1): TDD = T1 WITH [T:=(suffix(T1'T, 1)),
                         D:=(suffix(T1'D, 1))]
```

4   Probabilistic Channels and Operators

The modeling of some basic probabilistic/random channels and composition operators that are used to construct probabilistic connectors is presented in this section.

4.1   Random and Probabilistic Channels

The behavior of probabilistic/random channels are specified in PVS with the disjunction or conjunction of different predicates and constraints on the *TDD* sequences at source and sink nodes. We consider one random channel, *randomized synchronous channel*, and four probabilistic channels: *message-corrupting synchronous channel, probabilistic lossy synchronous channel, faulty FIFO1 channel* and *lossy FIFO1 channel*.

RSync: Randomized synchronous channel ($A \xrightarrow{rand(0,1)} B$) is the randomized variant of synchronous channel. When the channel is activated through an arbitrary write operation at source node A, it generates a random number $b \in \{0,1\}$ at sink node B. Sink node synchronously takes the random number with equal probability for 0 (*zero*) and 1 (*one*). In *RSync*, *zero* and *one* are declared as random variables. Their specifications generated two TCCs for expected type *random variable*, which is proved interactively with the PVS theorem prover. To prove both TCCs, we used already defined judgment *constant_is_measurable* in the *measure space definition* theory that can be found in the library *measure_integration*. The proofs for both TCCs are omitted here because of the page limitation and can be found at [20]. *RSync* is specified as follows:

```
zero: random_variable = (LAMBDA t: 0)
one:  random_variable = (LAMBDA t: 1)

RSync(Input, Output): bool = FORALL(n:nat):
        Output'D(n) = (zero, oah) OR
        Output'D(n) = (one, oah) &
            Teq(Input, Output)
```

The universal quantification and the first disjunction capture the random behavior being observed at the sink node. Each data element in the *TDD* sequence at the sink node can be either *zero* or *one* with probability *oah*, which is defined as:

```
oah(x): probability = 1/2
```

The synchronous behavior for this channel is satisfied with the predicate *Teq*, which shows that the time for the occurrence of data elements being observed at both channel ends are equal.

CSync: Message corrupting synchronous channel ($A -p\rightarrow B$) is the probabilistic variant of synchronous channel, where with probability p, the delivered message can be corrupted. In such a channel, if a data element is written to the source end, then the probability that the exact correct data value will be obtained at the sink end is $1 - p$. A corrupted data value, represented with c in the specification, will be obtained with probability p.

```
CSync(Input, Output)(p:probability):
  INDUCTIVE bool = (Output'T(0) = Input'T(0) &
  Output'D(0) = (Input'D(0)'1,(1-p)*Input'D(0)'2))
   OR (EXISTS(c:Data): Output'D(0) = (c,(p)*Input'D(0)'2)
   & CSync(next(Input), next(Output))(p))
```

The *CSync* channel is defined inductively. Inductive definitions in PVS, which are predicates with eventual range type *boolean*, are similar to recursive definitions as both involve induction and must satisfy some constraints to guarantee that they are total. The first formula is for the time equality constraint for the synchronous behavior. We can also model the first constraint with *Teq* predicate. The second and third formula with the disjunction reflects the probabilistic behavior. The sink node receives the same data that was written at the source node with the updated probability, where $1 - p$ is multiplied with the probability for data at source node. On the other hand, sink node receives the corrupted value (c) with probability p multiplied with the probability for the written data. The last formula is for the recursive step that channel takes.

PLSync: In the probabilistic lossy synchronous channel ($A \xrightarrow{q} B$), the transmission of the message from the source to sink fails with probability q. And with probability $1 - q$, *PLSync* acts like a standard *Sync* channel where the message is successfully transmitted from the source end to the sink end. In PVS, the *PLSync* channel is modeled as follows:

```
PLSync(Input, Output)(q:probability):
  INDUCTIVE bool = (Output'T(0) = Input'T(0) &
  Output'D(0) = (Input'D(0)'1,(1-q)*Input'D(0)'2)
   & PLSync(next(Input), next(Output))(q)) &
   (Output'D(0)'2 = (q)*Input'D(0)'2 => PLSync(next(Input),Output)(q))
```

The *PLSync* channel is defined inductively but unlike *CSync*, it may take two different routes in each step. Three conjuncted formulas are for the case when the data is successfully received by the sink end. First formula satisfies the time constraint that ensures the synchronous behavior. Second formula reflects that the data item is received by the sink end with probability $1 - q$ multiplied to the probability for that data at the source end. The third formula is the recursive step that channel takes when a data is transmitted successfully. For the case when the transmitted data is lost, the recursive behavior of the channel is reflected by the last two formulas with implication between them. In such case, no data is obtained at the sink end.

FFIFO1: Faulty FIFO1 channel ($A \cdot \overset{r}{\cdot} \overline{\square} \rightarrow B$) is a probabilistic variant of *FIFO1* channel, that might loose (with probability r) the message when it is inserted into the buffer and the buffer remains empty. It can also behave as a normal *FIFO1* channel where the insertion of the data into the buffer is successful with probability $1 - r$.

```
FFifo(Input, Output)(r:probability):
  INDUCTIVE bool = (Output'T(0) > Input'T(0) &
  Output'T(0) < Input'T(1) & Output'D(0) =
  (Input'D(0)'1, (1-r)*Input'D(0)'2) &
   FFifo(next(Input), next(Output))(r)) &
    (Output'D(0)'2 = (r)*Input'D(0)'2 => FFifo(next(Input), Output)(r))
```

The *FFIFO1* channel is also defined inductively and like *PLSync*, it may take two different routes in each step. For the case when data written at source end is inserted successfully into the buffer, the channel should satisfy four constraints which are specified with the conjunction of four predicates. The first two formulas are for the time constraints, where the first formula is for the time delay between data at source and sink ends. As *FIFO1* has a buffering capacity of 1, next data item waits till the current data item in the buffer is taken out at the sink end. This is specified with the second formula that the time of the next data item is greater than the time for the current data item in the buffer. The last two formulas are for the recursive behavior that channel takes when the written data is lost before its insertion in the buffer. Like *PLSync*, no data is received at the sink end in such case.

LFIFO1: Another probabilistic variant called lossy FIFO channel ($A \text{---}\square\text{---}^{r}\text{->} B$) might loose each stored data item with some fixed probability (r) in any step. Compared to *FFIFO1*, this channel may loose the data in the process of taking the data from the buffer. As channels are modeled by the relations between observations on source and sink ends, therefore, the specifications for *LFIFO1* and *FFIFO1* are same.

With this modeling approach, we can easily adjust the specifications for untimed and timed channels in a proper way, where the observations on source and sink ends of all channels are specified by *TDD* sequences. Then the probabilistic/random channels as well as untimed/timed channels can be combined together to build connectors. A connector is probabilistic if it constitutes at least one probabilistic or random channel.

4.2 Operators

Compositional operators can be applied on channels in various topological order for the construction of complex connectors. As already discussed in Sect. 2, there are three kinds of composition operators: (1) *flow-through*, (2) *replicate* and (3) *merge*.

The *flow-through* operator simply allows the data items to pass through mixed node(s) without any change. A component connected to a connector can write data items at source node and can obtain data items from the sink node. The *replicate* operator puts the source ends of different channels together into one source node. A write operation by a component on source node succeeds only if all coinciding channels ends accept the data item. The behavior of *flow-through* and *replicate* operators does not depend on the context of the data-flow. The approach for the modeling of these two operators in [18] can be adopted here without any change. The structure of connectors allow us to specify both operators implicitly by means of nodes renaming and conjunction instead of writing a new function.

This is explained with simple examples. For two channels *PLSync(A, B)* and *FIFO1(B, C)*, the *flow-through* operator acting on node *B* is implemented already. For two channels *PLSync(A, B)* and *FIFO1(C, D)*, the *replicate* operator can be implemented explicitly by renaming the *C* with *A* for the *FIFO1* channel. Using conjunction and node renaming for these two operators make it possible to specify connectors directly as lemmas and theorems.

Unlike *flow-through* and *replicate*, the *merge* operator depends on the content of the data-flow. The time and data dimension is same for *TD* and *TDD* sequences, which means that these two dimensions do not need any change. As we are dealing with data distribution, so the equality relation for data is changed to the equality relation on data distribution. Thus, both data items and their associated probabilities should be equal. Merge is modeled as follows in PVS:

```
Merge(s1,s2,s3:TDD): INDUCTIVE bool =
  (NOT s1'T(0) = s2'T(0)) & (s1'T(0) < s2'T(0) => s3'T(0) = s1'T(0) &
    s3'D(0) = s1'D(0) & Merge(next(s1),s2,next(s3))) & (s1'T(0) > s2'T(0)
    => s3'T(0) = s2'T(0) & s3'D(0)= s2'D(0) & Merge(s1,next(s2),next(s3)))
```

The modeling approach provided in this section for probabilistic/random channels and composition operators can be used to construct different probabilistic connectors according to their topological orders.

5   Reasoning

After connectors modeling, we can analyze and prove their properties. In this section, some examples are provided for the reasoning about probabilistic/random connectors as well as the refinement and equivalence relations between them.

Example 1. Figure 3 shows a probabilistic Reo connector that distributed components can use for message communication. Component 1 can deliver its messages to the connector via connecting to node *in*, while component 2 is connected to the node *out* to obtain the message from the connector. Messages are transmitted from component 1 to component 2 with FFIFO1 channel (AB). Other primitive channels (Sync, SyncD, FIFO1, LossySync) are organized in the connector to repeat component 1 message as often as necessary. The property that component 2 almost surely obtain the message via *out* from *in* is established with the following theorem in PVS.

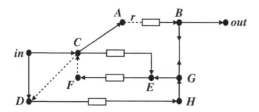

Fig. 3. A probabilistic Reo connector

Theorem 1. `Sync(in,D)` & `Sync(in,C)` & `Sync(C,A)` & `Fifo1(C,E)` & `Fifo1(E,F)` & `LSync(C,D)(n)` & `LSync(F,C)(n)` & `FFifo(A,B)(r)` & `Fifo1(D,H)` & `Sync(H,G)` & `SyncD(G,B)` & `Sync(G,E)` & `Sync(B,out)` => `out'D(0)'1 = in'D(0)'1` & `Tle(in,out)`

Proof. Mathematical induction is used to prove Theorem 1. After applying induction on n, main goal is split into two sub-goals. The first sub-goal is for the base case and the other one is for the inductive case.

For the base case, the antecedent formula is simplified by creating a free *skolem* variable and removing *implies*. The definitions of channels and predicates are expanded. Some irrelevant formulas in the antecedent are suppressed with the *hide* command. The sub-goal is divided into two more sub-goals: one for the data dimension and other for the time dimension. Both sub-sub-goals are proved with PVS proof commands and decision procedures.

For the inductive case, the sequent formula is first simplified with repeated *skolemization* and *flattening*. In the first antecedent formula, the universal quantifiers are instantiated automatically with *inst?* commands. Sometimes a single *inst?* can only find a partial instantiation where successive invocations of *inst?* can succeed in fully instantiating all of the quantified variables. The rest of the proof is similar to the base case, where the sub-goal is split to two more sub-goals for data and time dimension. The detailed PVS proof for Theorem 1 can be found at [20].

The notion of refinement has been adopted widely in development of complex systems. Refinement relation provides guarantee for the correctness of implementation with respect to the abstract specification of the same system, and thus helps in bridging the gap between requirements and the final implementations.

Here, we use the refinement relation for connectors defined in [23], where the refinement order over connectors is established on the basis of the implication relation of predicates. As discussed already, connectors are represented by conjunction of a set of predicates, where the variables are bound by the universal and existential quantification. Let C_1 and C_2 represent two connectors that are modeled by set of predicates. C_2 is a refinement of C_1 only if $C_2 \rightarrow C_1$, meaning the behavioral properties of C_1 can be derived from the properties of C_2. C_2 properties are regarded as hypothesis and the properties of connector C_1 as conclusion. The refinement relation between C_1 and C_2 is denoted as $C_1 \sqsubseteq C_2$. Next, we provide an example for refinement relation between probabilistic connectors.

Example 2 (Refinement). For the two connectors shown in Fig. 4, connector P is a refinement of connector Q ($Q \sqsubseteq P$).

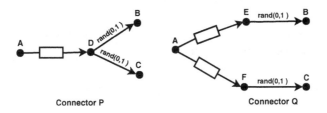

Fig. 4. Connectors refinement example

Given arbitrary input *TDD* sequence at node A and output *TDD* sequences at nodes B and C, connector P is a refinement of another connector Q only if the behavior property of Q can be derived from the connector P property. In connector Q, the outputs are not synchronized and data is received asynchronously by the sink ends B and C respectively. There is no constraints on the relationship between the time sequence of the two output events. On the other hand, P refines the behavior of Q by synchronizing the two sink nodes, which ensures that the two output events must happen simultaneously. We use a, b, c to denote the time sequence at nodes A, B and C respectively. Let d denotes the random number $d \in \{0,1\}$, that ranges over all data items. Let β, γ represent the data sequence being observed at sink nodes B and C respectively. Probabilistic connector P satisfies the condition $a < b \wedge a < c \wedge b = c \wedge \beta = d^*$ $\wedge \gamma = d^*$. Whereas, Q satisfies $a < b \wedge a < c \wedge \beta = d^* \wedge \gamma = d^*$. The refinement relation between Q and P is verified with following theorem.

Theorem 2. $\forall$ (A,B,C:TDD):

> ($\exists$ (D:TDD): Fifo1(A,D) & RSync(D, B) & RSync(D,C)) $\Rightarrow$ ($\exists$
> (E,F:TDD): (Fifo1(A,E) & RSync(E,B)) & (Fifo1(A,F) &
> RSync(F,C)))

Proof. The first suitable formula in the sequent ($\forall/\exists\ A, B, C : TDD$) is replaced to $TDD[A!1/A1, B!1/B1, C!1/C1]$ by creating three skolem constants. Implies is removed from consequent with *flattening*. Now we have one existentially quantified formula in both antecedent and consequent. Quantified formula in antecedent is reduced by automatic introduction of skolem constant with *skolem!* command. In consequent, we need to find the *TDD* sequences that specify the data flow through mixed nodes E and F for connector Q. In other words, we need to find an appropriate E and F that satisfies $(Fifo1(A, E) \wedge RSync(E, B))$ $\wedge (Fifo1(A, F) \wedge RSync(F, C))$. With (*inst 1 "D!1" "D!1"*), the first formula in consequent is instantiated where both E and F are substituted with $D!1$. Antecedent is divided into three formulas by removing logical &'s. Finally, the formula in the consequent is split into four sub-goals. All four sub-goals are trivially true and PVS proved those sub-goals automatically with *propax* propositional axioms. PVS proof tree for Theorem 2 is shown in Fig. 5.

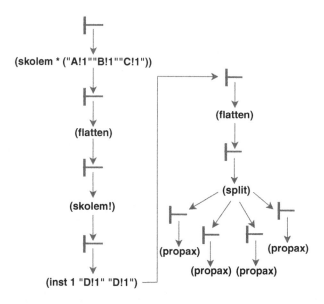

Fig. 5. Proof tree for connectors refinement proof

Generally, an equivalence relation is defined as a binary relation that holds the reflexivity, symmetric as well as transitivity properties. The equivalence relation between two connectors C_1 and C_2 is defined with mutual refinement:

$$C_1 \equiv C_2 \quad \textbf{iff} \quad C_1 \sqsubseteq C_2 \wedge C_2 \sqsubseteq C_1$$

Here, the equivalence relation is represented with implications that goes both ways, such as $C_2 \leftrightarrow C_1$.

Example 3 (Equivalence). Figure 6 shows two probabilistic connectors that are constructed by composing five channels RSync, FIFO1, t-Timer, SyncD and Sync in different topological orders. Both probabilistic connectors are equivalent $(R_1 \leftrightarrow R_2)$, which is proved in PVS.

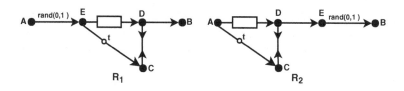

Fig. 6. Connectors equivalence example

The three untimed (*Sync, SyncD* and *FIFO1*) channels and one timed channel (*t-Timer*) can be combined together to make a timed connector known as *tFIFO1*, that was also studied in [13]. In a primitive *FIFO1* channel, the data distributions for the sequences at sink and source nodes are same with arbitrary time delay. On the other hand, the time delay is fixed by the parameter t in *tFIFO1*. Here, we call the *tFIFO1* a sub-connector and is modeled as:

```
Tfifo(A, B)(t:Time)(d:Data): bool =
  EXISTS (R,S:TDD): Fifo1(A, R) & SyncD(R, S)
      & Timert(A, S)(t)(d) & Sync(R, B)
```

In general, the connectors build from same set of sub-connectors in commutative orders are not equivalent as the configuration of connectors do not satisfy the commutative law. However, connectors R_1 and R_2 are equal for the above example.

Unlike the general approach that we adopted previously to construct a connector from basic channels, connectors R_1 and R_2 are composed by connecting the *tFIFO1* sub-connector with the *RSync* channel in different topological order. The main reason to use the reduced method (where a sub-connector is combined with a channel) for connectors construction is to make the proof process simpler and easier to understand. The equivalence relations between a channel linked with a sub-connector in different positions are first proved as lemmas.

Lemma 1. $\forall$ (A,B:TDD)(t:Time)(d:Data)*:*

$\exists$ (E:TDD): RSync(A,E) & Tfifo(E,B)(t)(d) <=> RSync(A,E) & $\exists$
(C,D:TDD): Fifo1(E,D) & SyncD(D,C) & Timert(E,C)(t)(d) &
Sync(D,B)

Lemma 1 shows the equivalence relation between the reduced construction of a connector and a connector constructed from basic channels for R_1. Similarly for R_2, another lemma is provided.

Lemma 2. $\forall$ (A,B:TDD)(t:Time)(d:Data)*:*

$\exists$ (E:TDD): Tfifo(A,E)(t)(d) & RSync(E,B) <=> $\exists$ (C,D:TDD):
Fifo1(A,D) & SyncD(D,C) & Timert(A,C)(t)(d) & Sync(D,E) &
RSync(E,B)

The main goal of equivalence relation between R_1 and R_2 is proved with following theorem:

Theorem 3. $\forall$(A,B:TDD)(t:Time)(d:Data)*:*

$\exists$ (E:TDD): RSync(A, E) & Tfifo(E,B)(t)(d) <=>
$\exists$ (R:TDD): Tfifo(A,R)(t)(d) & RSync(R,B)

Both lemmas are used to prove Theorem 3 and the complete proof can be found at [20]. It is important to point out that one of the main limitations of using proof assistants such as PVS is that heavy user intervention is required in the proof development. For a non-trivial theorem, the user does lots of repetitive work to prove the theorem. For example, Theorem 3 proof required repeated proof commands to prove the main proof-goal, which is divided later into sub-goals. To avoid this, PVS offers a powerful decision procedures such as *grind* that can be used to complete the proof that does not require induction and only requires the expansion of definitions in the model and reasoning for equality, arithmetic and quantification.

6   Conclusion

The formalization approach for untimed/timed Reo connectors in PVS is extended in this paper to model and reason about probabilistic/random connectors that are constructed from channels with random and probabilistic behavior. Probabilistic/random channels are modeled as relations on TDD sequences being observed at the source and sink nodes. Untimed/timed channels specifications are adjusted accordingly from TD sequences to TDD sequences. The specifications for probabilistic/random channels generated seven TCCs in total. Two TCCs are proved automatically by the prover and five are proved interactively. With formalised compositional operators and channels, complex connectors are modeled and their properties as well as the refinement and equivalence relation between them are proved with the help of PVS proof-commands, inference rules and decision procedures.

For future work, we would like to add more complex probabilistic and stochastic constraints in the connectors and reason about them. We also plan to extend the formalization approach further to deal with hybrid connectors, QoS (Quality of Service) and resource consumption aspects on connectors.

Acknowledgement. The work has been supported by the National Natural Science Foundation of China under grant no. 61772038, 61532019 and 61272160, and the Guandong Science and Technology Department (Grant no. 2018B010107004).

References

1. Arbab, F.: The IWIM model for coordination of concurrent activities. In: Ciancarini, P., Hankin, C. (eds.) COORDINATION 1996. LNCS, vol. 1061, pp. 34–56. Springer, Heidelberg (1996). https://doi.org/10.1007/3-540-61052-9_38
2. Arbab, F.: Reo: a channel-based coordination model for component composition. Math. Struct. Comput. Sci. **14**(3), 329–366 (2004)
3. Arbab, F., Baier, C., de Boer, F.S., Rutten, J.J.M.M.: Models and temporal logical specifications for timed component connectors. Softw. Syst. Model. **6**(1), 59–82 (2007)

4. Arbab, F., Chothia, T., van der Mei, R., Meng, S., Moon, Y.J., Verhoef, C.: From coordination to stochastic models of QoS. In: Field, J., Vasconcelos, V.T. (eds.) COORDINATION 2009. LNCS, vol. 5521, pp. 268–287. Springer, Heidelberg (2009). https://doi.org/10.1007/978-3-642-02053-7_14

5. Baier, C.: Probabilistic models for Reo connector circuits. J. Univers. Comput. Sci. **11**(10), 1718–1748 (2005)

6. Baier, C., Blechmann, T., Klein, J., Klüppelholz, S., Leister, W.: Design and verification of systems with exogenous coordination using vereofy. In: Margaria, T., Steffen, B. (eds.) ISoLA 2010. LNCS, vol. 6416, pp. 97–111. Springer, Heidelberg (2010). https://doi.org/10.1007/978-3-642-16561-0_15

7. Baier, C., Chrszon, P., Dubslaff, C., Klein, J., Klüppelholz, S.: Energy-utility analysis of probabilistic systems with exogenous coordination. In: de Boer, F., Bonsangue, M., Rutten, J. (eds.) It's All About Coordination - Essays to Celebrate the Lifelong Scientific Achievements of Farhad Arbab. LNCS, vol. 10865, pp. 38–56. Springer, Cham (2018). https://doi.org/10.1007/978-3-319-90089-6_3

8. Baier, C., Sirjani, M., Arbab, F., Rutten, J.: Modeling component connectors in Reo by constraint automata. Sci. Comput. Program. **61**, 75–113 (2006)

9. Baier, C., Wolf, V.: Stochastic reasoning about channel-based component connectors. In: Ciancarini, P., Wiklicky, H. (eds.) COORDINATION 2006. LNCS, vol. 4038, pp. 1–15. Springer, Heidelberg (2006). https://doi.org/10.1007/11767954_1

10. Daumas, M., Lester, D.R.: Stochastic formal methods: an application to accuracy of numeric software. In: Proceedings of HICSS 2007, p. 262. IEEE (2007)

11. Halmos, P.R.: The foundations of probability. Am. Math. Mon. **51**(9), 493–510 (1944)

12. He, K., Hermanns, H., Chen, Y.: Models of connected things: on priced probabilistic timed Reo. In: Proceedings of COMPSAC 2017, pp. 234–243. IEEE (2017)

13. Hong, W., Nawaz, M.S., Zhang, X., Li, Y., Sun, M.: Using Coq for formal modeling and verification of timed connectors. In: Cerone, A., Roveri, M. (eds.) SEFM 2017. LNCS, vol. 10729, pp. 558–573. Springer, Cham (2018). https://doi.org/10.1007/978-3-319-74781-1_37

14. Khosravi, R., Sirjani, M., Asoudeh, N., Sahebi, S., Iravanchi, H.: Modeling and analysis of Reo connectors using alloy. In: Lea, D., Zavattaro, G. (eds.) COORDINATION 2008. LNCS, vol. 5052, pp. 169–183. Springer, Heidelberg (2008). https://doi.org/10.1007/978-3-540-68265-3_11

15. Kokash, N., Krause, C., de Vink, E.: Reo+mCRL2: a framework for model-checking dataflow in service compositions. Formal Asp. Comput. **24**(2), 187–216 (2012)

16. Li, Y., Zhang, X., Ji, Y., Sun, M.: A formal framework capturing real-time and stochastic behavior in connectors. Sci. Comput. Program. **177**, 19–40 (2019)

17. Moon, Y., Silva, A., Krause, C., Arbab, F.: A compositional semantics for stochastic Reo connectors. In: Proceedings of FOCLASA 2010. EPTCS, vol. 30, pp. 93–107 (2010)

18. Nawaz, M.S., Sun, M.: Reo2PVS: formal specification and verification of component connectors. In: Proceedings of SEKE 2018, pp. 391–396. KSI Research Inc. (2018)

19. Owre, S., Shankar, N., Rushby, J.M., Stringer-Calvert, D.W.J.: PVS system Guide, PVS prover Guide. PVS language reference. Technical report, SRI International, November 2001

20. PVS dump file. github.com/saqibdola/PReo-PVS/blob/master/preo

21. Sun, M.: Connectors as designs: the time dimension. In: Proceedings of TASE 2012, pp. 201–208. IEEE Computer Society (2012)

22. Meng, S., Arbab, F.: On resource-sensitive timed component connectors. In: Bonsangue, M.M., Johnsen, E.B. (eds.) FMOODS 2007. LNCS, vol. 4468, pp. 301–316. Springer, Heidelberg (2007). https://doi.org/10.1007/978-3-540-72952-5_19

23. Sun, M., Arbab, F., Aichernig, B.K., Astefanoaei, L., de Boer, F.S., Rutten, J.: Connectors as designs: modeling, refinement and test case generation. Sci. Comput. Program. **77**(7–8), 799–822 (2012)

24. Sun, M., Zhang, X.: A relational model for probabilistic connectors based on timed data distribution streams. In: Jansen, D.N., Prabhakar, P. (eds.) FORMATS 2018. LNCS, vol. 11022, pp. 125–141. Springer, Cham (2018). https://doi.org/10.1007/978-3-030-00151-3_8

25. Zhang, X., Hong, W., Li, Y., Sun, M.: Reasoning about connectors using Coq and Z3. Sci. Comput. Program. **170**, 27–44 (2019)

26. Zhang, X., Sun, M.: Towards formal modeling and verification of probabilistic connectors in Coq. In: Proceedings of SEKE 2018, pp. 385–390. KSI Research Inc. (2018)

Greenify: A Game with the Purpose of Test Data Generation for Unit Testing

Sharmin Moosavi, Hassan Haghighi, Hasti Sahabi,
Farzam Vatanzade, and Mojtaba Vahidi Asl$^{(\boxtimes)}$

Faculty of Computer Science and Engineering,
Shahid Beheshti University, G. C., Evin, Tehran, Iran
mo_vahidi@sbu.ac.ir

Abstract. One of the most important, but tedious and costly tasks of software testing process is test data generation. Several methods for automating this task have been presented, yet due to their practical drawbacks, test data generation is still widely performed by humans in industry. In our previous work, we employed the notion of Game With A Purpose (GWAP) and introduced Rings as a GWAP to reduce time and costs of human-based test data generation and increase its appeal to engage even nontechnical people. In this paper, we propose a new game, called Greenify, with the purpose of test data generation so that it solves the main issues of Rings. The environment of this game is built based on a program's control flow graph. To evaluate the proposed approach, we designed several game levels based on six different C++ programs and gave them to volunteering players. The results show that in comparison to both conventional human-based approach and Rings, Greenify generates test data with less rime for all feasible paths of the given benchmark programs. In addition, Greenify identifies the smaller set of likely infeasible paths.

Keywords: Test data generation · Game With A Purpose ·
Human-based computation game · Human-based software testing

1 Introduction

Most software systems have numerous possible choices for test data when being tested. Thus, various criteria have been defined to find as small as possible subset of input values that result in more effective tests, i.e., those tests which lead to finding more failures of the Software Under Test (SUT). This process is called test data generation [1].

Three different categories of automatic test data generation methods have been presented including the random-based, symbolic execution, and search-based methods. These approaches have some drawbacks [3, 4, 12, 17] that makes them still incomplete and ineffective in producing test data [5], and therefore, test data generation is still typically carried out by human experts. Generating test data by humans has several advantages among which is the ability of humans to understand and interpret the code being tested while the computing power of human mind helps him solve problems with

© IFIP International Federation for Information Processing 2019
Published by Springer Nature Switzerland AG 2019
H. Hojjat and M. Massink (Eds.): FSEN 2019, LNCS 11761, pp. 77–92, 2019.
https://doi.org/10.1007/978-3-030-31517-7_6

high levels of complexity. However, generating data for large SUT is very difficult for humans. In addition, test data generation by humans is a very tedious, time-consuming and costly task in the software development process [1, 2].

Nowadays, one of the well-known methods for solving problems is broadcasting them to the crowd. Some of the crowdsourcing models use computer games in which mind challenges are one of their most important elements. As player thinks and deducts in the process of a game, he can implicitly and through no knowledge of his own, help solve other problems (for example, test data generation) which do not have entertainment goals, by their own. In these situations, crowdsourcing and human-based computation help extracting a significant amount of information from a large number of players and users [7, 11, 14, 16]. This approach to solve problems introduces the concept of Game With A Purpose (GWAP). Based on this idea, the method suggested in this paper for test data generation involves designing a game and extracting test data based on solutions each non-technical player finds implicitly when playing the game.

The first and only attempt for employing GWAP for test data generation was through the "Rings" game introduced in [13]. The puzzles of Rings are designed based on symbolic execution technique. For each path constraint in a program unit's Control Flow Graph (CFG), a Rings's puzzle is generated. When a player solves the puzzle, he is implicitly generating appropriate input values that lead to the execution of the chosen CFG path.

Rings alleviates some problems of human-based test data generation. Since the shape of the game is not technical, bigger problems can be solved using crowdsourcing (by nontechnical people without getting paid) with a major reduction in costs of test data generation. Furthermore, the lack of motivation is compensated with the amusement of the game. The main drawback of Rings is incapability of visualizing programs with complex conditional statements. The other shortcoming is the disposal of wrong solutions although they could be right solutions of other paths.

In this paper, we aim at designing a GWAP based on concrete execution that does not suffer from the Ring's problems. In the proposed game, called Greenify, the environment is built based on CFG of a given program. The CFG's nodes are displayed by light bubbles, and a path of the CFG is represented by a string of connected light bubbles. The players should change the input power flows of the string until the color of all connected bubbles turns to green. During the gameplay, players are actually generating necessary data to cover the given test paths. Greenify can mitigate the main drawbacks of Rings since:

1- It is not based on symbolic execution.
2- It stores all acquired data of player quests, even if it does not lead to success.
3- By checking all data extracted from different players' play, the likely infeasible paths could be identified.

We have conducted an experiment to evaluate the Greenify performance in comparison to Rings, the conventional human-based and random approaches. We have selected six programs and developed the puzzles of both Greenify and Rings for all paths of these programs. Then, we asked a group of players to play the puzzles, and also, a group of programmers to manually generate data. The highlights of the experimental results are as follows:

- When players play Greenify, they generate data faster than other approaches.
- Many Greenify puzzles are solved by wrong data obtained for other puzzles.
- All feasible paths are covered by Greenify.
- The smaller set of probable infeasible paths is identified by Greenify.

In the following, we glance through related work in Sect. 2. The design of Greenify is presented in Sect. 3. In Sect. 4, we have provided the experimental results. Finally, Sect. 5 is devoted to the conclusions and some directions for future work.

2   Related Work

One of the methods for crowdsourcing is using game thinking. Hence, in this section, some important works that apply the concept of crowdsourcing and game thinking in the field of software testing are presented (Fig. 1).

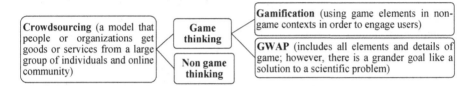

Fig. 1. The methods for crowdsourcing

Crowdsourcing- Nowadays crowdsourcing is a popular method in the domain of software testing. In [26, 27], some complex testing tasks in functional testing and verification such as cross-browser verification have been given to the crowd. The results show that test performance is improved in terms of time and bug detection compared to traditional software testing [28]. The research in [29, 30] use crowdsourced software testing (CST) for validation and acceptance testing and the results indicate that CST improves quality while being more flexible. CST is shown to be reliable, cost-efficient with high quality [30, 31] in usability testing, as well. To our knowledge, there is no CST for test data generation in the literature.

Gamification- The researchers in [20] have conducted an experiment on a gamified unit testing process including two groups of individuals, gamified and non-gamified, and showed that the gamified group has had a significant outperformance in locating faults compared to the non-gamified group. Arnarsson and Johannesson in [21] reported that developers engaged in their experiment were motivated by their gamified system to create more effective unit tests and emphasized that the software testing skills of developers have been considerably improved. The authors of [22] introduced a game called "*Code Defenders*" that engages students in a competitive way to do mutation testing. In the game, the players can be defenders or attackers and SUT has a central role.

GWAP- In [24], a GWAP, called *Xylem, The Code of Plant*, was introduced for formal verification. In this game, the invariants of program loops are presented as strange plants. *Pipe Jam* is another game, introduced in [25], that carries out software verification by converting the task into a game puzzle and then converting back the solutions to a correctness proof. The first research to use GWAP in test data generation has been introduced in [13]. The game, called Rings, generates test data based on symbolic execution. In Rings, a CFG path is shown as a pipe network to players. At the network entry, there are several rings that fall in the network of pipes during the play. There are also some filters in the network. If the attributes of the rings are set correctly, the rings transit between the filters, successfully. The program conditional statements resemble the filters in the game and the input parameters of the source code map to the rings of the game. When the players solve the puzzles, they indeed generate data for the given source code. Although according to the evaluation results, it is successful as a GWAP, Rings has several problems, including:

- Mathematical complexity: Rings cannot visualize nonlinear and complex path constraints.
- Disposal of wrong solutions: if players are unsuccessful in solving a puzzle, all of their data are wasted, even if a wrong solution for the puzzle could be the correct solution for another puzzle.
- A large set of probable infeasible-test paths: Corresponding paths of puzzles that are not solved by players in the threshold time, are considered as a set of likely infeasible paths. However, a large set of likely infeasible paths is recommended by Rings while many of these paths are feasible.

In the present paper, we propose a new game which has the Rings' advantages while solves the above-mentioned problems, as well.

3   The Game Design of Greenify

The goal of Greenify is to generate test data based on the program's corresponding CFG with the aim of covering special test paths. To this end, the player somehow changes the input values to satisfy or dissatisfy the conditional statements of the program, implicitly, in order to cover a specific test path without any technical knowledge of the program variables, program control flow, and the conditions used in the branch statements.

3.1   Display the Elements of a Program Unit in the Game

In this section, we explain how the components of a program (CFG and input variables) are displayed by game elements.

The Display of CFG in Greenify- The first step of designing Greenify is formulating CFG of SUT in a form of gameplay (or game environment). After extracting the CFG from the source code, it is displayed on the screen with some graphical appeal. Light bubbles that can present different colors are placed on the branches which are correspondent to the program's conditional statements. When a light bubble's color turns to green, it means that the corresponding conditional statement of the branch is evaluated as true, and when it turns to red, it means that the conditional statement is evaluated as false. For each level of the game, the player is asked to solve a path in the CFG.

The Display of Variables in Greenify- The SUT's input variables are mapped into sliders (for Integers, Floats and ASCII codes of characters) and checkboxes (for Booleans). The sliders are appropriate for both continuous and discrete variables. A player can change the input values by twiddling the sliders or checking and unchecking the checkboxes, without getting involved with the actual values of the variables.

For example, consider the code segment in Fig. 2 and its corresponding CFG. The goal of this program is to calculate the common area of two concentric circles. The two Boolean variables *in1* and *in2* determine if the outer or the inner area of each circle is intended in the calculation of the common area. Considering the CFG of this code, take for instance *ABCEH* as the target path of the graph that should be covered by appropriate input values. A screenshot of the game's environment for this situation is shown in Fig. 2 in which two sliders are shown for the two float inputs as well as two checkboxes for the two Boolean inputs.

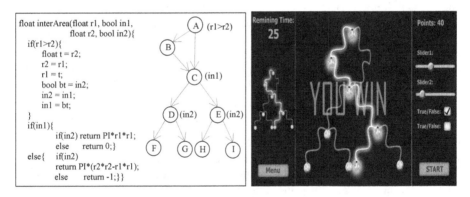

Fig. 2. The source code, CFG and game's environment of "interArea"

3.2   The Gameplay

A display of all described elements is shown to the player at the beginning of the game. The target path is shown to the player with blinking all the light bubbles of the path. The goal for the players is to adjust the input power flow by sliders or checkboxes to turn these light bubbles to green. At first, the player starts out just by randomly twiddling the sliders and checking the checkboxes. Each light bubble changes its color based on the corresponding values of the sliders and checkboxes. If a light bubble turns to green, this means the matching conditional is satisfied. However, if the bubble turns to red, the matching predicate is false (meaning that it is not covered by the corresponding input value). As the game goes by, the player can comprehend and learn patterns by viewing the results of his decisions and move the sliders and checkboxes in a more purposeful manner. Finally, when the player succeeds in turning all the light bubbles of the path to green, the level is passed and the player can move on to play other paths of the same graph or different graphs. The values with which the player completed the level are the generated test data resulting in the execution of the given test path for that level.

3.3   Logging the Events

As mentioned earlier, to complete each level of the game, all light bubbles in a specific path have to turn to green. However, during a play, some unwanted paths may be covered. When this happens, even though the level is incomplete, the values of the sliders may be appropriate test data for other test paths. These values can then be extracted as test data for those paths. This will not be told to the player since her target path is still uncovered. But, this feature is beneficial because test data can be produced for more than one test path in a single level. This way, a complete set of test data to achieve the coverage of all feasible test paths in a CFG is produced more quickly.

3.4   Special Cases in Test Data Generation with Greenify

The Inputs' Range: There is a challenge during the implementation of Greenify's sliders. The sliders, representing the input variables, have a limited length. Therefore, mapping an integer range to these sliders can be challenging. A solution considered in this article is to limit the input range in a more practical manner. For instance, in a program, it would be sufficient to consider only a part of the integer range. Based on the size of sliders on a mobile screen, we fitted the range from -10 to 10. As future work, we are planning to use another model instead of sliders, with which the player can change the precision simpler and choose the intended amounts, accordingly.

The Arrays: To simulate array data structures in the game, a new element is added to the game as shown in Fig. 3. If a player adds a new slider, indeed he adds a new element to the input array. The value of the array element is adjusted by changing the value of the new slider. Since the array in a program could have many elements, adjusting all elements for the players is very hard. Our solution to this challenge is generating data to all elements by random in the first time, and then the player could change each of the elements. To display a lot of sliders in the game, we use scroll bars such as Fig. 3.

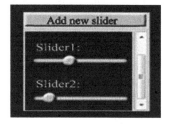

Fig. 3. A sample for considering program arrays in Greenify

Infeasible Test Path Detection: To guess infeasible test paths of the CFG, the approach used in this paper specifies a limited amount of time to complete a level (or cover a test path). If the player is not successful in that time period, she loses the level and another test path is given to her to cover. If the number of players who cannot solve the puzzle of a given path exceeds a specified threshold, the difficulty of that path increases and it will be given to higher-rated players. The more a path is given to players and is left unsolved, the higher the probability of it is infeasible.

Large CFGs: As the size of CFG increases, the game becomes harder to play. Since Greenify is merely designed to generate data for unit codes usually have small CFGs, large CFGs are not in our research scope. Nevertheless, to show the effectiveness of Greenify, in the next section, Triangle code is presented which has a large CFG with 57 paths such that their maximum length is 15. As the experiment showed, the players easily played the Triangle's game and did not engage in the apparent complexity of the game.

3.5   Players

Game flow and attracting players is important in Greenify. Therefore, in the following sub-sections, hinting and rating to players are discussed.

Hinting Players: It is important to design gameplay that is neither too easy nor too hard. Hints and clues could be used such that while the player is challenged, she doesn't lose hope and leave the game. A possible way to hint the player is to somehow show which light bubbles are affected when a slider is altered. For example, suppose the variable "A" is directly used in nodes labeled 15, 21, 23 and 30. So, if the player twiddles the slider representing "A", the corresponding light bubbles can blink, grow or change color. This way, the player is hinted which sliders should change to make a specific light bubble green. Furthermore, this would not make the game too easy because focusing on one light bubble to make it green can mess up the other light bubbles. Accordingly, the player has to use the hints wisely. To figure out which light bubbles are affected by each slider, we employed a scanner in our implementation to find the variables used in each program branch.

Rating Players: To make Greenify more attractive, players can be rated as they complete different levels. At first, players are rated as beginners, and they are asked to complete easier graphs with shorter test paths. As a player completes different levels, she gains more points and is rated higher. Players with higher rates are given harder and larger test paths. The difficulty of each test path is affected by the number of program branches (b), the number of the program's input variables (i) and the complexity of the program conditional statements in branches (c); the last parameter can be formulated as the number of variables or the number of clauses in a conditional statement. All of these parameters can be given proper weights by which the parameters' values are multiplied and averaged to come to a single value as the difficulty degree for a level. Equation 1 formulates the difficulty degree, were the corresponding weight for each parameter, $w1$, $w2$, and $w3$ can be chosen by the game designer.

$$DifficultyDegree = \frac{b(w1) + i(w2) + c(w3)}{w1 + w2 + w3} \qquad (1)$$

As an example, the *ABCEH* path of the graph shown in Fig. 2 has two branches, four input variables and the average branch complexity of 1.33 (The first branch's conditional statement includes two variables and the next two branches include 1 variable). If we respectively give a weight of $w1 = 2$, $w2 = 3$ and $w3 = 1$ to the parameters, the difficulty degree for this path would be 3.22.

3.6   Example: The Triangle Program

To better illustrate how Greenify works, an example is presented here. The example describes a game level based on a well-known program, called "Triangle", that by receiving three values as the three sides of a triangle, decides if the triangle is scalene, isosceles, equilateral or it is not a triangle at all. The source code of the program is shown in Fig. 4. This code has many infeasible test paths, and also its conditional statements are complex. Thus, many automatic test data generation approaches are unable to cover all feasible test paths.

The CFG of the "Triangle" program is illustrated in Fig. 5. The orange path, shown in Fig. 5, is the path that should be covered in this level of the game. In this path, it is determined that the triangle is isosceles. In Greenify, this path is first shown to the player. Then, by twiddling the three sliders, each corresponding to an input variable of the program, the player changes the input values. Each time the sliders are manipulated, the color of each node is changed, accordingly. For instance, if the player sets all the sliders to the same value, the path of the graph which leads to an equilateral triangle becomes green. Now, the player is supposed to play more with the sliders to turn the target path (shown in orange) to green. If she succeeds, she has finished the level and the values of the sliders are the test data generated as a result of completing this level.

```
private static int Triangle (int Side1, int Side2, int                              triOut = 4;
Side3)                                              else          triOut = 1;
{                                                       return (triOut);}
   int triOut;                                   if (triOut > 3)        triOut = 3;
   if (Side1 <= 0 || Side2 <= 0 || Side3 <= 0)   else if (triOut == 1 && Side1+Side2 > Side3)
     {  triOut = 4;                                                triOut = 2;
        return (triOut);}                          else if (triOut == 2 && Side1+Side3 > Side2)
   triOut = 0;                                                     triOut = 2;
   if(Side1 == Side2)      triOut = triOut + 1;    else if (triOut == 3 && Side2+Side3 > Side1)
   if(Side1 == Side3)      triOut = triOut + 2;                    triOut = 2;
   if(Side2 == Side3)      triOut = triOut + 3;    else      triOut = 4;
   if (triOut == 0)                                return (triOut);}

{
   if (Side1+Side2 <= Side3 || Side2+Side3<= 31
     Side1 || Side1+Side3 <= Side2)
```

Fig. 4. The source code of "Triangle"

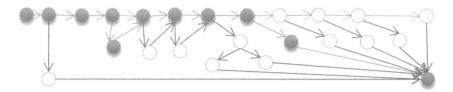

Fig. 5. CFG of "Triangle"

4   Evaluation

In this section, we compare the Greenify, with both Rings and conventional human-based test data generation, in terms of test data generation speed, coverage and proposed set of infeasible test paths. Since our purpose is improving the human-based approach, the automated approaches to test data generation are not in the scope of our research, and thus, we don't compare Greenify with these methods. Instead, we compare Greenify with random-based test data generation methods. In addition, we intend to evaluate the amount of entertainment of the game. So, the research questions are as follows:

1. Does Greenify generate test data faster in comparison to Rings, the conventional human-based and random-based approaches?
2. Is the path coverage of Greenify better in comparison to Rings, the conventional human-based and random-based approaches?
3. Does Greenify offer a smaller set for probable infeasible paths than Rings, the conventional human-based and random-based approaches?
4. Is Greenify more attractive than Rings for the players?

In the following subsections (Subsects. 4.1, 4.2, 4.3 and 4.4), answers to the questions 1 to 4 are described.

To conduct the experiment, simple versions of Greenify and Rings were designed for six benchmark programs (the benchmark programs are described in Table 1) and were given to 30 Computer Engineering students from the Faculty of Computer Science and Engineering of Shahid Beheshti University to perform a trial run. The average age of the participants was 21 years, 14 volunteers of them had programming experience, and 3 volunteers were familiar with concepts of software testing. The volunteers were divided into two groups each with 15 players. The players of the first group, first solved the Greenify puzzles, and after completing Greenify, they started to solve the puzzles of Rings; the participants of the second group solved the puzzles of the games in respectively reverse.

We also gave the six mentioned programs to five programmers and asked them to find input values manually, in a way to cover all the feasible paths of the code. In the end, we generated data for mentioned programs by the random-based test data generation approach. With the acquired data, we examined the amount of time consumed by the programmers, by the players in both games, and by the random method. We also computed the percentage of test paths covered by the test data generated via each method.

Table 1. The benchmark programs

#	Name	Description	Number of test paths
1	InterArea	The common area between two centric circles (Fig. 2)	8
2	Triangle	Determining type of a triangle (explained in Sect. 3)	57
3	Simple-Triangle	Determining type of a triangle	4
4	Binary-Search	Binary search algorithm	5
5	LCM	Determining least common multiplier	6
6	Reminder	Determining (x mod y)	4

4.1 Test Data Generation Time

According to the first research question, we compared Greenify with Rings, the manual and random approaches in terms of test data generation time.

The six benchmark programs contain 84 test paths, altogether, among which only 37 test paths are feasible. The total attempts of all the players in playing Greenify was 4263 times during which numerous test data was produced for all feasible test paths. In four competitors, the time taken for each feasible test path to be covered for the first time by any player was calculated in seconds, as displayed in Fig. 6. As shown in the figure, in the worst case, Greenify took 62.6275 s to complete a path. It is interesting that all other feasible paths were covered in less than 15 s. In the best case, it took 3.2250 s to complete a path. Both the best and the worst cases belong to the "Triangle" program. The path with the highest coverage time is the one through which it is determined that two of the inputs are equal, but the triangle inequality property is not held, and therefore, the three inputs cannot make out a valid triangle. The path with the least coverage time is the one through which it is concluded that at least one of the inputs is less than or equal to zero, and thus, the inputs cannot build a valid triangle. It is worth noting that some feasible paths were not covered by Rings and the random-based approach. The first time which players covered all paths for each program in four methods is shown in Table 2.

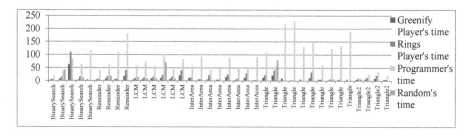

Fig. 6. Elapsed time (in seconds) for the first coverage of each feasible test path in Greenify, Rings, human-based and random testing

Table 2. Comparison of the first time that all paths are covered by the four test data generation approaches

	In Greenify (seconds)	In Rings (seconds)	By humans (seconds)	By random approach (the threshold time is 120 s)
InterArea	15.30	25.35	91	0.1
Triangle	21.25	40.34 (only 6 paths are covered)	231	120 (only 3 paths are covered)
simpleTriangle	9.03	20.454	34	120 (only 3 paths are covered)
Binary-Search	62.62	110.03	117	120 (only 4 paths are covered)
LCM	21.38	39.57	102	44.63
Reminder	17.90	40.214	181	7.74

As shown in Table 2, Greenify, Rings and the random-based approach have generated data for feasible paths faster than the human-based approach while Greenify outperformed Rings and the random-based method. The main reason for the better performance of Greenify compared with Rings is the use of wrong solutions obtained from Greenify players, which caused many paths to be covered by Greenify before they were proposed to the players. The random-based approach has generated data in less time for the two benchmarks while the speed of test data generation was less for other benchmarks compared to Greenify. In other words, Greenify generated data in less time for 66% of benchmarks.

To statistically analyze the time measured for covering paths by the four competitors (i.e., Greenify, Rings, human-based and random testing), we used the Anova test (Single Factor) method. A well-known test to compare the averages of two samples is T-test; but in case of more than two samples, it may be unreliable. Therefore, the Anova test could be a good choice to statistically analyze the time, elapsed to cover the paths, by the four competitors. By the Anova test, we can check whether there is a difference between the samples and it does not say which sample is better. Therefore, in the null hypothesis we indicate the averages of the samples are the same, and the alternative hypothesis is that the averages are different. We used the Anova test method in Excel Analysis Toolpak to compute all the needed data. In the results, F, F-critical, and P-value are equal to 46.64, 2.67 and 1.42E−20, respectively. Since F > Fcritical and P-value is less than the chosen significance level (P-value < 0.05), the null hypothesis is rejected. We compared the average elapsed times of Greenify and three other methods which seems to indicate that Greenify outperforms the competitors (Fig. 7).

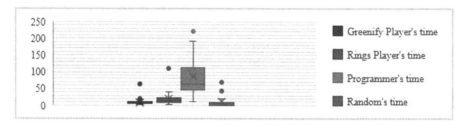

Fig. 7. Elapsed time comparison between the four test data generation approaches (Average times of Greenify, Rings, Programmers and Random are equal to 9.18, 18.83, 85.51 and 10.07, respectively)

Since the Anova test could not show Greenify has less average time than the three other methods, we use T-test to show that the difference between the average of the elapsed time of Greenify and the programmers is significant. The null hypothesis is "The average time of the programmers is less than the average time of Greenify". The calculated p-value is 2.58E−10. Since the p-value is less than the chosen significance level (0.05), the null hypothesis is rejected. Therefore, the average elapsed time for Greenify is less in comparison to the programmers.

4.2   Degree of Path Coverage

Based on the second research question, Greenify is compared with other approaches in terms of the path coverage criterion. Test data generated by Greenify and programmers covered all feasible paths. Rings covered 33 paths of 37 feasible paths and the random test data generation approach covered only 28 feasible test paths when the threshold time was 120 s. Feasible path coverage percentages are shown in Table 3.

Table 3. The results of path coverage percentage of the four competitors

	Greenify	Rings	Programmers	Random test data generation
Path coverage percentage	100%	89%	100%	75%

We used Kruskal-Walis test, a rank-based nonparametric test, to statistically analyze the number of covered paths of the benchmark programs by the four competitors. The null hypothesis in this analysis is "the number of covered paths for four categories is equal" and we want to see whether it is rejected. According to results, H and P-value are equal to 22.87 and 4.29E−5, respectively. Since H > P-value, the null hypothesis is rejected.

4.3   Estimation of Infeasible Paths

Based on the third research question, Greenify is evaluated in terms of the number of likely infeasible test paths. The "Triangle" program has 57 paths yet only 10 paths are feasible. This means that there is only a 17.5% chance for a player to be successful in completing the paths given to her. However, keep in mind that this program is a special case. In most other programs, the percentage of feasible paths is considerably higher.

Since the players have no idea whether a given level actually has an answer, they keep playing until they can win by passing as many levels as they can. If this problem was not handled by playing a game, developers obviously were not interested in spending this amount of time on it. Even if they were obligated to spend this time, they would not be satisfied with this part of their jobs. This somehow shows the engaging privileges of the game. Additionally, while the players in our experiment continuously tried to cover infeasible paths and failed, they unintentionally covered other paths by setting the game sliders to the input values needed to cover those paths. This way, even when they failed to complete the target path, they generated data for other feasible paths, and this scenario resulted in faster coverage of all feasible paths.

The players made 1050 attempts for the "Triangle" program and were able to find test data for 10 out of 57 test paths in the given time period set as the threshold for this game. Therefore, based on the idea mentioned, one can conclude that 47 paths of the "Triangle" program are most likely to be infeasible. The analysis of this program showed that these 47 paths were the exact set of existing infeasible paths of this program. On the other hand, Ring's players were only able to cover 6 test paths of all the 10 feasible test paths of the "Triangle". This means that the set of probable infeasible paths, proposed by Rings, was 41.

The number of proposed infeasible paths by the random method is 56. The random method generated 110000000 data in 100 s for the "Triangle" code but only 4 paths were covered while Greenify covered all feasible paths only by 1050 data. It shows that the generated test data by the random approach are ineffective due to its blindness while the players were smarter to generate test data.

4.4   Players' Viewpoints About Greenify

According to the last research question, we asked the players to present their viewpoints about Greenify and Rings.

To have a better understanding of the players' viewpoint on the game, a questionnaire was given to each of them after they finished playing. We asked players to rate their level of agreement about two questions on a five-point scale (1 = not at all, 5 = very) to compare the Rings and Greenify games in terms of their difficulty and enjoyability. Also, we asked them to choose a design goal to Greenify.

In Table 4 the average rates given by the players to both questions are shown. We use a statistical test (T-test) to show that difference between average rates of Greenify and Rings is significant. We selected the significance level of 0.05 and used the T-test function of Excel Analysis Toolpak to reject the null hypotheses shown in Table 4. The calculated p-values for both questions are shown in Table 4. Since these p-values are less than the chosen significance level, the null hypotheses are rejected. Therefore, the players chose Greenify, a more enjoyable and less complicated game to play.

Table 4. The result of players' answers to the questionnaire regarding enjoyability and difficulty of Greenify and Rings

Questions	Average rate to Greenify	Average rate to Rings	T-test parameters		
			Null hypothesis	Alternative hypothesis	P-value
1. The game was enjoyable.	3.86	2.63	Ring is more enjoyable	Greenify is more enjoyable	0.00053
2. The game was difficult to play	1.8	2.76	Playing Greenify is harder	Playing Rings is harder	0.00039

The interesting point in this survey was that even though the players were all students of computer engineering, only one of them guessed that Greenify had something to do with software quality or testing, and most of them thought it was designed just for entertainment (Fig. 8). The importance of this finding is that no basic knowledge is needed to play this game and anyone familiar with video games can easily play it.

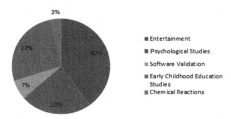

Fig. 8. Players' opinion about the design purpose of Greenify

5   Conclusions and Future Work

Based on the idea, explained in this paper, a game was designed and employed to generate test data. The main advantage of this idea is the use of inexpensive and copious agents (the players) that results in a decrease in costs and an increase in the speed as well as coverage of test data generation.

The results of the evaluation indicate that the proposed game outperforms Rings, the conventional human-based approach and the random method. Furthermore, the proposed game identifies a smaller set of likely infeasible paths. At last, the results of the conducted experiment reveal that the players mention Greenify as an attractive game.

As a direction for future work, we plan to provide more and larger benchmarks for better evaluation of Greenify. Another issue is finding a way to map the program's big input numbers into sliders. The solution we are considering is using another component instead of sliders, with which the player can change the precision, simpler, and choose the intended amount, accordingly.

A further issue that is worth considering is that the data collected from the behavior of the players as they attempt to cover paths can be very valuable for search-based methods. For instance, this data can be given to an appropriate learner and the behavior of the players can be analyzed to find further test data; therefore, the result can be a system for automatic test data generation. Because of the vast amount of data extracted from different players, a more powerful learner with higher precision and performance can be designed.

References

1. Ammann, P., Offutt, J.: Introduction to Software Testing. Cambridge University Press, New York (2016)
2. Utting, M., Pretschner, A., Legeard, B.: A taxonomy of model-based testing approaches. Softw. Test. Verif. Reliab. **22**(5), 297–312 (2012)
3. Chen, T.Y., Fei-Ching, K., Robert, G.M., Tse, T.H.: Adaptive random testing: the art of test case diversity. J. Syst. Softw. **83**(1), 60–66 (2010)
4. Cadar, C., et al.: Symbolic execution for software testing in practice: preliminary assessment. In: Proceedings of the 33rd International Conference on Software Engineering, pp. 1066–1071. ACM (2011)
5. Harman, M., McMinn, P., de Souza, J.T., Yoo, S.: Search based software engineering: techniques, taxonomy, tutorial. In: Meyer, B., Nordio, M. (eds.) LASER 2008-2010. LNCS, vol. 7007, pp. 1–59. Springer, Heidelberg (2012). https://doi.org/10.1007/978-3-642-25231-0_1
6. Weinstein, A.M.: Computer and video game addiction—a comparison between game users and non-game users. Am. J. Drug Alcohol Abus. **36**(5), 268–276 (2010)
7. Wightman, D.: Crowdsourcing human-based computation. In: Proceedings of the 6th Nordic Conference on Human-Computer Interaction: Extending Boundaries. ACM (2010)
8. Gong, D., Yao, X.: Automatic detection of infeasible paths in software testing. IET Softw. **4**(5), 361–370 (2010)
9. Werbach, K., Hunter, D.: For the win: How Game Thinking Can Revolutionize Your Business. Wharton Digital Press, Philadelphia (2012)
10. Deterding, S., Dixon, D., Khaled, R., Nacke. L.: From game design elements to gamefulness: defining gamification. In: Proceedings of the 15th International Academic MindTrek Conference: Envisioning Future Media Environments, pp. 9–15. ACM (2011)
11. Yuen, M.C., King, I., Leung. K.S.: A survey of crowdsourcing systems. In: 2011 IEEE Third International Conference on Privacy, Security, Risk and Trust (PASSAT) and 2011 IEEE Third Inernational Conference on Social Computing (SocialCom). IEEE (2011)
12. King, J.C.: symbolic execution and program testing. Commun. ACM **19**(7), 385–394 (1976)
13. AmiriChimeh, S., Haghighi, H., Vahidi-Asl, M., Setayesh-Ghajar, K., Gholami-Ghavamabad, F.: Rings: a game with a purpose for test data generation. Interact. Comput **30**, 1–30 (2017)
14. Mao, K., Capra, L., Harman, M., Jia, Y.: A survey of the use of crowdsourcing in software engineering. J. Syst. Softw. **126**, 57–84 (2017)
15. Schmitz, B., Felicia, P., Bignami, F.: An international survey In: Gamification in Education: Breakthroughs in Research and Practice, pp. 439–452. IGI Global (2018)

16. Reeves, N., West, P., Simperl, E.: "A game without competition is hardly a game": the impact of competitions on player activity in a human computation game. In: AAAI (2018)
17. Prabhakar, N., Singhal, A., Bansal, A., Bhatia, V.: A literature survey of applications of meta-heuristic techniques in software testing. In: Hoda, M.N., Chauhan, N., Quadri, S.M.K., Srivastava, P.R. (eds.) Software Engineering. AISC, vol. 731, pp. 497–505. Springer, Singapore (2019). https://doi.org/10.1007/978-981-10-8848-3_47
18. Baker, A., Navarro, E.O., Van Der Hoek, A.: An experimental card game for teaching software engineering processes. J. Syst. Softw. **75**(1), 3–16 (2005)
19. Sheth, S., Bell, J., Kaiser, G.: Halo (highly addictive, socially optimized) software engineering. In: 1st International Workshop on Games and Software Engineering, pp. 29–32 (2011)
20. Johansson, M., Ivarsson, E.: An experiment on the effectiveness of unit testing when introducing gamification. Ph.D. thesis, Master's thesis, Chalmers University of Technology (2014)
21. Arnarsson, D., Johannesson, I.H.: Improving unit testing practices with the use of gamification (2015)
22. Rojas, J.M., Fraser, G.: Code defenders: a mutation testing game. In: 11th International Workshop on Mutation Analysis. IEEE (2015)
23. Navarro, E.O., van der Hoek, A.: SIMSE: an interactive simulation game for software engineering education. In: CATE, pp. 12–17 (2004)
24. Logas, H., et al.: Software verification games: Designing Xylem, The Code of Plants". In: FDG (2014)
25. Dietl, W., et al.: Verification games: making verification fun. In: 14th Workshop on Formal Techniques for Java-like Programs, pp. 42–49 (2012)
26. Gómez, M., et al.: Reproducing context-sensitive crashes of mobile apps using crowd-sourced monitoring. In: 2016 IEEE/ACM International Conference on Mobile Software Engineering and Systems (MOBILESoft). IEEE (2016)
27. He, M., et al.: A crowdsourcing framework for detecting cross-browser issues in web application. In: Proceedings of the 7th Asia-Pacific Symposium on Internetware. ACM (2015)
28. Afzal, W., et al.: An experiment on the effectiveness and efficiency of exploratory testing. Empir. Softw. Eng. **20**(3), 844–878 (2015)
29. Leicht, N., et al.: When is crowdsourcing advantageous? The case of crowdsourced software testing (2016)
30. Schneider, C., Cheung, T.: The power of the crowd: performing usability testing using an on-demand workforce. In: Pooley, R., Coady, J., Schneider, C., Linger, H., Barry, C., Lang, M. (eds.) Information Systems Development, pp. 551–560. Springer, New York (2013). https://doi.org/10.1007/978-1-4614-4951-5_44
31. Gomide, V.H.M., et al.: Affective crowdsourcing applied to usability testing. Int. J. Comput. Sci. Inf. Technol. **5**(1), 575–579 (2014)

Learning

Active Learning of Industrial Software with Data

Lisette Sanchez[1,2], Jan Friso Groote[1,2(✉)],
and Ramon R. H. Schiffelers[1,2]

[1] Eindhoven University of Technology,
5612 AZ Eindhoven, The Netherlands
j.f.groote@tue.nl
[2] ASML, 5504 DR Veldhoven, The Netherlands
{lisette.sanchez,ramon.schiffelers}@asml.com

Abstract. Active automata learning allows to learn software in the form of an automaton representing its behavior. The algorithm SL*, as implemented in RALib, is one of few algorithms today that allows learning automata with data parameters. In this paper we investigate the suitability of SL* to learn software in an industrial environment.

For this purpose we learned a number of industrial systems, with and without data. Our conclusion is that SL* appears to be very suitable for learning systems of limited size with data parameters in an industrial environment. However, as it stands, SL* is not scalable enough to deal with more complex systems. Moreover, having more data theories available will increase practical usability.

Keywords: Active automata learning · SL* · Industrial environment

1 Introduction

For large and complex software systems, tasks like optimization and re-design tend to be time-consuming as they require an in-depth knowledge of the behavior of the system. Though such behavior ought to be properly documented, reality shows such documentation to often be incomplete, outdated or inconsistent. To be able to more efficiently execute said tasks, one would ideally, be able to obtain a good understanding of the behavior of a software system with minimum effort and within a limited time period.

Automata learning offers a solution to this problem, allowing one to learn the behavior of a system by sending commands to the system and observing its response. It allows for the automatic generation of formal models by applying this technique to either known systems (white-box) or unknown systems (black-box). This can be done in a passive sense by collecting and studying traces or in an active sense by firing input at the system and waiting for a response. All approaches have their pros and cons. While this research field is active in all these directions, this paper focuses only on black-box active automata learning.

© IFIP International Federation for Information Processing 2019
Published by Springer Nature Switzerland AG 2019
H. Hojjat and M. Massink (Eds.): FSEN 2019, LNCS 11761, pp. 95–110, 2019.
https://doi.org/10.1007/978-3-030-31517-7_7

A lot of the black-box active automata learning techniques ignore data parameters as they concentrate on the control flow avoiding the intricacies of data. Such techniques offer some insight into the behavior of the system but they do not show the effect that data parameters may have on this behavior, while in reality such knowledge can be crucial to effectively optimize or re-design a system.

One of the few algorithms that allow learning with data is SL*, an extension of the famous L* algorithm of [4], presented by [8] and implemented in RALib (by H.M. Falk and P.F. Brostean, available at bitbucket.org/learnlib/ralib/). In contrast with the finite state machines that L* infers, SL* infers register automata, a type of extended finite state machine (EFSM) which holds registers and transition guards that compare registers with data parameters.

The research question this paper is concerned with is how suitable SL* is for learning software behavior including data parameters through active automata learning in an industrial environment. In particular we want to know what its shortcomings are and how complex the systems are that it can cope with.

For this purpose we learn a number of systems at ASML, which is a company in Veldhoven, The Netherlands, making wafer scanners. Wafer scanners repeatedly project images on silicium wafers to produce integrated circuits at a nano meter scale. The challenge is to project each image exactly on top of each other. These scanners consist of highly advanced hardware controlled by 50Mline of code. ASML wants to replace parts of the existing code base by model based software. Therefore, ASML explores whether such models can be learned automatically from the code. We symbolically learned both standalone components, and combinations of them. We compare this with learning the system without data parameters by instantiating data parameters with a few concrete values.

Modulo some effort to adapt the tools to the industrial environment and struggling with implementations errors, we can conclude that SL* is suitable for learning software behavior with data parameters in an industrial environment for systems with limited complexity. For more complex systems learned partial results may also provide useful insights into the behavior of the system and potentially indicate errors in the implementation. However, as it stands, learning full industrial systems, constellations of components, and even complex individual components is not within reach.

In order to make learning more applicable in an industrial context, it is very useful that SL* is extended with additional theories, especially those that allow the use of constants, lists and queues. Furthermore, scalability needs to be addressed, for instance by dividing the learning process into steps, containing subsets of the input alphabet or subsets of the data parameters and combining the results somehow.

Related Work. Looking at the field of black-box active automata learning we see that many efficient algorithms produced over time are based on Dana Angluin's approach as presented in [4].

Angluin presented an algorithm L* that is capable of inferring deterministic finite state machines from an unknown system, also referred to as a system under learning (SUL). Her technique uses the concepts of a learner and a teacher, where the teacher knows the SUL and the learner initially only knows the input alphabet and the output alphabet of the SUL. By firing two types of queries, namely (1) membership queries asking if a provided sequence of inputs and outputs is accepted by the SUL or not, and (2) equivalence queries asking whether or not the model learned so far is equivalent to the SUL, the learner is able to eventually learn the SUL.

Over time, improvements and adaptations of this algorithm have been designed, of which a short summary is given in [18]. Such improvements include research on how to perform membership queries [10,16] as well as equivalence queries [14], but also data structure improvements [11–13,17], and research to improve scalability [3,5,9].

However, it is not until recently that effort has been put into the design of learning techniques that also consider the data flow of a system when learning its behavior [1,8]. Previous algorithms can only learn behavior depending on data when data is encoded into control by instantiating data to a few concrete data values. We make use of the SL^* algorithm of [8] where data is assumed to stem from data domains with very specific properties, such as $\langle \mathbb{N}, \{=\} \rangle$, i.e., the natural numbers with only equality, or $\langle \mathbb{R}, \{=, <, >\} \rangle$, i.e., the real numbers with an ordering.

So far, besides SL^* there is only one other major method, namely Tomte [1,2], that can deal with data. Tomte uses a similar technique but a different framework architecture where a separate mapper component maps abstract data to concrete values. This makes the learning algorithm independent from handling the data. In SL^* data is completely integrated into the learning algorithm. This is why we chose to use SL^* in our investigation.

Outline. We first provide some preliminaries in Sect. 2 after which we summarize how SL^* works in Sect. 3. Section 4 reports on the suitability of the adapted version of SL^* in an industrial environment after which Sect. 5 follows with a discussion and conclusion.

2 Preliminaries

The SL^* algorithm uses several important concepts [7,8] that are summarized in this section before the algorithm itself is explained in the next section.

2.1 Theories and Data Languages

The automata learning algorithm SL^* learns automata with data registers and data input and output. The data ranges over specific theories that have the following shape.

Definition 2.1. A theory is a pair $\langle \mathcal{D}, \mathcal{R} \rangle$ where

1. $\mathcal{D}$ is a possibly unbounded domain of data values.
2. $\mathcal{R}$ is a set of relations on D.

We say that two sequences of data values $\langle d_1, \ldots, d_n \rangle$ and $\langle d'_1, \ldots, d'_n \rangle$, with $d_1, \ldots, d_n, d'_1, \ldots, d'_n \in \mathcal{D}$, cannot be distinguished by the relations in $\mathcal{R}$ iff for all $R \in \mathcal{R}$, we have that $R(d_{i_1}, \ldots, d_{i_j}) \iff R(d'_{i_1}, \ldots, d'_{i_j})$ with $i_1, \ldots, i_j$ being indices between 1 and n.

We assume that all elements of any $\mathcal{D}$ in this paper are denotable. The current implementation of SL* comes with two theories, namely the *IntegerEquality* theory $\langle \mathbb{N}, \{=\} \rangle$ and the *DoubleInequality* theory $\langle \mathbb{R}, \{=, <, >\} \rangle$.

An alphabet $\mathcal{E}$ is a set of actions which can be split into an input alphabet $\mathcal{E}_{in}$ and an output alphabet $\mathcal{E}_{out}$, with $\mathcal{E} = \mathcal{E}_{in} \cup \mathcal{E}_{out}$ and $\mathcal{E}_{in} \cap \mathcal{E}_{out} = \emptyset$. A parameterized symbol $\alpha(p)$ is an action $\alpha \in \mathcal{E}$ with a formal parameter p. For some fixed theory $\langle \mathcal{D}, \mathcal{R} \rangle$, a data word is a concatenation of data symbols $\alpha(d)$ with $\alpha \in \mathcal{E}$ and $d \in \mathcal{D}$, i.e., $\alpha_1(d_1) \cdot \alpha_2(d_2) \cdots \alpha_n(d_n)$ with $\alpha_1, \alpha_2, \ldots, \alpha_n \in \mathcal{E}$ and $d_1, d_2, \ldots, d_n \in \mathcal{D}$. Similarly, a parameterized word is a concatenation of parameterized symbols $\alpha(p)$ with $\alpha \in \mathcal{E}$ and a formal parameter p.

Two data words w and w' are said to be $\mathcal{R}$-indistinguishable, denoted by $w \approx_{\mathcal{R}} w'$, iff their action sequences are the same and their data parameters cannot be distinguished by the relations in $\mathcal{R}$. For example, for some action $a \in \mathcal{E}$, $\mathcal{D} = \mathbb{Z}$ and $\mathcal{R} = \{<\}$, we have that data words $\alpha(2) \cdot \alpha(1)$ and $\alpha(3) \cdot \alpha(2)$ are $\mathcal{R}$-indistinguishable, since their action sequences $\alpha \cdot \alpha$ are the same and since we have $2<2 \iff 3<3$, $1<1 \iff 2<2$, $2<1 \iff 3<2$ and $1<2 \iff 2<3$.

Definition 2.2. Given a theory $\langle \mathcal{D}, \mathcal{R} \rangle$ and $k \in \mathbb{N}$, we say that a data word u is *k-extendable* iff either

- k = 0, or
- for any data word u' with $u \approx_{\mathcal{R}} u'$ and any data symbol $\alpha(d')$ with $\alpha \in \mathcal{E}$ and $d' \in \mathcal{D}$, we have that there is a data symbol $\alpha(d)$ with $d \in \mathcal{D}$ such that $u \cdot \alpha(d) \approx_{\mathcal{R}} u' \cdot \alpha(d')$, and such that $u \cdot \alpha(d)$ is $(k-1)$-extendable.

For example consider some theory $\langle \mathbb{N}, \{<\} \rangle$ and a data word $u = \alpha(1) \cdot \alpha(2)$. We have that u is not 1-extendable, because for $u' = \alpha(2) \cdot \alpha(4)$ we have $u \approx_{\mathcal{R}} u'$ but for $\alpha(d') = \alpha(3)$ there is no $\alpha(d)$ such that $\alpha(1) \cdot \alpha(2) \cdot \alpha(d) \approx_{\mathcal{R}} \alpha(2) \cdot \alpha(4) \cdot \alpha(3)$.

A theory is said to be *strongly extendable* iff all data words are ∞-extendable and a theory is said to be *weakly extendable* iff for all data words u and for all $k \in \mathbb{N}$, there is a data word u' with $u' \approx_{\mathcal{R}} u$ that is k-extendable.

Note. SL* requires a theory to be either weakly extendable or strongly extendable. The two theories currently implemented in RALib, namely $\langle \mathbb{N}, \{=\} \rangle$ and $\langle \mathbb{R}, \{=, <, >\} \rangle$ are both strongly extendable.

A data language $\mathcal{L}$ is a set of data words, such that for all two words w and w' that are $\mathcal{R}$-indistinguishable, we have that $w \in \mathcal{L} \iff w' \in \mathcal{L}$. A word w is said to be *accepted* by $\mathcal{L}$ iff $w \in \mathcal{L}$, and *rejected* otherwise.

Furthermore, we make the following assumptions about any data language $\mathcal{L}$ (w.r.t. a theory $\langle \mathcal{D}, \mathcal{R} \rangle$)

- $\mathcal{L}$ is prefix-closed, i.e., for any two words w, w' we have that if $w \cdot w' \in \mathcal{L}$ then also $w \in \mathcal{L}$.

- $\mathcal{L}$ is input/output alternating, i.e., all data words in $\mathcal{L}$ contain alternating input and output data symbols and start with an input data symbol.
- $\mathcal{L}$ is output-deterministic, i.e., for any word w ending in an input symbol, we have, for all $\alpha(d), \alpha(d')$ with $\alpha \in \mathcal{E}_{out}$ and $d, d' \in \mathcal{D}$, that if both $w \cdot \alpha(d)$ and $w \cdot \alpha(d')$ are in $\mathcal{L}$ then words $w \cdot \alpha(d)$ and $w \cdot \alpha(d')$ are $\mathcal{R}$-indistinguishable.

A system under learning (SUL) as used in this paper is an implementation of a data language.

2.2   Register Automata

Register automata (RA) are a type of extended finite state machines that can be used to model data languages.

We assume a theory $\langle \mathcal{D}, \mathcal{R} \rangle$, an alphabet $\mathcal{E}$ and a set of registers $\mathcal{G} = \{x_1, \ldots, x_n\}$. A guard is a conjunction of negated or unnegated relations from $\mathcal{R}$ over registers and formal parameters p used in parameterized symbols $\alpha(p)$. A register automaton is then defined as follows.

Definition 2.3. A register automaton is a tuple $\mathcal{A} = (\mathcal{S}, s_0, \mathcal{X}, \Gamma, \lambda)$ where

- $\mathcal{S}$ is a finite set partitioned in input states $\mathcal{S}_{in}$ and output states $\mathcal{S}_{out}$.
- $s_0 \in \mathcal{S}$ is the initial state.
- $\mathcal{X} : \mathcal{S} \to \mathcal{G}$ is a mapping that maps each state to a finite set of registers.
- Γ is a finite set of transitions, each of the form $(s, \alpha(p), g, \pi, s')$ where
  - s is the source state.
  - $\alpha(p)$ is a parameterized symbol. If s is an input state, $\alpha \in \mathcal{E}_{in}$ and s' is an output state. Otherwise, i.e., if s is an output state, then $\alpha \in \mathcal{E}_{out}$ and s' is an input state.
  - g is a guard over p and $\mathcal{X}(s)$.
  - π is an assignment that updates registers in $\mathcal{X}(s')$ with values of p and registers in $\mathcal{X}(s)$.
  - s' is the target state.
- $\lambda : \mathcal{S} \to \{+, -\}$ is a mapping that maps each state to either $+$ or $-$, indicating whether a state is accepting.

We write $s \xrightarrow{\alpha(p), g, \pi} s'$ iff $(s, \alpha(p), g, \pi, s') \in \Gamma$. We write $s \xrightarrow{\alpha(p), g, \pi}$ iff there is an $s' \in \mathcal{S}$ such that $s \xrightarrow{\alpha(p), g, \pi} s'$.

We assume that the RAs in this paper are deterministic, i.e., there are no data words that lead to both accepting and rejecting states and we say that a register automaton has runs over all data words iff every input state has outgoing transitions for all actions in $\mathcal{E}_{in}$ and every output state has outgoing transitions for all actions in $\mathcal{E}_{out}$. In this case unwanted actions lead to rejected states.

In general the initial state s_0 is an input state, i.e., $s_0 \in \mathcal{S}_{in}$. However, we employ symbolic decision trees that are instances of register automata where the initial state can also be an output state.

We use SRAs to represent a SUL:

Definition 2.4. A simple register automaton (SRA) is a register automaton $\mathcal{A} = (\mathcal{S}, s_0, \mathcal{X}, \Gamma, \lambda)$ with $\mathcal{X}(s_0) = \emptyset$ that has runs over all data words.

Note. When visualizing RAs in this paper, input states are indicated by solid lines and output states by dotted lines. Accepted states are indicated by double lines and rejected states by singular lines. Furthermore, input actions are typically prepended with a question mark and output actions are typically prepended with an exclamation mark.

2.3   Symbolic Decision Trees

One of the most distinguishing differences between SL* and its predecessor L* is that SL* uses symbolic decision trees to represent sets of data words.

Definition 2.5. A symbolic decision tree (SDT) is a register automaton $\mathcal{T} = (\mathcal{S}, s_0, \mathcal{X}, \Gamma, \lambda)$ where $\mathcal{S}$ and Γ form a tree with root s_0. We write $\mathcal{X}(\mathcal{T})$ to denote $\mathcal{X}(s_0)$.

An SDT models (part of) the data language based on the valuation of $\mathcal{X}(\mathcal{T})$. For example, consider the theory $\langle \mathbb{R}, \{=, <, >\} \rangle$. There are two registers x_1 and x_2 of which only the latter is used. A symbolic decision tree can express that traces ϵ and $\alpha(p)$ can be accepted provided $p \geq x_2$. This SDT with a depth 1 is depicted in Fig. 1. For any sequence of actions σ, an SDT of depth $|\sigma|$ can be constructed.

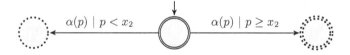

Fig. 1. SDT created for the prefix and suffix as shown in Table 1

Equivalence. To test the equivalence of two SDTs, the following notion of isomorphism is used.

Definition 2.6. Let $\mathcal{T} = (\mathcal{S}, s_0, \mathcal{X}, \Gamma, \lambda)$ and $\mathcal{T}' = (\mathcal{S}', s_0', \mathcal{X}', \Gamma', \lambda')$ be two SDTs with sets of registers $\mathcal{G}$ and $\mathcal{G}'$ respectively. Let $\gamma : \mathcal{G} \to \mathcal{G}'$ be a bijection. We say that $\mathcal{T}$ and $\mathcal{T}'$ are isomorphic under γ, denoted $\mathcal{T} \simeq_\gamma \mathcal{T}'$, iff there is a bijection $\phi : \mathcal{S} \to \mathcal{S}'$ such that:

- $\phi(s_0) = s_0'$,
- $\gamma(\mathcal{X}(s)) = \mathcal{X}'(\phi(s))$ for all $s \in \mathcal{S}$,
- $\lambda(s) = \lambda'(\phi(s))$ for all $s \in \mathcal{S}$, and
- $(s_1, \alpha(p), g, \pi, s_2) \in \Gamma \iff (\phi(s_1), \alpha(p), g^\gamma, \pi^\gamma, \phi(s_2)) \in \Gamma'$

where g^γ and π^γ are respectively a guard and an update with the registers replaced according to γ.

Definition 2.7. Let $\mathcal{T}$ and $\mathcal{T}'$ be two SDTs with $\mathcal{T} \simeq_\gamma \mathcal{T}'$. We say that $\mathcal{T}$ and $\mathcal{T}'$ are isomorphic, denoted $\mathcal{T} \simeq \mathcal{T}'$, iff γ is a bijection.

2.4   Observation Table

An observation table is a data structure used to store results on which data words are accepted by the SUL and which are not.

Definition 2.8. Let $\mathcal{F}$ represent the set of all SDTs. Given an alphabet $\mathcal{E}$ and a theory $\langle \mathcal{D}, \mathcal{R} \rangle$, an observation table is a tuple $\mathcal{O} = (\mathcal{U}, \mathcal{U}^+, \mathcal{V}, \mathcal{Z})$ where

- $\mathcal{U}$ is a prefix-closed set of data words, referred to as short prefixes.
- $\mathcal{U}^+ = \{u \cdot \alpha(d) \mid u \in \mathcal{U} \text{ and } \alpha \in \mathcal{E}\}$ (adhering to the input/output alternating assumption (Sect. 2.1)) and for some $d \in \mathcal{D}$, is a set of extended prefixes.
- $\mathcal{V}$ is a set of parameterized words, referred to as symbolic suffixes.
- $\mathcal{Z} : (\mathcal{U} \cup \mathcal{U}^+) \to \mathcal{F}$, is a mapping that maps each prefix to an SDT.

An observation table is considered *closed* iff for every $u' \in \mathcal{U}^+$ there is a $u \in \mathcal{U}$ and a γ such that $\mathcal{Z}(u') \simeq_\gamma \mathcal{Z}(u)$. Intuitively this means that for every extended prefix there should be a short prefix such that their SDTs are isomorphic under some γ. In this way, the number of states required to represent $\mathcal{L}$ is limited to $|\mathcal{U}|$.

An observation table is considered *register-consistent* iff for every $u \cdot \alpha(d) \in \mathcal{U}^+$ that requires an initial register, i.e., $x_i \in \mathcal{X}(\mathcal{Z}(u \cdot \alpha(d)))$, we also have $x_i \in \mathcal{X}(\mathcal{Z}(u))$. Intuitively this means that if some SDT requires an initial register, this register should have been stored previously.

Intuitively, an SDT $\mathcal{Z}(u)$ indicates in a generic way how a SUL responds after it is requested to perform a data word u. This response matches the actions from a suffix, and it is formulated abstractly in terms of registers and conditions, where the respective data values in u correspond to the registers in $\mathcal{Z}(u)$.

Creating SDTs. Given a theory $\langle \mathcal{D}, \mathcal{R} \rangle$, a prefix $u \in (\mathcal{U} \cup \mathcal{U}^+)$ and a set of symbolic suffixes $\mathcal{V}$, let $\mathcal{D}'$ represent the set of (instantiated) data values in the prefix and let $\mathcal{P}'$ represent the set of (uninstantiated) formal parameters in $\mathcal{V}$. A set of test cases $R(p', d') \cup R(d', p')$ is then created for all $R \in \mathcal{R}$, $d' \in \mathcal{D}'$ and $p' \in \mathcal{P}'$. For each such test case, all $p' \in \mathcal{P}'$ are instantiated with appropriate data values $d \in \mathcal{D}$.

For example, consider a SUL that disallows decreasing numbers and consider the theory $\langle \mathbb{R}, \{=, <, >\} \rangle$, a data word $u = \alpha(1) \cdot ok \cdot \alpha(3) \cdot ok$ for which the data values 1 and 3 are stored in registers x_1 and x_2 respectively, and $\mathcal{V} = \{\alpha(p)\}$. We then have $\mathcal{D}' = \{1, 3\}$ and $\mathcal{P}' = p$.

Table 1. Test cases for a specific prefix and symbolic suffix

Prefix	Symbolic suffix	Test cases	Instantiated suffix	Accepted
$\alpha(1) \cdot ok \cdot \alpha(3) \cdot ok$	$\alpha(p)$	$p < 1$	$\alpha(0)$	no
		$1 < p < 3$	$\alpha(2)$	no
		$p = 1$	$\alpha(1)$	no
		$p = 3$	$\alpha(3)$	yes
		$3 < p$	$\alpha(4)$	yes

Table 1 shows the test cases generated for this example. For each test case an instantiation is created formed by the concatenation of the prefix and the instantiated suffix that satisfies the test case. The instantiated suffix is also depicted in Table 1. The instantiation is sent to the SUL which either accepts or rejects it (also indicated in Table 1). From these results an SDT can then be created as is shown in Fig. 1. This SDT indicates that all data words $\alpha(1)\cdot ok\cdot\alpha(3)\cdot ok\cdot\alpha(p)$ with $p \geq x_2$ are accepted by the SUL and all data words $\alpha(1)\cdot ok\cdot\alpha(3)\cdot ok\cdot\alpha(p)$ with $p < x_2$ are rejected by the SUL.

3   The Algorithm SL*

3.1   Algorithm

The algorithm SL^* presented by Cassel et al. is an extension of Dana Angluin's algorithm L^*. For a more detailed description of either algorithm we refer to the original papers [4,8]. In this section we provide a brief summary of SL^* which should contain sufficient information for the purpose of this paper.

The main idea of SL^* is similar to that of L^*, where concepts of a learner and teacher are used. The learner attempts to learn a black-box system under learning (SUL) that models a data language $\mathcal{L}$ with alphabet $\mathcal{E}$. The SUL is represented as a register automaton (RA, Sect. 2.2) and $\mathcal{L}$ is inferred by asking the teacher so-called membership queries and equivalence queries.

The learner makes use of an observation table (Sect. 2.4) to create, and store the results of membership queries and to build a hypothesis automaton based on this table. The rows of an observation table consist of a set of prefixes, containing specific data values, and the columns consist of a set of symbolic suffixes, which are abstracted from specific data values. Every cell represents a membership query, which is a data word w (Sect. 2.1), where w is the concatenation of the prefix and suffix of the cell. The answers from the teacher to each membership query are transformed into a symbolic decision tree (SDT, Sect. 2.3), which represents, for a given prefix, for which instantiations of parameters in the suffix the SUL accepts the query (Sect. 2.3).

The learner continues to update the observation table by asking the teacher membership queries until the observation table is both closed and register-consistent (Sect. 2.4), at which point it creates a hypothesis automaton from the table, represented as an RA, and sends it to the teacher in the form of an equivalence query. Should the hypothesis automaton be equivalent to the SUL the reply will be positive. Otherwise the teacher will provide a counterexample in the form of a query that is accepted by the hypothesis but not by the SUL or vice versa, after which the learner will continue with an updated observation table and another set of membership queries until it creates the correct hypothesis automaton.

Given an RA with t transitions and at most r registers per state, that models a data language $\mathcal{L}$, SL^* infers $\mathcal{L}$ with $O(tr)$ equivalence queries and $O(t^2r+trm)$ membership queries, where m is the length of the longest counterexample [8].

3.2 Example

In this section, we demonstrate the algorithm SL^* by means of an example over the data theory $\langle \mathbb{R}, \{=, <, >\}\rangle$.

Consider the SUL as presented in Fig. 2, with input alphabet $\mathcal{E}_{in} = \{enter(p)\}$ with $p \in \mathbb{N}$, and output alphabet $\mathcal{E}_{out} = \{ok, nok\}$. Any transitions not shown in the figure lead to sink states which are omitted from the figure.

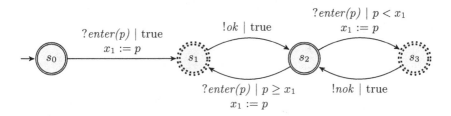

Fig. 2. Example SUL as described above

The observation table is initialized with $\mathcal{U} = \{\epsilon\}$ and $\mathcal{V} = \{\epsilon\} \cup \mathcal{E}_{out}$, as is shown in Table 2. True guards are omitted. Transitions that do not follow the assumption of alternating input and output symbols are not processed.

Table 2. Observation table after the first round

		$\mathcal{V} = \{\epsilon,\ ok,\ nok\}$
$\mathcal{U}$	ϵ	→◯
$\mathcal{U}^+$	$enter(1)$	◯ ←!ok ⟲ !nok→ ◯

The top SDT shown in the table indicates that the empty data word is accepted by the SUL (indicated by the doubly lined state) but it does not show the results for data words ok and nok as they do not follow the assumption of alternating input and output symbols.

The bottom SDT shown in the table indicates with its initial, doubly dotted state that the data word $enter(1)$ leads to an accepting output state, i.e., a state that requires the next action to be from the output alphabet (Sect. 2.2). Furthermore, the SDT indicates that the data word $enter(1) \cdot ok$ is accepted by the SUL and the data word $enter(1) \cdot nok$ is rejected by the SUL (indicated by the singly lined state). Since $\mathcal{V}$ only contains the data symbols ϵ, ok and nok, no other transitions are processed for this SDT.

Table 3. Observation table after the fourth round

$\mathcal{U}$		$\mathcal{V} = \{\epsilon,\ ok,\ nok\}$
	ϵ	
	$enter(1)$	
	$enter(1) \cdot nok$	
	$enter(1) \cdot nok \cdot enter(2)$	
$\mathcal{U}^+$	$enter(1) \cdot ok$	same as ϵ
	$enter(1) \cdot nok \cdot enter(2) \cdot ok$	same as $enter(1) \cdot nok$
	$enter(1) \cdot nok \cdot enter(2) \cdot nok$	same as $enter(1) \cdot nok$

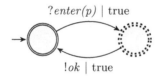

?enter(p) | true

!ok | true

Fig. 3. The hypothesis automaton based on the observation table shown in Table 3

Table 2 is not closed however, since for row $enter(1)$ in $\mathcal{U}^+$ there is no equivalent row in $\mathcal{U}$, hence row $enter(1)$ is added to $\mathcal{U}$ and $\mathcal{U}^+$ is adapted appropriately. Table 3 shows the observation table that is eventually obtained, which is both closed and register-consistent.

A hypothesis automaton is created based on this table (Fig. 3). This results in the following counterexample from the SUL: $enter(1) \cdot ok \cdot enter(2) \cdot ok \cdot enter(0) \cdot nok$, which is accepted by the SUL but not by the hypothesis automaton.

Eventually, the algorithm obtains another closed and register-consistent table, for which a new hypothesis automaton $\mathcal{H}$ is created (Fig. 4) and sent to the teacher, resulting in a positive reply, meaning the learning process is complete and the learner has learned the SUL. Looking past some syntactic differences we can see that the automata in Figs. 2 and 4 are isomorphic under $x_1 \rightarrow r_1$.

4   Industrial Setting

4.1   Experimental Setup

As the main purpose of this paper is to investigate the suitability of SL^* in an industrial environment, the algorithm has been applied to several case studies extracted from the coding environment of ASML. In this section we elaborate on the case studies themselves and on applying the algorithm to these case studies.

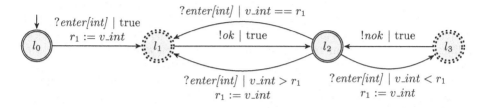

Fig. 4. Result of SL^* after learning the SUL of Fig. 2

Case Studies. In some departments within ASML, a modelling environment called ASD:Suite [6] (see also [15] in this proceedings for a compact explanation of ASD) is used to model the behavior of software from which the source code is generated. Using ASD:Suite, a major component can be decomposed into many smaller components. In particular there is a very large component within the code base of ASML that is decomposed into 200–300 smaller components. For the purpose of this paper, several of these smaller components are considered as case studies.

It is important to note that components modeled in the ASD:Suite use guards to make control flow decisions based on state variables, i.e., variables used to describe the state of a system, as the use of such state variables provides a more compact model of the behavior of the component. Any component using state variables however, can also be modeled as a component without state variables, resulting in a more extensive behavioral model with more explicit states. Visually, this means that the second model has a layered structure, where different layers of states represent the different values of an otherwise present state variable. Models learned by SL^* do not contain state variables and thus contain such a layered structure when inferring ASD:Suite components that do contain state variables.

The case studies we use in this paper are components referred to as c_1, c_2 and c_3, of which only the last one contains behavior that is influenced by its data parameters. These components communicate with each other as shown in Fig. 5. For confidentiality reasons the names of these components are omitted in this section, but we provide a short summary of their behavior.

Component c_3 constitutes a rather typical list implementation, with behavior that allows adding items to the list, removing items from the list, adapting

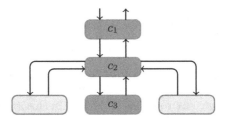

Fig. 5. Communication between the three components c_1, c_2 and c_3

items on the list and viewing items on the list. The behavior of this component is influenced by data parameters passed to the component and is therefore chosen for this case study. Component c_3 communicates only with c_2, which receives calls from c_1 concerning the list and forwards them to c_3 whilst also communicating with two other components, indicated in gray in Fig. 5. Component c_1 is the simplest component of these three, as it only functions as a communicator between other components and c_2.

Each component is learned separately, observing the running times and studying the results, as well as a combination of c_1 and c_2, and a combination of all three components, to observe the learning results and running times when dealing with increased complexity.

To illustrate the strength of SL* when it comes to learning software behavior with (abstract) data parameters, the same set of test cases is learned with concrete data parameters. For this purpose, the input alphabet of each test case is extended such that for each parameterized input i, five concrete but arbitrary inputs are created instead, with concrete values $v_1, v_2, \ldots, v_5$.

Preparation. In preparation of applying the algorithm, code is generated for all components in the SUL and for the direct environment of the SUL, i.e., the components in the wrapper. The input and output alphabet are provided, as is allowed in the black-box model, and a wrapper component is created.

Furthermore, due to the restrictions of theories $\langle \mathcal{D}, \mathcal{R} \rangle$, each parameter in both the SUL and the stub code is transformed into a parameter $d \in \mathcal{D}$. Should there be no access to the code of the SUL, then the wrapper has to map parameters $d \in \mathcal{D}$ to the appropriate parameter types as they are in the SUL. For the purpose of this paper, this extension is omitted, however. The IntegerEqualityTheory is used in all cases.

Environment. The experiments are conducted on a machine with the following properties:

- System: Windows 7, 64 bit, 8 GB RAM, 2.4 GHz CPU.
- JVM: Eclipse Neon 4.6.3, 64 bit, -Xms512m, -Xmx7144m.

4.2 Results

The results are shown below in Table 4, which contains the following information:

- $\#\mathcal{E}_{in}$: the number of inputs in $\mathcal{E}_{in}$.
- $\#\mathcal{E}_{out}$: the number of outputs in $\mathcal{E}_{out}$ prior to the final round of the algorithm, i.e., when no new outputs are added to $\mathcal{E}_{out}$ anymore.
- **sv:** the number of state variables used in the implementation.
- **time:** the total running time of the algorithm averaged over 10 runs. The word 'om' indicates that the learning process was interrupted due to an out of memory error. For these cases the last obtained results are listed.
- **states:** the number of states in the resulting model.
- **transitions:** the number of transitions in the resulting model.
- **mq:** the number of membership queries performed, averaged over 10 runs.
- **eq:** the number of equivalence queries performed, averaged over 10 runs.
- **correct:** whether or not the learned result is correct. This correctness is evaluated by visual inspection. Notations 'N.A'. and '??' denote cases that do not have a final model to inspect or cases that are too big to evaluate by visual inspection, respectively.

For each test case, two values are listed to indicate the result for the test case with abstract and with concrete data parameters. The absence of two values indicates a similar result for both cases. In the test cases that resulted in an out of memory, the DoubleInequalityTheory has also been tried, resulting in the same outcome.

For two out of five test cases the experiments with data parameters led to out of memory. In both cases one parameterized input (the same input in both cases) was removed from the input alphabet in order to be able to obtain a partial result. This input dealt with obtaining the next item from an iterator. These adapted test cases are indicated by the use of asterisks and their results are shown in Table 5.

All in all, the results mostly indicate a problem with scalability as increased complexity quickly leads to out of memory when including data parameters. For those cases that were successfully learned though, the success of SL* becomes apparent. For components that do not contain behavior based on data parameters, learning with SL* uses much less membership queries to learn the same number of states with fewer transitions, resulting in more visual models. For components that do contain behavior based on data parameters, an even more distinguishing result becomes visible. Note that the test cases without data parameters contain only 5 hard-coded values, where the cases with data parameters allow for values in an infinite domain, thereby attesting to the strength of SL* when it comes to learning software behavior with data parameters.

Table 4. Results of applying SL* to several case studies from an industrial environment

	$\#\mathcal{E}_{in}$	$\#\mathcal{E}_{out}$	sv	Time (sec)	States	Transitions	mq	eq	Correct
c_1	18	25	2	9/6	31/31	114/254	3984/9307	11/10	yes
c_2	22	39	5	12K/6.9K	660/660	4.9K/12.2K	1.4M/3.3M	135/117	yes/??
c_3	12	15	1	om/8.3K	127/2.7K	350/18K	19K/4.9M	38/245	N.A./??
c_1, c_2	20	33	6	137/66	108/108	752/1.7K	58k/132k	34/36	yes
c_1, c_2, c_3	10	17	6	om/32K	328/2.4K	1.3K/30K	177K/11.5M	77/239	N.A./??

Table 5. Results of applying SL* to several simplified case studies from an industrial environment

	Time (sec)	States	Transitions	mq	eq	Correct
c_3 *	136/3.2K	87/842	227/5.4k	10k/895k	13/145	yes/??
c_1, c_2, c_3 *	490/3835	109/838	383/9.1K	26k/2.2M	36/147	yes/??

5   Conclusion

Learning well known software with data parameters using SL* that fit the available theories is quite impressive. Applying SL* in an industrial environment can be of use, but there are quite some limitations to consider.

First of all, two direct shortcomings were found that prevented SL* from learning the correct results. Industrial systems do not have a strict alternation of input and output. Furthermore, there are too many software flaws in the available implementation of SL*. Both had to be dealt with in order to allow SL* to correctly learn the results of the industrial case studies. Especially, the latter is not only very time consuming, but it also obfuscates conclusions about the quality of SL*.

While applying SL* to said industrial cases, another weakness became apparent, namely the limited availability of data theories, forcing the use of integers and doubles and limiting the operators usable in guards to equality, $<$ and $>$. In general other data types such as lists and sets are used in SULs but cannot be learned. More importantly, the source code of a SUL may not be accessible, and in such a case it is generally not known which data types are used; one can only hope that they match the available theories.

Another problem is the scalability of the algorithm. Where smaller sized systems can be learned quite fast, an increased complexity quickly results in out of memory errors. Unfortunately, it is not always clear in such cases whether the problems find their origin in the size of the SUL, the quality of the implementation or in the data types that must be learned.

Despite these weaknesses, the strength of SL* has become apparent when applying the algorithm to industrial case studies in comparison to learning these case studies without data parameters. Under the right circumstances, SL* can learn the behavior of a component with data much more efficiently and with a much more compact result, thereby providing valuable insights to engineers requiring to gain knowledge of this behavior. Even when using SL* to learn the behavior of a component that only employs trivial, finite data, the results can be gained more efficiently and are in such a case more compact, by representing this finite data using an infinite data domain.

It is clear that learning industrial software with data still has a long way to go. But under the right circumstances, it can certainly work. And in such cases the learned result generally offers a great amount of insight into the behavior of a system, reducing the amount of time and effort required to gain knowledge about the behavior of the system manually.

References

1. Aarts, F.: Tomte: bridging the gap between active learning and real-world systems. Ph.D. thesis, Radboud University, Nijmegen, The Netherlands (2014)
2. Aarts, F., Fiterau-Brostean, P., Kuppens, H., Vaandrager, F.: Learning register automata with fresh value generation. In: Leucker, M., Rueda, C., Valencia, F.D. (eds.) ICTAC 2015. LNCS, vol. 9399, pp. 165–183. Springer, Cham (2015). https://doi.org/10.1007/978-3-319-25150-9_11
3. Aarts, F., Jonsson, B., Uijen, J., Vaandrager, F.: Generating models of infinite-state communication protocols using regular inference with abstraction. Formal Methods Syst. Des. **46**(1), 1–41 (2015)
4. Angluin, D.: Learning regular sets from queries and counterexamples. Inf. Comput. **75**(2), 87–106 (1987)
5. Bratus, S., Lindner, F. (eds.): 8th USENIX Workshop on Offensive Technologies, WOOT 2014, San Diego, CA, USA, 19 August 2014. USENIX Association (2014)
6. Broadfoot, G., Hopcroft, P.: Analytical software design (2003). Uploaded to researchgate.net
7. Cassel, S., Howar, F., Jonsson, B.: RALib: a LearnLib extension for inferring EFSMs. DIFTS (2015)
8. Cassel, S., Howar, F., Jonsson, B., Steffen, B.: Active learning for extended finite state machines. Formal Asp. Comput. **28**(2), 233–263 (2016)
9. Cho, C., Babic, D., Shin, E., Song, D.: Inference and analysis of formal models of botnet command and control protocols. In: Proceedings of the 17th ACM Conference on Computer and Communications Security, CCS 2010, Chicago, Illinois, USA, 4–8 October 2010, pp. 426–439 (2010)
10. Groce, A., Peled, D., Yannakakis, M.: Adaptive model checking. Log. J. IGPL **14**(5), 729–744 (2006)
11. Isberner, M.: Foundations of active automata learning: an algorithmic perspective. Ph.D. thesis, Technical University Dortmund, Germany (2015)
12. Isberner, M., Howar, F., Steffen, B.: The TTT algorithm: a redundancy-free approach to active automata learning. In: Bonakdarpour, B., Smolka, S.A. (eds.) RV 2014. LNCS, vol. 8734, pp. 307–322. Springer, Cham (2014). https://doi.org/10.1007/978-3-319-11164-3_26
13. Kearns, M., Vazirani, U.: An Introduction to Computational Learning Theory. MIT Press, Cambridge (1994)
14. Lee, D., Yannakakis, M.: Principles and methods of testing finite state machines - a survey. Proc. IEEE **84**, 1090–1123 (1996)

15. Neele, T., Rol, M., Groote, J.F.: Verifying system-wide properties of industrial component-based software. In: Hojjat, H., Massink, M. (eds.) FSEN 2019. LNCS, vol. 11761, pp. 158–175. Springer, Cham (2019)
16. Peled, D., Vardi, M., Yannakakis, M.: Black box checking. J. Autom. Lang. Comb. **7**(2), 225–246 (2002)
17. Rivest, R., Schapire, R.: Inference of finite automata using homing sequences. Inf. Comput. **103**(2), 299–347 (1993)
18. Vaandrager, F.: Model learning. Commun. ACM **60**(2), 86–95 (2017)

An Experimental Study on Flakiness and Fragility of Randoop Regression Test Suites

Samad Paydar$^{(\boxtimes)}$ and Aidin Azamnouri

Ferdowsi University of Mashhad, Mashhad, Iran
s-paydar@um.ac.ir, aidin.noori@mail.um.ac.ir

Abstract. Randoop is a well-known tool that proposes a feedback-directed algorithm for automatic and random generation of unit tests for a given Java class. It automatically generates two test suites for the class under test: (1) an error-revealing test suite, and (2) a regression test suite. Despite successful experiences with applying Randoop on real world projects like Java Development Kit (JDK) which have led to creation of error-revealing tests and identification of real bugs, it has not been investigated in the literature how useful are the regression test suites generated by Randoop. In this paper, we have investigated flakiness and fragility of Randoop's regression tests during evolution of 5 open source Java projects with a total of 78 versions. The results demonstrate that the flakiness of the regression tests is not generally noticeable, since in our dataset, only 5% of the classes have at least one flaky regression tests. In addition, test fragility analysis reveals that in most versions of the projects under study, the regression tests generated by Randoop could be successfully executed on many of later versions. Actually, for 2 out of 5 projects in the experiments, the regression tests generated for each version could be successfully executed on all the later versions of the project.

Keywords: Random testing · Randoop · Fragility · Flaky tests

1 Introduction

Randoop [16] is a well-known tool in the domain of random testing which employs a feedback-directed algorithm for automatically generating unit tests for Java programs. It takes a Java class as the class under test (CUT) and creates random sequences of method calls on the objects of that class. Further, by executing each generated method sequence, it decides whether the sequence is appropriate for being extended to generate longer sequences. During sequence generation, Randoop tries to execute sequences to check the CUT against a set of predefined contracts that every Java class is expected to be compatible with. Should a contract is violated, Randoop stores the corresponding method sequence as an

© IFIP International Federation for Information Processing 2019
Published by Springer Nature Switzerland AG 2019
H. Hojjat and M. Massink (Eds.): FSEN 2019, LNCS 11761, pp. 111–126, 2019.
https://doi.org/10.1007/978-3-030-31517-7_8

error-revealing test. If a sequence does not violate any contract, it is stored as a regression test that has captured the current behavior of the system. Finally, Randoop generates two test suites from these two types of test: (1) an error-revealing test suite, and (2) a regression test suite.

Based on our experience (including the experiments discussed in this paper) with running Randoop on well-known open-source projects, we have observed that usually the error-revealing test suite is empty for a CUT, since the default contracts considered by Randoop are very general and they are not violated by those projects which are implemented by professional programmers. Therefore, for a test practitioner, the main output of Randoop is usually the regression test suite that it generates. This test suite is aimed at revealing regressions during the evolution of the CUT. In other words, if the behavior of the CUT which is captured by Randoop regression tests is changed in the later versions, the corresponding regression tests are expected to fail. Then, the tester needs to analyze the code to see whether the new behavior is correct or it is the result of an error introduced in the new version.

It is interesting to investigate how effective is the generated regression test suite during the evolution of the CUT. In this paper, we discuss an experimental study which mainly focuses on flakiness and fragility of Randoop's regression tests generated for real-world Java programs. The results are expected to shed light on the required improvements on Randoop that can increase the potentials of its application in real-world projects.

There are some works in the literature that study flaky tests [9], i.e. the tests that their pass or fail result is not deterministic and hence, they fail in some executions and pass in some other executions. In addition, a fragile test is a test that is successfully executed on a version of the CUT, but it fails to execute, e.g. due to a compile error, on the successive version of the CUT. Studying the causes for a test to become fragile during the evolution of the software, and also the possible automated fixes, have set the stage for a line of research, specifically in GUI testing domain [2]. While studying the flaky tests and fragile tests has been considered in the literature, there is not yet an established definition for measuring the level of flakiness and fragility in a given test suite. Consequently, in this paper, we first provide a set of metrics for this purpose, and then we use them to analyze the flakiness and fragility of Randoop regression test suites for open-source projects.

The reason why we focus on test flakiness and test fragility lies in the fact that the more a regression test suite generated by Randoop contains fragile or flaky tests, the less successful it would be in serving its main purpose, which is assuring the quality of software during its evolution. A flaky test fails to capture a consistent behavior of the CUT, and hence it cannot be used as a reference to determine whether the behavior is changed during the evolution of the CUT. Moreover, a fragile test first needs to be analyzed and modified so that it can be successfully executed. Identifying flaky or fragile tests and performing possible fixes on them might take a lot of time and effort, and hence, should Randoop generates a large number of flaky or fragile tests, its applicability in real world projects becomes quite questionable. The main purpose of this paper is to investigate this issue.

The rest of the paper is organized as follows. Section 2 briefly reviews the related works on Randoop. In Sect. 3, the experimental study and its elements are discussed, followed by the analysis of the results and discussion of the findings of the experiments in Sect. 4. Finally, Sect. 5 concludes the paper.

2   Related Work

In this section, we briefly review some works that are aimed at improving Randoop effectiveness in unit test generation. First and foremost, the low code coverage of the Randoop tests has attracted many researchers [8,10,21,23]. Due to the fact that the method sequences are created randomly and without any background knowledge or human intervention, it is quite difficult for Randoop to provide the methods under test with the appropriate inputs so that various states of the objects are covered. As a result, different parts of the code that require specific inputs are not covered by Randoop tests.

To address this limitation, GRT [10] provides noticeable improvements over Randoop by employing a two-step analysis method. In the first step, static analysis is performed to collect the required information from the class under test. In the second step, a dynamic analysis is performed with regards to the feedback received from the execution of the method sequences in addition to the information collected in the first step that lead to making a good decision on choosing which sequences should be extended. In [8], the idea of mutating an object under test is employed for the purpose of improving code coverage of the tests.

Another limitation of Randoop is that it cannot properly generate sequences from useful methods; thus, as a solution in [22], Seeker is introduced which employs dynamic and static analysis to create more useful sequences.

Due to the importance of generating appropriate input arguments for method calls, in [23], the TestMiner tool is introduced which extracts literals from the source code of the tests and uses them to create the required input strings. In [12], reusing the test cases from the libraries of the software under test, which resulted in the better generation of test cases, were investigated. Another issue with Randoop is that it does not test the private methods of CUT. In this regard, the authors in [1] suggest using Java Reflection and having access to private fields, which can result in false positives, but better code coverage. This issue of code visibility is also considered in [11].

Regarding the flaky tests, i.e. the tests that their pass/fail behavior is non-deterministic, the authors in [9] have discussed an empirical analysis of flaky tests in real world projects. Their main goal has been to identify the root causes for test flakiness, determine how and when the flaky behavior is manifested, and also to describe the mechanisms that are usually used by developers to fix the flaky tests. The focus in [9] is on flakiness of manually-written tests, while in this paper, we specifically target the tests automatically generated by Randoop.

There are also some works that focus on repairing failed unit tests. For instance in [4], the ReAssert technique is introduced which uses both static and dynamic analysis to suggest a repair for a failed unit test. The suggested repair is mainly in terms of modification in the assertion statements, for instance, replacing assertTrue with assertFalse, or replacing literal values in the assert statements. It is worth noting that ReAssert is not intended to repair those tests that cannot be compiled due to recent changes in the program under test. In other words, it does not modify the unit tests to eliminate compile errors, but just to make a failing test pass.

There is another line of works that have focused on evaluating automated unit test generation tools. For instance, in [15], the methodology and the results of the 6th JUnit testing tool competition is discussed. In this competition, a total of 59 CUTs from 7 open-source Java projects are selected and four automated JUnit tests generation tools, i.e. EvoSuite [5], JTexpert [19], T3 [17] and Randoop are executed with different time budgets to generate test suites for these CUTs. Finally, the performance of the tools are evaluated in terms of structural code coverage metrics and through mutation analysis. In a similar work [3], Randoop is also compared with EvoSuite and 4 other test input generator tools, again in terms of code coverage, efficiency and mutation adequacy.

In another work [20], the authors have evaluated effectiveness of three automated test generation tools Randoop, EvoSuite and AgitarOne in terms of being able to detect real faults in the Defects4J dataset. They have also analyzed the flaky tests generated by these automated tools. The results have shown that on average, 21% of the Randoop tests were flaky, i.e. their pass/fail behavior is non-deterministic. In [7], the authors have discussed their experiences with deploying Infer, a static analysis tool, and Sapienz, a dynamic analysis tool, at Facebook. They have described the open problems that need to be considered by software testing researchers, one of which is the flakiness of tests. In this regard, the authors emphasize the highly stochastic behavior of the systems deployed in real-word situations, and propose that we need to "Assume all Tests Are Flaky". Proposing the theoretical discussions behind this idea, a set of research questions are provided on how to deal with flaky tests based on this assumption. In [18], the authors have discussed their experience with applying Randoop for automated test generation for GUI testing of an industrial project. It is mentioned that integrating Randoop with the build process for the purpose of regression testing has resulted in many false positives. In other words, due to the high rate of intended changes, most of the failing regression tests do not indicate a real bug, but an intended change. However, the paper does not provide quantitative analysis of this problem.

The review of the related work shows that while the limited coverage, readability, and other aforementioned factors regarding Randoop and other automated unit test generation tools is taken into consideration by many researchers, the flakiness and fragility of the Randoop regression tests during the evolution of a project is not considered. This paper seeks to conduct the first investigation in this regard.

3   Experimental Study

In this section, different elements of the experimental study of Randoop regression tests are described. First, the research questions are introduced and then, the preparation of the dataset used in the experiments is described. Finally, the experiment procedures and the evaluation metrics are presented.

3.1   Research Questions

The goal of the current study is to investigate how effective are Randoop regression tests in terms of being able to reveal potential regressions during software evolution. For this purpose, we have focused on evaluating flakiness and fragility of Randoop regression tests. However, a prerequisite for this assessment is to determine whether Randoop is able to create any regression test for the CUT. In other words, if Randoop fails to create any regression test for a large ratio of the classes in a program under test, then the effectiveness of the generated regression test suites is questionable since they might not cover an appropriate amount of the program's code base. As a result, we first seek to determine for what percentage of the input classes, Randoop has been able to create at least one regression test.

Next, we consider two types of problems affecting the effectiveness of the regression tests: (1) flakiness and (2) fragility of the tests. Assuming that a regression test T is created over version i of the program under test, T is flaky if the result of executing T on the same version of the program, i.e. version i, is non-deterministic and hence varies over different executions [9,14]. A flaky test is not useful from the point of view of regression tests, since it has not captured a stable behavior of the CUT, and hence, it is unable to judge about regressions in future versions of the CUT. In addition, T is a fragile test with regards to a successive version j, $j > i$, if it cannot be executed on version j of the program under test due to a compile error in T. The more flaky or fragile tests exist in the test suite generated by Randoop, the less is effectiveness of the test suite.

It is worth noting that flakiness is an inherent weakness of a regression test, since when a regression test which is created on version i is failed on the same version, it has not been able to correctly and consistently capture the behavior of that version of the CUT. Therefore, addressing the test flakiness issue requires improving the Randoop algorithm details to prevent generation of the flaky tests. Test fragility, on the other hand, is not necessarily rooted in the weakness of Randoop or the regression tests it generates, since it is caused by the changes made in the successive versions of the program under test. For instance, if Randoop has created a regression test for class C_1 in version i of the program under test, and this class is renamed in version j, $j > i$, then the corresponding test will fail to compile on version j and hence it becomes a fragile test with regard to this version. However, this cannot be considered as the weakness of that test. Actually, it depends on how we define a change in the behavior of the program under test. If we consider renaming of a class as a change in the behavior of the program under test, it can be argued that having the test failed is exactly what we expect, since the regression test is expected to fail to reveal the change in the behavior of the program under test. If we exclude this kind of change from the definition of behavior change, then the test is not expected to fail. Regardless of which argument a test is in favor of, it is more appealing if it was possible to repair the test so that it can be compiled and executed to see whether it passes or fails. For instance, if it is possible to make the test executable just by renaming the corresponding class in the test code, it is interesting to keep the test in the regression test. However, this requires analyzing the source code to see what is the reason for the compile error and what changes are required to eliminate the error so that the test is compiled successfully. Apparently, this is not an easy task and it might be quite challenging and time-consuming, specifically for a large test suite. This increases the cost of using Randoop for practitioners, and hence, this is why we consider test fragility to indirectly reduce the effectiveness of the Randoop's regression tests.

Based on the viewpoint described above, the main research question in this research is:

RQ. How useful are the regression tests generated by Randoop? To answer this question, the following specific research questions are considered:

RQ$_1$. For what percentage of the classes under test, Randoop is able to generate any regression test?

RQ$_2$. What percentage of the Randoop regression tests are flaky?

RQ$_3$. What percentage of the Randoop regression tests generated for a version i of a CUT can be executed on the version $i + 1$ of that CUT?

RQ$_4$. How long does a Randoop regression test last as a non-fragile test during the evolution of the program under test? In other words, what is the maximum value of $k - j$ so that the regression tests generated over version j can successfully execute over version k, $k > j$?

In this paper, we have conducted an experimental study to answer these questions using a dataset of real world open source projects. While the results of the experiments are not meant to be applicable to every project, we believe they can provide a general understanding of the effectiveness of Randoop over similar projects.

3.2   Dataset

For the purpose of the experimental evaluations, first, a dataset is prepared including different versions of five Java open source projects from the Apache Commons family. Table 1 shows the basic information about the selected projects. We have selected these projects since they are well-known real-world projects, each having released more than 10 version. Actually, on average, about 16 versions have been available for each project and the size of each project, in terms of the number of classes, is increased by a factor of 10 from its first version to its last version. Hence, while the number of projects included in the data set is small, but the volume of the changes in these projects is noticeable and they are good candidates for representing the concept of evolution in a real-world project.

In addition, to create a dataset of Randoop regression tests, for every public class in each version of each project, we have executed Randoop with a time limit of 10 s and the resulting regression tests are stored in the dataset. It is worth noting that the default time limit of Randoop for test generation for a single class is 100 s, however due to the large number of classes in the dataset, we have used a smaller time limit to keep the execution cost of the experiments reasonable. Further, we have set *testsperfile* parameter of Randoop to 1, so that each regression test is created as a separate Java file declaring a test class with a single test method. The information about the generated regression tests is shown in Table 1.

Table 1. Dataset used in the experiments

Project	Project name	Versions			Number of classes with test			Avg. test per class
		First	Last	Count	Min	Max	Total	
P_1	BeanUtils	1.0	1.9.3	19	3	78	1025	338
P_2	Codec	1.1	1.11	11	9	49	336	278
P_3	Collections	1.0	4.4.1	11	21	220	1264	190
P_4	Compress	1.0	1.16.1	20	36	126	1709	294
P_5	Digester	1.0	3.3.2	17	11	67	599	353

3.3 Experiments

In order to answer the first research question, it is needed to analyze the regression tests generated by Randoop and identify the cases where it has failed to generate any test for a given class. As for answering the next research questions, i.e. RQ_2 to RQ_4, we designed two experiments:

1. Flakiness Experiment. Since a flaky test has different behaviors in different executions, in order to determine the flaky tests, we have executed every regression test generated for each version i of each project, on the same version i of the same project until whether the test is failed or it is executed for 10 times. If the test is failed in one of its executions, it is considered to be a flaky test. This experiment is designed for answering RQ_2. Actually, repeating a test for 10 times is not guaranteed to reveal its flakiness, however, to control the execution cost of the experiment, we have used the value of 10 as a reasonable threshold, since this strategy of 10 reruns is common in practice [6,13].

2. Fragility Experiment. In this experiment, we have executed every regression test generated on each version j of each project, on all the versions k (k > j) of the same project. However, we have ignored the flaky tests identified in the previous step. This experiment is considered to answer RQ_3 and RQ_4.

3.4   Metrics

In order to analyze the results of the experiments, we have defined a set of metrics which are introduced below.

- *TestGenSuccess* of Randoop on a specific version of a project P is the percentage of the classes in that version for which Randoop has successfully generated at least one regression test.
- *Flakiness* of a class is the percentage of the tests generated for that class that are flaky.
- *Fragility*$_{j,k}$ of a class is the percentage of the non-flaky tests generated for a class in version j of the corresponding project which are fragile with respect to version k, $k > j$.
- *Fragility-Free Length* of a project is the maximum value of $k - j$ where the regression tests generated for version j can be executed on version k. A great value for this metric points to a long period in the evolution of the project during which the regression tests of older versions have no fragility with regards to later versions.

4   Result Analysis

In this section, we analyze and discuss the results of the experiments and answer the research questions described in the previous section.

4.1   Regression Test Suite Generation

In order to answer RQ_1, we have computed for each version of each project the percentage of the classes in that version for which Randoop has been successful in generating at least one regression test. The results are shown in Table 2. For instance, the results demonstrate that considering different versions of P_1, Randoop has been able to create regression tests for 94% to 100% of the CUTs. Furthermore, across all the versions, on average, Randoop has created regression tests for about 97% of the classes in P_1. The worst performance of Randoop is associated with P_3 where Randoop has created regression tests for only 72% of the classes in version 3.0. Some sample classes with no regression tests are mentioned in Table 3. Finally, over all the projects, Randoop has created regression tests for an average of 95% of the classes under test. As a results, it is reasonable to answer RQ_1 by concluding that Randoop is powerful in creating regression tests for most of the classes under test.

It is interesting to analyze why Randoop has not been able to create regression tests for some of the classes. Our initial analysis demonstrates that we can attribute this issue to the inability of Randoop in preparing required arguments for calling the methods, including constructors, of the CUTst, since they require complex objects, not primitive values, as input parameter. Hence, Randoop has not been able to create any object from these class and call methods on

Table 2. Test generation results

Project	TestGenSuccess for different versions (%)		
	Min	Max	Average
P_1	94	100	97
P_2	97	100	99
P_3	72	100	85
P_4	97	100	99
P_5	85	100	95
Total	72	100	95

Table 3. Sample classes with no regression tests

Project	Version	Class name
P_1	1.4	org.apache.commons.beanutils.ResultSetIterator
P_2	1.10	org.apache.commons.codec.binary.BaseNCodecInputStream
P_3	3.0	org.apache.commons.collections.list.LazyList
P_4	1.10	org.apache.commons.compress.archivers.dump.DumpArchiveSummary
P_5	3-3.0	org.apache.commons.digester3.binder.CallMethodBuilder

those objects. However, we admit that more precise analysis is required to identify any other possible cause for this problem.

Finally, it is interesting to mention that Randoop has created a non-empty Error Test Suite only for 89 classes[1], counting for about 1% of the classes in the dataset. In addition, the average number of error tests generated for these classes is 27. This supports our previous claim that from a practical point of view, Randoop rarely generates any error-revealing for the class under test.

4.2   Flakiness Analysis

Next, we have analyzed the results of the flakiness experiment by computing Flakiness for each CUT in each version of the projects in the dataset. The results, shown in Table 4, demonstrate that for different projects, between 3% to 9% of the classes have Flakiness > 0. Specifically, for those classes in P_1 with Flakiness > 0, the minimum, maximum and average Flakiness is respectively 1%, 79% and 11%. For other projects, the average flakiness of those classes with Flakiness > 0 is greater, compared to P_1. Finally, across the entire dataset, 5% of the classes have Flakiness > 0 and the average Flakiness of these classes is 54%. Based on these results, we can answer RQ_2 by concluding that for a low ratio of the CUTs Randoop generates any flaky tests, but for such classes, on

---

[1] This includes 26 distinct classes, since some classes have error test suite in different versions.

average, about half of the generated tests are flaky. Some sample classes for which Randoop has generated flaky tests are introduced in Table 5.

Table 4. Results of the flakiness experiment for classes with flakiness > 0

Project	Count	Ratio (%)	Count (Unique)	Flakiness		
				Min	Max	Avg.
P_1	49	5	5	1	79	11
P_2	30	9	6	1	93	48
P_3	44	3	10	1	99	43
P_4	106	6	6	15	100	80
P_5	38	6	9	5	100	55
Total	267	5	36	1	100	54

We have not performed a detailed root causes analysis of the flaky tests. However, our initial investigation reveals that the way Randoop deals with side effect of modifying static members of the CUT needs to be improved. A good case in point is class *org.apache.commons.beanutils.ConvertUtils* in P_1, where during test generation, a method sequence modifies the static members defined in this class, e.g. *defaultDouble* and *defaultInteger*, and later a second method sequence reads the value of these members and uses them in the assertions. Later, when a test that is created from the second method sequence is executed, it is executed with no history of the changes that are performed by the first method sequence, and hence, the assertions fail. Listing 1.1 shows a sample regression test that is flaky due to this reason. It is worth mentioning that *test order dependency* is identified in [12] as the third most frequent cause of test flakiness, and *static field in CUT* is determined as one of the three identified sources of this dependency.

Table 5. Sample classes with flaky tests

Project	Version	Class name
P_1	1.0	org.apache.commons.beanutils.ConvertUtils
P_2	1.10	org.apache.commons.codec.digest.Crypt
P_3	1.0	org.apache.commons.collections.BeanMap
P_4	1.0	org.apache.commons.compress.archivers.zip.ZipArchiveEntry
P_5	2.1	org.apache.commons.digester.Digester

Listing 1.1. A sample flaky test generated by Randoop for version 1.0 of P_1

```
@Test public void test1() throws Throwable {
    org.apache.commons.beanutils.ConvertUtils convertUtils0 =
        ↪ new org.apache.commons.beanutils.ConvertUtils();
    float f1 = convertUtils0.getDefaultFloat();
    org.junit.Assert.assertTrue(f1 == 10.0f);
}
```

4.3 Fragility Analysis

In order to analyze the results of the fragility experiment, we have first measured $Fragility_{j,k}$ for each class under test in a source version j with respect to all subsequent versions k, $k > j$. Next, we have computed the average value of $Fragility_{j,k}$ over all the classes in version j. The results are shown via the heat maps in Figs. 1, 2 and 3. In these heat maps, a cell with a red color represents the maximum value among all the cells and a green cell shows the minimum value. For the purpose of brevity, the heat maps related to projects P_1 and P_4 are not shown since all their cells have a value of 0.

Source Version (j)	\multicolumn{10}{c}{Target Version (k)}									
	1.2	1.3	1.4	1.5	1.6	1.7	1.8	1.9	1.10	1.11
1.1	11	11	11	17	17	17	17	17	17	17
1.2		0	0	4	4	4	4	4	4	4
1.3			0	6	6	6	6	6	6	6
1.4				3	3	3	3	3	3	3
1.5					0	0	0	0	0	0
1.6						0	0	0	0	0
1.7							0	0	0	0
1.8								0	0	0
1.9									0	0
1.10										0

Fig. 1. Average $fragility_{j,k}$ for P_2 (Color figure online)

The results demonstrate that the average fragility of the regression tests generated for every version of P_1 with regards to every later version is 0%. This interesting observation means that if Randoop was used to generate regression tests for each version of P_1, those test would have been executable on every successive version of P_1 to control any change in the behavior during the evolution of the P_1. The same is true about P_4 where the average fragility of the regression tests of each version with regards to successive versions is 0%. For P_3, the average fragility of the regression test of version 1.1 with regard to version 1.2 is 11%, meaning that 11% of the tests generated for version 1.1 cannot be compiled and hence executed on version 1.2. Further, 17% of these tests cannot be compiled on version 1.5 and later versions. However, the tests that are generated for version 1.5 and later, have no fragility with regard to all their successive versions. For P_3, the tests generated for versions before 4.4.0, all have a noticeably high fragility with version 4.4.0 and later versions. This is a symptom of a noticeable change in version 4.4.0. Actually, our investigation reveals that this is due to renaming the main package of P_3 from *collections* to *collections4*. This has made all the tests generated for previous versions fail to compile. For P_5, the results are similar to P_3, and the regression tests generated for versions before 3.3.0 have almost complete fragility with regard to the version 3.3.0 and later versions. Similar to P_3, this can be attributed to the fact that the main package of P_5 is renamed from *digester* to *digester3*.

Finally, among 18 versions of P_1 (the last version is not considered since it has no successive version), all have the characteristic that their regression tests have no fragility on their immediate successive version. For P_2, P_3, P_4 and P_5, this is respectively 8 out of 10, 7 out of 10, 19 out of 19, and 14 out of 16.

Based on the discussion above, we can answer RQ3 by saying that fragility of the regression test of a version is usually 0% or low with regard to at-least a few successive versions. Consequently, we can conclude that if Randoop is being used for regression testing during the evolution of a project, it could be of great help in controlling regressions. However, as mentioned for P_3 and P_5, in some points during the evolution of the project, the previous regression tests might become fragile due to major changes introduced in a new version. What is needed in that situation, is an effective technique for automatically performing the possible repairs on the regression tests so that they can be compiled on the new versions. We believe development of such a repair technique is both feasible and valuable in improving the effectiveness of Randoop regression tests.

Source Version (j)	Target Version (k)									
	2.0	2.1	2.1.1	3.0	3.1	3.2	3.2.1	3.2.2	4-4.0	4-4.1
1.0	6	6	6	40	40	40	40	40	95	95
2.0		0	0	36	36	36	36	36	97	97
2.1			0	21	21	21	21	21	98	98
2.1.1				24	21	21	21	21	98	98
3.0					0	0	0	0	99	99
3.1						0	0	0	99	99
3.2							0	0	99	99
3.2.1								0	99	99
3.2.2									99	99
4-4.0										0

Fig. 2. Average fragility$_{j,k}$ for P_3 (Color figure online)

It is interesting to identify the cause of the fragility of the tests. Through analysis of the compilation results of the tests, we have identified the top-5 errors most frequently raised by the compiler during the fragility experiment.

Source Version (j)	Target Version (k)															
	1.1	1.1.1	1.2	1.3	1.4	1.4.1	1.5	1.6	1.7	1.8	1.8.1	2.0	2.1	3.3.0	3.3.1	3.3.2
1.0	0	0	0	0	0	0	0	36	36	36	36	36	36	100	100	100
1.1		0	0	0	0	0	0	29	29	29	29	29	29	100	100	100
1.1.1			0	0	0	0	0	29	29	29	29	29	29	100	100	100
1.2				0	0	0	0	19	19	19	19	19	19	100	100	100
1.3					0	0	0	19	19	19	19	19	19	100	100	100
1.4						0	0	17	17	17	17	17	17	100	100	100
1.4.1							0	19	19	19	19	19	19	100	100	100
1.5								20	20	20	20	20	20	95	95	95
1.6									0	0	0	0	0	98	98	98
1.7										0	0	0	0	98	98	98
1.8											0	0	0	98	98	98
1.8.1												0	0	98	98	98
2.0													0	98	98	98
2.1														99	99	99
3.3.0															0	0
3.3.1																0

Fig. 3. Average fragility$_{j,k}$ for P_5 (Color figure online)

The results are shown in Table 6. In this table, the compiler errors are abstracted by replacing the project-specific identifiers, e.g. class name or package names. While this requires thorough investigation to identify the types of changes that have led to these compiler errors, our initial analysis have demonstrated that changing package names, moving classes to new packages and changing access level of the class members (e.g. from public to private) are among the most frequent changes that have caused compiler errors and test fragility. For instance, in version 3.0 of P_3, the class *FilterIterator* is moved from *org.apache.commons.collections* package to *org.apache.commons.collections.iterators* package. This change makes all the regression tests that are created for previous versions and use *FilterIterator* to fail to compile on version 3.0. We believe it is promising to seek to develop new techniques for automatically repairing the regression tests to cope with these changes. This is the main direction of our future work. To answer RQ$_4$, it is required to compute Fragility-Free Length for each project. This can be achieved by identifying the length of the longest sequence of zeros in the rows of Figs. 1, 2 and 3. The Fragility-Free Length for each project is shown in Table 7. The results emphasize the effectiveness of Randoop regression tests since it demonstrates that the regression tests that are generated for the versions in which the fragility-free period starts, could have been used to perform regression testing on an interesting number of later versions.

Table 6. Top-5 compiler errors for fragile tests

Compiler error template
cannot find symbol {identifier}
incompatible types: {type1} cannot be converted to {type2}
package {package} does not exist
reference to {identifier} is ambiguous
{class member} has private access in {class}

Table 7. Results of fragility experiment

Project	P_1	P_2	P_3	P_4	P_5
Fragility-free length	18	6	4	19	7

5   Conclusion

In this paper, we have discussed an experimental evaluation of the effectiveness of the regression tests generated by Randoop. Specifically, we have investigated flakiness and fragility of Randoop's regression tests during evolution of 5 open source Java projects with a total of 78 versions. The results demonstrate that the flakiness of the regression tests is not generally noticeable, since in our dataset, only 5% of the classes have at least one flaky regression tests. In addition, test fragility analysis reveals that in most versions of the projects under study, if Randoop has been used to generate regression tests, those tests could be successfully executed on a noticeable number of later versions. Actually, for 2 out of 5 projects that are used in the experiments, the regression tests generated for each version could be successfully executed on all the later versions of the project. For some of the projects, there are some points during the evolution of the project in which the previous regression tests become fragile. We believe that it is possible to develop repair algorithms to automatically do the required modifications on some of the fragile tests to eliminate their fragility. Our future work is mainly focused on development of such a repair technique.

References

1. Arcuri, A., Fraser, G., Just, R.: Private API access and functional mocking in automated unit test generation. In: 2017 IEEE International Conference on Software Testing, Verification and Validation, ICST 2017, Tokyo, Japan, 13–17 March 2017, pp. 126–137 (2017)
2. Coppola, R., Morisio, M., Torchiano, M.: Mobile GUI testing fragility: a study on open-source android applications. IEEE Trans. Reliabil. **68**(1), 67–90 (2019). https://doi.org/10.1109/TR.2018.2869227
3. Cseppento, L., Micskei, Z.: Evaluating code-based test input generator tools. Softw. Test. Verif. Reliab. **27**(6), e1627 (2017)

4. Daniel, B., Jagannath, V., Dig, D., Marinov, D.: Reassert: suggesting repairs for broken unit tests. In: ASE, pp. 433–444. IEEE Computer Society (2009)
5. Fraser, G., Arcuri, A.: Evosuite: automatic test suite generation for object-oriented software. In: SIGSOFT/FSE 2011 19th ACM SIGSOFT Symposium on the Foundations of Software Engineering (FSE-19) and 13th European Software Engineering Conference (ESEC 2013), Hungary, 5–9 September 2011, pp. 416–419 (2011)
6. Gupta, P., Ivey, M., Penix, J.: Testing at the speed and scale of Google. Google Engineering Tools Blog (2011)
7. Harman, M., O'Hearn, P.W.: From start-ups to scale-ups: opportunities and open problems for static and dynamic program analysis. In: SCAM, pp. 1–23. IEEE Computer Society (2018)
8. Jaygarl, H., Kim, S., Xie, T., Chang, C.K.: OCAT: object capture-based automated testing. In: Proceedings of the Nineteenth International Symposium on Software Testing and Analysis, ISSTA 2010, Italy, 12–16 July 2010, pp. 159–170 (2010)
9. Luo, Q., Hariri, F., Eloussi, L., Marinov, D.: An empirical analysis of flaky tests. In: Proceedings of the 22nd ACM SIGSOFT International Symposium on Foundations of Software Engineering (FSE-22), Hong Kong, China, 16–22 November 2014, pp. 643–653 (2014)
10. Ma, L., Artho, C., Zhang, C., Sato, H., Gmeiner, J., Ramler, R.: GRT: program-analysis-guided random testing (T). In: 30th IEEE/ACM International Conference on Automated Software Engineering, ASE 2015, Lincoln, NE, USA, 9–13 November 2015, pp. 212–223 (2015)
11. Ma, L., Zhang, C., Yu, B., Sato, H.: An empirical study on the effects of code visibility on program testability. Softw. Qual. J. **25**(3), 951–978 (2017)
12. Ma, L., Zhang, C., Yu, B., Zhao, J.: Retrofitting automatic testing through library tests reusing. In: 24th IEEE International Conference on Program Comprehension, ICPC 2016, Austin, TX, USA, 16–17 May 2016, pp. 1–4 (2016)
13. Micco, J.: Continuous integration at Google scale, 2013 (2013)
14. Micco, J.: Flaky tests at Google and how we mitigate them (2016)
15. Molina, U.R., Kifetew, F.M., Panichella, A.: Java unit testing tool competition: sixth round. In: Proceedings of the 11th International Workshop on Search-Based Software Testing, ICSE 2018, Sweden, 28–29 May 2018, pp. 22–29 (2018)
16. Pacheco, C., Ernst, M.D.: Randoop: feedback-directed random testing for Java. In: Companion to the 22nd ACM SIGPLAN Conference on Object-Oriented Programming Systems and Applications Companion, pp. 815–816. ACM (2007)
17. Prasetya, I.S.W.B.: T3i: a tool for generating and querying test suites for Java. In: ESEC/SIGSOFT FSE, pp. 950–953. ACM (2015)
18. Ramler, R., Klammer, C., Buchgeher, G.: Applying automated test case generation in industry: a retrospective. In: 2018 IEEE International Conference on Software Testing, Verification and Validation Workshops, ICST Workshops, Västerås, Sweden, 9–13 April 2018, pp. 364–369 (2018)
19. Sakti, A., Pesant, G., Guéhéneuc, Y.: JTExpert at the fourth unit testing tool competition. In: SBST@ICSE, pp. 37–40. ACM (2016)
20. Shamshiri, S., Just, R., Rojas, J.M., Fraser, G., McMinn, P., Arcuri, A.: Do automatically generated unit tests find real faults? An empirical study of effectiveness and challenges (T). In: ASE, pp. 201–211. IEEE Computer Society (2015)
21. Thummalapenta, S., Xie, T., Tillmann, N., de Halleux, J., Schulte, W.: MSeqGen: object-oriented unit-test generation via mining source code. In: Proceedings of the 7th joint meeting of the European Software Engineering Conference and the ACM SIGSOFT International Symposium on Foundations of Software Engineering, Amsterdam, The Netherlands, 24–28 August 2009, pp. 193–202 (2009)

22. Thummalapenta, S., Xie, T., Tillmann, N., de Halleux, J., Su, Z.: Synthesizing method sequences for high-coverage testing. In: Proceedings of the 26th Annual ACM SIGPLAN Conference on Object-Oriented Programming, Systems, Languages, and Applications, OOPSLA 2011, Portland, OR, USA, 22–27 October 2011, pp. 189–206 (2011)
23. Toffola, L.D., Staicu, C., Pradel, M.: Saying 'hi!' is not enough: mining inputs for effective test generation. In: Proceedings of the 32nd IEEE/ACM International Conference on Automated Software Engineering, ASE 2017, Urbana, IL, USA, 30 October–03 November 2017, pp. 44–49 (2017)

Verification

Formalizing and Analyzing Security Ceremonies with Heterogeneous Devices in ANP and PDL

Antonio González-Burgueño$^{(\boxtimes)}$ and Peter Csaba Ölveczky

University of Oslo, Oslo, Norway
antonigo@ifi.uio.no

Abstract. *Security ceremonies* extend cryptographic protocols with models of human users to allow us to take human behaviors into account when reasoning about security. *Actor-network procedures* (ANPs) are a well-known formal model of security ceremonies, and *procedure derivation logic* (PDL) allows us to reason logically about ANPs. In a security ceremony, different nodes may have different *capabilities*: computers can encrypt and decrypt messages, whereas humans cannot; a biometric device can capture biometric information, whereas a random number generator used in e-banking cannot; and so on. Furthermore, even if a node has the *decryption* capability, it must also know the encryption key to decrypt a message. ANPs do not support explicitly specifying node capabilities. In this paper, we extend ANPs to deal with heterogeneous devices by explicitly specifying the nodes' capabilities. We also modify PDL to take into account the knowledge of participants at different points in time. All this allows us to reason about secrecy and authentication in ceremonies with different kinds of devices and human users.

1 Introduction

Most security breaches nowadays occur not by breaking cryptographic protocols or because of buffer overflow, but through various forms of "social engineering attacks," such as phishing emails, malicious apps and web sites, browser status/address bar spoofing attacks [6], and so on. Furthermore, web applications typically interact with human users. To reason about security, we must therefore include humans as key parts of the security process, which requires defining new models of such processes. For example, in standard crypto-protocol formalisms, the behavior of each actor is typically given as a (deterministic) *sequence* of actions, whereas humans may exhibit *nondeterministic* behaviors (does the user click on the link? does she perform an action in the wrong way?).

Security ceremonies [8] extend cryptographic protocols with models of human users. *Actor-network procedures* (ANPs), introduced by Meadows and Pavlovic, are one of the more popular ways of formalizing security ceremonies (see, e.g., [1, 5,11,12,14,15]), and *procedure derivation logic* (PDL) [11,15] allows us to reason

© IFIP International Federation for Information Processing 2019
Published by Springer Nature Switzerland AG 2019
H. Hojjat and M. Massink (Eds.): FSEN 2019, LNCS 11761, pp. 129–144, 2019.
https://doi.org/10.1007/978-3-030-31517-7_9

logically about ANPs. ANPs define the possible behaviors as partial orders over events, and PDL formulas allow nodes to assert the order of events in a protocol run. ANP and PDL have been used to formalize and reason about a wide range of systems, including physical access to secure areas of airports and office buildings, multi-factor multi-channel authentication, and key agreement procedures.

A security ceremony typically includes different kinds of nodes, such as computers, different kinds of humans (expert users, novices, intruders, etc.), and authentication devices like smart cards, random number generators, biometric devices, and so on. Different actors may have very different capabilities: a computer can encrypt and decrypt messages whereas humans cannot; a biometric device can capture biometric information, whereas a random number generator used in e-banking cannot; and so on.

The ANP formalism is fairly abstract, and does not support specifying that different nodes have different capabilities. In this paper, we therefore define *ANPs with capabilities* (ANP-Cs), which extend ANPs with an explicit specification of the capabilities of the different nodes. ANP-Cs also add the following events to APNs' *send* and *receive* events: (a) *learning* events for obtaining information (messages, keys, etc.) from previously received messages, and (b) events *creating* new terms from existing knowledge and the node's capabilities. Learning events are needed to express secrecy: did the intruder learn m from overhearing some (encrypted) message m'?

PDL is a logic for reasoning about the temporal order of *events*, and does not allow us to reason about the *knowledge* of the nodes at certain times. However, a node that has the capability to decrypt an encrypted message can only do so if it currently knows the decryption key for the message. To reason more accurately about security ceremonies, we should keep track of the knowledge of each node throughout the run of the ceremony. We therefore modify PDL to allow reasoning about ANP-Cs. Our new logic PDL-CK allows us to reason about the dynamically evolving knowledge of the participants, and can be used, for example, to reason logically about under what circumstances (i.e., what are the necessary capabilities of the different actors and what must they know initially?) a certain action, such a node decrypting a message, can take place.

The rest of this paper is structured as follows: Sect. 2 gives some background on ANP and PDL. Section 3 shows how different capabilities can be axiomatized as operations in an equational algebraic theory, introduces the new events for learning and creating, and defines ANP-Cs as ANPs with an explicit mapping from devices to capabilities. Section 4 introduces PDL-CK. Finally, Sect. 5 discusses related work, and Sect. 6 gives some concluding remarks.

2   Preliminaries

Meadows and Pavlovic have developed *actor-network procedures* (ANPs) [13, 15] to formally specify security ceremonies. This is a quite abstract model, where the possible local behaviors of a group ("configuration") of nodes is specified as a partial order of *localized events*. A localized event is either $\mathsf{send}(t)_P$ or $\mathsf{receive}(t)_P$, where t is a term of a user-defined algebraic theory (Σ, E) of operations (consisting of an algebraic signature Σ declaring sorts and operations/functions, and a set E of equations axiomatizing those operations), and P is a node or group of collaborating nodes.[1] The set of possible runs in an entire system are then given as the partial order of localized events that "combine" the different local partial orders in a send/receive-consistent way.

Procedure derivation logic (PDL) [13,15] is a logic for localized reasoning about the temporal order of events in an ANPs; for example, "node p knows that if it has received the message t, then some node X previously sent t".

Although ANP and PDL have been used on a number of applications [12,13,15,16], there is currently no tool support for ANP and PDL.

Actor-Network Procedures. The "static" structure of an ANP is defined as an *actor-network*. A *configuration* is a set of nodes and/or (sub)configurations where all participants need each other to achieve a common goal. A smart card and a card reader may be seen as a configuration: both are needed to validate someone's identity. An actor-network is a network of such (possibly hierarchical) configurations, *principals* that control the configurations, and *channels* between configurations, where each channel has a *type*, and is defined as follows in [15]:

Definition 1 ([15]). *An actor-network consists of: a set $\mathcal{J}$ (of principals); a set $\mathcal{N}$ (of nodes); a set $\mathcal{P}$ of configurations, where a configuration can be a finite set of nodes, or a finite set of configurations; a set $\mathcal{C}$ (of channels); a set Θ (of channel types); a partial map $\copyright : \mathcal{P} \to \mathcal{J}$ (denoting the principal controlling a configuration); functions $\delta, \varrho : \mathcal{C} \to \mathcal{P}$ denoting the source and destination of a channel; and a function $\vartheta : \mathcal{C} \to \Theta$ (assigning to each channel its type).*

An algebraic theory (Σ, E) defines the operations, such as encryption, decryption, creating a nonce, etc. An *event* or *action* has the form $a(t)$, where a is an event identifier (such as send or receive) and the term t is its parameter.

An *actor-network procedure* extends an actor-network by adding a *process*, which defines the local behaviors of each configuration as a partially ordered multiset of *localized events*:

Definition 2 ([15]). *A process $\mathcal{F}$ is a partially ordered multiset of localized events, $\mathcal{F} = \langle \mathcal{F}_{\mathbb{E}}, \mathcal{F}_{\mathcal{P}} \rangle : \mathbb{F} \to \mathbb{E} \times \mathcal{P}$, where*

- *$(\mathbb{F}, \to)$ is a well-founded partial order, representing the structure time,*
- *$\mathbb{E}$ is a family of events, and*
- *$(\mathcal{P}, \subseteq)$ is the partial order of configurations*

such that if $\phi \to \varphi$ in $\mathbb{F}$ then $\mathcal{F}_{\mathcal{P}}\phi \subseteq \mathcal{F}_{\mathcal{P}}\varphi$ or $\mathcal{F}_{\mathcal{P}}\varphi \subseteq \mathcal{F}_{\mathcal{P}}\phi$.

Although a process is defined as a partially ordered *multiset* of localized events, for simplicity, Meadows and Pavlovic assume that each event takes place at most once. We therefore write $e_{1P} \to e_{2Q}$ to denote that there are (time points)

---

[1] $\mathsf{send}(t)_P$ and $\mathsf{receive}(t)_P$ are written $\langle \cdot t \cdot \rangle_P$ and $(\cdot t \cdot)_P$, resp., in [13,15].

ϕ and φ in $\mathbb{F}$ with $\phi \to \varphi$ such that $\mathcal{F}(\phi) = (e_1, P)$ and $\mathcal{F}(\varphi) = (e_2, Q)$. Informally, this means that e_1 takes place in configuration P before e_2 takes place in configuration Q. The last requirement in Definition 2 implies that a process just orders events *inside* the configuration P (or Q, if $P \subseteq Q$), and hence only define the local behaviors.

A *run* of a process ρ assigns to each receive event $\mathsf{receive}(t)_Q$ a unique *flow* $\mathsf{send}(t)_P \xrightarrow{\tau} \mathsf{receive}(t)_Q$. A run can be seen as a partially ordered (multi)set of localized events that extends the partial order $\to$ in ρ by adding these flows $\mathsf{send}(t)_P \to \mathsf{receive}(t)_Q$. That is, a run extends the internal synchronization in a configuration to the whole network. A network procedure is then defined in [15] as a pair $(\rho, \mathcal{S})$ where ρ is a process and $\mathcal{S}$ is a set of runs of ρ (denoting the "secure" runs).

Procedure Derivation Logic. *Procedure derivation logic* (PDL) [13] is a logic for reasoning about security properties in actor-network procedures. The reasoning of protocol participants is concerned mostly with the order of events in a protocol run. A PDL statement has the form $A : \Phi$, where $A \in \mathcal{J}$ is a participant, and Φ is a predicate asserted by A. The predicate Φ is formed by applying the usual quantifiers and logical connectives (we write $\Longrightarrow$ for implication) to the atomic predicates, which can be: e_P, meaning "the (localized) event e_P happened," or $e_P \to e'_Q$, meaning "the event e_P happened before the event e'_Q". In PDL, the valid statements are derived from the few "generic" PDL axioms, the protocol specification, and protocol-specific assumptions.

One of the generic PDL axioms says that any message that is received must have been sent. That is, if the principal $©P$ controlling P knows $\mathsf{receive}(t)_P$, this principal also knows that there was a corresponding send event $\mathsf{send}(t)$ by some configuration X:

$$©P : \mathsf{receive}(t)_P \Longrightarrow \exists X.\ \mathsf{send}(t)_X \to \mathsf{receive}(t)_P$$

Other PDL axioms axiomatize freshly generated random numbers and continuous flows. In addition, the user can axiomatize her own assumptions about her system. The paper [15] shows many examples of the use of PDL.

3   ANPs with Explicit Device Capabilities

Different devices taking part in a security ceremony can have different capabilities. For example, a security ceremony could include smart cards, biometric devices such as fingerprint readers or iris scanners, a fob device used in online banking to generate one-time passwords, different kids of human users (superuser, standard user, amateur user), computers, and so on.

A security ceremony including many such devices could involve a smart card (or passport) which stores some biometric data of a user. When the user swipes the smart card/passport, the smart card reader sends the biometric data to a central computer, and a biometric device such as a face recognition system takes a photo of the human user and sends a hash of that information to a central computer. If the biometric data on the smart card and the one taken by the biometric device match, and everything else is OK according to the computer, the user is allowed to enter a certain area/country.

These devices have different capabilities: a fingerprint reader can generate a number by reading your fingerprint, whereas a human or computer cannot; a computer can encrypt and decrypt messages, and a human cannot; only the e-banking one-time password generator can generate one-time passwords; etc.

In this section we extend ANPs to explicitly define and include the capabilities of the different actors in a security ceremony. The two main reasons for making the capabilities explicit are:

- Specification: making explicit the capabilities of nodes in a ceremony.
- Most importantly, knowing the capabilities of the nodes is necessary to reason about the (dynamically evolving) knowledge of the participants (e.g., a node that cannot decrypt messages cannot know/obtain the plaintext from an encrypted message), as well as reasoning under what circumstances certain runs are possible.

In this section we first show how the different capabilities of different devices can be given as functions in an algebraic theory (Σ, E). We then define an *actor-network procedure with explicit capabilities* (ANP-C) as an actor-network procedure with an associated map from nodes to sets of operations/capabilities. Finally, to make the reasoning about obtained knowledge in Sect. 4 simpler, and in general to make the knowledge obtained or created explicit, ANP-Cs add two new kinds of events to ANPs: *create* event use a node's capability and current knowledge to create new informations, and *learning* events models explicitly obtaining knowledge from other pieces of knowledge. The learning event makes it possible to reason about secrecy and authentication; for example, secrecy means that an intruder cannot obtain certain information m *from an overheard encrypted message*—it does not mean that the intruder does not know m. Therefore, just relying on knowledge is not enough to reason about secrecy; we need to make the learning *from* something explicit.

3.1   Specifying Device Capabilities

We show in this section how different capabilities that devices may have can be given as functions in the algebraic theory (Σ, E) of ANP operations.

Smart Cards. A smart card is a small device that typically can:

- Send and receive information to/from a smart card reader.
- Store (and possibly update) data, such as, e.g., the identity and credentials of a user, a PIN code, the remaining amount of money on the card, and the smart card's public key and private key.
- Encrypt and decrypt data using its private and public keys.

We can specify public-key encryption/decryption as the following algebraic theory, written in the style of the Maude language [7], where the keyword op introduces an operator/function, and eq introduces an equation:

```
sorts Node Msg EncMsg PbKey PvKey Key .     subsort  PbKey PvKey < Key .
op pv : Node -> Key .                         op pb : Node -> Key .
op enc : Msg PvKey -> EncMsg .                op dec : EncMsg PbKey  -> Msg .
vars X : Msg .                                var Y : Node .
eq dec(enc(X,pb(Y)),pv(Y)) = X .              eq dec(enc(X,pv(Y)),pb(Y)) = X .
```

where the sorts Msg, EncMsg, PbKey, PvKey, Key, and Node denote, respectively, messages, encrypted messages, private keys, public keys, keys in general (including both public and private keys), and node identities. $pv(n)$ and $pb(n)$ denote, respectively, the private key of n and the public key of n. Finally, enc and dec denote public-key encryption and decryption, respectively.

Biometric Devices. A biometric device is an authentication device that verifies the identity of a person based on physiological or behavioral characteristics, such as fingerprints, facial or iris images, and/or voice recognition. A biometric device compares the pre-stored biometric information about the user[2] with the biometric information captured by the sensor of the device during the authentication process. In addition to authenticating a person, biometric keys are also used to encrypt/decrypt sensitive information, for example in smart phones.

The following operations define the capability of turning an "image" (of a person's iris or fingerprint) into biometric data, as well as an operation for checking whether the biometric data of two "images" refer to the same person:

```
sorts Image BioData .
ops fingerPrint irisScan ... : Image -> BioData .
op compare : BioData BioData -> Bool .
```

If biometric data are also used for, say, shared-key encryption, there is an operation *bioKey* that generates a shared key from biometric data; we also axiomatize shared-key cryptography with shared-key encryption and decryption operations *skEnc* and *skDec*:

```
sorts  SharedKey  Key .                       subsort SharedKey < Key .
op bioKey : BioData -> SharedKey .
op skEnc : Msg SharedKey -> EncMsg .          op skDec : EncMsg SharedKey -> Msg .
var SK : SharedKey .                          eq skDec(skEnc(X,SK),SK) = X .
```

One-Time PIN Generators. A one-time PIN generator is a device that generates a sequence of "random" numbers used for example in online banking as well as in online services like Google, Facebook, or Dropbox. These devices use a formula that generates pseudo-random numbers based on a seed, e.g., a shared key (such as the device serial number) and the moment in time in which the

---

[2] The biometric information of the user can be pre-stored at the device itself, e.g., a phone with a biometric sensor, or in an external support such as a passport.

transaction/operation is performed. Since the device (whose owner must push a button or perform an action to activate the device and generate the random value) and the entity at which the user wants to be authenticated both know the seed and the time, both can obtain the same number and hence (partially) authenticate the user. Alternatively, the generated random is instead a function of the seed and the previous random number (or a counter). Since we use an *untimed* framework, we can only define the second option:

```
sort Seed .    subsort Seed < Nat .    op pin : Seed Nat -> Nat .
```

Our longer report [10] defines many more operations used in security ceremonies.

3.2 Actor-Network Procedures with Capabilities

We define an *ANP with capabilities* (ANP-C) to be a pair $(\mathcal{A}, \mathbb{C})$ where $\mathcal{A}$ is an ANP and $\mathbb{C}$ assigns to each node n in $\mathcal{A}$ its capabilities:

Definition 3. *An* ANP *with capabilities (ANP-C) is a pair* $(\mathcal{A}, \mathbb{C})$ *where:*

- $\mathcal{A} = (\mathcal{J}, \mathcal{N}, \mathcal{P}, \mathcal{C}, \Theta, \delta, \varrho, \vartheta, \mathcal{F})$ *is an ANP such that the different capabilities of the devices and their algebraic properties are included in its underlying algebraic theory* (Σ, E), *and*
- $\mathbb{C}$ *is a capability distribution* $\mathbb{C} : \mathcal{N} \to \wp(\Sigma)$ *assigning to each node n in $\mathcal{A}$ its capabilities.*

3.3 Learn and Create Events

As mentioned, to reason about secrecy (what did a bad guy learn by overhearing a message M?), we need some way of saying that someone learnt a particular piece if information from a certain message. Just reasoning about the knowledge of the intruder is not sufficient, since the intruder may know the secret from before, but could not learn it *from the overheard message*. We therefore introduce a new type of event, called a *learning event*, which has the form

$$\text{apply } op \text{ to } t \text{ toLearn } t',$$

where op is a function in our signature ($op \in \Sigma$) and $t, t' \in \mathcal{T}_\Sigma$ are two Σ-terms. In this event, an actor which has the capability to perform the operation op applies op to the term t (which could be the overheard message) and learns t'. This event may take additional parameters $u_1, \dots, u_n$; the actor performing such a learning event should already know t and $u_1, \dots, u_n$, and $op(t, u_1, \dots, u_n) =_E t'$; that is $op(t, u_1, \dots, u_n)$ and t' are equivalent terms in the equational theory (Σ, E). For example, an intruder that has overheard (and hence knows) a message $skEnc(m, sk)$, knows the (shared) encryption key sk, and has the capability to shared-key decrypt messages, can then perform the learning event apply $skDec$ to $skEnc(m, sk)$ toLearn m to learn m from $skEnc(m, sk)$, since $skDec(skEnc(m, sk), sk) =_E m$.

The creation of a term t in ANP, used e.g., for creating fresh nonces, in [15] does not take into account the capabilities of the node which creates a term. We therefore define a new kind of *create event* which makes explicit also the capability used to create the event. Such a create even has the form

$$\text{apply } op \text{ to } t_1, \ldots, t_n,$$

where $op \in \Sigma$ and $t_1, \ldots, t_n \in \mathcal{T}_\Sigma$ are terms of appropriate sorts. Introducing such an event also facilitates the reasoning about how the knowledge of actors evolves during a run. We therefore assume that nodes create terms before using them; e.g., a node knowing both m and sk should perform the event/create the term apply $skEnc$ to m, sk before sending this encrypted message.

3.4   Example: Establishing Shared Keys Using SSL/TSL

Figure 1 shows a graphical representation of an ANP-C for the SSL/TSL procedure involving a user, her smartphone with a fingerprint reader, and a computer belonging to, e.g., the bank, for establishing a secret shared key.

The different nodes are represented as filled circles at the far left of the figure. Each time point ϕ_k is written ⓚ and is decorated with the event $\mathcal{F}_E(\phi_k)$ that takes place at the time point. The actor/configuration that performed the event is the actor to the left of the time point.

A run has an internal synchronization inside the same node/configuration; these are written with a standard arrow $\rightarrow$ between two time points. The external synchronization between two different configurations happens when one configuration receives a message sent by another. We write $ⓘ \overset{m}{\Longrightarrow} ⓚ$ for such a communication event, where m is the message transferred. We do *not* write that the events taking place at ϕ_i and ϕ_j are send(m) and receive(m), respectively.

According to [13], a node may perform local operations. Specifically, if a node applies a Boolean operation, then it can branch to different time points, depending on whether the result of the previous operation equals *true* or *false*. We use the arrows $\overset{true}{\dashrightarrow}$ and $\overset{false}{\dashrightarrow}$ in this case. Finally, to save space, some expressions are abbreviated, and given as equations $s = t$.

In the example, the user U can check whether a certificate from the bank C looks OK; the smartphone P can read fingerprints and generate biometric data from them, and can generate shared keys and do public-key cryptography; the computer can compare two (biometric data associated to) two fingerprints and decide whether they belong to the same person (finger?), and can generate certificates for the user. The new capabilities added to (Σ, E) are therefore:

```
sort Cert .   subsort Cert < Msg .  op genCert : Bool Node -> Cert .
op visCheck : Cert -> Bool .        op genSk : Bool Node Node -> SharedKey .
```

The ceremony has the following steps: The user U sends her fingerprint *image* to the smartphone P (time points ϕ_0 and ϕ_1); P then uses the operation *fingerprint* to create the biometric data *fingerprint(image)*, which is abbreviated

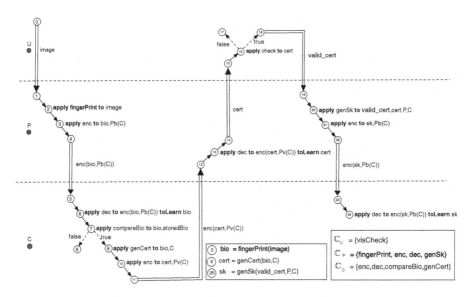

Fig. 1. An ANP-C showing an SSL/TLS procedure involving a user (U), a smartphone with a biometric device (P), and the bank's computer (C).

to *bio* (ϕ_2); *P* then applies the function *enc* to *bio* and the computer's public key $Pk(C)$ (ϕ_3), and then sends *enc*(*bio*, $Pk(C)$) at time point ϕ_4. This message is read by the computer *C* at time point ϕ_5. *C* then applies the *dec* function to learn *bio* (ϕ_6). If this received biometric information *bio* equals the bank's stored biometric data *storedBio* (time point ϕ_7), which the bank hopefully knows before (see Sect. 4 for a discussion on defining initial knowledge), we continue to time point ϕ_9, where *C* applies *genCert* to generate *C*'s certificate, which is encrypted at time point ϕ_{10} and sent to *P* at time point ϕ_{11}. The smartphone *P* receives this message (ϕ_{12}), decrypts the message to learn the certificate (ϕ_{13}), and sends/shows the certificate to the user *U* (ϕ_{14}). The user receives/sees this certificate (ϕ_{15}) and then checks the certificate visually (ϕ_{16}). If the certificate looks good, the user goes to time point ϕ_{18} where she "sends" an OK message to the smartphone. The smartphone *P* gets this OK "message" (ϕ_{19}), applies *genSk* to generate a shared key between *P* and *C* (ϕ_{20}), encrypt this message (ϕ_{21}) and sends this encrypted message to *C* (ϕ_{22}). Finally, *C* receives this message at time point ϕ_{23} and decrypts it at ϕ_{24} to learn the shared key.

4   PDL-CK: Reasoning About ANP-Cs and Knowledge

In this section we define a variation of the PDL logic, called PDL-CK, for reasoning about ANP-Cs.

PDL is typically used to reason about *secure runs*, that is, behaviors that we know are possible. However, one of the main goals of making capabilities explicit is exactly to reason about what runs are possible. For example, can an intruder obtain a secret? More precisely, under what circumstances can the intruder obtain a secret? And under what circumstances is a security ceremony with the desired event actually possible? For example, in the SSL-TSL example above, under what circumstances is the shared key actually established?

Making capabilities explicit goes half ways towards answering these questions: to perform an action (like decrypting a message), a node needs both a certain capability (such as decrypting messages) *and* certain knowledge (such as knowing the decryption key). We therefore propose to reason about ANP-Cs using a logic which takes into account both the capabilities and the (dynamically evolving) knowledge of the participants of the ceremony. We call this logic PDL-CK ("PDL with capabilities and knowledge"). With this logic we can reason about under what circumstances something can happen or a property holds. More precisely, which capabilities and what initial knowledge are needed for a (good or bad) event to take place? That is, in addition to reasoning about events and their temporal relationship as in PDL, PDL-CK allows us to reason also about the knowledge of the actors when the different events take place.

Notation: assuming that each event only takes place once, we denote by $\mathbb{K}_e$ the knowledge of the nodes at the end of the time point at which e takes place.

This section first introduces such global knowledge. Then we introduce the logic PDL-CK and its axioms, before showing examples of reasoning in PDL-CK.

4.1   Knowledge Distributions and Knowledge Histories

Keys, messages, nonces, and so on, are usually modeled as ground terms in the algebra (Σ, E), and are not identified with their actual numerical values. Therefore, we can represent a node's knowledge as a set of Σ-terms. A *knowledge distribution* defines the current knowledge of each node in the network:

Definition 4. *A* knowledge distribution κ *for a set of nodes* $\mathcal{N}$ *is a function* $\kappa : \mathcal{N} \to \wp(\mathcal{T}_\Sigma)$ *assigning to each node* n *the set* $\kappa(n)$ *of ground terms it knows.*

A *knowledge history* assigns such a knowledge distribution to each time point in the procedure:

Definition 5. *Given a process* $\mathcal{F}$ *with an underlying structure time* $(\mathbb{F}, \to)$*, a* knowledge history $\mathbb{K}$ *for* $\mathcal{F}$ *is a function* $\mathbb{K} : \mathbb{F} \to (\mathcal{N} \to \wp(\mathcal{T}_\Sigma))$ *that assigns to each time point* $\varphi \in \mathbb{F}$ *a knowledge distribution. Furthermore, the function* $\mathbb{K}$ *must be monotonic w.r.t.* $\to$*, i.e.,* $\varphi_i \to \varphi_j \Rightarrow \mathbb{K}(\varphi_i)(n) \subseteq \mathbb{K}(\varphi_j)(n)$ *for all* n*.*

Intuitively, $\mathbb{K}(\phi)$ denotes the knowledge of the different actors at the "end" of time point ϕ; that is, it includes knowledge acquired at time point ϕ.

Notation. Under the usual assumption that an event e takes place at most once, at time point ϕ, we write $\mathbb{K}_e$ for the knowledge distribution $\mathbb{K}(\phi)$.

The initial knowledge of the nodes plays a key role. We denote by $\mathbb{K}_{init}$ the *initial knowledge* in a knowledge history $\mathbb{K}$. Mathematically, this can be seen as adding a new event *init* which takes place at a new time point ϕ_{init} so that $init \to \phi$ for any other time point ϕ (in the run).

Example 1. A possible initial knowledge of the ANP-C in Fig. 1 could be

$$\mathbb{K}_{init}(U) = \{image, ok\}$$
$$\mathbb{K}_{init}(P) = \{Pb(C), Pv(P), Pb(P)\}$$
$$\mathbb{K}_{init}(C) = \{true, false, Pb(C), Pv(C), Pb(P), storedBio\}.$$

For example, the computer initially knows a (pre-stored) biometric key of the user. This history at time point ϕ_9, after the event apply *genCert* to *true, C*, is:

$$\mathbb{K}_{apply\ldots}(U) = \mathbb{K}_{init}(U)$$
$$\mathbb{K}_{apply\ldots}(P) = \mathbb{K}_{init}(P) \cup \{bio(= fingerprint(image)), image, enc(bio, Pb(C))\}$$
$$\mathbb{K}_{apply\ldots}(C) = \mathbb{K}_{init}(C) \cup \{bio, enc(bio, Pb(C)), cert\}.$$

4.2 PDL-CK

The *procedure derivation logic with capabilities and knowledge* (PDL-CK) modifies and extends PDL to reason not only about the temporal order of events, but also of the participants' knowledge at each point in time. To simplify the exposition, in the rest of this paper we assume that we do not have "composite" configurations. That is, any configuration is a single node.

The difference between PDL and PDL-CK is that PDL reasons about an ANP $\mathcal{A}$, whereas PDL-CK reasons about a pair $((\mathcal{A}, \mathbb{C}), \mathbb{K})$, where $(\mathcal{A}, \mathbb{C})$ is an ANP-C and $\mathbb{K}$ is a knowledge history for $\mathcal{A}$. (In practice, we are interested in whether *there exists* a $\mathbb{K}$ such that $\Phi(\mathbb{K})$ holds for a given $(\mathcal{A}, \mathbb{C})$).

Therefore, e_p (the event e took place at p) and $e_{1p} \to e_{2q}$ (the event e_1 took place at p before e_2 took place at q) are still atomic propositions in PDL-CK; the difference is that the PDL-CK formulas also may include $\mathbb{C}$ and $\mathbb{K}$. However, the axioms in PDL are replaced with others to take also the capacities and the knowledge into account.

Some generic PDL-CK axioms for global (bird's-eye view) reasoning are given in Table 1 (where we use the symbol $\implies$ for logical implication). The axiom **Equality** says that if p knows t_1, and t_1 and t_2 are E-equivalent, then p must also know t_2. The axiom **Send** says that if p sends z, then p must have known z before, and that nothing new was learnt anywhere as a result of performing this action. The **Receive** axiom says that if p receives z, then: p knows z at the end of this time point, that the only thing learnt globally during this time point is that z learnt p, and the receive event must have been preceded by the corresponding send event at some actor q. The axiom **Learn** says that if p applies O to a term u to learn t, then p knows t at (the end of) this time point, that p has the capability to perform O, that p knows u before, that there are additional parameter values $u_1, \ldots, u_n$ previously known by p so that $O(u, u_1, \ldots, u_n) =_E t$, and that the only thing learnt by performing this event is that p learnt t. Likewise, **Creation** says that if you "generate" a new term $O(t_1, \ldots, t_n)$, then you have learnt this new term, must have the capability O and must know $t_1, \ldots, t_n$ earlier, and that the only new knowledge added is that p has learnt the generated term. Finally, we add new axioms for test-and-branch.

(Note that the nodes do not learn anything by taking a branch. We can encode such knowledge by adding two new capabilities $valid, inValid : \texttt{Bool} \rightarrow Flag$ and transform a branch $boolExp \overset{true}{\dashrightarrow} e'$ to $e \overset{true}{\dashrightarrow}$ apply $valid$ to $boolExp \rightarrow e'$, and transforming $boolExp \overset{false}{\dashrightarrow} e''$ to $e \overset{false}{\dashrightarrow}$ apply $inValid$ to $boolExp \rightarrow e''$).

Table 1. PDL-CK Axioms.

Equality	$\forall t_1, t_2, e, p.\ t_1 =_E t_2 \implies t_1 \in \mathbb{K}_e(p) \Leftrightarrow t_2 \in \mathbb{K}_e(p)$
Send	$\mathsf{send}(z)_p \implies p\ \mathbf{knows}\ z\ \mathbf{before}\ \mathsf{send}(z)_p \ \wedge\ nothingLearnt(\mathsf{send}(z)_p)$
Receive	$\mathsf{receive}(z)_p \implies z \in \mathbb{K}_{\mathsf{receive}(z)}(p)\ \wedge\ onlyLearnt(\mathsf{receive}(z)_p, z, p)$ $\wedge\ \big(\exists q.\ \mathsf{send}(z)_q \rightarrow \mathsf{receive}(z)_p\big)$
Learn	$(\mathsf{apply}\ O\ \mathsf{to}\ u\ \mathsf{toLearn}\ t)_p$ $\implies t \in \mathbb{K}_{(\mathsf{apply}\ O\ \mathsf{to}\ u\ \mathsf{toLearn}\ t)}(p)\ \wedge\ O \in \mathbb{C}(p)$ $\wedge\ p\ \mathbf{knows}\ u\ \mathbf{before}\ (\mathsf{apply}\ O\ \mathsf{to}\ u\ \mathsf{toLearn}\ t)_p$ $\wedge\ \exists\ u_1, \ldots, u_n.\ \big(O(u, u_1, \ldots, u_n) =_E t$ $\wedge\ \forall_{1 \le i \le n}.\ p\ \mathbf{knows}\ u_i\ \mathbf{before}\ (\mathsf{apply}\ O\ \mathsf{to}\ u\ \mathsf{toLearn}\ t)_p\big)$ $\wedge\ onlyLearnt((\mathsf{apply}\ O\ \mathsf{to}\ u\ \mathsf{toLearn}\ t)_p, t, p)$
Creation	$(\mathsf{apply}\ O\ \mathsf{to}\ t_1, \ldots, t_n)_p$ $\implies O(t_1, \ldots, t_n) \in \mathbb{K}_{(\mathsf{apply}\ O\ \mathsf{to}\ t_1, \ldots, t_n)}(p)\ \wedge\ O \in \mathbb{C}(p)$ $\wedge\ \forall_{1 \le i \le n}.\ p\ \mathbf{knows}\ t_i\ \mathbf{before}\ (\mathsf{apply}\ O\ \mathsf{to}\ t_1, \ldots, t_n)_p$ $\wedge\ onlyLearnt((\mathsf{apply}\ O\ \mathsf{to}\ t_1, \ldots, t_n)_p, O(t_1, \ldots, t_n), p)$
Branch.True	$bExpr_p \overset{true}{\dashrightarrow} e_q \implies (e_q \implies bExpr)\ \wedge\ nothingLearnt(bExpr_p)$
Branch.False	$bExpr_p \overset{false}{\dashrightarrow} e_q \implies (e_q \implies \neg bExpr)\ \wedge\ nothingLearnt(bExpr_p)$

The formulas $p\ \mathbf{knows}\ z\ \mathbf{before}\ e_q$ (p must know z before then localized event e_q takes place), $onlyLearnt(e_q, t, p)$ (the only knowledge added to the system as a result of performing the event e is that p learnt t), and $nothingLearnt(e_q)$ (nothing was learnt by performing the event e) are defined as follows:

$$p\ \mathbf{knows}\ z\ \mathbf{before}\ e_q \triangleq z \in \mathbb{K}_{init}(p) \vee \exists e', r.\ (e'_r \rightarrow e_q\ \wedge\ z \in \mathbb{K}_{e'}(p))$$

$$onlyLearnt(e_q, z, p) \triangleq$$
$$\forall x, r.\ x \in \mathbb{K}_e(r) \implies (x =_E z\ \wedge\ p = r) \vee r\ \mathbf{knows}\ x\ \mathbf{before}\ e_q$$

$$nothingLearnt(e_p) \triangleq \forall t, q.\ t \in \mathbb{K}_e(q) \implies q\ \mathbf{knows}\ t\ \mathbf{before}\ e_p.$$

4.3 Examples

This section gives some small examples of reasoning with PDL-CK.

Example 2. Figure 2 shows an ANP-C run where a computer C_A sends a shared-key encrypted message $skEnc(msg_1, sk_1)$ to a smart card reader R which decrypts the message (e.g., to receive an update). The encrypted message is overheard/received by a Trojan virus T. The algebraic theory (Σ, E) of operations is (a subset of) the one in Sect. 3.1. The run of this ANP-C is as follows:

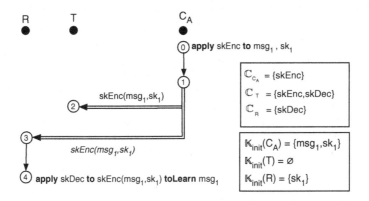

Fig. 2. An actor-network run for updating information.

0. The computer C_A creates the encrypted message $skEnc(msg_1, sk_1)$.
1. C_A sends the shared-key encrypted message $skEnc(msg_1, sk_1)$.
2. The trojan virus T receives/overhears the message $skEnc(msg_1, sk_1)$.
3. The smart card reader R receives the message $skEnc(msg_1, sk_1)$.
4. R learns sk_1 from the message $skEnc(msg_1, sk_1)$ by applying the $skDec$ capability with parameter sk_1.

The desired property is that if R learns msg_1 from the shared-key encrypted message $skEnc(msg_1, sk_1)$, then *initially* R knows the shared key, $sk_1 \in \mathbb{K}_{init}(R)$, and R can perform the shared-key decryption operation, $skDec \in \mathbb{C}(R)$:

(apply $skDec$ to $skEnc(msg_1, sk_1)$ toLearn $msg_1)_R \implies skDec \in \mathbb{C}(R) \land sk_1 \in \mathbb{K}_{init}(R)$.

Example 3. An interesting property to prove about the ceremony in Fig. 1 is that if a shared key is established between the phone and the bank, then:

- the bank *initially* knows U's biometric data: $storedBio \in \mathbb{K}_{init}(C)$; and
- the biometric data of the user matches the biometric data stored by the bank: $compare(fingerPrint(image), storedBio)$.

That is, the formula to prove is:

(apply dec to $enc(sk, Pb(C))$ toLearn $sk)_C$
$\implies storedBio \in \mathbb{K}_{init}(C) \land compare(fingerPrint(image), storedBio)$.

Our longer report [10] contains many more examples, including reasoning about secrecy and authentication.

5   Related Work

Most papers on ANP and PDL [5,11,12,14] show how ANP and PDL can be applied to reason about *protocol runs*, but do not use a dynamic representation of the knowledge of the different actors, and do not differentiate between the capabilities of different devices. Fiadeiro et al. [9] use ANP to describe a logic for reasoning about the different states and state transitions of an actor network. In this formalization, the different actors, interaction channels and knowledge are static, whereas in our work, the knowledge of each actor evolves during the execution of the run.

Basin et al. [3] use a node topology for the analysis of security protocols that specifies the node's capabilities, initial knowledge, honesty, and available communication channels. They group the different agents in three different groups based on their capabilities and knowledge, i.e., honest, dishonest and restricted, but do not distinguish between different types of restricted agents (human participants) and their capabilities and knowledge. Their security ceremony formalization is linked to the Tamarin tool, whereas our work is not yet linked to a tool.

Bella and Coles-Kemp [4] present a security ceremony model focused on the human-computer interoperation, whereas our framework deals with the interactions between different kinds of devices and humans, and we explicitly define the different participants of the security ceremony (human and non-humans) whereas they use a general model to represent the different actors.

Radke et al. [17] define an attacker model for security ceremonies in which they use a recognize function to formalize human capabilities. In contrast to our work, they do not focus on representing knowledge (explicitly).

Finally, Belfanz et al. [2] and Creese et al. [18] define different threat models in different communications channels, but do not define the capabilities nor the knowledge or the participants. We do not take into account channel features, but we explicitly define the different participants and analyze a communication process independently of the kind of channel used.

6   Concluding Remarks

Many different kinds of devices and humans, with different rights and capabilities, participate in today's security processes. We have therefore extended the well-known and general model of security ceremonies by Meadows and Pavlovic by explicitly representing the user-definable capabilities of each actor. We have also defined a new logic, PDL-CK, to reason about our models. This logic allows reasoning about the dynamically changing knowledge of the participants. We believe that this is the first formalism for security ceremonies that makes explicit the different user-definable capabilities of the participants. PDL-CK allows us to reason, for example, under what circumstances (i.e., initial knowledge and capabilities) certain actions, such as decrypting a message, can be performed.

Much work remains. Like the work of Meadows and Pavlovic that we extend, our model does not yet have an executable formal semantics, and hence no tool support. We should develop verification strategies and should apply our methods on state-of-the-art applications. We should also consider non-monotonic knowledge and dynamic node capabilities.

References

1. Anlauff, M., Pavlovic, D., Waldinger, R., Westfold, S.: Proving authentication properties in the Protocol Derivation Assistant. In: FCS-ARSPA 2006. ACM (2006)
2. Balfanz, D., Smetters, D.K., Stewart, P., Wong, H.C.: Talking to strangers: authentication in ad-hoc wireless networks. In: NDSS 2002. The Internet Society (2002)
3. Basin, D.A., Radomirovic, S., Schläpfer, M.: A complete characterization of secure human-server communication. In: CSF 2015. IEEE Computer Society (2015)
4. Bella, G., Coles-Kemp, L.: Layered analysis of security ceremonies. In: Gritzalis, D., Furnell, S., Theoharidou, M. (eds.) SEC 2012. IAICT, vol. 376, pp. 273–286. Springer, Heidelberg (2012). https://doi.org/10.1007/978-3-642-30436-1_23
5. Cervesato, I., Meadows, C.A., Pavlovic, D.: An encapsulated authentication logic for reasoning about key distribution protocols. In: CSFW 2005, vol. 1. IEEE (2005)
6. Chen, S., Sasse, R., Meseguer, J., Wang, H., Wang, Y.M.: A systematic approach to uncover security flaws in GUI logic. In: IEEE SSP 2007. IEEE (2007)
7. Clavel, M., et al.: All About Maude - A High-Performance Logical Framework: How to Specify, Program and Verify Systems in Rewriting Logic. LNCS, vol. 4350. Springer, Heidelberg (2007). https://doi.org/10.1007/978-3-540-71999-1
8. Ellison, C.: Ceremony design and analysis. IACR Cryptology ePrint Archive (2007)
9. Fiadeiro, J., Țuțu, I., Lopes, A., Pavlovic, D.: Logics for actor networks: a case study in constrained hybridization. In: Madeira, A., Benevides, M. (eds.) DALI 2017. LNCS, vol. 10669, pp. 98–114. Springer, Cham (2018). https://doi.org/10.1007/978-3-319-73579-5_7
10. Gonzalez-Burgueño, A., Ölveczky, P.C.: Formalizing and analyzing security ceremonies with heterogeneous devices in ANP and PDL (2018). http://folk.uio.no/antonigo/Security_Ceremonies_Heterogeneous_Devices.pdf
11. Meadows, C., Pavlovic, D.: Deriving, attacking and defending the GDOI protocol. In: Samarati, P., Ryan, P., Gollmann, D., Molva, R. (eds.) ESORICS 2004. LNCS, vol. 3193, pp. 53–72. Springer, Heidelberg (2004). https://doi.org/10.1007/978-3-540-30108-0_4
12. Meadows, C., Pavlovic, D.: Formalizing physical security procedures. In: Jøsang, A., Samarati, P., Petrocchi, M. (eds.) STM 2012. LNCS, vol. 7783, pp. 193–208. Springer, Heidelberg (2013). https://doi.org/10.1007/978-3-642-38004-4_13
13. Pavlovic, D., Meadows, C.: Actor-network procedures. In: Ramanujam, R., Ramaswamy, S. (eds.) ICDCIT 2012. LNCS, vol. 7154, pp. 7–26. Springer, Heidelberg (2012). https://doi.org/10.1007/978-3-642-28073-3_2
14. Pavlovic, D., Meadows, C.: Deriving secrecy in key establishment protocols. In: Gollmann, D., Meier, J., Sabelfeld, A. (eds.) ESORICS 2006. LNCS, vol. 4189, pp. 384–403. Springer, Heidelberg (2006). https://doi.org/10.1007/11863908_24
15. Pavlovic, D., Meadows, C.: Actor-network procedures: modeling multi-factor authentication, device pairing, social interactions. CoRR abs/1106.0706 (2011)
16. Pavlovic, D., Meadows, C.: Deriving ephemeral authentication using channel axioms. In: Christianson, B., Malcolm, J.A., Matyáš, V., Roe, M. (eds.) Security Protocols 2009. LNCS, vol. 7028, pp. 240–261. Springer, Heidelberg (2013). https://doi.org/10.1007/978-3-642-36213-2_27

17. Radke, K., Boyd, C., Nieto, J.G., Manulis, M., Stebila, D.: Formalising human recognition: a fundamental building block for security proofs. In: AISC 2014. CRPIT, vol. 149. Australian Computer Society (2014)
18. Roscoe, A.W., Goldsmith, M., Creese, S.J., Zakiuddin, I.: The attacker in ubiquitous computing environments: formalising the threat model. In: FAST 2003 (2003)

Logics for Petri Nets with Propagating Failures

Leandro Gomes[1(✉)], Alexandre Madeira[2], and Mario Benevides[3]

[1] HASLab INESC TEC - Univ. Minho, Braga, Portugal
leandro.r.gomes@inesctec.pt
[2] CIDMA - Univ. Aveiro, Aveiro, Portugal
[3] COPPE/PESC - Instituto de Matemática/DCC,
Universidade Federal do Rio de Janeiro, Rio de Janeiro, Brazil

Abstract. Petri nets play a central role in the formal modelling of a wide range of complex systems and scenarios. Their ability to handle with both concurrency and resource awareness justifies their spread in the current formal development practices. On the logic side, Dynamic Logics are widely accepted as the *de facto* formalisms to reason about computational systems. However, as usual, the application to new situations raises new challenges and issues.

The ubiquity of failures in the execution of current systems, interpreted in these models as triggered events that are not followed by the corresponding transition, entails not only the adjustment of these structures to deal with this reality, but also the introduction of new logics adequate to this emerging phenomenon.

This paper contributes to this challenge by exploring a combination of two previous works of the authors, namely the Propositional Dynamic Logic for Petri Nets [1] and a parametric construction of multi-valued dynamic logics presented in [13]. This exercise results in a new family of Dynamic Logics for Petri Nets suitable to deal with firing failures.

1 Introduction

Petri nets are semantic structures widely used in computer science. Their adequacy to model, specify and analyze complex systems dealing with concurrency and resource awareness is well known. At the core of this success is their rich and intuitive graphical syntax. Nevertheless, for property oriented specification

This work is financed by the ERDF – European Regional Development Fund through the Operational Programme for Competitiveness and Internationalisation - COMPETE 2020 Programme and by National Funds through the Portuguese funding agency, FCT - Fundação para a Ciência e a Tecnologia, within projects POCI-01-0145-FEDER-016826, POCI-01-0145-FEDER-029946 and UID/MAT/04106/2019. The second author is supported in the scope of the framework contract foreseen in the numbers 4, 5 and 6 of the article 23, of the Decree-Law 57/2016, of August 29, changed by Portuguese Law 57/2017, of July 19.

© IFIP International Federation for Information Processing 2019
Published by Springer Nature Switzerland AG 2019
H. Hojjat and M. Massink (Eds.): FSEN 2019, LNCS 11761, pp. 145–157, 2019.
https://doi.org/10.1007/978-3-030-31517-7_10

and verification purposes, it is useful to consider logic systems having this structure as a semantics. The first attempt in such direction was done by the linear logic community (e.g. [6]). A number of other logics were then proposed in the literature for standard and timed versions of Petri nets eg. [3].

Propositional dynamic logic (PDL) [8], a very versatile logic for verification of computational systems, was also explored in this context. Particularly, Petri-PDL [12] was introduced as an extention of PDL to give logical semantics to Petri nets. In such variant, the programs are marked Petri nets expressed by a textual syntax (with a choice and a composition operators). Another approach was taken in [5], where the well established theory of modal semirings was used to develop a generic modal algebra for reasoning about reachability properties in Petri nets. The BI resource based semantics presented in [16] introduces another proposal to allow comparison of "amounts of information" modelled by the possible worlds of the model. In this work, Petri nets are presented as concrete instances of this semantics. Later, the work of [12] was extended [1] to include the iteration operator. This logic is expressive enough to describe properties of systems like the one shown in the example below:

Example 1. Let us present the following situation, based on the example presented in [1], which illustrates the behaviour of a chocolate vending machine. The system works as follows: we turn the machine on (l) and put one coin (m) and then it releases the chocolate (c).

Its behaviour can be specified by the Petri net of Fig. 1. The upper left place (ℓ) is the power button of a vending machine; the bottom left is the coin inserted (m) and the bottom right is the chocolate output (c); if the vending machine is powered on, always when a coin is inserted you will have a chocolate released. We can express that *once we turn the machine on and put one coin we can obtain a chocolate* by the formula $\langle (\ell, m), (\ell m t_2 x \odot x t_3 y c) \rangle \top$, meaning that, if we are in a state were states ℓ and m are marked, after executing the Petri net program $\ell m t_2 x \odot x t_3 y c$, we reach a state were $\top$ is satisfied.

The above formula can be proved using the proof system presented in [1].

Fig. 1. Execution of the program $\ell m t_2 x \odot x t_3 y c$ in the chocolate machine

The complexity of modern systems, namely the heterogeneity of the environments where they live, entails a more demanding approach in their design and building processes. The inevitability that human beings eventually make mistakes in such processes extols the advantage of adopting formalisms which deal with the possibility of failures at the outset.

Recalling again the previous example, we would bet that the reader already experienced undesirable situations like *after putting a coin in a vending machine, the desired chocolate gets stuck behind of the glass.* The analysis of such kinds of failures would require a formalism able to express statements like *once we turn the machine on and put one coin we have an assurance α that we will obtain a chocolate.* A possible model for handling theses scenarios would be a variation of the classical definition of Petri nets, where the triggering of a transition happens with some reliability degree. The resulting assurance would depend on two aspects: on one side, the reliability degree associated to the execution of a program; on the other, an appropriate evaluation of a formula in a many-valued truth space. Despite their adequacy in the reasoning about several properties of Petri nets, none of the approaches presented in [5,11] or [16] aim to formalise the attribution of such degrees.

In order to achieve a Dynamic Logic analogous to [1], but suitable to this scenario, we base this work on the construction of multi-valued dynamic logics introduced in [13,14]. First, we introduce a new variant of the Petri Nets, the *Petri nets with* **A**-*failures*, which explicitly assumes that the modelled system may eventually fail, supporting a claim of reliability to each firing of a transition. In the case where a failure occurs, the firing event is consumed without the occurrence of the expected transition. Depending on the system modelled, it would make sense to measure these reliability degrees in a discrete scale, in a continuous interval, or simply in an universe only with the values *true* and *false.* Hence, instead of fixing the domain of the assurances degrees as the usual real interval $[0, 1]$, we will be more generic: the proposed models are parametric to the nature of the reliability degrees that are most suitable for each concrete situation. This flexibility is realised by assuming, as parameter, an (action) lattice **A**. Some additional considerations on this parameter are in order.

As in standard PDL, the interpretation of programs in Petri-PDL [11] relies on the Kleene algebra of relations (as we will see in the next section, firing functions are interpreted as binary relations). However, firing functions in Petri nets with **A**-failures are based on reliability degrees given by elements of an action lattice, and not on the interpretation of classic binary relations.

To give meaning to Petri net programs in this new formalism, this paper adopts a class of Kleene algebras, parameterised by an action lattice **A**. These algebraic structures base the interpretation of (composed) programs in Petri nets with **A**-failures, by reflecting how failures in transitions are propagated into the whole execution of a program. This is also reflected in the kind of assertions we can express in the logic, as well as in the outcome we expect for the validity of a Dynamic Logic formula in a Petri net with **A**-failures. For that purpose, we follow a strategy similar to that used in [13,14], where an action lattice will follow a similar role in our method, namely as a computational model (by representing weighted fails) and as a truth universe (by giving a (possible) many-valued truth space to the addressed logics). The proposed method for constructing graded dynamic logics is parametric on whatever truth/computational domain is the most suitable to the system under consideration.

Outline. The remaining of this paper is organized as follows. Section 2 presents all the background needed about the Petri-PDL* formalism and the concept of action lattice. Section 3 is devoted to Petri Net with **A**-failures, as well as, to suitable Kleene Algebras to interpret programs in these structures. In Sect. 4, we introduce a parametric construction of dynamic logics for Petri nets with **A**-failures, and proper illustrations for such a method. Finally, Sect. 5 concludes the paper with some final remarks on future work.

2   Background

In this section, we present a brief overview of two topics on which the later development is based. First, we review the syntax and semantics of Petri-PDL* [1]. Second, we recall the main notions behind the method introduced in [13], for the generation of many-valued dynamic logics parametrized by an action lattice. This parameter supports both the (possible non-bivalent) truth spaces and the base computational model.

2.1   Propositional Dynamic Logic for Petri Nets with Iteration

This subsection recalls the syntax and semantics of Petri-PDL*, as presented in [1]. The language of Petri-PDL* consists of

Propositional symbols: $Prop = \{p, q, \ldots\}$
Place names: $a, b, c, d, \ldots$
Transition types: $T_1 : xt_1y$, $T_2 : xyt_2z$ and $T_3 : xt_3yz$
Petri net Composition symbol: $\odot$
PDL operator: $\_^\star$ (iteration)
Markings: $S = \{\epsilon, s_1, s_2, \ldots\}$, where ϵ is the empty sequence. The notation $a \in s$ is used to denote that the place name a occurs in s. The expression $\#(s, a)$ is the number of occurrences of place name a in s. It is said that a sequence r is a subsequence of s, denoted $r \preceq s$, if for any place name a, if $a \in r$ implies $a \in s$.

Definition 1. *Petri-PDL* Programs for a set of places P*

Basic programs: *set $\Pi_0(P)$ defined by the grammar*

$$\pi ::= at_1b \mid abt_2c \mid at_3bc$$

where t_i is of type T_i, $i = 1, 2, 3$ and $a, b, c \in P$.
Petri net Programs: *set $\Pi(P)$ defined by the grammar*

$$\eta ::= \pi \mid \pi \odot \eta \mid \eta^\star$$

for $\pi \in \Pi_0(P)$

Definition 2. *Let* Prop *be a set of propositions. The set of Petri-PDL* * *formulas for* Prop, *denoted by* $\mathrm{Fm}^{\mathrm{Petri-PDL}^\star}(\mathbf{A})$, *is defined by the grammar*

$$\rho ::= p \mid \top \mid \neg\rho \mid \rho \wedge \rho \mid \langle s, \eta \rangle \rho$$

where $p \in$ Prop.

We use the standard abbreviations $\bot \equiv \neg\top$, $\rho \vee \rho \equiv \neg(\neg\rho \wedge \neg\rho)$, $\rho \to \rho \equiv \neg(\rho \wedge \neg\rho)$ and $[s, \eta]\rho \equiv \neg\langle s, \eta \rangle \neg\rho$.

The definition below introduces the *firing* function. It defines how the marking of a basic Petri net changes after a firing.

Definition 3. *For a set of markings* S, *we define the firing function* $f : S \times \Pi_0 \to S$ *as follows*

$$- f(s, at_1b) = \left\{ \begin{array}{l} s_1bs_2, \; if \; s = s_1as_2 \\ \epsilon, \; if \; a \notin s \end{array} \right\}$$

$$- f(s, abt_2c) = \left\{ \begin{array}{l} s_1cs_2s_3, \; if \; s = s_1as_2bs_3 \\ \epsilon, \; if \; a \notin s \; or \; b \notin s \end{array} \right\}$$

$$- f(s, at_3bc) = \left\{ \begin{array}{l} s_1s_2bc, \; if \; s = s_1as_2 \\ \epsilon, \; if \; a \notin s \end{array} \right\}$$

The definitions of frame, model and satisfaction, that we recall below, are adapted from PDL to deal with the firing of basic Petri nets.

Definition 4. *A frame for Petri-PDL* * *is a triple* $\langle W, R_\pi, M \rangle$, *where*

- W *is a non-empty set of states;*
- $M : W \to S$;
- R_π *is a binary relation over* W, *for each basic program* π, *satisfying the following condition: let* $s = M(w)$
    - *if* $f(s, \pi) \neq \epsilon$, *if* $wR_\pi v$ *then* $f(s, \pi) \preceq M(v)$
    - *if* $f(s, \pi) = \epsilon$, $(w, v) \notin R_\pi$
- *we inductively define a binary relation* R_η, *for each Petri net program* η, *as follows:*
    - $R_{\eta^*} = R_\eta^*$, *where* R_η^* *denotes the reflexive transitive closure of* R_η.
    - $\eta = \eta_1 \odot \eta_2 \odot \cdots \odot \eta_n$

    $$R_\eta = \{(w, v) \mid \text{ for some } \eta_i, \exists u \text{ such that } s_i \in M(u) \text{ and } wR_{\eta_i}u \text{ and } uR_{\eta_i}v\}$$

    where $s = M(w)$, η_i *are Petri net programs and* $s_i = f(s, \eta_i)$, *for all* $1 \leq i \leq n$.

Definition 5. *A* model *for Petri-PDL* * *is a pair* $\mathcal{M} = \langle \mathcal{F}, \mathbf{V} \rangle$, *where* $\mathcal{F}$ *is a Petri-PDL frame and* $\mathbf{V}$ *is a valuation function from a set of propositions* Prop, $\mathbf{V} : \text{Prop} \to 2^W$.

The semantic notion of satisfaction for Petri-PDL* is defined below.

Definition 6. *Let* $\mathcal{M} = (\mathcal{F}, \mathbf{V})$ *be a model. The notion of satisfaction of a formula* ρ *in a model* $\mathcal{M}$ *at a state* w, *notation* $\mathcal{M}, w \models \rho$, *can be inductively defined as follows:*

- $\mathcal{M}, w \models p$ *iff* $w \in \mathbf{V}(p)$;
- $\mathcal{M}, w \models \top$ *always*;
- $\mathcal{M}, w \models \neg\rho$ *iff* $\mathcal{M}, w \not\models \rho$;
- $\mathcal{M}, w \models \rho \wedge \rho'$ *iff* $\mathcal{M}, w \models \rho$ *and* $\mathcal{M}, w \models \rho'$;
- $\mathcal{M}, w \models \langle s, \eta \rangle \rho$ *if there exists* $w' \in W$, $w R_\eta w'$, $s \subseteq M(w)$ *and* $\mathcal{M}, w' \models \rho$.

If $\mathcal{M}, v \models A$ for every state v, we say that A is *valid in the model* $\mathcal{M}$, notation $\mathcal{M} \models A$. And if A is valid in all $\mathcal{M}$ we say that A is *valid*, notation $\models A$.

2.2   Kleene Algebras and Action Lattice

We review in this section the notion of Action Lattice [10] as it was used in [13].

Definition 7 (Kleene Algebra and Action lattice). *An* action lattice *is a tuple* $\mathbf{A} = (A, +, ;, 0, 1, *, \rightarrow, \cdot)$, *where* A *is a set,* 0 *and* 1 *are constants,* $*$ *is an unary operation in* A *and* $+, ;, \rightarrow$ *and* $\cdot$ *are binary operations in* A *satisfying the axioms enumerated in Fig. 2, where the relation* $\leq$ *is induced by* $+$: $a \leq b$ *iff* $a + b = b$. *An* integral action lattice *consists of an action lattice satisfying* $a \leq 1$, *for all* $a \in A$. *A* Kleene Algebra *is a structure* $(A, +, ;, 0, 1, *)$ *satisfying* (1)-(13).

$$a + (b + c) = (a + b) + c \tag{1}$$

$$a + b = b + a \tag{2}$$

$$a + a = a \tag{3}$$

$$a + 0 = 0 + a = a \tag{4}$$

$$a; (b; c) = (a; b); c \tag{5}$$

$$a; 1 = 1; a = a \tag{6}$$

$$a; (b + c) = (a; b) + (a; c) \tag{7}$$

$$(a + b); c = (a; c) + (b; c) \tag{8}$$

$$a; 0 = 0; a = 0 \tag{9}$$

$$1 + (a; a^*) = a^* \tag{10}$$

$$1 + (a^*; a) = a^* \tag{11}$$

$$a; x \leq x \Rightarrow a^*; x \leq x \tag{12}$$

$$x; a \leq x \Rightarrow x; a^* \leq x \tag{13}$$

$$a; x \leq b \Leftrightarrow x \leq a \rightarrow b \tag{14}$$

$$a \cdot (b \cdot c) = (a \cdot b) \cdot c \tag{15}$$

$$a \cdot b = b \cdot a \tag{16}$$

$$a \cdot a = a \tag{17}$$

$$a + (a \cdot b) = a \tag{18}$$

$$a \cdot (a + b) = a \tag{19}$$

Fig. 2. Axiomatisation of action lattices (from [10])

As stated in the introduction, the structure of an action lattice is explored in this paper along a double dimension: as a computational model and as a truth space. The intuitions for some of its operations shall be taken from both of these perspectives. Such is the case of operation $+$, which plays the role of non-deterministic choice, in the interpretation of programs, and of logical disjunction, in the interpretation of sentences. However, there are operations whose intuition is borrowed from just in one of these domains. For instance, while operations $*$ and ; are taken as iterative execution and sequential composition of actions, operations $\to$ and $\cdot$ play the role of logical implication and conjunction, respectively.

The following structures are examples of action lattices:

Example 2 (2 - linear two-values lattice). As a first action lattice example, we consider the two valued boolean lattice $\mathbf{2} = (\{\top, \bot\}, \vee, \wedge, \bot, \top, *, \to, \wedge)$ with the standard boolean connectives defined as follows:

$$
\begin{array}{c|cc}
\vee & \bot & \top \\
\hline
\bot & \bot & \top \\
\top & \top & \top
\end{array}
\quad
\begin{array}{c|cc}
\wedge & \bot & \top \\
\hline
\bot & \bot & \bot \\
\top & \bot & \top
\end{array}
\quad
\begin{array}{c|cc}
\to & \bot & \top \\
\hline
\bot & \top & \top \\
\top & \bot & \top
\end{array}
\quad
\begin{array}{c|c}
* & \\
\hline
\bot & \top \\
\top & \top
\end{array}
$$

Example 3 ($\mathbf{W}_k$ finite Wajsberg hoops). We consider now an action lattice endowing the finite *Wajsberg hoops* [2] with a suitable star operation. Hence, for a fix natural $k > 0$ and a generator a, we define the structure $\mathbf{W}_k = (W_k, +, ;, 0, 1, *, \to, \cdot)$, where $W_k = \{a^0, a^1, \cdots, a^k\}$, $1 = a^0$ and $0 = a^k$, and for any $m, n \leq k$: $a^m + a^n = a^{min\{m,n\}}$, $a^m; a^n = a^{min\{m+n,k\}}$, $(a^m)^* = a^0$, $a^m \to a^n = a^{max\{n-m,0\}}$ and $a^m \cdot a^n = a^{max\{m,n\}}$.

Example 4 (Ł - the Łukasiewicz arithmetic lattice). The *Łukasiewicz arithmetic lattice* is the structure $\mathbf{Ł} = ([0,1], \max, \odot, 0, 1, *, \to, \min)$, where $x \to y = \min(1, 1 - x + y)$, $x \odot y = \max(0, y + x - 1)$ and $x^* = 1$.

More examples and properties of action lattices can be found in [13].

3 Petri Nets with Failures

This section introduces the notion of Petri net with **A**-failures, as well as suitable Kleene algebras to interpret (composed) programs. As referred in the introduction, the use of an action lattice **A** as parameter is due to the necessity of supporting a double dimension: (i) attribute a reliability degree to the firing of a transition, referring to the interpretation of Petri net programs; (ii) state a degree for a specific property of a Petri net, on the logical side.

As stated, this work is concerned with Petri nets where transitions between markings may fail. This assumption entails adjusting the system dynamics of classical Petri nets: while, in such case, we argue that a system evolves to another markings if a transition is enabled, in our approach, a transition to a new marking occurs with a reliability degree α, where α is an element of the lattice **A**. In cases where the Petri net does not transit to another marking, the transition is still consumed. Formally:

Definition 8. *Given an action lattice* $\mathbf{A} = (A, +, ;, 0, 1, *, \to, \cdot)$, *a set* S *of markings (over a set of place names P) and a basic Petri net program* $\pi \in \Pi_0$, *an α-firing function, for $\alpha \in A$, is a function* $f_\pi^\alpha : S \times S \to A$ *defined as*

$$- \text{ for any } a\,t_1\,b \in \Pi_1,\ f^\alpha_{at_1b}(s,s') = \begin{cases} \alpha, & \text{if } a \in s \text{ and } b \in s' \\ \alpha \to 0, & \text{if } a \in s \text{ and } a \in s' \\ 0 & \text{if } a \notin s \end{cases}$$

$$- \text{ for any } ab\,t_2\,c \in \Pi_2,\ f^\alpha_{abt_2c}(s,s') = \begin{cases} \alpha, & \text{if } a,b \in s \text{ and } c \in s' \\ \alpha \to 0, & \text{if } a,b \in s \text{ and } a,b \in s' \\ 0 & \text{if } a,b \notin s \end{cases}$$

$$- \text{ for any } a\,t_3\,bc \in \Pi_3,\ f^\alpha_{at_3bc}(s,s') = \begin{cases} \alpha, & \text{if } a \in s \text{ and } b,c \in s' \\ \alpha \to 0, & \text{if } a \in s \text{ and } a \in s' \\ 0 & \text{if } a \notin s \end{cases}$$

where $\Pi_i(P)$ are the following partitions of the atomic programs: $\Pi(P)$, $\Pi_1(P) = \{x\,t_1\,y \mid x,y \in P\}$, $\Pi_2(P) = \{xy\,t_2\,z \mid x,y,z \in P\}$ and $\Pi_3(P) = \{x\,t_3\,yz \mid x,y,z \in P\}$.

Note that, in this work, we do not take into consideration the order of the tokens in the markings. Hence, those are represented as multisets, instead of sequences as done for Petri-PDL* [1].

Now, we have conditions to introduce the intended model.

Definition 9 (Petri net with A-failures). *Let $\mathbf{A} = (A,+,;,0,1,*,\to,\cdot)$ be an action lattice. A Petri net with $\mathbf{A}$-failures consists of a tuple $\mathcal{P} = (P,S,\Pi_0,I,M_0)$ where P is a set of places; $S \subseteq P^*$ is the set of (admissible) markings; $\Pi_0 \subseteq \Pi(P)$ is the set of atomic programs; $I : \Pi_0 \to A$ is the atomic programs reliability degree and $M_0 \in S$ is the initial marking. The interpretation of an atomic program $\pi \in \Pi_0$ is given by the firing function $f^{I(\pi)}_\pi$.*

In this work, as in [13], the underlying Kleene algebra of $\mathbf{A}$ (c.f. Definition 7) provides a generic computational model for interpreting programs. However, differently form such work, we interpret computations as α-firing functions of Definition 8, which carry the information about their effect when executed. Hence, we define the following algebra:

Definition 10. *Let $\mathbf{A} = (A,+,;,0,1,*,\to,\cdot)$ be an action lattice and S be a finite set. The algebra of $\mathbf{A}$-firing functions is the structure $\mathbf{F} = (F,\cup,\circ,\varnothing,\chi,*)$ where:*

- *F is the universe of all the α-firing functions, for all $\alpha \in A$*
- *$(f^{\alpha_1}_{\pi_1} \cup f^{\alpha_2}_{\pi_2})(s,s') = f^{\alpha_1}_{\pi_1}(s,s') + f^{\alpha_2}_{\pi_2}(s,s')$*
- *$(f^{\alpha_1}_{\pi_1} \circ f^{\alpha_2}_{\pi_2})(s,s') = \sum\limits_{s'' \in S} f^{\alpha_1}_{\pi_1}(s,s''); f^{\alpha_2}_{\pi_2}(s'',s')$*
- *$\varnothing(s,s') = 0$*
- *$\chi(s,s') = \begin{cases} 1, & \text{if } s = s' \\ 0, & \text{otherwise} \end{cases}$*
- *$(f^\alpha_\pi)^*(s,s') = \bigvee\limits_{i \geq 0} (f^\alpha_\pi)^i(s,s') = (f^\alpha_\pi)^0(s,s') + (f^\alpha_\pi)^1(s,s') + (f^\alpha_\pi)^2(s,s') + \ldots$*

The next theorem states that **F** represents an adequate structure to interpret Petri net programs for Petri nets with **A**-failures[1].

Theorem 1. F *is a Kleene Algebra*

Proof. This proof is analogous to the proof of the classical result [4], stating that the algebra of $n \times n$ matrices over a Kleene algebra is a Kleene algebra.

With this Kleene algebra, we are able to interpret regular programs in Petri nets with **A**-failures, i.e. regular expressions of atomic transitions in **A**:

Definition 11 (A-interpretations of programs). *Let* $\mathbf{A} = (A, +, ; , 0, 1, *, \rightarrow, \cdot)$ *be an action lattice and* (P, S, Π_0, I, M_0) *a Petri net with* **A***-failures. The interpretation of a Petri net program* η *is a firing function recursively defined as follows:*

- *for any atomic program* $\pi \in \Pi_0$, $[\![\pi]\!](s, s') = f_\pi^{F(\pi)}(s, s')$
- $[\![\pi_1; \pi_2]\!](s, s') = ([\![\pi_1]\!] \circ [\![\pi_2]\!])(s, s')$,
- $[\![\eta^*]\!](s, s') = [\![\eta]\!]^*(s, s')$, *for* $[\![\eta]\!]^*(s, s') = \sum_{i \geq 0} [\![\eta]\!]^i(s, s')$ *where* $[\![\eta]\!]^0(s, s') = \chi(s, s')$ *and for any* $i \geq 0$, $[\![\eta]\!]^{i+1}(s, s') = ([\![\eta]\!]^i \circ [\![\eta]\!])(s, s')$
- $[\![\eta + \eta']\!](s, s') = [\![\eta]\!](s, s') + [\![\eta']\!](s, s')$, *for* η, η' *Petri net programs.*

The interpretation of Petri Net composed programs, as presented in Definition 1, where the *global composition* $\odot$ is considered rather than the *sequential composition* ;, can be handled in our logic indirectly by defining $\odot$ as

$$\eta \odot \eta' \equiv \eta; (\eta + \eta')^* + \eta'; (\eta + \eta')^* \tag{20}$$

where η and η' are Petri net programs.

4 Parametric Construction of Dynamic Logics for Petri Nets with Failures

This section introduces a parametric method to build Petri-PDL to reason about Petri nets with **A**-failures, inspired by the construction proposed in [13]. The semantic and satisfaction of these logics are built on top of an arbitrary action lattice $\mathbf{A} = (A, +, ; , 0, 1, *, \rightarrow, \cdot)$ (c.f. Definition 7). Hence, the resulting logics will be denoted by $\mathbf{GP(A)}$. Petri-PDL*, as introduced in [12], is captured as an instance of this construction (by using, as parameter, the lattice **2** of Example 2). Beyond the reliability degrees for transitions, the action lattice also supports the truth space for the (possible multi-valued) outcomes of the logic.

The language for $\mathbf{GP(A)}$ is the same of Petri-PDL*, except for *formulae*, that we define below.

---

[1] A more generic algebraic structure, suitable to deal with generic weighted computations was recently introduced by the authors in [7].

Definition 12. *Let* Prop *be a set of propositions. The set of* **GP**(**A**) *formulas for the set of propositions* Prop *and for the set of place names* P, *denoted by* $\mathrm{Fm}^{\mathrm{GP}(\mathbf{A})}(\mathrm{Prop}, P)$, *is defined by the grammar*

$$\rho ::= p \mid \top \mid \bot \mid \rho \wedge \rho \mid \rho \vee \rho \mid \rho \to \rho \mid \langle \xi \rangle \rho \mid [\xi]\rho$$

where $p \in \mathrm{Prop}$, $\xi ::= \pi \mid \pi; \xi \mid \xi^\star \mid \xi + \xi$ *for* $\pi ::= at_1b \mid abt_2c \mid at_3bc$, *and* $a, b, c \in P$.

Observe that we denoted the regular programs (with the sequential composition ;) by letter ξ instead of η used for the Petri-net programs (with global composition $\odot$). However, in the sequel, we will relax this convention by using η for both cases. The symbol $\odot$ will also be used as meta-syntax of our logic, to be interpreted according to (20). For instance, the expression $\langle \eta \odot \eta' \rangle \varphi$ is just notation for the formula $\langle \eta; (\eta + \eta')^* + \eta'; (\eta + \eta')^* \rangle \varphi$.

Note that, differently from previous work [1], we do not include the negation as a primitive operator, and use, instead, the defined negation $\neg x \equiv x \to \bot$. Actually, as stated, we intend to deal with generic truth spaces for possible non bivalent interpretation of assertions (e.g. we are not requiring negative involution).

Definition 13. *A model for* **GP**(**A**) *is a pair* $\mathcal{M} = \langle \mathcal{P}, \mathbf{V} \rangle$, *where* $\mathcal{P}$ *is a Petri net with* **A***-failures and* **V** *is a valuation function over a set of propositions* Prop, *defined as* $\mathbf{V} : \mathrm{Prop} \times S \to A$.

Now, we define the semantic notion of satisfaction for **GP**(**A**).

Definition 14. *Let* $\mathbf{A} = (A, +, ;, 0, 1, *, \to, \cdot)$ *be an action lattice. The* (graded) *satisfaction* $\models: (\mathcal{M} \times S) \times \mathrm{Fm}^{\mathrm{GP}(\mathbf{A})}(\mathrm{Prop}) \to A$ *for* **GP**(**A**) *is recursively defined for each model* $\mathcal{M}$, *any marking* $s \in S$ *and for any formula* $\rho \in \mathrm{Fm}^{\mathrm{GP}(\mathbf{A})}(\mathrm{Prop})$ *as follows:*

- $(\mathcal{M}, s \models p) = \mathbf{V}(p, s)$;
- $(\mathcal{M}, s \models \top) = \top$;
- $(\mathcal{M}, s \models \bot) = \bot$;
- $(\mathcal{M}, s \models \rho \wedge \rho') = (\mathcal{M}, s \models \rho) \cdot (\mathcal{M}, s \models \rho')$;
- $(\mathcal{M}, s \models \rho \vee \rho') = (\mathcal{M}, s \models \rho) + (\mathcal{M}, s \models \rho')$;
- $(\mathcal{M}, s \models \rho \to \rho') = (\mathcal{M}, s \models \rho) \to (\mathcal{M}, s \models \rho')$;
- $(\mathcal{M}, s \models \langle \eta \rangle \rho) = \sum_{s' \in S} \left([\![\eta]\!](s, s'); (\mathcal{M}, s' \models \rho) \right)$;
- $(\mathcal{M}, s \models [\eta]\rho) = \bigwedge_{s' \in S} \left([\![\eta]\!](s, s') \to (\mathcal{M}, s' \models \rho) \right)$

Example 5. Let us start by revisiting Example 1, by using **GP**(**2**) (see Example 2). For that, we denote $f^{\top}_{\ell m t_2 x}(\ell m, x)$ by a and $f^{\top}_{x t_3 y c}(x, yc)$ by b and, in this situation $a = b = \top$. So, we can write the sentence of Example 1 as *once we turn the machine on and put one coin we have the (total) reliability that we will obtain a chocolate*. This expression can, then, be represented in **GP**(**2**) by the formula $(\mathcal{M}, \ell m \models \langle \ell m t_2 x \odot x t_3 y c \rangle \top) = \top$. Hence (Fig. 3):

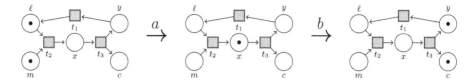

Fig. 3. A Petri net for a (possibly) defective chocolate vending machine

$$\mathcal{M}, \ell m \models \langle \ell mt_2 x; xt_3 yc \rangle \top$$

$$= \sum_{s \in S} \Big(\llbracket \ell mt_2 x; xt_3 yc \rrbracket (\ell m, s); (\mathcal{M}, s \models \top) \Big)$$

$$= \sum_{s \in S} \Big((\llbracket lmt_2 x \rrbracket \circ \llbracket xt_3 yc \rrbracket)(\ell m, s); (\mathcal{M}, s \models \top) \Big)$$

$$= \sum_{s \in S} \Big((\sum_{s' \in S} (\llbracket \ell mt_2 x \rrbracket (\ell m, s'); \llbracket xt_3 yc \rrbracket (s', s))); (\mathcal{M}, s \models \top) \Big)$$

$$= \sum_{s \in S} \Big((\llbracket \ell mt_2 x \rrbracket (\ell m, x); \llbracket xt_3 yc \rrbracket (x, s) + \llbracket \ell mt_2 x \rrbracket (\ell m, \ell m); \llbracket xt_3 yc \rrbracket (\ell m, s)); (\mathcal{M}, s \models \top) \Big)$$

$$= (\llbracket \ell mt_2 x \rrbracket (\ell m, x); \llbracket xt_3 yc \rrbracket (x, yc) + \llbracket \ell mt_2 x \rrbracket (\ell m, \ell m); \llbracket xt_3 yc \rrbracket (\ell m, yc)); (\mathcal{M}, yc \models \top)$$

$$+ (\llbracket \ell mt_2 x \rrbracket (\ell m, \ell m); \llbracket xt_3 yc \rrbracket (\ell m, \ell m)); (\mathcal{M}, \ell m \models \top)$$

$$+ (\llbracket \ell mt_2 x \rrbracket (\ell m, x); \llbracket xt_3 yc \rrbracket (x, x) + \llbracket \ell mt_2 x \rrbracket (\ell m, \ell m); \llbracket xt_3 yc \rrbracket (\ell m, x)); (\mathcal{M}, x \models \top) = \top$$

Assume now that this machine has a technical problem and it can not assure with total reliability the release of a chocolate every time a coin is inserted. Suppose also that we can express such reliability degrees in a $1 \ldots 10$ discrete scale. Hence, using $\mathbf{GP}(W_{10})$ (see Example 3), we can express that the machine transits from marking lm to x with a reliability 8 and from x to yc with 9, i.e. $a = 8$ and $b = 9$. Now, the verification of the property *once we turn the machine on and put one coin we have a reliability 7 out of 10 that we will obtain a chocolate*, from the marking ℓm, can be computed by

$$\mathcal{M}, \ell m \models \langle \ell mt_2 x; xt_3 yc \rangle \top = (8; 9 + (8 \rightarrow 0); 0); 10 + ((8 \rightarrow 0); 0); 10 + (8; (9 \rightarrow 0) + (8 \rightarrow 0); 0); 10 = 7.$$

Nevertheless, for some situations, it could be more appropriate to use a continuous scale. Suppose, for instance, that we want to be more precise, by stating that the reliability degree of the machine to evolve from marking lm to x is 0.78 and from x to yc is 0.93, which corresponds to $a = 0.78$ and $b = 0.93$. This can be expressed using $\mathbf{GP}(L)$ (see Example 4). In this case we have:

$$\mathcal{M}, \ell m \models \langle \ell mt_2 x; xt_3 yc \rangle \top = max\{max\{0.78 \odot 0.93, (0.78 \rightarrow 0) \odot 0\} \odot 1, ((0.78 \rightarrow 0) \odot 0) \odot 1, max\{0.78 \odot (0.93 \rightarrow 0), (0.78 \rightarrow 0) \odot 0\} \odot 1\} = 0.71.$$

Let us now use the global composition operator $\odot$, in place of the simple sequential composition $;$. Given the Petri net program $\eta = \ell mt_2 x \odot xt_3 yc$, we compute the reliability degree of the formula $\langle \ell m t_2 x \odot x t_3 y c \rangle \top$, using **GP(2)**, as follows:

$$\mathcal{M}, \ell m \models \langle \ell m t_2 x \odot x t_3 y c \rangle \top$$

$$= \sum_{s \in S} \Big([\![\ell m t_2 x \odot x t_3 y c]\!](\ell m, s); (M, s \models \top) \Big)$$

$$= \sum_{s \in S} \Big([\![\ell m t_2 x; \eta^* + x t_3 y c; \eta^*]\!](\ell m, s); (M, s \models \top) \Big)$$

$$= \sum_{s \in S} \Big(([\![\ell m t_2 x; \eta^*]\!](\ell m, s) + [\![x t_3 y c; \eta^*]\!](\ell m, s)); (M, s \models \top) \Big)$$

$$= \sum_{s \in S} \Big(((([\![\ell m t_2 x]\!] \circ [\![\eta^*]\!])(\ell m, s) + ([\![x t_3 y c]\!] \circ [\![\eta^*]\!])(\ell m, s)); (M, s \models \top) \Big)$$

$$= \sum_{s \in S} \Big((\sum_{s' \in S} ([\![\ell m t_2 x]\!](\ell m, s'); [\![\eta^*]\!](s', s)) + \sum_{s' \in S} ([\![x t_3 y c]\!](\ell m, s'); [\![\eta^*]\!](s', s))); (M, s \models \top) \Big)$$

$$= \sum_{s \in S} \Big(([\![\ell m t_2 x]\!](\ell m, x); [\![\eta^*]\!](x, s) + [\![\ell m t_2 x]\!](\ell m, \ell m); [\![\eta^*]\!](\ell m, s) + [\![x t_2 y c]\!](\ell m, x); [\![\eta^*]\!](x, s)$$

$$+ [\![x t_3 y c]\!](\ell m, \ell m); [\![\eta^*]\!](\ell m, s)); (M, s \models \top) \Big)$$

$$= ((\top \wedge \top) \vee (\bot \wedge \top) \vee (\bot \wedge \top) \vee (\bot \wedge \top)) \wedge \top \vee (\bot \wedge \top) \wedge \top \vee ((\top \wedge \top) \vee (\bot \wedge \top)) \wedge \top = \top$$

5 Conclusions and Further Work

In this work, we contributed with the generalisation of the logic presented in [1], by considering that the firing of a Petri net may fail. The approach taken in order to handle this variation was based on previous work done in [13], where an action lattice is considered to model both the notion of reliability degree of transitions in models and to support the (possible) multi-valued truth degree of a formula. This goal was accomplished by introducing: (i) a new definition of Petri net, where transitions between markings may fail; (ii) an underlying class of Kleene algebras (parametric on an action lattice), suitable for interpreting (composed) Petri net programs; (iii) a parametric method to build Dynamic logics with these semantics.

The extension of this work can be done in several directions. First, the necessity to have supporting computational tools for these logics suggests the development of a proof calculi and model checking algorithms, with their computational complexity. In this line, we expect to obtain characterizations, parametric to the base action lattice adopted in each situation. Moreover, comparing these logics with the literature is also in our agenda, namely to establish a formal relation between the models of **GP**(L) and the *Fuzzy Petri nets* [17].

The behaviour of Petri nets is concurrent by nature, being defined by the simultaneous firing of sets of transitions. However, in the method introduced, global composition is presented as a derived operator from the base (sequential composition, choice and reflexive transitive closure) Kleene operations. Hence, in future, we intend to adapt the presented construction to another parameter supporting a concurrent computational model like, for instance, a Concurrent Kleene Algebra [9]. An approach in this direction was already addressed in [5], which is based on the well known work on modal semirings [15]. Note however that, although such approach is capable of handling concurrency, it lacks the expressiveness for generating a logic able to reason in a multi-valued truth space.

References

1. Benevides, M.R.F., Lopes, B., Haeusler, E.H.: Propositional dynamic logic for Petri nets with iteration. In: Sampaio, A., Wang, F. (eds.) ICTAC 2016. LNCS, vol. 9965, pp. 441–456. Springer, Cham (2016). https://doi.org/10.1007/978-3-319-46750-4_25
2. Blok, W.J., Ferreirim, I.: On the structure of hoops. Algebra Universalis **43**(2–3), 233–257 (2000)
3. Blondin, M., Finkel, A., Haase, C., Haddad, S.: The logical view on continuous Petri nets. ACM Trans. Comput. Log. **18**(3), 24:1–24:28 (2017)
4. Conway, J.H.: Regular Algebra and Finite Machines. Printed in GB by William Clowes & Sons Ltd., London (1971)
5. Dang, H.-H., Möller, B.: Modal algebra and Petri nets. Acta Inf. **52**(2–3), 109–132 (2015)
6. Engberg, U., Winskel, G.: Linear logic on Petri nets. In: de Bakker, J.W., de Roever, W.-P., Rozenberg, G. (eds.) REX 1993. LNCS, vol. 803, pp. 176–229. Springer, Heidelberg (1994). https://doi.org/10.1007/3-540-58043-3_20
7. Gomes, L., Madeira, A., Barbosa, L.S.: Generalising KAT to verify weighted computations. Technical report submition under consideration
8. Harel, D., Kozen, D., Tiuryn, J.: Dynamic Logic. Foundations of Computing Series. MIT Press, Cambridge (2000)
9. Hoare, T., et al.: Developments in concurrent Kleene algebra. In: Höfner, P., Jipsen, P., Kahl, W., Müller, M.E. (eds.) RAMICS 2014. LNCS, vol. 8428, pp. 1–18. Springer, Cham (2014). https://doi.org/10.1007/978-3-319-06251-8_1
10. Kozen, D.: On action algebras. In: Logic and Information Flow, pp. 78–88 (1994)
11. Lopes, B., Benevides, M., Haeusler, E.H.: Extending propositional dynamic logic for Petri nets. ENTCS **305**(11), 67–83 (2014)
12. Lopes, B., Benevides, M., Haeusler, H.: Propositional dynamic logic for Petri nets. Log. J. IGPL **22**, 721–736 (2014)
13. Madeira, A., Neves, R., Martins, M.A.: An exercise on the generation of many-valued dynamic logics. J. Log. Algebraic Methods Program. **1**, 1–29 (2016)
14. Madeira, A., Neves, R., Martins, M.A., Barbosa, L.S.: A dynamic logic for every season. In: Braga, C., Martí-Oliet, N. (eds.) SBMF 2014. LNCS, vol. 8941, pp. 130–145. Springer, Cham (2015). https://doi.org/10.1007/978-3-319-15075-8_9
15. Möller, B., Struth, G.: Modal Kleene algebra and partial correctness. In: Rattray, C., Maharaj, S., Shankland, C. (eds.) AMAST 2004. LNCS, vol. 3116, pp. 379–393. Springer, Heidelberg (2004). https://doi.org/10.1007/978-3-540-27815-3_30
16. Pym, D.J., O'Hearn, P.W., Yang, H.: Possible worlds and resources: the semantics of BI. Theor. Comput. Sci. **315**(1), 257–305 (2004)
17. Zhou, K.-Q., Zain, A.M.: Fuzzy Petri nets and industrial applications: a review. Artif. Intell. Rev. **45**(4), 405–446 (2016)

Verifying System-Wide Properties
of Industrial Component-Based Software

Thomas Neele[(✉)], Marijn Rol, and Jan Friso Groote

{T.S.Neele,J.F.Groote}@tue.nl

Eindhoven University of Technology, Eindhoven, The Netherlands

Abstract. Analytical Software Design (ASD) enables model-based development of component software systems. Until now, functional verification of ASD systems is only possible on a per-component basis. There is no functional verification engine for ASD itself, so this verification relies on a translation of individual components to mCRL2, a process-algebraic model checker. We show how to extend the ASD-mCRL2 translation to support multiple components in order to enable checking of system wide functional properties. With our extended translation, we perform a case-study on a newly developed industrial system consisting of 26 communicating components. The results indicate that it is feasible to model check functional properties on this scale.

1 Introduction

Modern high-tech industry relies more and more on software to implement supervisory control logic. With the large number of software components in a typical machine, the software can become very complex. The industry not only wants software that meets high quality standards to assure safety and reliability, but the reduction of the costs and time of development also plays an important role. This is assured by model based software design accompanied with formal analysis where software problems are eradicated as soon as possible in the development process. Comparative research shows that it is possible to reduce the number of bugs by a factor 10 and the development time by a factor 3 [14].

Analytical Software Design (ASD) [3,4] is one of the model based engineering tools being used in industrial environments. Using ASD, software engineers develop models which can be checked for various properties such as deadlock/livelock freedom and interface compliance with a single press of a button. From the models, ASD generates executable code, e.g. Java or C++, that can be run in a production environment.

In contrast to many other tools that apply model checking techniques, ASD does not suffer severely from the *state-space explosion* problem. This is achieved

---

The original version of this chapter was revised: Definition 2 was corrected. The correction to this chapter is available at https://doi.org/10.1007/978-3-030-31517-7_18

© IFIP International Federation for Information Processing 2019
Published by Springer Nature Switzerland AG 2019
H. Hojjat and M. Massink (Eds.): FSEN 2019, LNCS 11761, pp. 158–175, 2019.
https://doi.org/10.1007/978-3-030-31517-7_11

through the application of compositional verification techniques: each component in a system is checked individually by comparing its implementation and interface using *failure divergence refinement* (FDR) [17]. A pleasant property of FDR is that deadlock/livelock freedom of each component guarantees deadlock/livelock freedom of the complete system. The ASD approach has been used to develop systems with over 200 components [12] (more than 300 models if interface and design models are counted separately), where total verification takes around 20 min.

It is also possible to check a broader range of properties on single components through a translation to mCRL2 [5,11]. The process algebraic description language mCRL2 comes with a toolset for simulating, visualising, manipulating and model checking behavioural specifications. We call the functional properties that span a single component *local properties*.

There are however many global properties, also called 'end-to-end' properties, that are not covered by only checking local properties. Typical examples are:

- If the software control is instructed to manufacture a product, then the appropriate associated low level instructions are always issued.
- If one of the actuators reports an error, the control system always reports the error to the higher software layers.
- If the control software reports that the machine is off, it will never instruct any of its controlled actuators to move.

In this paper we report on how we verify such global properties on newly developed industrial control software. For this purpose we extend the existing mCRL2 translation to support multiple components. Firstly, communication has to be restricted to take place between the right components. Furthermore, important functionality that was implemented in C++, instead of ASD, needs to be translated manually to mCRL2. Finally, we must add several mechanisms to preserve the single-threaded execution as defined by the semantics, *i.e.*, we must ensure that only one component is active at a time.

We evaluate the approach by translating an ASD system that is newly developed and which consists of 26 components (together containing 5054 so called rule cases). On the resulting mCRL2 model, we check a complete set of end-to-end properties. Because the state-space of the system only consisted of 178 million states, we were able to establish whether each requirement was satisfied.

Our expectation was that we would encounter many hardships in the verification, especially because the state spaces would be excessively large. But the contrary turned out to be true. The state space remained well within acceptable limits for the available computer equipment. The reason for this appears to lie in the run-to-completion semantics employed in ASD, together with the strict use of interfaces. These coincide with design rules for systems to avoid the state space explosion [10]. There were a number of minor issues that had to be overcome, such as speeding up writing intermediate results to disk. It also turned out that applying a branching bisimulation reduction to the intermediate state space before applying model checking was much more time efficient than following the ordinary workflow.

Our conclusion is that it is very well possible to verify actual industrial-size software while it is under development. But for success, it needs to be written in an appropriate domain specific language whose semantics avoids a state space explosion.

Overview. Section 2 introduces the basic concepts on which this paper is built. We explain our approach to multi-component translation in Sect. 3. The case study is introduced in Sect. 4 together with the properties we verify and Sect. 5 contains the results of the experiments we conducted. In Sect. 6, we give an overview of some related work. Finally, Sect. 7 presents a conclusion.

2   Background Information

This section provides a short introduction to ASD, mCRL2 and the modal µ-calculus, which form the bases of our approach.

2.1   Analytical Software Design

Analytical Software Design (ASD) [4], developed by Verum, enables the development of software based on communicating components. The components are designed and verified using the ASD:Suite. Furthermore, the ASD:Suite can generate the executable code that can be used in a production environment. In ASD, there are two types of components:

- *Standard ASD component.* A standard component consists of an *interface* and a *design* model. The interface model specifies the externally visible behaviour of a component. It provides a more abstract view on the behaviour of a component. The design model specifies the inner working of a component, including how it interacts with lower level components. The design model always refines the interface model under failure-divergence refinement [17].
- *Foreign component.* A foreign component consists of only an interface model. It typically models the behaviour of a hardware component or another system that is implemented outside of ASD, *e.g.*, in C++.

If a component A relies on another component B for certain tasks, then we say A is a *client* of B and B is a *server* of A. Intuitively, an interface model serves as a contract on the behaviour of the corresponding design model. The interface model specifies exactly in which order a client can send calls to a server and which responses it can expect.

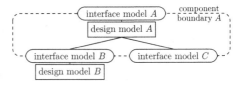

Fig. 1. An example system composed of two standard components, A and B, and a foreign component C.

Most of the decision logic of a component is contained in the design model. In ASD, the components must be structured as a tree, *i.e.*, a component cannot have more than one client. See Fig. 1.

Within ASD, we distinguish four types of communication: *call events*, *reply events*, *notification events* and *modelling events*. A call event happens when a client wants to request certain information or a certain action from one of its servers. While the server is handling that call event, it may choose to send one or more notification events to its client. These notifications are stored in the *notification queue* of the client until control is given back to the client. The notification queue will be explained in detail later. When the server is finished with a call event, it will always send a reply event to the client. When a reply contains data, we call it a *valued reply*, otherwise it is called a *void reply*.

A modelling event typically represents low level input, such as an interrupt, which can be guaranteed to come, or which can incidentally take place. It can only be performed by a foreign component. Similar to notification events, they are sent from a server to a client. However, whereas notification events always happen as the result of a call event, modelling events only happen spontaneously.

All ASD models are described using a formalism similar to *extended finite state machines*, which are state machines augmented with data. Software engineers develop these state-machines in the ASD:Suite in a format called *Sequence-based Specification* (SBS). A model can contain *state variables*, which store information about the state of the component. State variables can be Booleans or any other finite enumeration type. Transitions can be guarded with expressions over the state variables, and state variables can be updated after every transition. A guarded transition can only be taken when the guard evaluates to *true* given the current values of the state variables. A row in an SBS is called a *rule case*. We give a formal definition of a design model, which we will use later to highlight the most important aspects of the translation to mCRL2.

Definition 1. A design model is a tuple $DM = (S, V, T, (\hat{s}, \hat{v}))$, where

- S is a set of states;
- V is a set of state variables $v_1{:}D_1, \ldots, v_n{:}D_n$, and their types D_i are finite enumeration types;
- T is a set of transitions, defined as

$$T \subseteq S \times \Phi(V) \times Call \times (Event^* \times (Reply \cup \{\varnothing\}) \times \mathcal{A}(V)^* \times S \cup \{Illegal\})$$
$$S \times \Phi(V) \times (Reply \cup Notif) \times (Event^* \times \mathcal{A}(V)^* \times S \cup \{Illegal\})$$

  A transition has a source state and a guard, and can originate either from a call event, from a notification that is stored in the queue or from a valued reply. If the transition is not illegal, it results in zero or more calls and/or notifications, a reply (when necessary), assignments to the state variables and a state update.
- $\hat{s} \in S$ and $\hat{v} \in D_1 \times \cdots \times D_n$ define the initial state and the initial value of the state variables, respectively.

Here, *Call* and *Notif* are the set of all call events and notifications respectively, *Event* = *Call* $\cup$ *Notif* is the set of all event, $\Phi(V)$ is the set of all possible guards over V, *Reply* is the set of all valued replies, $\varnothing$ is a void reply and $\mathcal{A}(V)$ is the set of all possible assignments over V.

To simplify the reasoning, in the theory that is presented here, we assume that none of the events carry data values. In ASD, the data that is carried by events can only be forwarded and not inspected, so the assumption in the definition is not restrictive. In the case study of Sect. 4, we do consider all of ASD's features including communication of data.

Example 1. We consider a component A that can be activated and deactivated and also paused and resumed. Component A is a client of component B, which always needs to be deactivated before component A can become inactive. A sequence-based specification of the design model of component A is given in Fig. 2: it shows the four rule cases of state *Active* and one rule case of the state *Inactive*. When one of the actions *Pause* or *Resume* is performed, an empty reply (*VoidReply*) is returned and the variable *Enabled* is updated (rule cases 4 and 5). Component A can only be deactivated when it is not *Enabled* (rule cases 1 and 2). Upon deactivation, it first sends a message to component B, and only then deactivates itself by going to the state *Inactive*. Activation from the state *Inactive* happens in a similar way. We assume the actions not shown for one of the states are *blocked* in that state, *i.e.*, they cannot happen.   □

There are two possible semantics for ASD: the *multi-threaded execution model* and the *single-threaded execution model* [12]. In this paper, we only consider the latter. In the single-threaded execution model events cannot happen in parallel, but only in sequence. Therefore, these semantics should define clearly in which order events are processed. According to the documentation of ASD, the following actions take place in order when a component receives an event from a client:

- All actions from the SBS rule case are processed in order.
- State variables are updated.
- The transition to the target state is taken.
- The notifications in the queue are processed. No events other than those caused by these notifications may occur before the queue has been emptied.
- A void or valued reply takes place to give control back to the client.

Case	Event	Guard	Actions	Variable update	Target state
State: *Active*					
1	A.Deactivate	enabled == false	B.Deactivate; A.Deactivated; A.VoidReply	-	*Inactive*
2	A.Deactivate	Otherwise	Illegal	-	-
3	A.Activate	-	NoOp	-	*Active*
4	A.Pause	-	A.VoidReply	enabled = false	*Active*
5	A.Resume	-	A.VoidReply	enabled = true	*Active*
State: *Inactive*					
6	A.Activate	-	B.Activate; A.Activated; A.VoidReply	-	*Active*
7	A.Deactivate	-	NoOp	-	*Inactive*

Fig. 2. Example of an SBS for the design model of a component called A.

These rules are also referred to as *run-to-completion semantics*, meaning that a component completes all of its tasks before relinquishing control to another component. Note that since events and notifications can arrive in different orders, there are still many potential runs in an ASD model.

Wrapper Components. The tree structure of ASD is quite restrictive in practice, since it does not allow a component to have more than one client. That makes it impossible to implement bidirectional communication channels that have two clients, or database-like components that have many clients. One can work around this issue by manually implementing foreign components, as we explain below.

In the case study that we consider, wrapper components are used to implement symmetric communication channels, see Fig. 3. In this case, there are three components A, B and C. The components A and B are both a client of C, albeit through two separate interfaces. The router – written manually in C++ – implements both these interfaces. Since ASD is not aware of the connection between both

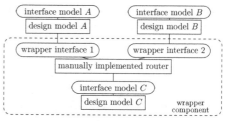

Fig. 3. The structure of a wrapper component.

interfaces, this structure does not violate ASD's single-client constraint.

The router forwards all requests from components A and B to C, and also sends responses from C back to the correct client. For all requests component C receives from component A, it sends a notification to B, and vice versa. In this way, the wrapper component C serves as a bidirectional communication channel.

2.2 mCRL2

The language mCRL2 is a process-algebraic language [11] which can be analysed using the accompanying toolset [5]. The main aim of mCRL2 is model checking of parallel processes. Additionally, mCRL2 can generate, reduce, compare and visualise state-spaces.

The mCRL2 modelling language is very flexible and despite a limited set of language primitives, very expressive. Therefore, it is very well suited as a target language for automatic translations. Several basic operators that we deal with in this paper are sequential composition (operator $\cdot$), choice (operator $+$), sum (operator $\sum$, which generalises choice) and conditional (operator $\_ \rightarrow \_ \diamond \_$).

Example 2. To illustrate some of the concepts behind mCRL2, we consider the following specification.

act $tick, reset, press;$
proc $Clock(n{:}Nat) = tick.Clock(n{+}1) + reset.Clock(0);$
          $Button = press.reset.Button;$
init **allow**$(\{tick, reset, press\},$
          comm$(\{reset|reset \rightarrow reset\},$
          $Clock(0) \parallel Button));$

In this system, we have two processes, a *Clock* and a *Button*. The clock can perform an action *tick*, after which it increases the time (stored in parameter n). When the button is pressed, it subsequently communicates with the clock via the action *reset*, and the clock resets its counter. Communication is enforced through the combination of the **allow** and **comm** operators, which in this case express that both *reset* actions much happen synchronously. For a more complete overview of the mCRL2 language, see [11]. □

2.3 Modal μ-calculus

To express formal properties, the mCRL2 toolset relies on the modal μ-calculus [13] with data, which is suitable to express virtually any conceivable behavioural property. It is far more expressive than LTL/CTL, but it is equally efficient when it comes to establishing those properties [6]. Here, we provide the core grammar of the μ-calculus, *i.e.*, without the use of data:

$$\phi ::= \textit{false} \mid \textit{true} \mid \neg\phi \mid \phi \vee \phi \mid \phi \wedge \phi \mid \phi \Rightarrow \phi \mid \langle a \rangle \phi \mid [a]\phi \mid \mu X.\,\phi \mid \nu X.\,\phi \mid X$$

Here a is an action, X is a fixpoint variable representing a set of states and $\mu X.\,\phi$ and $\nu X.\,\phi$ are the least and greatest fixpoints over X respectively. Formulae in the μ-calculus are interpreted over labelled transition systems. The semantics is roughly as follows. The Boolean operators have their usual semantics. The diamond modality $\langle a \rangle \phi$ is *true* if and only if an a-step is possible after which ϕ holds. The box modality $[a]\phi$ expresses that after every possible a-step, ϕ must hold. The least fixpoint $\mu X.\,\phi$ is true for the smallest set of states X such that ϕ holds for all states in X. Note that X can occur in ϕ. Dually, $\nu X.\,\phi$ is true for the largest set X that satisfies ϕ. The least fixpoint operator expresses that a property must be valid within a finite number of iterations, whereas the greatest fixpoint also allows for infinitely repeating behaviour.

The mCRL2 toolset also allows specifying modalities with sets of actions via so-called *action formulas*: *true* represents the set of all actions and *false* represents the empty set of actions. Supported operators are union, intersection and inverse ($\bar{a}$ is the set of all actions other than a). Furthermore, sequences of actions can be specified with *regular formulas*, which give the possibility to concatenate sequences (with the . operator), take their union (operator +) or iterate over them (operator *). The action formula a^* represents zero or more occurrences of the sequence a, and $true^*$ represents any sequence of actions. For example, $[a.b]false$ means that a sequence $a\,b$ is not possible (since if it is possible, *false* must hold in the resulting state) and $\langle a^*.b \rangle true$ means that a sequence consisting of zero or more a's followed by a b is possible. Action formulas and regular formulas can always be expressed using the fixed point operators, but they are generally more convenient to specify concrete behavioural properties.

In this work, we do not consider μ-calculus formulae with data. In mCRL2, data variables can be bound in quantifiers, *i.e.*, ∃ or ∀, or as parameter of a fixpoint variable. They are used in conditions, and as parameters of actions and fixpoint variables. See [11] for a complete overview of the modal μ-calculus.

3   Approach

The existing translation from ASD to mCRL2 is only capable of translating the models within one component boundary at a time [12]. This translation yields two mCRL2 specifications: one containing the topmost interface model and one containing the design model and the interface models below it. On the latter specification, we can check local properties that concern only that component.

We define a new translation that yields a single mCRL2 specification that represents the behaviour of the complete system. The new translation takes as input all the design models and also the interface models of foreign components. Before we introduce the challenges introduced by the new translation in detail, we first introduce the basic single-component translation.

3.1   Translating Single Components

Due to the expressivity of mCRL2, ASD components can be mapped almost directly to mCRL2. First, for every state of the component, a recursive process is created. This process carries one parameter for each state variable of the ASD model. For each rule case, this process has one *action summand*, which contains the condition, actions, variable updates and target state deduced from the rule case. Furthermore, the mCRL2 specification contains a *Queue* process that represents the behaviour of the notification queue. A complete definition of the translation can be found in [12].

Definition 2. Given a design model $DM_A = (S, V, T, (\hat{s}, \hat{v}))$, the mCRL2 process that corresponds to its initial state is defined according to the function Tr:

$$Tr(S, (v_1{:}D_1, \ldots, v_n{:}D_n), T, (\hat{s}, \hat{v})) = P_{\hat{s}}(\hat{v}, \bot)$$

where for each state $s \in S$, the corresponding recursive process in mCRL2 is defined as $P_s(v_1{:}D_1, \ldots, v_n{:}D_n, rv{:}Reply) = \sum_{t \in T} Tr(t)$, with

$$Tr(s, \varphi, e^r, (e_1^s, \ldots, e_m^s), r, (a_1, \ldots, a_k), s') =$$
$$\quad \varphi \to e^r \cdot Tr_s(e_1^s) \cdot \ldots \cdot Tr_s(e_m^s) \cdot$$
$$\quad\quad (qEmpty \cdot sendReply(r) \cdot P_{s'}(a_1, \ldots, a_k) +$$
$$\quad\quad qNonEmpty \cdot P_{s'}(a_1, \ldots, a_k, rv = r))$$
$$Tr(s, \varphi, e^r, (e_1^s, \ldots, e_m^s), (a_1, \ldots, a_k), s') =$$
$$\quad \varphi \to Tr_r(e^r) \cdot Tr_s(e_1^s) \cdot \ldots \cdot Tr_s(e_m^s) \cdot$$
$$\quad\quad (qEmpty \cdot ((rv \not\approx \perp) \to sendReply(rv) \diamond skip) \cdot P_{s'}(a_1, \ldots, a_k, rv = \perp) +$$
$$\quad\quad qNonEmpty \cdot P_{s'}(a_1, \ldots, a_k))$$
$$Tr(s, \varphi, e^r, Illegal) = \varphi \to Tr_r(e^r) \cdot illegal \cdot \delta$$

$$Tr_s(e) = \begin{cases} outwardNotif(e) & \text{if } e \in Notif \\ e \cdot recReply(\varnothing) & \text{if } e \text{ is a void call event} \\ e & \text{if } e \text{ is a valued call event} \end{cases}$$

$$Tr_r(e) = \begin{cases} e & \text{if } e \in Call \\ readNotif(e) & \text{if } e \in Notif \\ recReply(e) & \text{if } e \in Reply \end{cases}$$

In the definitions above, rv is a process parameter that stores the reply value that needs to be returned after the queue is emptied. A special value, $\perp$, indicates that no reply is due to be sent. Whereas all call events are translated into communicating actions, notifications and replies are translated into arguments of the actions $outwardNotif$ and $readNotif$, and $sendReply$ and $recReply$ respectively. Checking whether the queue is empty or not happens through the communicating actions $qEmpty$ and $qNonEmpty$. Lastly, $skip$ is the empty process and δ is the deadlock process.

Example 3. Recall component A from Example 1. We give the translation of the rule cases 1, 2 and 4 according to Definition 2:

$$A_{Active}(enabled{:}Bool, rv{:}Reply)$$
$$\quad = (enabled \approx false) \to A\_deactivate\_called \cdot invoke\_B\_Deactivate \cdot recReply(\varnothing) \cdot$$
$$\quad\quad outwardNotif(A\_Deactivated) \cdot$$
$$\quad\quad (qEmpty \cdot sendReply(\varnothing) \cdot A_{Inactive}() + qNonEmpty \cdot A_{Inactive}(rv = \varnothing))$$
$$\quad + (enabled \approx true) \to A\_deactivate\_called \cdot illegal \cdot \delta$$
$$\quad + A\_Pause\_called \cdot (qEmpty \cdot sendReply(\varnothing) \cdot A_{Inactive}(enabled = false)$$
$$\quad + qNonEmpty \cdot A_{Inactive}(enabled = false, rv = \varnothing)) + \ldots$$

For the state *Active*, we have a process definition A_{Active}, which carries the state variable *enabled*. The different types of events each have a prefix or suffix to distinguish them: received call events have the suffix *called* and sent call events have the prefix *invoke*. After an illegal event, the process deadlocks (operator δ). □

3.2   Communication

In the existing single-component translation, a void reply is represented with the action $sendReply(\varnothing)$. Since the scope of this translation is very limited – it only translates one design model and several interface models from one component boundary (cf. Fig. 1) – synchronization on this action can only take place in one way: between the design model and one of the interface models. However, in the multi-component setting, we have to explicitly enforce synchronization to happen between the proper components. Therefore, every occurrence of an action $sendReply$ does not only have an argument for the type of the reply, but also two arguments to indicate the source and destination of the reply. In this way, only those components will synchronize on that action. The same approach is applied to notifications.

3.3   Manual Translations

The automatic translation to mCRL2 cannot handle wrapper components, since their router is implemented in C++ instead of ASD. The behaviour of a wrapper component as a symmetric communication channel is essential to the behaviour of the complete system. Therefore, it is desirable that the wrapper components are also present in the translation of the complete system. We manually translated the router to mCRL2, because this is far more efficient than performing an automatic translation from C++.

There is another component, called *AsyncCall*, of which the behaviour is manually translated from C++ to mCRL2. The component *AsyncCall* can be requested by any component to send a response at some later time. This is a workaround such that ASD components can awaken themselves to finish residual duties. Internally, these requests are stored in a queue in *AsyncCall*. The queue can only contain one request per component and components also have the option to cancel their request.

We remark that the wrapper components are partially generic and the *AsyncCall* component is completely generic. Therefore, they do not need to be implemented from scratch when verifying several systems. Ideally, the mCRL2 specification of the wrapper components can be generated by the same program that generates their C++ implementation.

3.4   Queues

As defined in the semantics of ASD, every component contains its own queue to store notifications. This implies that the complete mCRL2 specification will have a queue for every design model in the system. To ensure that the run-to-completion semantics is preserved, we add a lock to every queue. A queue is unlocked exactly when the corresponding component is active processing a call from a client or a modelling event. In this way a client can only process the content of a queue when it is active.

3.5 Framework

Not only the ASD components themselves, but also the outside world, which we will refer to as the *framework*, should behave according to certain constraints. For example, the framework cannot send out another call or modelling event when the system did not yet finish the previous task. To encode this, we add the following features to our translation:

- A new action *emptyQ* that can only be executed when all queues are empty; all queues synchronise on this action.
- An additional process *Thread* controls the sending of calls to the uppermost components and sending of modelling events by the foreign components. At the moment it sends a call or modelling event, it checks whether the queues are empty. It can only send another message after the previous one completed processing.

4 Case Study

We perform a case study to investigate the feasibility of our approach and to determine its applicability to industrial-size systems. The case study is based on a real-life ASD system found in the model stack of our industrial partner. Components and events have been renamed for confidentiality reasons. Figure 4 shows the high-level structure of the system. The system consists of two loosely-coupled subsystems, called *A* and *B*. *A* and *B* have to cooperate to execute an action together, which we will call *Exec*. The clients of *A* and *B* independently decide whether they are ready to do so. Moreover, after a client has requested for *Exec* to be performed, it can repeal its decision by sending a *Cancel* message.

Both sides synchronize using wrapper components located on the *cancel layer* and the *control layer*. The cancel layer consists of the components responsible for cancelling the execution of *Exec* and the control layer is responsible for performing *Exec*. The cancel and control layers, including their direct server components, consist of 14 components. The complete system consists of 26 components, which contain 5054 rule cases in total.

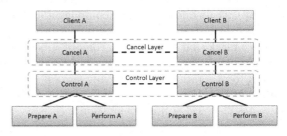

Fig. 4. The structure of the case study system. The dashed lines indicates bidirectional communication through wrapper components.

In the initial state, the clients of *A* and *B* can decide whether they want to perform *Exec* or cancel it. When both clients request to do *Exec* without sending a *Cancel* at some point, then this action is performed. If at least one client requests a cancellation before they both request *Exec*, then the action

Cancel is performed. If a client asks for *Exec* to be cancelled after *Exec* has started, then it will not be cancelled. Both clients will receive a notification when an *Exec* or a *Cancel* has been completed. After a client requests *Exec*, it will immediately start preparing for *Exec* to happen. When *Exec* or *Cancel* has finished, the system should return to the initial state. We call the process between the first message and the performing of *Exec* or *Cancel* a *round*.

4.1   Subsystems

In our analysis, we consider four different variants of this system, to get a rough idea of the scalability. Firstly, we have the *layers subsystem*, which consists of the cancel layer, the control layer, the components directly below them and the wrapper components in between. We consider two variants of the layers subsystem: the regular implementation and an implementation where no *Cancel* request can be performed. Secondly, we have two variants of the complete system: one that does not allow errors to occur and one that does allow errors. We will call the former *good-weather behaviour* (GWB) and the latter *bad-weather behaviour* (BWB). The bad-weather behaviour system is rather rudimental, which means that clients can raise errors which are subsequently dealt with by the system to cause the least disturbance in the normal process operation.

Table 1. Properties of the layers system written in modal μ-calculus

	Property	Formula
0	Initial state	$(\langle A\_Request\_Exec \rangle true \wedge \langle A\_Request\_Cancel \rangle true \wedge$
		$\langle B\_Request\_Exec \rangle true \wedge \langle B\_Request\_Cancel \rangle true)$
1	Cannot do *Exec* without two requests	$[true^*](\text{Initial state} \Rightarrow [(\overline{A\_Request\_Exec}^* + \overline{B\_Request\_Exec}^*).Exec]false)$
2	Cannot request execution after a cancel request	$[true^*.A\_Request\_Cancel.\overline{(outwardNotification(Cancelled))}^*.A\_Request\_Exec]false$
3	Must perform execution after two execute requests	$[true^*](\text{Initial state} \Rightarrow [A\_Request\_Exec.\overline{(A\_Request\_Cancel}$ $\overline{+ B\_Request\_Cancel)}^*.B\_Request\_Exec]\mu X.([\overline{Exec}]X \wedge \langle true \rangle true))$
4	Raise cancel notification after two cancel requests	$[true^*.A\_Request\_Cancel.\overline{(outwardNotification(Cancelled))}^*.B\_Request\_Cancel]$ $\mu X.([\overline{outwardNotification(Cancelled)}]X \wedge \langle true \rangle true)$
5	After a cancel request, *Cancel* is performed	$[true^*](\text{Initial state} \Rightarrow [A\_Request\_Cancel + B\_Request\_Cancel]$ $\mu X.([\overline{A\_Cancel}]X \wedge \langle true \rangle true))$
6	Cannot make multiple *Exec* requests in a round	$[true^*.A\_Request\_Exec.\overline{(outwardNotification(Exec\_finished))}^*.A\_Request\_Exec]false$
7	No synchronization error during an execution	$[true^*](\text{Initial state} \Rightarrow [A\_Request\_Exec.\overline{(B\_Request\_Exec)}^*.B\_Request\_Exec$ $.\overline{(A\_Request\_Exec + B\_Request\_Exec)}^*.Sync\_Error(A)]false)$
8	Synchronization error after requesting an execute too soon	$[true^*]((\langle A\_Request\_Exec \rangle true \wedge \langle B\_Get\_Results \rangle true) \Rightarrow$ $[\overline{(B\_Get\_Results)}^*.A\_Request\_Exec]\mu X.([\overline{Sync\_Error(A)}]X \wedge \langle true \rangle true))$

4.2 Properties

After consulting the domain experts, we identified several system-wide properties that the system under study should adhere to. For the layers subsystem, we have eight properties, which are listed in Table 1. Furthermore, we have three properties that involve the complete system; they are listed in Table 2. Note that some properties are symmetric for both clients; in that case we only listed one of the two μ-calculus formulae. Many properties are concerned with behaviour from the moment that neither client has sent a message yet until the moment that *Exec* or *Cancel* is performed. Since we are dealing with a system that runs continuously, we should not only check what happens from the initial state, but in every round. Therefore, we formulated a property in the μ-calculus that expresses whether the system is at the start of a round (property 'Initial state' in Tables 1 and 2). This formula is used within other properties to check behaviour in all rounds. Most action names in these properties should be self-explanatory. The actions *outwardReply* and *outwardNotification* respectively represent a reply and a notification sent to one of the two clients. The inserting of a notification into the queue of a certain component is represented by the action *raiseNotification*.

Table 2. Properties of the full system written in modal μ-calculus

	Property	Formula
0	Initial state	$\langle A\_Request\_Exec.\overline{(Protocol\_Error(A))}^*.outwardReply(VoidReply)\rangle true \wedge$
		$\langle A\_Request\_Cancel.\overline{(Protocol\_Error(A))}^*.outwardReply(VoidReply)\rangle true \wedge$
		$\langle B\_Request\_Exec.\overline{(Protocol\_Error(B))}^*.outwardReply(VoidReply)\rangle true \wedge$
		$\langle B\_Request\_Cancel.\overline{(Protocol\_Error(B))}^*.outwardReply(VoidReply)\rangle true)$
1	Must perform execution after two execute requests	$[true^*](Initial\ state \Rightarrow [A\_Request\_Exec.\overline{(A\_Request\_Cancel + B\_Request\_Cancel)}^*.$ $B\_Request\_Exec]\mu X.([\overline{Exec}]X \wedge \langle true\rangle true))$
2	Prepare steps are done before perform steps	$[true^*](Initial\ state \Rightarrow [A\_Request\_Exec.\overline{(A\_Request\_Cancel + B\_Request\_Cancel)}^*.$ $B\_Request\_Exec.\overline{(raiseNotification(A\_Prepare\_Step\_Done))}^*.Exec]false)$
3	Perform steps are done before raising an execution notification	$[true^*](Initial\ state \Rightarrow [A\_Request\_Exec.\overline{(A\_Request\_Cancel + B\_Request\_Cancel)}^*.$ $B\_Request\_Exec.\overline{(raiseNotification(A\_Perform\_Step\_Done))}^*$ $.outwardNotification(Exec\_finished)]false)$

In these properties, we use several common patterns. First, it is very common to write a property of the shape $[true^*]\varphi$, meaning that after any sequence of actions, φ has to hold. Building on that, the property $[true^*.a]false$ expresses that action a cannot occur anywhere and the property $[true^*.a.\bar{b}^*.c]false$ expresses that after every action a, an action b must happen before the action c happens.

A more complex, but important, pattern is $\mu X.([\bar{a}]X \wedge \langle true\rangle true)$, which means that action a unavoidably happens within a finite amount of steps. The intuition is as follows: as long as we do something other than a (subformula $[\bar{a}]$), we recurse through variable X. That may only happen finitely often, due to the least fixpoint (μX). Therefore, we must at some point end up in a state where actions other than a are not possible. This state cannot be a deadlock, since that is explicitly forbidden by $\langle true \rangle true$. Hence, we end up in a state where only a actions can be done, and at least one a is possible. This is the same as saying that ultimately, a must be done.

5   Results

In our experiments, we applied the workflow of Fig. 5 to check each of the properties. First, the mCRL2 specification is normalised into a *linear process* (LPS), from which we generate the state space in the shape of a *labelled transition system* (LTS). This LTS is subsequently minimised under divergence-preserving branching bisimulation using the Groote-Jansen-Keiren-Wijs algorithm [9]. Combined with a μ-calculus formula, we construct a *Boolean equation system* (BES), which can be solved to obtain an answer to the model checking question. A benefit of using this particular workflow is that the state space does not need to be generated repeatedly for every property we want to check.

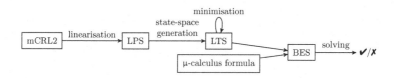

Fig. 5. The workflow used for model checking.

To run the experiments, we used a machine with multiple Xeon E5520 processors (56 cores in total), clocked at 2.27 GHz and 935 GB of memory. The mCRL2 version we installed has Git commit hash `73241e378e`[1]. The mCRL2 analysis tools are all single threaded.

Table 3 gives an overview of the time required for state-space generation and the size of each of the state spaces. The time reported does not include the time required for bisimulation reduction, which is about 45 min for the BWB system. The full system under bad-weather behaviour is almost on the limit of what can be generated in a reasonable amount of time with 178.6 million states. At the same time, bisimulation reduction is very effective, and manages to bring the number of states back to 12.4 million.

---

[1] Sources are available at https://github.com/mCRL2org/mCRL2.

Figure 6 shows a visualisation of the minimised state space of the layers subsystem. The initial state is at the top and every disk represents a (non-deterministic) choice. Initially, the system contains little branching behaviour (the red, yellow and green parts at the top). Only deeper in the state space, there is more choice to perform different actions (blue and purple parts at the bottom). The low amount of branching can be ascribed to the run-to-completion semantics of ASD.

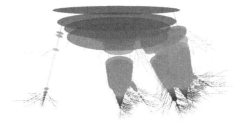

Fig. 6. Visual representation of the minimised state space of the layers subsystem. (Colour figure online)

Table 3. Time required for state-space generation and number of states and transitions for the systems before and after divergence-preserving branching bisimulation minimisation.

System	Time (s)	Mem	#states	#transitions	After bisim. red.		
					#states	#transitions	%red
Layers no *Cancel*	7	28 MB	9,107	9,472	7,085	7,422	22.2
Layers subsystem	46	63 MB	109,608	114,310	55,361	58,338	49.5
Complete system GWB	14,713	1.7 GB	17,179,798	19,098,495	3,787,974	4,298,103	75.0
Complete system BWB	154,397	14 GB	178,603,107	196,784,882	12,451,325	14,879,416	93.0

Table 4 records for each of the four variants of the system the average time required to check one of the properties. All properties hold, except when checked on the bad-weather behaviour system, since that has not been fully implemented. The time required for the full system is significant: almost one hour for the good weather version and close to five hours per property for the bad weather system.

While running these large experiments, we observed that a lot of time and memory is spent on storing and loading intermediate files from disk. For a typical property of the BWB system, `lts2pbes` spends more than three quarters of the time on storing the PBES on disk. This problem could be by-passed by implementing an integrated tool that combines the functionality of `lts2pbes` and `pbessolve`. The amount of memory required to verify a property of the BWB system is roughly 180 GB; this peak is also reached while writing the output in `lts2pbes`.

6   Related Work

The successor of ASD is Dezyne[2], also developed by Verum. Similar to the ASD-mCRL2 translation, there is also a translation from Dezyne to mCRL2 [2].

---

[2] See https://www.verum.com/, accessed 13-05-2019.

Table 4. Average time spent to verify a single property on each of the four (sub)systems.

	Time (s)			
	Layers no cancel	Layers system	Full system GWB	Full system BWB
lts2pbes	2.06	9.82	2,317	14,126
pbessolve	0.44	3.74	890	4,150
Total	2.50	13.56	3,207	18,276

This translation is also limited to single components, so it does not support verification of end-to-end properties.

mCRL2 has also been used in other studies to analyse systems with a very large state space. For example, in [1], the train control system ERTMS Hybrid Level 3 is analysed with mCRL2. They apply the same workflow as we do: minimise the transition system with bisimulation before checking any property. The largest state space they verified contains close to 34 million states.

Remenska *et al.* [15] also work with an automated translation. They convert the behaviour captured in UML2.0 sequence diagrams to mCRL2 specifications. Their technique is applied on DIRAC, the computing grid framework of CERN's LHCb experiment. Although the state-space is too large to generate completely, they do find a counter-example to the desired property with depth-first search.

The idea of generating code from formal models that have been checked with model checking is also applied in [7]. The authors present a tool called DLC, Distributed LNT Compiler, which can produce C code from an LNT specification. The generated code is suited for running om multiple machines concurrently, synchronization between the machines is achieved with a rendezvous protocol. LNT specifications can be analysed with the existing tools from the CADP toolset [8].

7   Conclusion

We showed how to translate a component system implemented in ASD to mCRL2. This enables checking of end-to-end properties on ASD, which is important for mission-critical software. Furthermore, we demonstrated with a case-study that this approach is applicable to an actual industrial system. For the two variants of the layers subsystem, the time and space required to run the model checker is sufficiently small to enable interactive verification during development. This is due to the semantics of ASD that avoids a major state-space explosion. The results exceeded our own expectations and give us hope that model checking of complete systems can be applied more often in industrial settings. Based on these results, we aim to develop an environment in which all industrial controllers, newly developed in ASD, can be completely verified during their development process.

One of the challenges that needs to be tackled before wider adoption of this approach is possible, is the complexity of modal μ-calculus. Currently, specifying properties with μ-calculus requires expertise, and it is not uncommon for formulas to contain mistakes. A possible solution is to supply developers with natural-language templates in which they enter the correct action names. The corresponding formula will then be generated from the template [16].

References

1. Bartholomeus, M., Luttik, B., Willemse, T.: Modelling and analysing ERTMS hybrid level 3 with the mCRL2 toolset. In: Howar, F., Barnat, J. (eds.) FMICS 2018. LNCS, vol. 11119, pp. 98–114. Springer, Cham (2018). https://doi.org/10.1007/978-3-030-00244-2_7

2. van Beusekom, R., et al.: Formalising the Dezyne modelling language in mCRL2. In: Petrucci, L., Seceleanu, C., Cavalcanti, A. (eds.) FMICS/AVoCS -2017. LNCS, vol. 10471, pp. 217–233. Springer, Cham (2017). https://doi.org/10.1007/978-3-319-67113-0_14

3. Broadfoot, G.H.: ASD case notes: costs and benefits of applying formal methods to industrial control software. In: Fitzgerald, J., Hayes, I.J., Tarlecki, A. (eds.) FM 2005. LNCS, vol. 3582, pp. 548–551. Springer, Heidelberg (2005). https://doi.org/10.1007/11526841_39

4. Broadfoot, G.H., Hopcroft, P.J.: Analytical software design. Technical report, Verum Consultants B.V. (2003)

5. Bunte, O., et al.: The mCRL2 toolset for analysing concurrent systems. In: Vojnar, T., Zhang, L. (eds.) TACAS 2019. LNCS, vol. 11428, pp. 21–39. Springer, Cham (2019). https://doi.org/10.1007/978-3-030-17465-1_2

6. Cranen, S., Groote, J.F., Reniers, M.A.: A linear translation from CTL* to the first-order modal μ-calculus. Theor. Comput. Sci. **412**(28), 3129–3139 (2011). https://doi.org/10.1016/j.tcs.2011.02.034

7. Evrard, H., Lang, F.: Automatic distributed code generation from formal models of asynchronous processes interacting by multiway rendezvous. J. Log. Algebraic Methods Program. **88**, 121–153 (2017). https://doi.org/10.1016/j.jlamp.2016.09.002

8. Garavel, H., Lang, F., Mateescu, R., Serwe, W.: CADP 2011: a toolbox for the construction and analysis of distributed processes. STTT **15**(2), 89–107 (2013). https://doi.org/10.1007/978-3-540-73368-3_18

9. Groote, J.F., Jansen, D.N., Keiren, J.J.A., Wijs, A.J.: An O(m log n) algorithm for computing stuttering equivalence and branching bisimulation. ACM Trans. Comput. Logic **18**(2) (2017). https://doi.org/10.1007/978-3-662-49674-9_40

10. Groote, J.F., Kouters, T.W.D.M., Osaiweran, A.: Specification guidelines to avoid the state space explosion problem. Softw. Test. Verif. Reliab. **25**(1), 4–33 (2015). https://doi.org/10.1002/stvr.1536

11. Groote, J.F., Mousavi, M.R.: Modeling and Analysis of Communicating Systems. MIT Press, Cambridge (2014)

12. Jonk, R.: The semantics of ALIAS defined in mCRL2. Master's thesis, Eindhoven University of Technology (2016)

13. Kozen, D.: Results on the propositional μ-calculus. Theor. Comput. Sci. **27**(3), 333–354 (1982). https://doi.org/10.1007/BFb0012782

14. Osaiweran, A., Schuts, M., Hooman, J., Groote, J.F., van Rijnsoever, B.J.: Evaluating the effect of a lightweight formal technique in industry. STTT **18**(1), 93–108 (2016). https://doi.org/10.1007/s10009-015-0374-1

15. Remenska, D., et al.: From UML to process algebra and back: an automated approach to model-checking software design artifacts of concurrent systems. In: Brat, G., Rungta, N., Venet, A. (eds.) NFM 2013. LNCS, vol. 7871, pp. 244–260. Springer, Heidelberg (2013). https://doi.org/10.1007/978-3-642-38088-4_17

16. Remenska, D., Willemse, T.A.C., Templon, J., Verstoep, K., Bal, H.: Property specification made easy: harnessing the power of model checking in UML designs. In: Ábrahám, E., Palamidessi, C. (eds.) FORTE 2014. LNCS, vol. 8461, pp. 17–32. Springer, Heidelberg (2014). https://doi.org/10.1007/978-3-662-43613-4_2

17. Roscoe, A.W.: On the expressive power of CSP refinement. Form. Asp. Comput. **17**(2), 93–112 (2005). https://doi.org/10.1007/s00165-005-0065-x

Distributed Algorithms

Case Study on Certifying Distributed Algorithms: Reducing Intrusiveness

Samira Akili$^{(\boxtimes)}$ and Kim Völlinger

Humboldt University of Berlin, Berlin, Germany
akilisam@cms.hu-berlin.de, voellinger@hu-berlin.de

Abstract. Certifying distributed algorithms (CDAs) are a runtime verification method for distributed systems. A CDA computes additionally a *witness* to an input-output pair – a correctness argument for the pair. The witness is verified at runtime by a distributed *checker* algorithm. In this paper, we apply CDAs to an industrial case study of collaborative transport robots serving machines in a factory. In particular, we present a certifying variant of a distributed bidding algorithm executed by the robots to assign transport jobs amongst each other. Furthermore, we introduce overlays in order to organize the communication of the distributed checker, and compare them regarding their intrusiveness.

1 Introduction

We consider certifying distributed algorithms (CDAs) – a runtime verification method for distributed systems. A CDA computes a *witness* w additionally to an input-output pair (i, o) such that if a *witness predicate* holds for the triple (i, o, w), the pair (i, o) is correct. A *distributable* witness predicate states a property in the system by stating properties for each component, and hence can be decided by a *distributed* checker algorithm at runtime. As an example, consider a distributed algorithm where the components of a network decide if the network graph itself is bipartite. In the case of a non-bipartite network graph, an odd cycle in the graph is a witness since an odd cycle is not bipartite itself. The witness predicate states that an odd cycle exists in a network for which the distributed algorithm outputs that its non-bipartite. In [7] a distributable witness predicate for the example is described. In the typical setup of runtime verification, a system is instrumented to compute outputs for a monitor deciding if a given property holds. Analogously, a CDA is instrumented to compute a witness for the checker deciding if an input-output pair is correct. In this paper, we investigate a case study of transport robots serving machines in a factory [1]. Since the robots execute distributed algorithms to achieve collaborative goals, they can be classified as a multi-agent system. We apply CDAs to verify a distributed bidding algorithm used to assign transport jobs at runtime. Moreover, we consider overlays (i.e. communication topologies imposed on the components of the system) for the distributed checker, and compare them regarding their intrusiveness (i.e. the degree to which runtime verification affects the system).

© IFIP International Federation for Information Processing 2019
Published by Springer Nature Switzerland AG 2019
H. Hojjat and M. Massink (Eds.): FSEN 2019, LNCS 11761, pp. 179–185, 2019.
https://doi.org/10.1007/978-3-030-31517-7_12

Related Work. Certifying *sequential* algorithms are established [5] but there is little work on certifying *distributed* algorithms [7–10]. CDAs can be classified as a distributed and choreographed monitoring approach since the checker is a distributed algorithm, and as a synchronous monitoring approach since the system waits for the checker to accept [2]. Overlay networks are a well established research strand offering sophisticated solutions for various applications [3]. However, to our knowledge, there is no approach of using overlays to reduce intrusivenes for runtime verification.

2   Preliminaries: Certifying Distributed Algorithms

We model the communication topology of a distributed system as a connected undirected graph $G = (V, E)$: a vertex represents a component, an edge a communication channel. A *distributed algorithm*, running on a distributed system, consists of a sub-algorithm for each component such that all components together solve one problem [4]. The input i is distributed such that each component $v \in V$ has a sub-input i_v with $i = \cup_{v \in V} i_v$; analogously for the output. A CDA computes a *witness* w additionally to its input-output pair (i, o) such that if a predicate – the *witness predicate* – holds for the triple (i, o, w), the pair (i, o) is correct [10]. We call a predicate that is defined over a component's sub-input, sub-output and sub-witness a *local predicate*. A predicate Γ is *universally distributable* with a local predicate γ if for all triples (i, o, w) holds: $\forall v \in V : \gamma(i_v, o_v, w_v) \longrightarrow \Gamma(i, o, w)$, and *existentially distributable* if: $\exists v \in V : \gamma(i_v, o_v, w_v) \longrightarrow \Gamma(i, o, w)$. A predicate is *distributable* if one of the former applies, or if it is implied by conjuncted and/or disjuncted universally/existentially distributable predicates [7]. The witness predicate has to be distributable such that it can be decided by a distributed *checker* algorithm at runtime. The *sub-checker* of component v decides all local predicates over (i_v, o_v, w_v). Using a spanning tree, the sub-checkers aggregate the evaluated local predicates upwards and combine them by logical conjunction or disjunction depending on whether the according predicate is universally or existentially distributable; the root decides the witness predicate by combining the evaluated distributable predicates [9]. Hence, if the distributed checker accepts, the distributed input-output pair (i, o) is correct. The user of a CDA does not have to trust the actual algorithm but the checker which is simpler for a well-chosen witness. Using the framework proposed in [8,9] an implemented checker can be verified.

3   Case Study: Certifying Distributed Bidding

We conduct a case study on a fleet of collaborative transport robots serving machines in a factory, provided by INSYSTEMS [1]. In particular, we investigate distributed bidding which is executed whenever a machine signals that it needs to be served. The robots communicate via a wireless network by sending broadcast or unicast messages.

Specification. W.l.o.g. let $ID = \{1, ...n\}$ be the set of the robots' unique identifiers. We refer to a robot with ID $k \in ID$ as robot k. For a robot k, the sub-input is its ID ($i_k := k$) and the sub-output is its winner-tuple ($o_k := (winnerID_k, winnerBid_k)$). The correctness of a distributed bidding is specified by the following postconditions: all robots agree on the winner *(agreement)*, the winner exists *(existence)*, and the bid of the winner is the maximum of all bids *(maximum)*. INSYSTEMS provides different variants for distributed bidding. However, we treat the algorithm as a black box and ground its certifying variant on the specification.

In the following, we give a certifying variant of distributed bidding by introducing a witness, a witness predicate and distributed checker algorithm. Moreover, we compare different overlays organizing the communication of the distributed checker regarding their intrusiveness.

Distributed Witness. The sub-witness of robot k is its own bid and a set containing the sub-outputs of the other robots. Hence, $w_k = (bid_k, \{o_l | l \in ID$ and $l \neq k\}$. The sub-witnesses are computed during bidding by bookkeeping; no additional computation is necessary.

Local Predicates. Let γ_{agree}, γ_{exist} and γ_{max} be local predicates over robot k's sub-input i_k, sub-output o_k, and sub-witness w_k. The predicate γ_{agree} holds iff $o_k = o_l$ for all $k \neq l \in ID$, i.e. if k's winner-tuple equals the winner-tuples of all other robots. The predicate γ_{exist} holds iff $k = winnerID_k$, i.e. if k chose itself as a winner. The predicate γ_{max} holds iff $bid_k \leq winnerBid_k$, i.e. if $k's$ bid is less than or equal to the bid of its chosen winner.

Distributable Predicates. Let Γ_{agree}, Γ_{exist}, Γ_{max} be predicates over the distributed input i, output o and witness w stating the three properties of the specification, e.g. if Γ_{agree} holds *agreement* is ensured. We forego a formalization. The three predicates are distributable with the introduced local predicates. The predicate Γ_{agree} is universally distributable with γ_{agree} since for all triples (i, o, w) holds: $\forall k \in ID, \gamma_{agree}(i_k, o_k, w_k) \longrightarrow \Gamma_{agree}(i, o, w)$. The predicate Γ_{exist} is distributable with γ_{agree} and γ_{exist} since for all triples (i, o, w) holds: $(\exists k \in ID, \gamma_{exist}(i_k, o_k, w_k) \wedge \Gamma_{agree}(i, o, w)) \longrightarrow \Gamma_{exist}(i, o, w)$. The predicate Γ_{agree} ensures that there is exactly one winner. The predicate Γ_{max} is distributable with γ_{agree} and γ_{max} since for all triples (i, o, w) holds: $(\forall k \in ID, \gamma_{exist}(i_k, o_k, w_k) \wedge \Gamma_{agree}(i, o, w)) \longrightarrow \Gamma_{max}(i, o, w)$. The predicate Γ_{agree} ensures that each robot compares its bid with the same winner-bid.

Witness Predicate. A logical conjunction of the predicates Γ_{agree}, Γ_{exist} and Γ_{max} is a witness predicate for the specification of distributed bidding.

Distributed Checker. The sub-checker of each robot runs as a separate process on the robot, and sub-checkers communicate with each other using the robots' IDs. The sub-checker of a robot k executes the following tasks:

(1) collecting the winner-tuples for its robot's sub-witness w_k, and deciding the local predicates γ_{agree}, γ_{exist} and γ_{max} on the triple (i_k, o_k, w_k),

(2) participating in deciding the distributable predicates Γ_{agree}, Γ_{exist} and Γ_{max} on the triple (i, o, w),

(3) and participating in deciding the witness predicate on the triple (i, o, w).

Note that for an arbitrary (connected) overlay, it is sufficient to consider the winner-tuples of neighbors in the overlay for task (1) since agreement is ensured by transitivity over neighborhoods. Hence, for task (1), a sub-checker collects the winner-tuples of neighboring robots. As the chosen overlay determines the number of neighbors, it affects the intrusiveness of the tasks. We investigate the tasks in more detail for each overlay at the end of this Section.

Criteria for Intrusiveness. Intrusiveness denotes the degree to which runtime verification affects the original system [2]. We evaluate intrusiveness by the message overhead, runtime and local computation time of the distributed checker. We measure message overhead as the number of received messages to reflect the processing overhead a message inflicts, e.g. a broadcast message is counted once per receiving component. As usual for asynchronous systems, we measure runtime by assuming that a message is delivered in one time unit [6]. Local computation time denotes the sequential computation time of a robot. In distributed algorithm analysis, local computation time is neglected when reasonably low but pointed out if a component performs a "global" computation (i.e. in our case, if the local computation depends on the number of robots) [6]. As message overhead, runtime and local computation of the checker delay the system and take resources of the robots, we consider these measurements to be reasonable criteria for intrusiveness.

Communication of Sub-Checkers. We investigate three topologies to organize the communication of the distributed checker: the original system without an overlay (complete graph), and two overlays, a star tree and a balanced binary tree. For each topology, we evaluate the intrusiveness of the tasks (1)–(3). The results are summed up in the table in Fig. 1. We denote if the number of sub-checkers having a certain local computation time is constant or linear in the number of components; e.g. $\Theta(n)_1$ denotes that a constant number of sub-checkers has the local computation time $\Theta(n)$, and $\Theta(n)_n$ that the number of sub-checkers having $\Theta(n)$ is linear in the number of components. Moreover, we denote if some sub-checkers have nothing to do with a 0 instead of $\Theta(1)$ to point out how fairly work is distributed between the sub-checkers. For the overlays, the first row of local computation is root's (one of the sub-checkers) effort with the exception of task (2) for the binary tree where it is the effort of all non-leave sub-checkers. Note that the complexity classes of task (1) depend on the particular local predicate, while the complexity classes for the tasks (2) and (3) are the same for each distributable witness predicate.

	Complete Graph			Star			Balanced Binary Tree		
	(1)	(2)	(3)	(1)	(2)	(3)	(1)	(2)	(3)
Local Computation	$\Theta(n)_n$	$\Theta(n)_n$	$\Theta(1)_n$	0_1	$\Theta(n)_1$	$\Theta(1)_1$	0_1	$\Theta(1)_n$	$\Theta(1)_1$
	-	-	-	$\Theta(1)_n$	0_n	0_n	$\Theta(1)_n$	0_n	0_n
Message Overhead	$\Theta(n^2)$	$\Theta(n^2)$	-	$\Theta(n)$	$\Theta(n)$	$\Theta(n)$	$\Theta(n)$	$\Theta(n)$	$\Theta(n)$
Runtime	$\Theta(1)$	$\Theta(1)$	-	$\Theta(1)$	$\Theta(1)$	$\Theta(1)$	$\Theta(1)$	$\Theta(\log n)$	$\Theta(\log n)$

Fig. 1. The intrusiveness of the tasks (1)–(3) for each topology.

Complete Graph. For task (1), each sub-checker broadcasts the winner-tuple of its robot and subsequently compares its robot's winner-tuple with all other tuples to decide the predicate γ_{agree}. Hence, local computation time is linear in the number of robots for each sub-checker. For task (2), each sub-checker broadcasts a triple with its evaluated local predicates, and decides the distributable predicates with the received triples. Note that by comparing its robot's winner-tuple with all other tuples, each sub-checker already decides the predicate Γ_{agree} by deciding γ_{agree} in task (1) since a robots sub-witness equals the distributed witness in this case. However to decide the distributable predicates for the maximum and existence property communication is still needed. For task (3), each sub-checker logically conjuncts the three evaluated distributable predicates.

Star Tree. For task (1), root broadcasts its winner-tuple and the other sub-checkers compare their winner-tuple with it. For task (2), each sub-checker sends the triple of its evaluated local predicates to root. As root decides the distributable predicates, root's local computation is linear in the number of robots. For task (3), root decides the witness predicate and informs the other sub-checkers by a broadcast.

Balanced Binary Tree. For task (1), each non-leaf sub-checker sends its winner-tuple to its children, and each child compares its winner-tuple with the winner-tuple of its parent. For task (2), starting by the leaves, each sub-checker gets the triple of the evaluated local predicates from its children and combines it with its own triple. The root holds a triple of the evaluated distributable predicates. Hence, the runtime is the tree's depth. For task (3), root decides the witness predicate and informs all others using the tree.

Comparison. The complete graph and star have the lowest runtime. However, regarding message overhead and local computation, the complete graph performs the worst. In the star, only root computes a global computation, while in the binary tree no global computation occurs. We conclude that the complete graph is not suitable to organize the communication of the sub-checkers, while the star and binary tree can be both justified. They reflect a trade-off between runtime and local computation time which respectively depend on the depth and the branching factor of a tree. A star is extreme in branching and therefore minimizes runtime. A chain would be extreme in depth. However, we chose a binary tree for comparison since its runtime is sub-linear while local computation time is still constant. A balanced tree additionally restricts the depth. Hence, the branching factor should be optimized according to the requirements of the system.

4   Discussion

We applied CDAs to an industrial case study [1]. Particularly, we presented a certifying variant of distributed bidding to verify it at runtime. Moreover, we introduced overlays to organize the communication of the sub-checkers, and compared them regarding their intrusiveness. We concluded that an overlay with a tree topology improves a quadratic message overhead to a linear one, and that by adjusting the branching factor, runtime and local computation time can be balanced out. Our results can be generalized to obtain a generic method to verify agreement at runtime (e.g. to be reused for consensus problems) using overlays.

Future Work. Note that for a universally distributable witness predicate, the distributed checker could stop after task (1) if a sub-checker raises an alarm when detecting that the according local predicate is not satisfied. When choosing an overlay, as many checkers as possible should be able to raise an alarm. We reflected that idea e.g. for the binary tree by letting the children check agreement with their parent. If parents check agreement with their children, leaves (about half of the components) cannot raise an alarm. For an existentially distributable witness predicate, a time out could be used: if no sub-checker decides that a local predicate holds before a time out is reached, the checkers conclude that the predicate does not hold. However, this could lead to false negatives. Another criteria for an overlay could be robustness against message loss, e.g. by choosing neighbors in the overlay according to the physical neighbors. Another direction is to consider overlays that can be efficiently updated in case of system dynamics.

References

1. proANT Transport Robots. http://www.insystems.de/en/produkte/proant-transport-roboter/
2. Francalanza, A., Pérez, J.A., Sánchez, C.: Runtime verification for decentralised and distributed systems. In: Bartocci, E., Falcone, Y. (eds.) Lectures on Runtime Verification. LNCS, vol. 10457, pp. 176–210. Springer, Cham (2018). https://doi.org/10.1007/978-3-319-75632-5_6
3. Lua, E.K., Crowcroft, J., Pias, M., Sharma, R., Lim, S.: A survey and comparison of peer-to-peer overlay network schemes. IEEE Commun. Surv. Tutor. **7**(2), 72–93 (2005)
4. Lynch, N.A.: Distributed Algorithms. Morgan Kaufmann Publishers Inc., San Francisco (1996)
5. McConnell, R.M., Mehlhorn, K., Näher, S., Schweitzer, P.: Certifying algorithms. Comput. Sci. Rev. **5**, 119–161 (2011)
6. Peleg, D.: Distributed Computing: A Locality-Sensitive Approach. Society for Industrial and Applied Mathematics, Philadelphia (2000)
7. Völlinger, K.: Verifying the output of a distributed algorithm using certification. In: Lahiri, S., Reger, G. (eds.) RV 2017. LNCS, vol. 10548, pp. 424–430. Springer, Cham (2017). https://doi.org/10.1007/978-3-319-67531-2_29
8. Völlinger, K., Akili, S.: Verifying a class of certifying distributed programs. In: Barrett, C., Davies, M., Kahsai, T. (eds.) NFM 2017. LNCS, vol. 10227, pp. 373–388. Springer, Cham (2017). https://doi.org/10.1007/978-3-319-57288-8_27

9. Völlinger, K., Akili, S.: On a verification framework for certifying distributed algorithms: distributed checking and consistency. In: Baier, C., Caires, L. (eds.) FORTE 2018. LNCS, vol. 10854, pp. 161–180. Springer, Cham (2018). https://doi.org/10.1007/978-3-319-92612-4_9

10. Völlinger, K., Reisig, W.: Certification of distributed algorithms solving problems with optimal substructure. In: Calinescu, R., Rumpe, B. (eds.) SEFM 2015. LNCS, vol. 9276, pp. 190–195. Springer, Cham (2015). https://doi.org/10.1007/978-3-319-22969-0_14

Taming Hierarchical Connectors

José Proença[1,2]([✉]) and Alexandre Madeira[1,2]

[1] CISTER, ISEP, Universidade do Minho & HASLab/INESC TEC, Braga, Portugal
pro@isep.ipp.pt
[2] CIDMA, Universidade de Aveiro & HASLab/INESC TEC, Aveiro, Portugal

Abstract. Building and maintaining complex systems requires good software engineering practices, including code modularity and reuse. The same applies in the context of coordination of complex component-based systems. This paper investigates how to verify properties of complex coordination patterns built hierarchically, i.e., built from composing blocks that are in turn built from smaller blocks. Most existing approaches to verify properties *flatten* these hierarchical models before the verification process, losing the hierarchical structure. We propose an approach to verify hierarchical models using *containers* as actions; more concretely, containers interacting with their neighbours. We present a dynamic modal logic tailored for hierarchical connectors, using Reo and Petri Nets to illustrate our approach. We realise our approach via a prototype implementation available online to verify hierarchical Reo connectors, encoding connectors and formulas into mCRL2 specifications and formulas.

1 Introduction

Coordination languages describe how to combine the behaviour of independently executing components, oblivious to each other. As the complexity of systems and their coordination increases, so does the need to structure these systems into reusable blocks of manageable size. In the context of coordination languages, we argue that a complex connector or protocol should be built using a hierarchy of reusable blocks, each in turn built by compositing more refined blocks.

This section motivates this notion of hierarchical construction using Reo [1] to describe a switcher connector (Fig. 1) that routes data from a source end a to either a sink end b or a sink end c. A second source end sw switches between the two possible data flows, i.e., initially all data flows from a to b, but after signalled by sw data will flow from a to c. Observe that the hierarchical construction can also be used with other connector models, such as process algebra communicating over shared channels [4], or with Petri Nets [5].

Connectors interact with components and with other connectors via their interfaces, depicted as 'o' in Fig. 1. Informally, the xor connector sends data atomically from its left port to either its top-right or bottom-right port. In turn, the alternator uses this connector alternate between sending data from its left

© IFIP International Federation for Information Processing 2019
Published by Springer Nature Switzerland AG 2019
H. Hojjat and M. Massink (Eds.): FSEN 2019, LNCS 11761, pp. 186–193, 2019.
https://doi.org/10.1007/978-3-030-31517-7_13

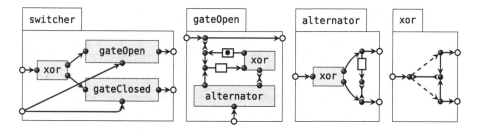

Fig. 1. Hierarchical construction of a `switcher` connector.

port to its top-right and to its bottom-right ports. The `gateOpen` connector controls the passage of data from the left port to the right port: initially data can flow; upon receiving a signal from its bottom port the data flow stops until a new signal is received from its bottom port. Finally, the `switcher` connector routes data to either the top or to the bottom right port, alternating whenever the left-bottom port is triggered.

Existing approaches to model-check Reo connectors consider only the flattened connector (see Fig. 2 for the flattened `switcher`). This paper addresses how to model-check hierarchical connectors, exploiting the hierarchical structure. E.g., allowing one to verify if, after ignoring the internals of the `alternator`, the `switcher` can output two consecutive values on its bottom-right port.

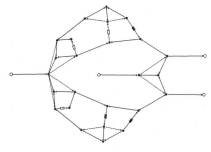

We present a *model* and a *modal* **Fig. 2.** Flattened `switcher` connector.
logic to specify hierarchical connectors, not restricted to the realm of Reo, whose alphabet of actions are the reusable *containers*. Containers can be either a primitive connector (e.g., ⊐→) or a connector built with other containers (e.g., `gateOpen` in Fig. 1). *Performing* a container c, from our perspective, means performing an action where c interacts with its exterior.

Summarising, the key contribution of this paper is a model (Sect. 2) and a logic (Sect. 3) to specify and model-check hierarchical connectors, using Reo as an example to specify connectors. A prototype implementation generates mCRL2 specifications and logical formulas of our proposed model and logic (Sect. 4).

2   Modelling Hierarchical Connectors

We define hierarchical models for connectors for which a compositional semantics exist. This semantics may be given, for example, by constraint automata [2] (in the case of Reo), by a process algebra [4], or by Petri nets (PN) [5]. The toy examples in Fig. 3, using Reo and PN, will be used to illustrate the concepts.

Table 1. Semantics of the containers in Fig. 3 (x and y) and container abstractions (∂).

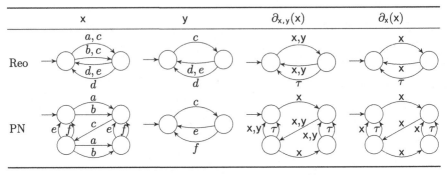

	x	y	$\partial_{x,y}(x)$	$\partial_x(x)$
Reo				
PN				

Using the constraint automata semantics [2] without data constraints [6] for Reo and the standard Petri Net semantics we derive their semantics in Table 1 (columns x and y). The two right columns exemplify container abstractions, replacing actions by the container names that use these to interact. The Reo and PN semantics are omitted because these are orthogonal to our approach.

A *hierarchical connector* (HiCon) is as a set of nested containers, each mapped to a labelled transition system whose labels consist of sets of actions. In turn, these actions are mapped to the set of their parent containers. As an example, the PN of Fig. 3 has containers x and y, whereas y is in x. The transition a belongs to x, c belongs to y, f does not belong to any container, and e belongs to both x and y. This notion of action belonging to containers is then used to formalise the container abstraction ∂ up to a given set of containers.

Formally, a **HiCon** is a tuple $H = (C, A, rt, \sigma, \rho)$ such that: C is a set of containers; A is a set of actions performed by containers; $rt \in C$ is the root container; σ is a function mapping each container c to a labelled transition system (LTS) $(Q_c, q_{0,c}, A_c, \rightarrow_c)$, with states Q_c, initial state $q_{0,c}$, actions $A_c \subseteq A$, and transition relation $\rightarrow \subseteq Q_c \times 2^{A_c} \times Q_c$; and $\rho = (\rho_C, \rho_A)$ is a pair of functions $\rho_C : C \rightarrow C$ and $\rho_A : A \rightarrow 2^C$, where ρ_C induces a total partial order with upper bound rt, and ρ_A maps actions to their parents such that $c \in \rho_A(a)$ implies $a \in A_c$. For example, the Reo connector depicted in Fig. 3 is formalised as (C, A, x, σ, ρ) where $C = \{x, y\}$, $A = \{a, b, c, d, e\}$, $\sigma(x)$ and $\sigma(y)$ are depicted in Table 1, $\rho_C = \{y \mapsto x, x \mapsto x\}$ and $\rho_A = \{a \mapsto \{x\}, b \mapsto \{x\}, c \mapsto \{x, y\}, d \mapsto \varnothing, e \mapsto \{x, y\}\}$.

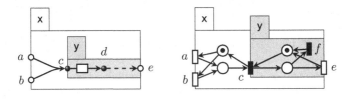

Fig. 3. Similar examples of hierarchical connectors, using Reo (left) and PN (right).

$$\partial_{\text{xor},\text{gOp},\text{gCl}}(\text{switcher}) \qquad \partial_{\text{xor},\text{alternator}}(\text{gateOpen}) \qquad \partial_{\text{xor}}(\text{alternator})$$

Fig. 4. Examples of container abstractions of the switcher connector from Fig. 3.

Given a HiCon H, a container c, and a subset C_H of its containers, we define the **container abstraction** of c up to the containers in C_H, written $\partial_{C_H}(c)$, as the LTS $(Q, q_0, C', \rightarrow')$ where $(Q, q_0, A, \rightarrow) = \sigma(c)$, $\rightarrow' = \{(q, \bigcup \rho(as), q') \mid (q, as, q') \in \rightarrow\}$, and $C' = \{c' \mid ((q, cs, q') \in \rightarrow) \wedge c' \in cs\}$. This definition matches $\partial_{x,y}(x)$ and $\partial_x(x)$ depicted in Table 1. The more complex example in Fig. 1, using Reo's Port Automata semantics, yields the container abstractions in Fig. 4.

3 Container Logic

This section introduces a logic to express and verify properties over hierarchical connectors. For that, let us consider the following syntax:

$$\psi := \text{true} \mid \text{false} \mid \langle \phi \rangle \psi \mid [\phi] \psi \mid @_c \psi \mid \partial \psi \qquad \text{(state formula)}$$
$$\phi := \varphi \mid \phi^* \mid \phi + \phi \mid \phi \cdot \phi \qquad \text{(regular formula)}$$
$$\varphi := c \mid \tau \mid \text{all} \mid \text{none} \mid \overline{\varphi} \mid \varphi + \varphi \mid \varphi \& \varphi \qquad \text{(action formula)}$$

This logic, based on a Hennessy-Milner with regular modalities (e.g. as the one adopted in the mCRL2 toolset [4]), is intended to express and verify properties of container abstractions $\partial_C(c)$. *Action formulas* build sets of actions over basic containers and abstract transitions τ (that abstracts actions not belonging to containers C). *Regular formulas* represent regular expressions over these sets. Finally, *state formulas* enrich standard dynamic (modal) formulas with two extra operators, aiming to navigate over the hierarchy of containers. Intuitively, @ operator allows to move down in the hierarchy by 'looking within' the view being analysed; conversely, ∂ operator goes up by 'looking outside' of it.

We start by formalising the *interpretation of regular formulas* in our semantic structures. A regular formula ϕ is inductively interpreted in a container abstraction $M = \partial_C(c) = (Q, q_0, C, \rightarrow)$ by the relation $M_\phi \subseteq Q \times Q$ defined below.

$$M_{\phi^*} = (M_\phi)^* \qquad M_{\phi+\phi'} = M_\phi \cup M_{\phi'} \qquad\qquad M_{\varphi \& \varphi'} = M_\varphi \cap M_{\varphi'}$$
$$M_{\phi \cdot \phi'} = \{(q, q') \mid \exists s \in Q \cdot (q, s) \in M_\phi \wedge (s, q') \in M_{\phi'}\} \qquad M_{\overline{\varphi}} = Q \times Q \setminus M_\varphi$$
$$M_{\text{all}} = \{(q, q') \mid (q, c, q') \in \rightarrow, c \in C\} \qquad M_\tau = \{(q, q') \mid (q, c, q') \in \rightarrow, c \notin C\}$$
$$M_{\text{none}} = Q \times Q \setminus M_{\text{all}} \qquad\qquad M_c = \{(q, q') \mid (q, c, q') \in \rightarrow, c \in C\}$$

Let $H = (C, A, rt, \sigma, \rho)$ be a hierarchical connector, $c \in C$ a container, and $C_H \subseteq C$ a set of containers. The **satisfaction of a formula** ψ in a state $q \in Q$ of a container abstraction $M = \partial_C(c) = (Q, q_0, C, \rightarrow)$ is defined as follows.

$$H, c, q \models \mathsf{true} \text{ is always true} \qquad H, c, q \models @_{c'} \psi \text{ if } H, c', q \models \psi$$
$$H, c, q \models \mathsf{false} \text{ is always false} \qquad H, c, q \models \partial \psi \text{ if } H, \rho_C(c), q \models \psi$$
$$H, c, q \models \langle \phi \rangle \psi \text{ if } \exists q' \in Q \cdot (q, q') \in M_\phi \land H, c, q' \models \psi$$
$$H, c, q \models [\phi] \psi \text{ if } \forall q' \in Q \cdot (q, q') \in M_\phi \Rightarrow H, c, q' \models \psi$$

Consider, for example, the formulas $\phi_1 = [\mathsf{all}^* \,.\, \mathsf{gateOpen} \,\&\, \mathsf{gateClose}]\,\mathsf{false}$ and $\phi_2 = \langle \mathsf{all}^* \,.\, \mathsf{gateOpen} \rangle @_{\mathsf{gateOpen}} \langle \overline{\mathsf{alternator}}^* \rangle \partial \langle \mathsf{gateOpen} \rangle \mathsf{true}$. The first states that $\mathsf{gateOpen}$ and $\mathsf{gateClose}$ cannot fire at the same time, and the second that $\mathsf{gateOpen}$ can fire twice in a row without its $\mathsf{alternator}$ firing. Both properties hold for $\mathsf{switcher}$; more specifically, it holds that $\partial_{\mathsf{gOp,gCl}}(\mathsf{switcher}), \mathsf{switcher}, q \models \psi_1$ and $\partial_{\mathsf{gOp,alt}}(\mathsf{switcher}), \mathsf{switcher}, q \models \psi_2$, where q is the initial state.

4 Model-Checking HiCon in Practice

We propose a concrete approach to model-check HiCon, in the context of Reo connectors, by using mCRL2 model-checking tools. This work is built over the encoding of a calculus of Reo [8] into the process algebra used to describe mCRL2 specifications [3,7], here extended to hierarchical connectors, and over the μ modal logic used by mCRL2's model-checker [4].

This section introduces (1) the hierarchical calculus of Reo connectors, (2) its encoding into mCRL2, and (3) an informal encoding of our logic into the standard modal logic used in mCRL2.

Hierarchical Calculus of Reo Connectors. The core language of hierarchical connectors is given by the grammar below, based on the core by Proença and Clarke [8], where n is a number and $\mathcal{P}$ is a set of primitive connectors.

$$c := p \in \mathcal{P} \mid \mathsf{id} \mid \mathsf{swap} \mid c \,;\, c' \mid c * c' \mid \mathsf{loop}(n)(c) \mid c\{def\}$$
$$def := s = c \mid [\mathsf{hide}]s = c \mid def, def'$$

The set $\mathcal{P}$ includes primitives dupl (to duplicate data), merger (to combine two inputs), fifo, lossy, and drain. In a nutshell, connectors are sequentially composed with ';' and composed in parallel with '*'. The connector id is the identity of ';', swap swaps the order of 2 inputs, and $\mathsf{loop}(1)(c)$ creates a feedback loop from the last output of c to its first input.

The example from Fig. 3 can be written as '$\mathsf{x} \{\mathsf{y=fifo;lossy, x=merger;y}\}$', meaning that the connector is the container x, defined as $\mathsf{merger;y}$, and y is defined as $\mathsf{fifo;lossy}$. We can define the container abstraction $\partial_{\mathsf{merger,y}}(\mathsf{x})$ by marking the specification of y with the prefix $[\mathsf{hide}]$.

Encoding into mCLR2 Specifications. We encode hierarchical Reo connectors into mCRL2 specifications based on a previous encoding of a calculus of flatten Reo connectors [3]. The hierarchy allows (1) the hiding of actions of containers marked as hidden, and (2) the inclusion of the names of the parent containers in the actions. We describe this encoding using as example the encoding of the connector 'x {[hide]y=fifo;lossy, x=merger;y}' from Fig. 3:

```
1   proc
2   Merger1 = (x_merger_1i1|x_merger_1m3 + x_merger_1i2|x_merger_1m3) . Merger1;
3   Fifo2 = x_y_2m4 . x_y_2m5 . Fifo2;
4   Lossy3 = (x_y_3m6 + x_y_3m6|x_y_3o1) . Lossy3;
5   Init1 = hide({x_y_2m5_x_y_3m6},
6           block({x_y_2m5, x_y_3m6},
7           comm({x_y_2m5|x_y_3m6 → x_y_2m5_x_y_3m6}, Lossy3 || Fifo2 )));
8   Init2 = block({x_merger_1m3, x_y_2m4},
9           comm({x_merger_1m3|x_y_2m4 → x_merger_1m3_x_y_2m4}, Init1 || Merger1));
10  init Init2;
```

Actions in this specification are ports of the Reo connectors. E.g. x_merger_1i2 denotes the 2nd input port of the merger in container x with unique identifier 1. The main process denoting this connector is Init2 (line 10), which is defined as the Init1 and Merger1 processes in parallel (line 9). In turn, Init1 consists of the Lossy3 and Fifo2 processes. In both Init processes communication is enforced by the block and comm constructs, but they differ in that Init1 also includes a hide construct (line 5) to hide communication between its lossy and fifo.

Encoding into mCRL2 Formulas. The encoding into mCRL2 specifications shown above quickly becomes unreadable for humans. To verify Reo connectors we use our container logic (Sect. 3) over containers (including primitive connectors), encoded into the modal logic used by mCRL2 to verify the encoded mCRL2 specifications. For example, the property $\langle \mathsf{all}^* \rangle$ @x⟨merger⟩ true can be read as *"at any moment the container merger inside x can interact"*, and is translated into the modal formula <true*> <x_merger_1i1|x_merger_1m3_x_y_2m4 || x_merger_1i2|x_merger_1m3_x_y_2m4> true. Informally, this encoding collects all possible actions and communications by traversing the internal representation of the mCRL2 specification, and uses this to infer in which actions the merger container can have interactions with its neighbours. It then expands merger occurrence by a disjunctions of its possibilities. Note that all constructs of our container logic are mapped directly into their mCRL2 counterparts, with the exception of @ and ∂ that are used to pinpoint the desired containers.

HiCon in the Arcatools Framework. Our approach is realised by a public prototype tool developed in Scala and JavaScript that can be executed via a web-browser, available to use and download at http://arcatools.org/#reo. Selecting the swicher connector under "Examples" yields the screenshot in Fig. 5. with the specification and the logical formulas on the left side, and the visualisation and the generated mCRL2 specification on the right size. The reader can load the

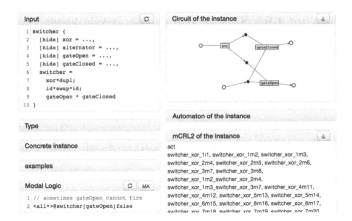

Fig. 5. Screenshot of the Arcatools framework to verify hierarchical Reo connectors.

formula and print the encoded mCRL2 formula, which can be used against the mCRL2 specification. It is also possible to download the tools and run a server locally that will also include the options to invoke mCRL2 tools directly from the browser to verify and visualise the specification.

5   Conclusions and Future Work

This paper presents an approach to reason about the behaviour of connectors built in a modular way. We empower the hierarchical structure of this construction, and propose a model that focuses on the containers of sub-connectors rather than on their interfaces. An action in the evolution of this model consists of a set of containers that interact with its neighbours at a given moment in time. We claim that this perspective over hierarchical connectors facilitates the writing and verification of properties of complex connectors.

In the future we plan to further explore the dedicated logic for hierarchical connectors. On one hand, we plan to exploit the existence of internal actions at different levels, leading to notions of weak and strong modalities and to new notions of behavioural equivalences. On the other hand, we plan to formalise the encodings described in Sect. 4, and to prove relevant results over our constructions, such as the preservation of behaviour during container abstractions.

Acknowledgements. This work is financed by the ERDF—European Regional Development Fund through the Operational Programme for Competitiveness and Internationalisation—COMPETE 2020 Programme and by National Funds through the Portuguese funding agency, FCT—Fundação para a Ciência e a Tecnologia, within projects POCI-01-0145-FEDER-029946 (1st author) and POCI-01-0145-FEDER-016692 (2nd author), in the scope of the framework contract foreseen in the numbers 4, 5 and 6 of article 23, of Decree-Law 57/2016, of August 29, changed by Portuguese Law 57/2017, July 19.

References

1. Arbab, F.: Reo: a channel-based coordination model for component composition. Math. Struct. Comput. Sci. **14**(3), 329–366 (2004)
2. Baier, C., Sirjani, M., Arbab, F., Rutten, J.J.M.M.: Modeling component connectors in Reo by constraint automata. Sci. Comput. Program. **61**(2), 75–113 (2006)
3. Cruz, R., Proença, J.: ReoLive: analysing connectors in your browser. In: Mazzara, M., Ober, I., Salaün, G. (eds.) STAF 2018. LNCS, vol. 11176, pp. 336–350. Springer, Cham (2018). https://doi.org/10.1007/978-3-030-04771-9_25
4. Groote, J.F., Mathijssen, A., Reniers, M., Usenko, Y., van Weerdenburg, M.: The formal specification language mCRL2. In: Brinksma, E., Harel, D., Mader, A., Stevens, P., Wieringa, R. (eds.) Methods for Modelling Software Systems (MMOSS), number 06351 in Dagstuhl Seminar Proceedings. Schloss Dagstuhl - Leibniz-Zentrum für Informatik, Germany (2007)
5. Jensen, K., Kristensen, L.M.: Coloured Petri Nets. Springer, Heidelberg (2009). https://doi.org/10.1007/b95112
6. Koehler, C., Clarke, D.: Decomposing port automata. In: Proceedings SAC 2009, pp. 1369–1373. New York, NY, USA, ACM (2009)
7. Kokash, N., Krause, C., de Vink, E.P.: Reo + mCRL2: a framework for model-checking dataflow in service compositions. FAC **24**(2), 187–216 (2012)
8. Proença, J., Clarke, D.: Typed connector families and their semantics. Sci. Comput. Program. **146**, 28–49 (2017)

Service Orchestration with Priority Constraints

Behnaz Changizi[1], Natallia Kokash[2(✉)], and Farhad Arbab[3]

[1] Leiden Institute of Advanced Computer Science,
Niels Bohrweg 1, Leiden, The Netherlands
behnaz.changizi@gmail.com

[2] Peoples' Friendship University of Russia (RUDN University),
6 Miklukho-Maklaya Street, Moscow 117198, Russian Federation
natallia.kokash@gmail.com

[3] Centrum Wiskunde & Informatica, Science Park 123, Amsterdam, The Netherlands
farhad.arbab@cwi.nl

Abstract. Business process management is an operational management approach that focuses on improving business processes. Business processes, i.e., collections of important activities in an organization, are represented in the form of a workflow, an orchestrated and repeatable pattern of activities amenable to automated analysis and control. Priority is an important concept in modeling workflows. We need priority to model cancelable and compensable tasks within transactional business processes. We use the Reo coordination language to model and formally analyze workflows. In this paper, we propose a constraint-based approach to formalize priority in Reo. We introduce special channels to propagate and block priority flows, define their semantics as constraints, and model priority propagation as a constraint satisfaction problem.

Keywords: Transaction · Priority · Constraints · Coordination

1 Introduction

Business Process Management (BPM) systems [20,23] are widely used to automate organizational business processes. Organizations rely on BPM to analyze, control or optimize their processes. BPM systems provide means for automated process analysis such as model validation, transformation, simulation, visualization of key performance indicators, and reporting [3]. Despite the variety of BPM systems [21,29], The foundation of BPMN is based on Petri Nets [1,32]. The choice of Petri Nets as foundation for BPMN implementation over other formal methods, often more expressive or specialized [13,14], is not surprising: hardly any model is as simple, intuitive, and naturally supports task traceability.

While Petri net-based models enable automated process analysis, they lack a few desirable characteristics: (i) They cannot naturally represent semantics

© IFIP International Federation for Information Processing 2019
Published by Springer Nature Switzerland AG 2019
H. Hojjat and M. Massink (Eds.): FSEN 2019, LNCS 11761, pp. 194–209, 2019.
https://doi.org/10.1007/978-3-030-31517-7_14

of component-based or service-based processes. Ideally, we would like to plug semantic models for individual components (often integrated dynamically at run time) to the semantic models of existing processes in a compositional way. (ii) The classical Petri Nets are not expressive enough and often are extended (e.g., with colors, reset and inhibitor arcs, priority transitions) to enable meaningful process analysis. Such extensions change the semantics of the model and generate incompatible dialects of process-specification languages adopted by various tools.

An alternative formalization to express the semantics of BPMN models is the Reo coordination language [5]. Reo has been used to formalize semantics of BPMN, UML Activity and Sequence Diagrams [15], to map BPEL fragments [33], to represent transactional workflows [27], and to implement service orchestrations [24] and service choreographies [30]. Reo allows composition of components and services in an intuitive way, and addresses the issue (i) mentioned above. Moreover, the open-ended nature of Reo allows us to introduce channels with specific properties required for some applications. Introducing new primitives may make it necessary to extend the formal semantics of Reo in order to include some new concepts. Several dozen variations of semantic models for Reo have been proposed [25]. They vary from rather simple ones that cover basic Reo behavior (e.g., constraint automata [8]) to more complex models that cover specific behavioral aspects, e.g., context-sensitivity [18]. In some of these models, computing the overall semantics of a system is computationally expensive. This hampers using the language for analyzing large real-world business processes.

In [16], the authors proposed to model the semantics of Reo as a constraint satisfaction problem (CSP). They define data flow in a Reo network in the form of mathematical expressions on data observed at Reo nodes. The main advantage of such representation is the possibility to use existing constraint solvers to infer the behavior of a network given the semantics of its constituent parts.

Priority flow is an important aspect of process modeling, which is not easily supported by existing formalisms. Analyzing compensation and error handling requires a mechanism to express priority of some flow alternatives over others. In this paper, we propose a constraint-based framework for priority flow. There is ongoing work on an existing automata based formal semantics of Reo to handle priority, but our practical needs for dealing with large models of realistic business processes currently complicates direct use of automata-based semantic models.

This paper is organized as follows: In Sect. 2, we briefly describe the Reo coordination language. In Sect. 3, we introduce priority flow in Reo along with a constraint-based semantics for it. In Sect. 4, we extend our approach to support numeric priorities. In Sect. 5, we show the application of our constraint-based approach via two classes of connectors: (a) priority-aware, and (b) connectors with a large number of states. In Sect. 6, we overview related work. Finally, in Sect. 7, we conclude the paper and outline future work.

2   Reo

In the realm of service-oriented computing, the behavior of a software system is not only defined by the functionality of its services, but also by their interactions. The code written to realize the latter is often called *glue code*. Writing and maintaining glue code is a tedious task, especially in complex systems wherein the size and rigidity of the glue code tend to grow over time. Coordination languages offer a more manageable alternative for generating glue code. Reo [5,6] is a channel-based coordination language for composition of software components and services. Using a small and open-ended set of predefined and user-defined constructs, Reo supports modeling of complex coordination behavior.

The primitive constructs in Reo are *channel*s and *node*s, whose composition yields *connector*s. A channel is an atomic connector with two *end*s and a *constraint* that relates the flow of data at these ends. Channel ends are either *source* ends that read data into the channel or *sink* ends that write the channel's data out. Channels can connect to each other through nodes. There are two types of channel ends; therefore, three types of nodes can exist: *source node*s where only source ends coincide, *sink node*s where only sink ends coincide, and *mixed node*s where both source and sink ends coincide. The mixed nodes of a connector are internal to the connector and not accessible for external data exchange. The source and sink nodes of a connector, collectively called its *boundary nodes* or *port*s, are used to connect to (the ports of) components to exchange data. A source node atomically replicates an incoming data items into all of its coincident channel ends, whenever they are all ready to accept. A sink node nondeterministically selects a data item out of one of its coincident channel ends and delivers it as its outgoing data item, leaving all other data items in its coincident channels intact. The behavior of a mixed node is an atomic combination of the behavior of a source node and that of a sink node: whenever all of its coincident source channels ends are ready to accept data items, it selects a data item out of one of its nondeterministically chosen coincident sink channel ends, and atomically replicates it into all of its source channel ends.

A *Sync* channel ⟶ has a source and a sink end. It accepts data from its source iff its sink can dispense it simultaneously. A *LossySync* ⤏ has a source and a sink end. It reads a data item from its source and writes it simultaneously to its sink. If the sink end is not ready to accept the data item, the channel loses it. A *SyncDrain* ⟶⟵ has two source ends and no sink end. It reads data from its two ends and discards it iff the ends are ready to interact simultaneously. A $FIFO_1$ ⟼⟢⟶ has a source end, a sink end, and capacity for only one data item. If it is empty, the channel accepts a data item from its source end and buffers it. If it is full, it is ready to dispense data through its sink end. Both ends of the channel cannot interact simultaneously. In addition to the primitive nodes, *Merger* and *Replicator*, here we use *Router* and *Cross-product*, which are shortcuts for derived connectors. The Reo nodes used in this work are explained as follows: A *Replicator* ⤙ has one source end and one or more sink ends. It replicates data coming from its source to its sinks simultaneously. A *Merger* ⤚ has one or more source ends and one sink end. It chooses one of its

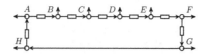

Fig. 1. 7-Sequencer

ready to interat source ends non-deterministically, receives a data item through this end, and writes it to its sink end simultaneously. A *Router* ─◁ has one source end and a number of sink ends. It accepts a data item from its source and simultaneously replicates it on one of its non-deterministically chosen sink, which is ready to accept data. A *Cross-product* ⟩▷ has a number of source ends and a sink end. It accepts a data item from each source, forms a tuple of them in the counter-clock-wise order with respect to its sink, where it writes the tuple, simultaneously.

3   Priority Flow

Here we define four channels to deal with priority in Reo.

A *PrioritySync* ⟶⟶ channel is similar to a *Sync* channel except it imposes priority on its flow, which propagates through the connector (unless it is blocked), and it can influence the non-deterministic choices in the containing connector by favoring data-flow alternatives that incorporate its ends. A *BlockSourceSync* channel ⟶⟶ is a *Sync* channel that blocks the propagation of priority from its source end towards its sink end. A *BlockSinkSync* channel ⟶⟵ is a *Sync* channel that stops propagation of priority from its sink end towards its source end. A *BlockSync* channel ⟶⤬⟵, a combination of *BlockSourceSync* and *BlockSinkSync*, stops the propagation of priority in both ways.

We model priority using the concepts of *innate* and *acquired* priority. Both ends of *priority sync* have *innate* priority. When an end with *innate* priority connects to another end that has no priority, the new end will obtain *acquired* priority. When one end of a synchronous type channel (e.g., *sync*, *lossy sync*, *sync drain*, ...) has *acquired* priority, the other end has *innate* priority.

However, in the case of non-synchronous channels (e.g., *FIFO*, *async drain*) and also the priority blocking channels, their ends can only have *acquired* priority. We update the constraint-based framework for Reo [16] to capture priority and the priority propagation mechanism, which we informally described above. In the rest of this paper, we omit data constraints when defining behavior of Reo elements. Data constraints are irrelevant for priority flow and were thoroughly covered in [16]. Motivated by the *constraint-based* nature of Reo itself, and the fact that constraint solving has advanced to the point that a number of practically useful constraint solvers exist today that can cope with realistically sized problems, we propose to define the behavior of Reo channels, as algebraic constraints that alter a set of variables.

Let $\mathcal{N}$ and $\mathcal{M}$ be global sets of ends and state memory variables, respectively. A free variable v has one of the following forms, where $n \in \mathcal{N}$ and $m \in \mathcal{M}$: $\tilde{n} \in \{\top, \bot\}$ shows presence or absence of data-flow on n; $\mathring{m}, \mathring{m}' \in \{\top, \bot\}$ denotes whether or not the state memory variable m is defined in the source and the target states of the transition, respectively; $n^{\triangleright} \in \{\top, \bot\}$ indicates the reason for lack of data-flow on n originating from the primitive or the context (of this primitive), respectively; $n^{!^{\bullet}}, n^{!^{\circ}} \in \{\top, \bot\}$ models priority flow denoting whether n has *acquired* or *innate* priority. An end n has priority iff $n^{!^{\bullet}} \vee n^{!^{\circ}} = \top$.

A constraint Ψ, which encodes the behavior of a Reo network is defined as: $a:: = \tilde{n} \mid n^{!^{\bullet}} \mid n^{!^{\circ}} \mid n^{\triangleright} \mid \mathring{m} \mid \mathring{m}'$ (atoms), $\Psi:: = \top \mid a \mid \neg\Psi \mid \Psi \wedge \Psi$ (formulae) A solution to Ψ is a map from the variable sets V to a value in $\{\bot, \top\}$. The satisfaction rules for a solution $\langle \delta \rangle$ are satisfaction in propositional logic. We denote the set of all solutions for Ψ as $\mathfrak{S}(\Psi)$.

Definition 1 (RCSP). *A Reo Constraint Satisfaction Problem (RCSP) is a tuple $\langle \mathcal{N}, \mathcal{M}, M_0, V, C \rangle$, where: $\mathcal{N}$ is a finite set of ends. $\mathcal{M}$ is a finite set of state memory variables. $M_0 \subseteq \mathcal{M}$ is a set of state memory variables that define the initial configuration of a network. V is a set of variables v defined by the grammar $v:: = \tilde{n} \mid n^{\triangleright} \mid \mathring{m} \mid \mathring{m}' \mid n^{!^{\circ}} \mid n^{!^{\bullet}}$ for $n \in \mathcal{N}$ and $m \in \mathcal{M}$. $C = \{C_1, C_2, ..., C_m\}$ is a finite set of constraints, where each C_i is a constraint given by the grammar Ψ involving a subset of variables $V_i \subseteq V$.*

Definition 2. (Composition $\odot$). *The composition of two RCSPs $\rho_1 = \langle \mathcal{N}_1, \mathcal{M}_1, M_{0,1}, V_1, C_1 \rangle$ and $\rho_2 = \langle \mathcal{N}_2, \mathcal{M}_2, M_{0,2}, V_2, C_2 \rangle$ is defined as follows: $\rho_1 \odot \rho_2 = \langle \mathcal{N}_1 \cup \mathcal{N}_2, \mathcal{M}_1 \cup \mathcal{M}_2, M_{0,1} \cup M_{0,2}, V_1 \cup V_2, C_1 \wedge C_2 \rangle$.*

Axiom 1 (Join axiom). *To propagate no-flow reasons, when a source end c and a sink end k from two networks, the following holds: $\neg\tilde{c} \Leftrightarrow \neg\tilde{k} \Leftrightarrow (c^{\triangleright} \vee k^{\triangleright})$.*

Axiom 2 (Priority join axiom). *When a source end c and a sink end k from two networks connect, this holds: $(c^{!^{\circ}} \vee c^{!^{\bullet}} \Leftrightarrow k^{!^{\circ}} \vee k^{!^{\bullet}}) \wedge (c^{!^{\circ}} \wedge k^{!^{\circ}} \Leftrightarrow c^{!^{\bullet}} \vee k^{!^{\bullet}})$.*

Axiom 3 (Non-deterministic choice axiom). *Let N be a set of ends from which a Reo primitive chooses one for communication non-deterministically. The following guarantees that a node y with no priority has flow only if no prioritized node, e.g., x, is ready to interact: $(\neg\tilde{x} \wedge (x^{!^{\circ}} \vee x^{!^{\bullet}}) \wedge \tilde{y} \wedge \neg(y^{!^{\circ}} \vee y^{!^{\bullet}})) \Rightarrow \neg x^{\triangleright}$.*

In [16], the authors described the constraints that a primitive imposes on a network as a CSP. We extend these constraints with priority capturing variables. If the variable $p^{!^{\bullet}}$ is *true*, the end p has *innate* priority. For example, in a *PrioritySync* channel, both ends have *innate* priority. A primitive end can also obtain *innate* priority via propagation. For instance, if one end of a *Sync* channel has *acquired* priority, which means it is prioritized because a primitive connected to it propagates priority, then the other end will have *innate* priority. We denote *acquired* priority for a primitive end p as: $p^{!^{\circ}} \wedge \neg p^{!^{\bullet}}$. The priority capturing constraint for a *Sync* channel with source end a and sink end b can be specified as follows: $\neg(a^{!^{\circ}} \vee a^{!^{\bullet}} \vee b^{!^{\circ}} \vee b^{!^{\bullet}}) \vee (a^{!^{\circ}} \wedge \neg a^{!^{\bullet}} \wedge b^{!^{\bullet}}) \vee (a^{!^{\bullet}} \wedge b^{!^{\circ}} \wedge \neg b^{!^{\bullet}})$.

```
1  Input: A Reo network R and its RCSP ψ, Output: Solutions for the given RCSP
2  fifoStates ← initial states of FIFOs from the given RCSP;
3  state₀ ← {⟨ fifoStates ⟩}; toExplore ← {state₀}; visited ← {}; solutions ← {};
4  while (toExplore ≠ {}) do
5  │    state ← toExplore.pop(); visited ← visited ∪ {state};
6  │    cnf ← updateStateAndMakeCNF(ψ, state);
7  │    solutions_B ← solve(cnf);
8  │    for sol_B ∈ solutions_B do
9  │    │    state'← next state of FIFOs extracted from sol_B;
10 │    │    if state' ∉ visited and state' ∉ toExplore then
11 │    │    │    toExplore ← toExplore ∪ {state'};
12 │    │    end
13 │    │    solutions ← solutions ∪ {⟨state, sol_B, state'⟩};
14 │    end
15 │    output ← {solutions, state₀};
16 end
```

Algorithm 1. Finding solutions for a given RCSP

The assertion $\neg p^{!^{\bullet}}$ blocks the priority propagation on p. Though, p can still have *acquired* priority through a potential connecting primitive when $p^{!^{\circ}} = \top$.

Table 1 shows the constraint encoding of Reo channels and nodes in presence of priority flow. The solutions to the CSP expressing the behavior of a Reo network encode possible data-flow through its nodes. Since a network may later connect to another network, the constraints should account for priority imposed by potential future connections. This information can be discarded when analyzing the behavior of a network in isolation. To exclude such cases, we should restrict the possible values of boundary ends.

Axiom 4 (Grounding axiom). *Let $B \subset N$ be the set of boundary nodes in a Reo network. We rule out the solutions that are only present for further expansion of the network by:* $\forall b \in B : b^{!^{\circ}} \Rightarrow b^{!^{\bullet}}$.

Solutions of the RCSP represent semantics of the corresponding Reo network, but they are specified as equations, which are much harder to interpret than an equivalent automata-based semantics. To tackle this issue, we introduce a new form of automata-like semantics for Reo, which we call Reo Labeled Transition System (RLTS). The purpose of the RLTS is to compactly represent solutions of RCSPs for visualization, model checking and simulation. Given a Reo network, its RCSP can be obtained by traversing the network and forming the conjunction the constraint encodings of its primitives. The procedure to solve an RCSP is presented in Algorithm 1. It takes a Reo connector and its RCSP and outputs the solutions set and the initial state of the connector. First, the algorithm initializes the global variables that keep the states of FIFO channels (*fifoStates*), the states to explore (*toExplore*), and the visited states (*visited*) (lines 2,3). While *toExplore* is not empty, Ψ is updated with the current state and its conjunctive normal form (CNF) is produced for computing the solutions of the Boolean predicates (lines 4,5). The ⟨*state'*⟩ indicates the new state of the connector and if it is not already explored or queued to be processed, it gets added to the list of states to be explored (lines 6–9). Then, the solutions set is updated with the current solution (line 13). The final output is the set of solutions and the initial state.

Table 1. Constraint encoding of Reo with priority

Channel	Constraints
a •——!—▸• b	$(\tilde{a} \Leftrightarrow \tilde{b}) \wedge \neg(a^{\triangleright} \wedge b^{\triangleright}) \wedge a^{!^{\bullet}} \wedge b^{!^{\bullet}}$
a •——)—▸• b	$(\tilde{a} \Leftrightarrow \tilde{b}) \wedge \neg(a^{\triangleright} \wedge b^{\triangleright}) \wedge \neg b^{!^{\bullet}}$
a •——(—▸• b	$(\tilde{a} \Leftrightarrow \tilde{b}) \wedge \neg(a^{\triangleright} \wedge b^{\triangleright}) \wedge \neg a^{!^{\bullet}}$
a •——)(—▸• b	$(\tilde{a} \Leftrightarrow \tilde{b}) \wedge \neg(a^{\triangleright} \wedge b^{\triangleright}) \wedge \neg a^{!^{\bullet}} \wedge \neg b^{!^{\bullet}}$
a •———————▸• b	$(\tilde{a} \Leftrightarrow \tilde{b}) \wedge \neg(a^{\triangleright} \wedge b^{\triangleright}) \wedge ((\neg a^{!^{\bullet}} \wedge \neg a^{!^{\circ}} \wedge \neg b^{!^{\bullet}} \wedge \neg b^{!^{\circ}}) \vee ((a^{!^{\circ}} \Rightarrow b^{!^{\bullet}}) \wedge (b^{!^{\circ}} \Rightarrow a^{!^{\bullet}})))$
a •----▸ b	$(\tilde{b} \Rightarrow \tilde{a}) \wedge \neg a^{\triangleright} \wedge \neg \tilde{a} \Rightarrow b^{\triangleright} \wedge ((\neg a^{!^{\bullet}} \wedge \neg a^{!^{\circ}} \wedge \neg b^{!^{\bullet}} \wedge \neg b^{!^{\circ}}) \vee ((a^{!^{\circ}} \Rightarrow b^{!^{\bullet}}) \wedge (b^{!^{\circ}} \Rightarrow a^{!^{\bullet}})))$
a •——▸◂—• b	$(\tilde{a}_1 \Leftrightarrow \tilde{a}_2) \wedge \neg(a_1^{\triangleright} \wedge a_2^{\triangleright}) \wedge ((\neg a^{!^{\bullet}} \wedge \neg a^{!^{\circ}} \wedge \neg b^{!^{\bullet}} \wedge \neg b^{!^{\circ}}) \vee (a^{!^{\circ}} \Rightarrow b^{!^{\bullet}}) \wedge (b^{!^{\circ}} \Rightarrow a^{!^{\bullet}}))$
a •—[ ]—▸ b	$(\tilde{a} \Rightarrow \neg \mathring{m} \wedge m') \wedge (\tilde{b} \Rightarrow \mathring{m} \wedge \neg \mathring{m}') \wedge (\neg \tilde{a} \wedge \neg \tilde{b}) \Rightarrow (\mathring{m} \Leftrightarrow \mathring{m}') \wedge (\neg \mathring{m} \Rightarrow b^{\triangleright}) \wedge (\mathring{m} \Rightarrow u^{\triangleright}) \wedge (\neg u^{!^{\bullet}} \wedge \neg b^{!^{\bullet}})$
a_1 ⊕▸b b◁ a_1 ; a_2 ... a_2	$\tilde{a} \Leftrightarrow (\tilde{b}_1 \wedge \tilde{b}_2) \wedge \neg \tilde{a} \Rightarrow ((\neg a^{\triangleright} \wedge b_1^{\triangleright} \wedge b_2^{\triangleright}) \vee (\neg b_1^{\triangleright} \wedge b_2^{\triangleright} \wedge a^{\triangleright}) \vee (\neg b_2^{\triangleright} \wedge b_1^{\triangleright} \wedge a^{\triangleright})) \wedge ((\neg a^{!^{\bullet}} \wedge \neg b_1^{!^{\bullet}} \wedge \neg b_2^{!^{\bullet}} \wedge \neg a^{!^{\circ}} \wedge \neg b_1^{!^{\circ}} \wedge \neg b_2^{!^{\circ}}) \vee ((a^{!^{\circ}} \Rightarrow (b_1^{!^{\bullet}} \wedge b_2^{!^{\bullet}}) \wedge (b_1^{!^{\circ}} \vee b_2^{!^{\circ}}) \Rightarrow a^{!^{\bullet}})))$
a—⊗ b_1, b_2 ; b_1 ▷a, b_2	$\tilde{a} \Leftrightarrow (\tilde{b}_1 \vee \tilde{b}_2) \wedge \neg(\tilde{b}_1 \wedge \tilde{b}_2) \wedge \tilde{a} \Leftrightarrow (\neg a^{\triangleright} \vee \neg(b_1^{\triangleright} \vee b_2^{\triangleright})) \wedge ((\neg a^{!^{\bullet}} \wedge \neg b_1^{!^{\bullet}} \wedge \neg b_2^{!^{\bullet}} \wedge \neg a^{!^{\circ}} \wedge \neg b_1^{!^{\circ}} \wedge \neg b_2^{!^{\circ}}) \vee (\tilde{a} \Rightarrow ((a^{!^{\circ}} \Rightarrow (b_1^{!^{\bullet}} \vee b_2^{!^{\bullet}})) \wedge (b_1^{!^{\circ}} \vee b_2^{!^{\circ}}) \Rightarrow a^{!^{\bullet}}) \wedge (\tilde{b}_1 \Rightarrow (a^{!^{\circ}} \Rightarrow b_1^{!^{\bullet}} \wedge b_1^{!^{\circ}} \Rightarrow a^{!^{\bullet}}) \wedge ((\neg b_1^{!^{\bullet}} \wedge \neg b_1^{!^{\circ}} \wedge \neg \tilde{b}_2 \wedge (b_2^{!^{\circ}} \vee b_2^{!^{\bullet}})) \Rightarrow \neg b_2^{\triangleright})) \wedge (\tilde{b}_2 \Rightarrow (a^{!^{\circ}} \Rightarrow b_2^{!^{\bullet}} \wedge b_2^{!^{\circ}} \Rightarrow a^{!^{\bullet}} \wedge (\neg b_2^{!^{\circ}} \wedge \neg b_2^{!^{\bullet}} \wedge \neg \tilde{b}_1 \wedge (b_1^{!^{\circ}} \vee b_1^{!^{\bullet}}) \Rightarrow \neg b_1^{\triangleright})))))$

Table 2. Updating Priority capturing constraints

	a •—!$_P$—▸• b $a^{!^{\bullet}} \geq P \wedge b^{!^{\bullet}} \geq P$	a •——)—▸• b $b^{!^{\bullet}} = 0$	a •——(—▸• b $a^{!^{\bullet}} = 0$	a •——)(—▸• b $a^{!^{\bullet}} = 0 \wedge b^{!^{\bullet}} = 0$	a —[ ]—▸ b $a^{!^{\bullet}} = 0 \wedge b^{!^{\bullet}} = 0$
a •----▸ b	$(a^{!^{\bullet}} = 0 \wedge a^{!^{\circ}} = 0 \wedge b^{!^{\bullet}} = 0 \wedge b^{!^{\circ}} = 0) \vee ((a^{!^{\circ}} > 0 \Rightarrow (a^{!^{\circ}} = b^{!^{\bullet}})) \wedge (b^{!^{\circ}} > 0 \Rightarrow (b^{!^{\circ}} = a^{!^{\bullet}}))) \wedge (b^{!^{\circ}} > 0 \Rightarrow \tilde{b})$				
a •———▸• b ; a •—▸◂—• b ; a —[ ]—▸ b	$(a^{!^{\bullet}} = 0 \wedge a^{!^{\circ}} = 0 \wedge b^{!^{\bullet}} = 0 \wedge b^{!^{\circ}} = 0) \vee ((a^{!^{\circ}} > 0 \Rightarrow (a^{!^{\circ}} = b^{!^{\bullet}})) \wedge (b^{!^{\circ}} > 0 \Rightarrow (b^{!^{\circ}} = a^{!^{\bullet}})))$ $a^{!^{\bullet}} = 0 \wedge b^{!^{\bullet}} = 0$				
a_1 ⊕▸b a_2 ; b◁ a_1 a_2	$((a^{!^{\bullet}} = 0 \wedge a^{!^{\circ}} = 0 \wedge b^{!^{\bullet}} = 0 \wedge b^{!^{\circ}} = 0) \vee ((b^{!^{\circ}} > 0 \Rightarrow (a_1^{!^{\bullet}} = b^{!^{\circ}} \wedge a_2^{!^{\bullet}} = b^{!^{\circ}})) \wedge (a_1^{!^{\circ}} > 0 \Rightarrow (a_2^{!^{\bullet}} = a_1^{!^{\circ}} \wedge b^{!^{\bullet}} = a_1^{!^{\circ}}) \wedge (a_2^{!^{\circ}} > 0 \Rightarrow (a_1^{!^{\bullet}} = a_2^{!^{\circ}} \wedge b^{!^{\bullet}} = a_2^{!^{\circ}})))))$				
a—⊗ b_1 b_2 ; b_1 ▷a b_2	$((a^{!^{\bullet}} = 0 \wedge a^{!^{\circ}} = 0 \wedge b^{!^{\bullet}} = 0 \wedge b^{!^{\circ}} = 0) \vee (\tilde{b}_1 \Rightarrow (b_1^{!^{\circ}} > 0 \Rightarrow (b_1^{!^{\circ}} = a^{!^{\bullet}}))) \wedge (\tilde{b}_2 \Rightarrow (b_2^{!^{\circ}} > 0 \Rightarrow (b_2^{!^{\circ}} = a^{!^{\bullet}}))) \wedge ((max(b_1^{!^{\circ}}, b_1^{!^{\bullet}}) > max(b_2^{!^{\circ}}, b_2^{!^{\bullet}})) \Rightarrow ((\tilde{b}_2 \wedge \neg \tilde{b}_1) \Rightarrow \neg b_2^{\triangleright})) \wedge ((max(b_2^{!^{\circ}}, b_2^{!^{\bullet}}) > max(b_1^{!^{\circ}}, b_1^{!^{\bullet}})) \Rightarrow ((\tilde{b}_1 \wedge \neg \tilde{b}_2) \Rightarrow \neg b_2^{\triangleright})))$				

Definition 3 (RLTS). *A Reo Labeled Transition System (RLTS) is a tuple $\mathcal{RLTS}=(\mathcal{N},\ \mathcal{M},\ Q,\ \rightarrow,\ q_0)$, where: $\mathcal{N}$ is a set of ends, $\mathcal{M}$ is a set of state memory variables, Q is a (finite) set of states of the form $\langle M \rangle$, M is the set of state memory variables that are valid in the given state, $\rightarrow\ \subseteq Q \times 2^{\mathcal{N}} \times 2^{\mathcal{N}} \times 2^{\mathcal{N}} \times Q$ is a transition relation, wherein N, R, and I in $(q,\ N,\ R,\ I,\ p) \in \rightarrow$ represent the ends that have flow, those without flow for which the reason for no flow is the end not being ready for interaction, and the ends with priority. Note that $n \notin N$ does not always mean $n \in R$ as the reason for data flow can be the network (then, n requires a reason for no flow). $q_0 \in Q$ is the initial state. We write $q \xrightarrow{N,\ R,\ I} p$ instead of $(q,\ N,\ R,\ I,\ p) \in \ \rightarrow$. For $n \in I, n \notin R \Leftrightarrow n \in N$.*

Definition 4 (Composition ▢). *We define the composition of $L_1 = (\mathfrak{N}_1,\ \mathcal{M}_1,\ Q_1,\ \rightarrow_1,\ q_{0_1})$ and $L_2 = (\mathfrak{N}_2,\ \mathcal{M}_2,\ Q_2,\ \rightarrow_2,\ q_{0_2})$ as: $L_1 \ ▢\ L_2 = (\mathcal{N}_1 \cup \mathcal{N}_2,\ \mathcal{M}_1 \cup \mathcal{M}_2,\ \rightarrow,\ q_{0_1} \times q_{0_2})$ where $\rightarrow$ is defined as:*

$$\frac{q_1 \xrightarrow{N_1,R_1,I_1}_1 t_1 q_2 \xrightarrow{N_2,R_2,I_2}_2 t_2 \ N_1 \cap \mathfrak{N}_2 = N_2 \cap \mathfrak{N}_1 \ R_1 \cap \mathfrak{N}_2 = R_2 \cap \mathfrak{N}_1 \ I_1 \cap \mathfrak{N}_2 = I_2 \cap \mathfrak{N}_1}{q_1 \times q_2 \xrightarrow{N_1 \cup N_2, R_1 \cup R_2, I_1 \cup I_2} t_1 \times t_2}$$

$$\frac{q_1 \xrightarrow{N_1,R_1,I_1}_1 t_1 q_2 \xrightarrow{N_2,R_2,I_2}_2 t_2 \ N_1 \cap \mathfrak{N}_2 = \emptyset}{q_1 \times q_2 \xrightarrow{N_1,R_1,I_1} t_1 \times t_2},\ \text{and its symmetric rule.}$$

We define few operations on a solution s for $\Psi = \langle \mathcal{N}_\Psi, \mathcal{M}_\Psi, M_{\Psi 0}, \mathcal{V}_\Psi, C_\Psi \rangle$: $\text{source}(s)=\langle\{m | m^\circ \in \mathcal{M}_\Psi : s(m^\circ) = \top\}\rangle$, $\text{target}(s)=\langle\{m | m'^\circ \in \mathcal{M}_\Psi : s(m'^\circ) = \top\}\rangle$, $\text{flow}(s)=\{n | n \in \mathcal{N}_\Psi : s(\tilde{n}) = \top\}$, $\text{reason-giving}(s)=\{n | n \in \mathcal{N}_\Psi : s(n^\triangleright) = \top\}$, $\text{priority}(s)=\{n | n \in \mathcal{N}_\Psi : (s(n^{!^\circ}) \vee s(n^{!^\bullet})) = \top\}$. We say $s \curvearrowright q \xrightarrow{N,R,I} p$, where q $= \text{source}(s)$, N $= \text{flow}(s)$, R=reason-giving(s), I $= \text{priority}(s)$, p $= \text{target}(s)$.

Definition 5 (Visualization). *The visualization function γ on $\Psi = \langle \mathcal{N}, \mathcal{M}, M_0, \mathcal{V}, C \rangle$ yields $\mathcal{L}=(\mathcal{N},\ \mathcal{M},\ Q,\ \rightarrow,\ q_0)$, where $\mathcal{M} = \{m | s(m^\circ) = \top \vee s(m'^\circ) = \top, s \in \mathfrak{S}(\Psi)\}$, $Q = \bigcup_{s \in \mathfrak{S}(\Psi)} \{source(s),\ target(s)\}$, $\rightarrow = \{(source(s),\ flow(s),\ reason\text{-}giving(s),\ priority(s),\ target(s))\ |s \in \mathfrak{S}(\Psi)\}$, $q_0 = source(s_0)$.*

Theorem 1. *Let Ψ_1 and Ψ_2 be two RCSPs, we show that $\gamma(\Psi_1 \odot \Psi_2) = \gamma(\Psi_1) \ ▢ \ \gamma(\Psi_2)$.*

Proof. Let $\gamma(\Psi_1)=(\mathfrak{N}_1, \mathcal{M}_1, Q_1, \rightarrow_1, q_{0_1})$, $\gamma(\Psi_2) = (\mathfrak{N}_2, \mathcal{M}_2, Q_2, \rightarrow_2, q_{0_2})$, and $\gamma(\Psi_1 \ \odot \ \Psi_2) = (\mathfrak{N}, Q, \rightarrow, q_0)$. It is trivial to see that $\mathfrak{N} = \mathfrak{N}_1 \cup \mathfrak{N}_2$, $\mathcal{M} = \mathcal{M}_1 \cup \mathcal{M}_2$, $Q = Q_1 \times Q_2$, $q_0 = q_{0_1} \times q_{0_2}$. Assume $\exists s \in \mathfrak{S}(\Psi_1 \odot \Psi_2)$, $s_1, \in \mathfrak{S}_1$, $s_2 \in \mathfrak{S}_2$, $t_1 : q_1 \xrightarrow{N_1,R_1,I_1}_1 p_1$, $t_2 : q_2 \xrightarrow{N_2,R_2,I_2}_2 p_2$ s.t. $s_1 \curvearrowright t_1$ and $s_2 \curvearrowright t_2$, but $\nexists \ t : q \xrightarrow{N,R,I} p \in \rightarrow$ s.t. $s \curvearrowright t$. Therefore, $N_1 \cap \mathfrak{N}_2 \neq N_2 \cap \mathfrak{N}_1 \wedge N_1 \cap \mathfrak{N}_2 \neq \emptyset$ or $(N_1 \cup N_2) \cap (R_1 \cup R_2) \neq \emptyset$. The latter is impossible. For the former, either $n \in N_1, n \notin N_2$ or $n \in N_2, n \notin N_1$, which is not possible as it means $s(n) = \top \wedge s(n) = \bot$. Similarly, we can show it is impossible to have a t in $\gamma(\Psi_1 \odot \Psi_2)$, when there is no $s \in \mathfrak{S}$ s.t. $s \curvearrowright t$.

RLTS is comparable with *Reo automata* [12], a context-dependent formal semantic of Reo. A transition in *Reo automata* is labeled with a *guard*, which is a

Boolean predicate in disjunctive normal form expressing positive and negative information about presence or absence of I/O requests, and a *firing* set that models the occurring I/O operations in the transition. The second set in RLTS transitions (the set of ends that provide reason for no flow) correspond to the negated elements of the guards in *Reo automata*, while the set of ends with flow relates to both the *firing* set and the positive elements of the guards. Unlike *Reo automata*, RLTS supports priority.

4   Numeric Priority

In BPMN, an *error* event has the highest priority, and the *exception* has priority over the normal flow. In this extension, the range for priority variables of an end n, $n^{!^\circ}$ and $n^{!^\bullet}$, is $\mathbb{N}$ (natural numbers) $\cup \{0\}$, where 0 indicates no priority. The larger number is the higher priority it represents. Each *PrioritySync* channel comes with a user defined priority value, which propagates through its ends. To propagation of a higher priority over a lower priority or no priority, we constrain priority variables to be greater than or equal to their initial values. Table 2 shows the priority related parts of the Reo constructs constraints. $\langle \delta \rangle \vDash x \geq P$ iff $\delta(x) \geq P$, $\langle \delta \rangle \vDash x > P$ iff $\delta(x) > P$, $\langle \delta \rangle \vDash x = P$ iff $\delta(x) = P$, where $x \in \{x^{!^\bullet}, x^{!^\circ}\}$, $P \in \mathbb{N} \cup \{0\}$. The new constraint-based encodings of the *replicator* and *router* nodes in this table are constructed in accordance with Axiom 3.

Definition 6 (NPRLTS). *A Numeric Priority Reo Labeled Transition System is a tuple ($\mathcal{N}$, $\mathcal{M}$, Q, $\rightarrow$, q_0), where: $\mathcal{N}$ is a set of ends, $\mathcal{M}$ is a set of state memory variables, Q is a (finite) set of states of the form $\langle M \rangle$, M is the set of state memory variables that are valid in the given state, $\rightarrow \subseteq Q \times 2^{\mathcal{N}} \times 2^{\mathcal{N}} \times \mathcal{N} \mapsto \mathbb{N} \times Q$ is a transition relation, wherein N, R, and f_I in (q, N, R, f_I, p) $\in \rightarrow$ are the ends having flow, those without flow for which the reason for no flow is the end not being ready for interaction, and a partial map of nodes with priority to their priority values, respectively. $q_0 \in Q$ is the initial state. We write $q \xrightarrow{N,R,f_I} p$ instead of (q, N, R, f_I, p) $\in \rightarrow$. For all $q \xrightarrow{N,R,f_I} p$: $f(n) > 0, n \notin N \Leftrightarrow n \in R$. We redefine priority($s$) as $\{(n, p) | n \in \mathcal{N}_\Psi : s(n^{!^\circ}) = p \vee s(n^{!^\bullet}) = p\}$.*

Definition 7 (Extended Visualization). *The visualization function γ on $\Psi = \langle \mathcal{N}_\Psi, \mathcal{M}_\Psi, M_{\Psi_0}, V, C \rangle$ yields $\mathcal{L} = (\mathcal{N}_L, \mathcal{M}_L, Q, \rightarrow, q_0)$, where $\mathcal{N}_L = \{n | s(\tilde{n}) = \top, s \in \mathfrak{S}(\Psi)\}$, $\mathcal{M}_L = \{m | s(m^\circ) = \top \vee s(m^{!\circ}) = \top, s \in \mathfrak{S}(\Psi)\}$, $Q = \bigcup_{s \in \mathfrak{S}(\Psi)} \{source(s), target(s)\}$, $\rightarrow = \{(source(s), flow(s), reason\text{-}giving(s), priority(s), target(s)) \mid s \in \mathfrak{S}(\Psi)\}$, $q_0 = source(s_0)$.*

5   Case Study

Here we demonstrate the application of our approach via an example and present a performance evaluation of our approach. Figure 2(a) depicts a sales process, which starts by receiving an order. It proceeds by reserving the ordered items for the customer. Then, the customer gets charged and her account is updated. Meanwhile if the payment encounters a problem, a *cancellation* event is triggered, which causes compensation for all of the performed activities. However, if an *error* event occurs, all tasks inside the transaction stop, the *boundary error catch* event redirects the flow to notifying the operator. Finally, if no problem occurs, the ordered items are shipped and the process ends.

Figure 2(c) shows a Reo network that simulates this process. The process starts by reading a token from the *writer* W_2, which resembles receiving an order. Though a Reo network can be used for modeling infinite data flow, in the BPMN standard, when a *start* event is triggered, a new instance of the process is instantiated. Therefore, the Reo network is designed to handle only one request. The end A_1 reads a token from the writer W_2 and directs it to *replicator* node B, which duplicates the token and forwards them to the BC and BE $FIFO_1$ channels. The token from BC continues to the CD $FIFO_1$ channel. If the payment succeeds, the flow from CD and BE $FIFO_1$ channels merge and a token enters the FG $FIFO_1$ channel. Then, it gets consumed by the *reader* R_3.

If the payment fails, performed activities need to be compensated. A token from W_1 simulates a payment failure, so the process needs to be canceled. The *prioritySync* channel IJ imposes a priority of *one* on the failure associated flow. The node J replicates the failure token into the *lossySync* channels JM and JU, depending on whether each of the $FIFO_1$ channels BC and CD is empty or full, the connected *lossySync* channels lose the incoming tokens or pass them to the adjacent *syncDrain* to consume the tokens of $FIFO_1$ channels, respectively. At the same time, the *replicator* node J writes into the $FIFO_1$ channels JK and JN, which simulate *cancel reservation* and *undo changes* tasks, respectively. The flow corresponding to *error*, starting from the *writer* W_3, is structurally similar to the failure flow, but it has a priority of 2 due to SQ *PrioritySync*.

To analyze the presented BPMN process, we convert it to a Reo network. The core mapping is presented in [7,17], which maps a *task* to a $FIFO_1$ channel, while it converts *message*, *cancel*, and *error* events to *writer* components simulating the incoming flows from the environment. A diverging *parallel* gateway is mapped to a *replicator*, while a converging *parallel* gateway is mapped to a *join*. The *sequence flows* are converted into *sync* channels. The mapping of *exception* and *error* handling flows are more complex and are presented in [27].

In this example, the *error* handling flow has the highest priority, while the *exception* handling has the medium priority, and the *success* flow has no priority. The choice between these three alternative flows is made by the *routers*. We obtain the NPRLTS as follows: First, we form the RCSP of the network by traversing through its primitives. Then, we solve the obtained RCSP and extract transitions from obtained solutions, as described in Algorithm 1.

To show the effect of priority on our example, we first investigate the behavior of the network in absence of priority, wherein the normal flow of the process can continue even in case of a payment failure. This is because the *router* node E chooses one of its outgoing flows non-deterministically. The following assets a priority-respecting routing of these alternative flows. $(\{BE\} \in source(t) \land (C_1 \in$

$flow(t) \lor E_1 \in flow(t))) \Rightarrow ((W_3 \notin reason-giving(t) \Leftrightarrow W_3 \in flow(t)) \land (W_3 \in reason - giving(t) \land W_1 \notin reason - giving(t)) \Leftrightarrow W_1 \in flow(t)).$

A typical way of verifying this property is to check it against the NPRLTS of the network. The given property is straight forward to check. Due to the number of ends in this example, the transition labels of the NPRLTS are lengthy. Thus for brevity, we apply an abstraction on the original NPRLTS, which leads to a more concise and readable model. To address a node end, we append a number index to the node name (e.g., B_1). We refer to a channel using the name of the nodes connected to its ends (e.g., BC). Similarly, we append a number index to a channel name to denote a channel end (e.g., BC_1). In addition, we group the ends with a similar name e.g., $B_{1,2}$ (referring to ends B_1 and B_2).

Since, the property solely mentions the ends C_1, E_1, W_1, and W_3 on the transitions originating from the states where $BE\ FIFO_1$ channel is full, we abstract from the rest of the ends in those transitions and from all the ends in other transitions. It is straight-forward to see that this abstraction does not affect the correctness of the validation due to the nature of the property.

Figure 2(b) shows the abstract NPRLTS of the network of Fig. 2(c) in absence of priority. The property that we are interested to check is that if from any state wherein BE holds, W_3 has flow unless it provides a reason for no flow itself, and if W_3 provides a reason for no flow, W_1 has flow unless it provides a reason for no flow itself. This property, however, does not hold on the current NPRLTS as it contains transitions originating from states $\{BC, BE\}$ and $\{CD, BE\}$, wherein either W_3 is absent in R (the set of ends providing a reason for now flow), yet it is not in N (the set of ends with data flow) or W_3 is in R, but W_1 is not in R, yet it is not in N.

Here we show how considering priority constraints rules out these transitions. We reason about one of the transitions (the transition from $\{BC, BE\}$ to $\{CD, BE\}$ with $N = \{C_1, ...\}$, $R = \{W_1, ...\}$). Similar reasonings hold for the rest.

$$0: \frac{\exists t \in NPRLTS: C_1 \in N(t), W_1 \in R(t), W_3 \notin N(t), W_3 \notin R(t)}{\exists\ s \in \mathfrak{S}(\Psi)\ s.t.\ s \Rightarrow \tilde{C_1} \land \neg \tilde{W_3} \land W_1{}^{\triangleright} \land \neg W_3{}^{\triangleright}}$$

$$1: \frac{0 \& \Psi_{PrioritySync_1}(SQ_{1,2})\ \&\ priority\ join\ on\ the\ network}{C_3^{!^\circ}=1},$$

$$2: \frac{0 \& \Psi_{PrioritySync_2}(IJ_{1,2})\ \&\ priority\ join\ on\ the\ network}{C_4^{!^\circ}=2}, \quad 3: \frac{2; \Psi_{router}(C_{1,2,3,4})}{\tilde{C_1} \land \neg \tilde{C_4} \Rightarrow C_4{}^{\triangleright}},$$

$$4: \frac{0\ \&\ join}{\neg \tilde{C_4}}, \quad 5: \frac{coloring\ \&\ join}{C_4{}^{\triangleright} \Rightarrow W_3{}^{\triangleright}},, \quad 6: \frac{0\ \&\ 3\ \&\ 4\ \&5}{W_3{}^{\triangleright}}, \quad 7: \frac{0\ \&\ 5}{\perp}$$

This disproves the existence of the aforementioned transition meaning that when $\{BC\}$ and $\{BE\}$ are full, the request from W_1 is not ignored.

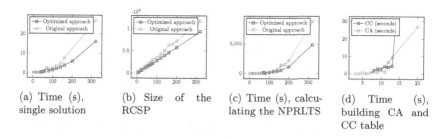

(a) Time (s), single solution

(b) Size of the RCSP

(c) Time (s), calculating the NPRLTS

(d) Time (s), building CA and CC table

Fig. 2. Performance evaluation of N-Sequencers

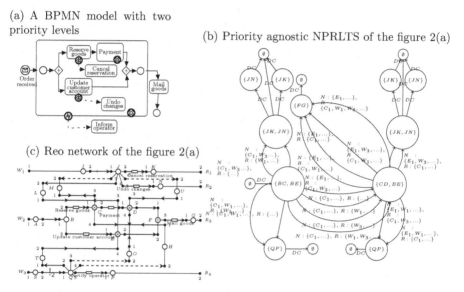

(a) A BPMN model with two priority levels

(b) Priority agnostic NPRLTS of the figure 2(a)

(c) Reo network of the figure 2(a)

The execution time of the Algorithm 1 depends on the number of states of the RCSP and the time to solve the RCSP. Thus, to study the performance of our framework and to compare it with the existing approaches, we choose *N-Sequencer*, which consists of N FIFO channels that are circularly connected. Adding each $FIFO_1$ channel doubles the number of states in the corresponding semantic model and increases the complexity of the constraints encoding the behavior of the network by adding new variables and new assertions on them. This makes the network a good choice for our benchmarking, where we would like to compare the solutions on state explosion. Since we are interested in comparing our approach with the existing tools, we do not include priority in our case study. This is justified by the fact that incorporating priority does not affect the number of states in the model and influences only the size of the constraint. In addition, adding more $FIFO_1$ channels to the network increases both the number of states and the size of the constraint capturing the semantics of the network. Since we use optimized third-library tools to solve the constraints, we do not distinguish between the various form of constraints obtained from different channels and instead we observe the approximate growth of the size of constraints.

Figure 1 shows a *7-sequencer*. Though the size of the operational semantics model of this network grows in a linear fashion in relation with N, the number of intermediate states to compute the final results grows exponentially. The benchmarks have been performed on Mac Book Pro OS X El Capitan with 2.8 GHz Intel Core i7 and 16 GB MHz DDR3 memory. Our approach is implemented in Java 8. We have used Reduce Algebra System revision number 2337 to compute the conjunctive normal form of the constraints and to solve them. We have experimented with an optimization on the number of variables used in the constraints by substituting equal variables with a single variable. Figure 2(a) presents the average time to compute a single solution of the RCSP of an *N-Sequencer*. Figure 2(b) shows the relation between N and the size of the RCSP's constraints of an *N-Sequencer*. This is an indication of the complexity of the constraint. Figure 2(c) illustrates the total time required to compute all solutions of a RCSP's constraint of an *N-Sequencer*. Figure 2(d) shows the time consumed to calculate the coloring semantics and the constraint automata semantics of *N-Sequencers* using the ECT toolset. The computation of the coloring semantics and the constraint automata fail with the stack overflow error for $N = 16$ and $N = 21$, respectively. The results shows that our approach handles larger models than the existing tools can. The effect of the optimization is more significant for larger N.

6   Related Work

Several works, e.g., [10,11,22] use priorities to model scheduling policies. Many workflow languages rely on Petri nets [2,4]. Priority flow in Petri net-based process models is managed with the help of inhibitor arcs and transition priorities [31]. Inhibitor arcs allow a transition to fire only if the adjacent place is empty. *Prioritized Petri nets* [9] introduce a partial order on transitions. Given a set of enabled transitions, the transitions with higher priority fire before the transitions with lower priority. Others, e.g., [28,34] use a partial order on transitions to model priority. Our earlier approach in modeling priority using binary variables supports a limited form of priority compared to the mentioned Petri nets approaches. However, the proposed extension bridges this gap by defining priorities as non-zero natural numbers. An advantage of our model is its compositionality. Compared to the aforementioned methods, Reo fits in the realm of component-based or service-oriented architecture in a compositional way. Reo is an extensible language, where new behavioral aspects can be added. An effort to express the behavior of Reo networks via constraints is reported in [19]. It demonstrates the efficiency of the constraint-based approach. It models synchronization and data flow constraints, but no priority flow was considered. In [16], a framework is presented to encode semantics of Reo networks as CSP with predicates in the form of binary propositions and numerical constraints. An advantage of this method is handling data constraints symbolically and, hence, mitigating the state explosion problem of automata models. We extended this framework to handle priority constraints, taking a step forward toward implementing a toolset that covers all behavioral aspects of Reo. Among the formal semantics of Reo, connector coloring comes with a limited notion of priority based on the context information. The context information affects otherwise non-deterministic data-flow choices. In [26], an automata-based semantics is proposed, which associates a preference for each transitions. A transition of lower preference is fired iff no more preferred transition can occur.

7 Conclusions and Future Work

In this paper, we addressed the problem of priority flow modelling using the Reo coordination language. We extended the unified constraint-based semantics of Reo with binary and numeric priority constraints, showed correctness of our approach for the binary case and evaluated the performance of the algorithm for solving the RCSP to derive the semantics of a Reo network given the behavior of its consituent elements. We also illustrated the use of our framework for modeling business processes with priority flow.

As part of our ongoing work, we are using this framework to encode other aspects of the semantics of Reo, specifically, timed behavior. A promising area for future work is to use our framework for constraint-based model checking of Reo networks with priority.

Acknowledgements. The publication has been prepared with the support of the "RUDN University Program 5–100" and funded by RFBR according to the research projects No. 12-34-56789 and No. 12-34-56789

References

1. Aalst, W.M.P.: Business process management demystified: a tutorial on models, systems and standards for workflow management. In: Desel, J., Reisig, W., Rozenberg, G. (eds.) ACPN 2003. LNCS, vol. 3098, pp. 1–65. Springer, Heidelberg (2004). https://doi.org/10.1007/978-3-540-27755-2_1
2. van der Aalst, W.M.P., ter Hofstede, A.H.M.: Yawl: yet another workflow language. Inf. Syst. **30**(4), 245–275 (2005)
3. van der Aalst, W.M.P., ter Hofstede, A.H.M., Weske, M.: Business process management: a survey. In: van der Aalst, W.M.P., Weske, M. (eds.) BPM 2003. LNCS, vol. 2678, pp. 1–12. Springer, Heidelberg (2003). https://doi.org/10.1007/3-540-44895-0_1
4. van der Aalst, W., Hofstede, A.H.M.T.: Workflow Patterns: On the Expressive Power of (Petri-net-based) Workflow Languages. Technical Report DAIMI PB-560 (2002)
5. Arbab, F.: Reo: a channel-based coordination model for component composition. Math. Struct. in Comput. Sci. **14**, 329–366 (2004)
6. Arbab, F.: Puff, the magic protocol. In: Formal Modeling: Actors, Open Systems, Biological Systems - Essays Dedicated to Carolyn Talcott on the Occasion of Her 70th Birthday. pp. 169–206 (2011)

7. Arbab, F., Kokash, N., Meng, S.: Towards using reo for compliance-aware business process modeling. In: ISoLA. pp. 108–123 (2008)
8. Baier, C., Sirjani, M., Arbab, F., Rutten, J.J.M.M.: Modeling component connectors in reo by constraint automata. Sci. Comput. Program. **61**(2), 75–113 (2006)
9. Balbo, G.: Introduction to stochastic petri nets. In: Brinksma, E., Hermanns, H., Katoen, J.-P. (eds.) EEF School 2000. LNCS, vol. 2090, pp. 84–155. Springer, Heidelberg (2001). https://doi.org/10.1007/3-540-44667-2_3
10. Bause, F.: Analysis of petri nets with a dynamic priority method. In: Azéma, P., Balbo, G. (eds.) ICATPN 1997. LNCS, vol. 1248, pp. 215–234. Springer, Heidelberg (1997). https://doi.org/10.1007/3-540-63139-9_38
11. Best, E., Koutny, M.: Petri net semantics of priority systems. Theor. Comput. Sci. **96**(1), 175–215 (1992)
12. Bonsangue, M., Clarke, D., Silva, A.: A model of context-dependent component connectors. Sci. Comput. Program. **77**(6), 685–706 (2012)
13. Bruni, R., Melgratti, H., Montanari, U.: Theoretical foundations for compensations in flow composition languages. In: Proceedings of the 32nd ACM SIGPLAN-SIGACT Symposium on Principles of Programming Languages. ACM (2005)
14. Butler, M., Hoare, T., Ferreira, C.: A trace semantics for long-running transactions. In: Proceedings of the International Conference on Communicating Sequential Processes: The First 25 Years. CSP 2004 (2005)
15. Changizi, B., Kokash, N., Arbab, F.: A unified toolset for business process model formalization. In: Proceedings of Formal Engineering Approaches to Software Components and Architectures. ENTCS, Elsevier (2010)
16. Changizi, B., Kokash, N., Arbab, F.: A constraint-based method to compute semantics of channel-based coordination models. In: Proceedings of the International Conference on Software Engineering Advances (ICSEA). IARIA (2012)
17. Changizi, B., Kokash, N., Arbab, F.: A unified toolset for business process model formalization. In: 7th International Workshop on Formal Engineering approaches to Software Components and Architectures (FESCA 2010), pp. 147–156. ENTCS (2010)
18. Clarke, D., Costa, D., Arbab, F.: Connector colouring I: synchronisation and context dependency. Sci. Comput. Program. **66**(3), 205–225 (2007)
19. Clarke, D., Proenca, J., Lazovik, A., Arbab, F.: Channel-based coordination via constraint satisfaction. Sci. Comput. Program. **76**(8), 681–710 (2011)
20. Dijkman, R., Hofstetter, J., Koehler, J. (eds.): BPMN 2011. LNBIP, vol. 95. Springer, Heidelberg (2011). https://doi.org/10.1007/978-3-642-25160-3
21. Dumas, M., Rosa, M.L., Mendling, J., Reijers, H.A.: Fundamentals of Business Process Management. Springer, Berlin (2013). https://doi.org/10.1007/978-3-662-56509-4
22. Füricht, R., Prähofer, H., Hofinger, T., Altmann, J.: A component-based application framework for manufacturing execution systems in c# and.net. In: Proceedings of the Fortieth International Conference on Tools Pacific: Objects for Internet, Mobile and Embedded Applications, pp. 169–178. CRPIT 2002, Australian Computer Society, Inc. (2002)
23. Havey, M.: Essential Business Process Modeling. O'Reilly Media Inc., Newton (2005)
24. Jongmans, S.-S.T.Q., Santini, F., Sargolzaei, M., Arbab, F., Afsarmanesh, H.: Automatic code generation for the orchestration of web services with Reo. In: De Paoli, F., Pimentel, E., Zavattaro, G. (eds.) ESOCC 2012. LNCS, vol. 7592, pp. 1–16. Springer, Heidelberg (2012). https://doi.org/10.1007/978-3-642-33427-6_1

25. Jongmans, S., Arbab, F.: Overview of thirty semantic formalisms for Reo. Sci. Ann. Comput. Sci. **22**, 201–251 (2012)

26. Kappé, T., Arbab, F., Talcott, C.L.: A compositional framework for preference-aware agents. In: Proceedings of the The First Workshop on Verification and Validation of Cyber-Physical Systems, V2CPS@IFM 2016, Reykjavík, Iceland, 4–5 June 2016, pp. 21–35 (2016)

27. Kokash, N., Arbab, F.: Formal design and verification of long-running transactions with extensible coordination tools. IEEE Trans. Serv. Comput. **6**(2), 186–200 (2013)

28. Lomazova, I.A., Popova-Zeugmann, L.: Controlling petri net behavior using priorities for transitions. Fundam. Inform. **143**(1–2), 101–112 (2016)

29. Lu, R., Sadiq, S.: A survey of comparative business process modeling approaches. In: Abramowicz, W. (ed.) BIS 2007. LNCS, vol. 4439, pp. 82–94. Springer, Heidelberg (2007). https://doi.org/10.1007/978-3-540-72035-5_7

30. Meng, S., Arbab, F.: Web services choreography and orchestration in Reo and constraint automata. In: Proceedings of the ACM Symposium on Applied Computing, pp. 346–353. ACM Press (2007)

31. Padberg, J.: Reconfigurable petri nets with transition priorities and inhibitor arcs. In: Parisi-Presicce, F., Westfechtel, B. (eds.) ICGT 2015. LNCS, vol. 9151, pp. 104–120. Springer, Cham (2015). https://doi.org/10.1007/978-3-319-21145-9_7

32. Reisig, W.: Understanding Petri Nets: Modeling Techniques, Analysis Methods, Case Studies. Springer, Berlin (2013). https://doi.org/10.1007/978-3-642-33278-4

33. Schumm, D., Turetken, O., Kokash, N., Elgammal, A., Leymann, F., van den Heuvel, W.-J.: Business process compliance through reusable units of compliant processes. In: Daniel, F., Facca, F.M. (eds.) ICWE 2010. LNCS, vol. 6385, pp. 325–337. Springer, Heidelberg (2010). https://doi.org/10.1007/978-3-642-16985-4_29

34. Valero, V., MaciÃ, H., Pardo, J.J., Cambronero, M.E., DÃaz, G.: Transforming web services choreographies with priorities and time constraints into prioritized-time colored petri nets. Sci. Comput. Program. **77**(3), 290–313 (2012). http://www.sciencedirect.com/science/article/pii/S0167642311001407, feature-Oriented Software Development (FOSD 2009)

Program Analysis

Modeling Non-deterministic C Code with Active Objects

Nathan Wasser[(✉)], Asmae Heydari Tabar, and Reiner Hähnle[iD]

Department of Computer Science, Technische Universität Darmstadt,
64289 Darmstadt, Germany
{wasser,heydaritabar,haehnle}@cs.tu-darmstadt.de
https://www.informatik.tu-darmstadt.de/se

Abstract. Cheap and ubiquitous availability of multi-processor hardware provides a strong incentive to parallelize existing software. We aim to annotate existing sequential applications written in C with OpenMP directives that can be processed by compilers on high performance parallel computers. We adopt a model-based approach, where from sequential C-code a software model is extracted in a largely automatic fashion. The target is the modeling language ABS (Abstract Behavioral Specification), an active objects-language with formal semantics. ABS has been designed to be statically analyzable. We focus on the first stages of model-based parallelization: model extraction and validation. We define a behavior-preserving, fully automatic translation of a large fragment of sequential C that explicitly renders all possible execution sequences, then use automated test case generation to produce validation test cases.

Keywords: Model extraction · Model validation · Parallelization

1 Introduction

The context of this paper is a project[1] concerned with the adaptation of legacy software due to changed requirements and technical advances. Specifically, cheap and ubiquitous availability of multi-processor hardware provides a strong incentive to parallelize existing software. In the long term we aim to annotate existing sequential applications written in C with OpenMP directives [14].

We adopt a *model-based* approach as illustrated in Fig. 1. From given sequential C-code a software model is extracted in a largely automatic fashion. The target is the modelling language ABS (Abstract Behavioral Specification) [7], an active objects-language [4] with formal semantics [9]. ABS is formally defined, free from ambiguity, and it has been designed to be statically analyzable [17].

---

[1] Software-Factory 4.0, see http://www.software-factory-4-0.de/.

This work was funded by the Hessian LOEWE initiative within the Software-Factory 4.0 project.

© IFIP International Federation for Information Processing 2019
Published by Springer Nature Switzerland AG 2019
H. Hojjat and M. Massink (Eds.): FSEN 2019, LNCS 11761, pp. 213–227, 2019.
https://doi.org/10.1007/978-3-030-31517-7_15

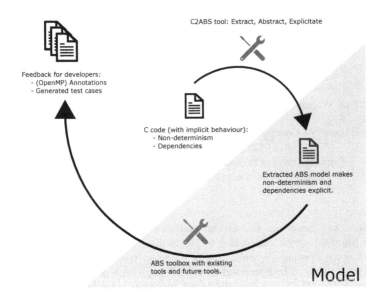

C2ABS tool: Extract, Abstract, Explicitate

Feedback for developers:
- (OpenMP) Annotations
- Generated test cases

C code (with implicit behaviour):
- Non-determinism
- Dependencies

Extracted ABS model makes
non-determinism and
dependencies explicit.

ABS toolbox with existing
tools and future tools.

Model

Fig. 1. Model-based parallelization

Therefore, it is possible to use software tools for exhibiting opportunities for parallelization and to generate suitable directives. In this paper we focus on the first stage: *model extraction* and *model validation*.

While abstraction of source code to a modelling language is a standard ingredient of many model checking tool chains (for example, [8]), here we pursue different goals: 1. we don't abstract away from behavior, but make non-deterministic behavior (a consequence of underspecification in C) explicit in the model; 2. non-deterministic execution sequences[2] and variable dependencies are precisely represented in a formal language and amenable to symbolic analysis; 3. the formal model with explicit non-determinism makes it possible to *validate* the model via automatically generated test cases and to give feedback to the author of the C-code about possibly unintended ambiguity.

Our main contributions are: 1. A behavior-preserving, fully automatic translation of a large fragment of sequential C that explicitly renders all possible execution sequences in ABS, and 2. application and adaptation of the ABS test case generator SYCO [3] to generate validation test cases. In Sect. 2 we define the C-fragment that we currently support and introduce a running example. In Sect. 3 we show how we extract an outline of the model based on the declarations of global variables and functions; how we extend the function-modelling classes with required helper methods in order to make non-determinism contained in C expressions within the function definition explicit in the model; and finally how we model the execution of the function call itself. In Sect. 4 we report on

---

[2] Most C compilers decide the evaluation order of subexpressions and side-effects at compile-time, but the C standard does not require this, so deciding at runtime is possible. Hence, this underspecified behavior is classified here as non-deterministic.

experiments performed with our tool, for model validation. Finally, we discuss related and future work in Sect. 5 and conclude in Sect. 6.

2   C-Fragment and Active Object Language

2.1   Input Language: C

The supported C-fragment is closely related to MISRA-C [12], a C subset widely used in embedded systems. We don't cover all features of MISRA-C (yet) which is not caused by principal limitations, but down to the fact that our tool is a research prototype rather than a commercial product. More importantly, in contrast to MISRA-C we explicitly *permit* non-deterministic computations and programs with underspecified C semantics that may lead to different behavior. In fact, our goal is to make such behavior explicit, so that it can be analyzed and taken into account in the parallelization stage.

Figure 2 contains the subset of C we use as an input language to explain our model extraction process.[3] A program is a list of declarations containing a function definition for main(). In addition to the assignment operator =, we restrict ourselves to the operator set $\{ +, -, *, ==, != =, >, >=, <, <= \}$. The semantics of a program from this subset of C are the same as the semantics of the C99 standard for the given program. In particular the unspecified evaluation order for side effects of assignments, as well as evaluation of arguments and subarguments to operators[4] and functions are preserved. Following the standard, evaluation of all function arguments and side effects caused by these is sequenced before the actual function call, while evaluation of arguments and side effects outside of the function call are indeterminately sequenced to it.[5]

Example 1. We consider an execution of the program in Listing 1.1. Execution of a C program always begins in the function main. First, a local variable y is initialized with the value −1. Then the condition of the **while** loop (x > reset(1)) is evaluated. The C standard imposes no order on the evaluation of the arguments x and reset (1) of the operator >.

Listing 1.1. A C program

```c
int  d = 0; int  x = 2;
int  reset (int  p)  {
    return  x = d;
}
int  main ()  {
    int  y = -1;
    while  (x >  reset (1))
        reset (d = y);
    return  x;
}
```

---

[3] Our model extraction tool C2ABS can process a much larger subset of C. The given subset, however, is sufficient to demonstrate the key focus of this paper: making non-deterministic unspecified behavior of a C program explicit through active objects.

[4] The subset of C under consideration does not contain operators which introduce sequence points, such as the comma operator (·,·) or the ternary operator (·?·:·).

[5] This means that the evaluation of arguments and side effects outside of the function call may happen before or after—but not during—the execution of the function call.

$$Decl_c ::= GlobalVarDecl_c \text{ ‘;’} \mid FuncDecl_c \text{ ‘;’} \mid FuncDef_c$$
$$GlobalVarDecl_c ::= \text{‘int’ } GlobalId_c \text{ ‘=’ } \mathbb{Z}$$
$$FuncDecl_c ::= \text{‘int’ } FuncId_c \text{ ‘(’ } ParamDecls_c \text{ ‘)’}$$
$$ParamDecls_c ::= \epsilon \mid \text{‘int’ } LocalId_c \{ \text{ ‘,’ ‘int’ } LocalId_c \}$$
$$FuncDef_c ::= FuncDecl_c \text{ ‘\{’ } \{ Stmt_c \} \text{ ‘return’ } Expr_c \text{ ‘;’ ‘\}’}$$
$$Stmt_c ::= \text{‘;’} \mid \text{‘\{’ } \{ Stmt_c \} \text{ ‘\}’} \mid LocalVarDecl_c \mid If_c \mid While_c \mid Expr_c \text{ ‘;’}$$
$$LocalVarDecl_c ::= \text{‘int’ } LocalId_c \text{ ‘=’ } Expr_c \text{ ‘;’}$$
$$If_c ::= \text{‘if’ ‘(’ } Expr_c \text{ ‘)’ } Stmt_c \text{ [‘else’ } Stmt_c \text{]}$$
$$While_c ::= \text{‘while’ ‘(’ } Expr_c \text{ ‘)’ } Stmt_c$$
$$Expr_c ::= \text{‘(’ } Expr_c \text{ ‘)’} \mid \mathbb{Z} \mid GlobalId_c \mid LocalId_c \mid Expr_c \text{ } Operator \text{ } Expr_c \mid$$
$$GlobalId_c \text{ ‘=’ } Expr_c \mid LocalId_c \text{ ‘=’ } Expr_c \mid FuncId_c \text{ ‘(’ } Args_c \text{ ‘)’}$$
$$Args_c ::= \epsilon \mid Expr_c \{ \text{ ‘,’ } Expr_c \}$$

Fig. 2. Syntax for a subset of C

Therefore, either of the following executions follow the standard:

1. reset (1) is called, setting x to 0 while returning the value 0, then x is evaluated to 0. Finally, $0 > 0$ is evaluated to 0,[6] thus the condition is deemed false, the **while** loop is exited and the program returns 0 (the value of x).
2. x is evaluated to 2, reset (1) is called, setting x to 0 while returning the value 0. Finally, $2 > 0$ is evaluated to 1, thus the condition is deemed true and the **while** loop entered. The expression statement reset (d = y); is executed by evaluating the expression. It is ensured that the value and side effect of d = y are evaluated before the function reset is called. Therefore d is set to -1 and reset (-1) is called, setting x to -1 (the value of d). Now the condition of the **while** loop is checked again and will evaluate to 0 regardless of evaluation order, thus exiting the loop. The program returns -1 (the value of x).

Execution of the program is thus underspecified, due to *implicit* non-determinism.[7]

2.2 Output Language: Active Objects

Languages such as Java or C feature low-level concurrency where a thread can be preempted at any time by another process running on the same processor and heap space. This leads to myriads of possible interleavings that cause complex data races being hard to contain and to characterize. On the opposite side of preemptive scheduling is actor-based, distributed programming [16], where all methods are executed atomically and concurrency occurs only among distinct

---

[6] In C relational operators return 1 for true, 0 for false; **if** and **while** treat the condition 0 as false, everything else as true.

[7] Potential results of unspecified behavior in C often go unnoticed by the programmer.

processors with disjoint heaps. In this scenario it is possible to specify behavior completely at the level of interfaces, typically in the form of behavioral invariants jointly maintained by an object's methods. The drawback is: this restrictive form of concurrency forces one to model and to specify systems at a highly abstract level, essentially in the form of protocols. It precludes modeling of concurrent behavior that is closer to real programs, such as waiting for results computed asynchronously on the same processor and heap.

Recently, *active object* languages [4] attempt to occupy a middle ground between preemption and full distribution. We focus on ABS [9] which is based on *cooperative scheduling* and has been used to model complex, industrial concurrent systems [2]. Cooperative scheduling implies that tasks cannot be preempted, but they may explicitly and voluntarily *suspend* their execution to allow a required result to be provided by another task: concurrent methods on the same processor and heap *cooperate* with each other to achieve a common goal.

The ABS language construct realizing this behavior has the form `await f?`, where `f` is a reference (called *future*) to the result of a method that may not have completed. Its effect is that the current task suspends itself and only resumes once the value of `f` is available. However, there might be more tasks except the one computing `f`'s value waiting for execution at this point. It is not determined in which sequence these waiting tasks are scheduled. Since they share the same memory, data races among them are possible.

Crucially, since the only ABS statement that can suspend execution is `await`, data races are *localized* in that they can *only* occur at await statements (or at the start of a method). Likewise, since all ABS methods run uninterruptedly either to completion or until they encounter an await statement, only the *final state* reached at the end of a method or before an await statement needs to be known when analyzing local data races. Hence, it suffices to reason about a very specific form of data race at few, explicitly specified code locations.

Given a program from our C subset we extract an ABS$_{lite}$ model from it. Figure 3 shows the syntax of ABS$_{lite}$.[8] For a brief overview of the semantics of ABS$_{lite}$, consider the model in Listing 1.2. The main block at the end is executed when the model is run. A new object o of class C is created with an initial value of 5 for the implicitly defined field **this**.x. Then two asynchronous calls are made to the object o: one call to add 2 to the field x and one call to return the value of field x. An asynchronous call immediately returns a future value, which can be polled through an **await** statement to see if the method call has returned. The **await** statement ensures that

Listing 1.2. A model in ABS$_{lite}$

```
class C( Int x) {
  Unit add( Int y) {
    this .x = this .x + y;
    return Unit ;
  }
  Int getX () {
    return this .x;
  }
}
{ // main block
  C o = new C(5);
  Fut<Unit> se = o!add(2);
  Fut<Int> fx = o!getX ();
  await se? & fx ?;
  Int z = fx . get ;
}
```

---

[8] C2ABS produces a model in ABS with additional features. ABS$_{lite}$ described here is chosen to show only what is actually required to extract a model from the C subset.

$$Model_a ::= \{ \; ClassDecl_a \; \} \; Block_a$$

$$ClassDecl_a ::= \text{'class'} \; ClassId_a \; \text{'('} \; ParamDecls_a \; \text{')'} \; \text{'\{'} \; \{ \; Decl_a \; \} \; \text{'\}'}$$

$$Decl_a ::= FieldDecl_a \; | \; MethodDecl_a$$

$$FieldDecl_a ::= Type_a \; FieldId_a \; \text{'='} \; PureExpr_a \; \text{';'}$$

$$Type_a ::= \text{'Int'} \; | \; \text{'Bool'} \; | \; \text{'Unit'} \; | \; \text{'Fut'} \; \text{'<'} \; Type_a \; \text{'>'} \; | \; ClassId_a$$

$$MethodDecl_a ::= Type_a \; MethodId_a \; \text{'('} \; ParamDecls_a \; \text{')'} \; RetBlock_a$$

$$ParamDecls_a ::= \epsilon \; | \; Type_a \; ParamId_a \; \{ \; \text{','} \; Type_a \; VarId_a \; \}$$

$$RetBlock_a ::= \text{'\{'} \; \{ \; Stmt_a \; \} \; \text{'return'} \; PureExpr_a \; \text{';'} \; \text{'\}'}$$

$$Stmt_a ::= \text{';'} \; | \; Block_a \; | \; VarDecl_a \; | \; Assign_a \; | \; If_a \; | \; While_a \; | \; Await_a \; | \; Expr_a \; \text{';'}$$

$$Block_a ::= \text{'\{'} \; \{ \; Stmt_a \; \} \; \text{'\}'}$$

$$VarDecl_a ::= Type_a \; VarId_a \; \text{'='} \; Expr_a \; \text{';'}$$

$$Assign_a ::= (VarId_a \; | \; \text{'this'} \; \text{'.'} \; FieldId_a) \; \text{'='} \; Expr_a \; \text{';'}$$

$$If_a ::= \text{'if'} \; \text{'('} \; PureExpr_a \; \text{')'} \; Stmt_a \; [\; \text{'else'} \; Stmt_a \;]$$

$$While_a ::= \text{'while'} \; \text{'('} \; PureExpr_a \; \text{')'} \; Stmt_a$$

$$Await_a ::= \text{'await'} \; PurcExpr_a \; \text{'?'} \; [\; \text{'\&'} \; PurcExpr_a \; \text{'?'} \;] \; \text{';'}$$

$$Expr_a ::= \text{'new'} \; ClassId_a \; \text{'('} \; Args_a \; \text{')'} \; | \; AsyncCall_a \; | \; GetExpr_a \; | \; PureExpr_a$$

$$AsyncCall_a ::= (\text{'this'} \; | \; VarId_a \; | \; \text{'this'} \; \text{'.'} \; FieldId_a) \; \text{'!'} \; MethodId_a \; \text{'('} \; Args_a \; \text{')'}$$

$$Args_a ::= \epsilon \; | \; PureExpr_a \; \{ \; \text{','} \; PureExpr_a \; \}$$

$$GetExpr_a ::= (VarId_a \; | \; \text{'this'} \; \text{'.'} \; FieldId_a) \; \text{'.'} \; \text{'get'}$$

$$PureExpr_a ::= \text{'('} \; PureExpr_a \; \text{')'} \; | \; VarId_a \; | \; \text{'this'} \; \text{'.'} \; FieldId_a \; | \; OpExpr_a \; | \; Literal_a$$

$$OpExpr_a ::= \text{'!'} \; PureExpr_a \; | \; PureExpr_a \; Operator \; PureExpr_a$$

$$Literal_a ::= \mathbb{Z} \; | \; \text{'True'} \; | \; \text{'False'} \; | \; \text{'Unit'}$$

Fig. 3. Syntax for ABS_{lite}

no further code in the main block is executed until both asynchronous calls have returned. In the meantime the active object o has received the two asynchronous calls. It begins to execute one of these calls. Once that call has returned, it will execute the other. Depending on the order it executes these calls, the value returned by getX() is either 5 or 7. The **get** returns the value of a future, blocking if neccessary until the value is available. Here the **await** ensures that the return value from the call to getX() is available. It is stored in the local variable z. Through the *explicit* non-determinism[9] of active objects (realized by the two asynchronous calls) the value of z is underspecified.

3   Model Extraction

An overview of the model extraction process is in Fig. 4. Each function definition is modelled as a class, while each executing function call is modelled as an active

---

[9] ABS code is atomically and deterministically executed by default. Non-determinism occurs only at scheduling points that are syntactically explicit in the code.

object of that class. Evaluation of (sub)expressions and side effects take place in asynchronous method calls to the same active object, while **await** statements at which forked asynchronous calls are joined model the sequencing rules of the C standard. If a function is called multiple times (whether recursively or iteratively), each of these calls is modelled by its own active object. As all functions have access to the global variables[10], a single active object which all other active objects have access to is used to model the state of all global variables. Blocking calls to the global object are used to access/modify the global variables. Additionally, blocking calls are used to pass control from one function call to a nested function call being executed, as the C standard ensures that subexpressions and side effects outside of a function call are indeterminately sequenced to it and, therefore, cannot occur during execution of the function call.

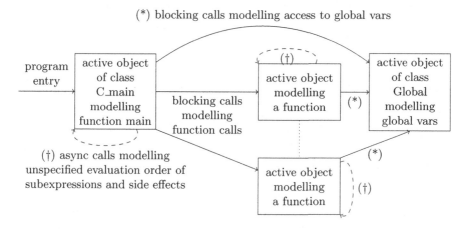

Fig. 4. Overview of model extraction

3.1   Modelling Global Variable Declarations and Initial Call to Main

Given a program p we construct the model shown in Listing 1.3. The function *extractFunctions* is described in Sect. 3.3 and *extractGlobalVars* is defined to create a class Global, which contains all global variables with their initial values as fields, with getter and setter methods for these fields:

$$extractGlobalVars : Decl_c{}^* \to Decl_a{}^*$$

$$\epsilon \mapsto \epsilon$$

$$decl\ decls \mapsto extractGlobalVars(decls),\ \text{if}\ decl \notin GlobalVarDecl_c$$

$$\textbf{int}\ gv = z;\ decls \mapsto \textbf{Int}\ gv = z;\ \textbf{Int}\ \text{get\_}gv()\ \{\ \textbf{return}\ gv;\ \}$$

$$\textbf{Unit}\ \text{set\_}gv(\textbf{Int}\ \text{x})\ \{\ \textbf{this}.gv = \text{x};\ \textbf{return Unit};\ \}$$

$$extractGlobalVars(decls)$$

---

[10] We ignore the potential for variable shadowing.

In the main block, we create an active object of class Global and pass this to an active object modelling the program entry. Whenever new active objects modelling function calls are created, we pass the Global object along, such that every modelled function call has access to the global variables. As an example, Listing 1.4 shows the extracted Global class from Listing 1.1.

Listing 1.3. Extracted model of p

```
class Global {
    extractGlobalVars(p)
}
extractFunctions(p)
{
    Global global = new Global();
    C_main o = new C_main(global);
    Fut<Int> fv = o!call();
    Int v = fv.get;
}
```

Listing 1.4. Example Global class

```
class Global {
    Int d = 0;
    Int get_d() { return d; }
    Unit set_d(Int x) {
        this.d = x;
        return Unit;
    }
    Int x = 2;
    Int get_x() { return x; }
    Unit set_x(Int x) {
        this.x = x;
        return Unit;
    }
}
```

3.2 Modelling Unspecified Evaluation Order Within Expressions

Evaluating an expression in C can exhibit unspecified behaviour due to the lack of a rigid evaluation order for subexpressions and side effects offered by the typical C standards (as opposed to, e.g., the Java language specification). To correctly model this unspecified behavior, we take advantage of the explicit non-determinism of active objects with respect to the execution order of asynchronous calls. Execution of a function call in C is modelled by an active object executing its call method. Within this method multiple asynchronous calls can be made to other methods of this active object followed by an **await** statement, such that these other methods can be executed in a non-deterministic fashion.

Definition 1. *A tuple* $(stmts, se, futVar) \in (VarDecl_a{}^* \times VarId_a{}^* \times VarId_a)$, *where* se *contains only local variables of type* **Fut<Unit>** *declared in* $stmts$ *(the side-effects of the evaluated expression) and* $futVar$ *is a local variable of type* **Fut<Int>** *declared in* $stmts$ *(the value of the evaluated expression) is defined as an* expression wrapper[11]. *The set of all expression wrappers is defined as* $\mathbb{EW}$.

We define the function *convert* in Fig. 5, which converts a C expression into an expression wrapper recursively, where $x, se \in VarId_a$ are fresh unused identifiers, $e_i \in Expr_c, z \in \mathbb{Z}, lv \in LocalId_c, gv \in GlobalId_c, (stmts_i, se_i, x_i) = convert(e_i), \oplus \in Operator$ and $f \in FuncId_c$.

As can be seen in the function *convert*, asynchronous calls to various methods of the current active object are made. The active object classes generated from a C function are thus required to implement the subset of methods in Fig. 6 which are used in the converted expression wrappers of all expressions contained in the function definition.

---

[11] In this paper we restrict expression wrappers to $(VarDecl_a{}^* \times VarId_a{}^* \times VarId_a)$, while in C2ABS they are in the superset $(Stmt_a{}^* \times VarId_a{}^* \times PureExpr_a)$.

$$(e_1) \mapsto convert(e_1)$$

$$z \mapsto (\textbf{Fut<Int>} \ \text{x} = \textbf{this}!\text{id}(z);, \ \epsilon, \ \text{x})$$

$$lv \mapsto (\textbf{Fut<Int>} \ \text{x} = \textbf{this}!\text{get\_}lv();, \ \epsilon, \ \text{x})$$

$$gv \mapsto (\textbf{Fut<Int>} \ \text{x} = \textbf{this}!\text{getGlobal\_}gv();, \ \epsilon, \ \text{x})$$

$$lv = e_1 \mapsto (stmts_1 \ \textbf{Fut<Unit>} \ \text{se} = \textbf{this}!\text{set\_}lv(x_1);, \ se_1 \ \text{se}, \ x_1)$$

$$gv = e_1 \mapsto (stmts_1 \ \textbf{Fut<Unit>} \ \text{se} = \textbf{this}!\text{setGlobal\_}gv(x_1);, \ se_1 \ \text{se}, \ x_1)$$

$$e_1 \oplus e_2 \mapsto (stmts_1 \ stmts_2 \ \textbf{Fut<Int>} \ \text{x} = \textbf{this}!op_{\oplus}(x_1, x_2);, \ se_1 \ se_2, \ \text{x})$$

$$f(e_1, \ldots, e_n) \mapsto (stmts_1 \cdots stmts_n \ \textbf{Fut<Int>} \ \text{x} = \textbf{this}!call\_f\_m(args);, \ \epsilon, \ \text{x})$$

$$\text{where } args = x_1, \ldots, x_n, se_{1_1}, \ldots, se_{n_{|se_n|}} \text{ and } m = \sum_{i=1}^{n} |se_i|$$

Fig. 5. The function $convert : Expr_c \rightarrow \mathbb{EW}$

```
Int id(Int x) { return x; }


Int get_lv() { return this.lv; }


Unit set_lv(Fut<Int> fx)
{
  await fx?;
  this.lv = fx.get;
  return Unit;
}

// for ⊕ ∈ {+, −, *}:
Int op⊕(Fut<Int> fx, Fut<Int> fy)
{
  await fx? & fy?;
  Int x = fx.get;
  Int y = fy.get;
  return x ⊕ y;
}
```

```
Int getGlobal_gv() {
  Fut<Int> fx = this.global!get_gv();
  // no await, blocking call
  Int result = fx.get;
  return result;
}


Unit setGlobal_gv(Fut<Int> fx) {
  await fx?; Int x = fx.get;
  Fut<Unit> se = this.global!set_gv(x);
  se.get; // no await, blocking call
  return Unit;
}


// for R ∈ { ==, != , >, >=, <, <= }:
Int opR(Fut<Int> fx, Fut<Int> fy) {
  await fx? & fy?;
  Int x = fx.get; Int y = fy.get;
  Int result = 0;
  if (x R y) result = 1;
  return result;
}
```

```
Int call_f_m(Fut<Int> fx₁,..., Fut<Int> fxₙ,
             Fut<Unit> se₁,..., Fut<Unit> seₘ) {
  await fx₁? & ... & fxₙ? & se₁? & ... & seₘ?;
  Int x₁ = fx₁.get; ... Int xₙ = fxₙ.get;
  C_f o = new C_f(this.global, x₁,..., xₙ);
  Fut<Int> fr = o!call();
  // no await, blocking call
  Int result = fr.get;
  return result;
}
```

Fig. 6. Families of required helper methods

Side effects are created only by assignments, while the side effects of an operator's operands are gathered and passed upwards. A function call has no side effects in this sense[12], but rather introduces a sequence point between evaluation of function arguments and any side effects produced therein, and the function call itself. For this reason the call to *call_f_m* contains the future values for all side effects of the function arguments, in addition to the arguments themselves. This allows an **await** statement to ensure that all side effects are completed, before the actual call to the function is modelled by creating a new active object of the appropriate type and calling its *call* method.

3.3 Modelling Function Definitions as Classes

The function *extractFunctions* called in Listing 1.3 extracts ABS_{lite} classes modelling C function definitions and is defined in Fig. 7, together with *extractFunction* and *extractLocalVars*. Here $(stmts', se'_1 \cdots se'_n, x') = convert(e)$ and *extractStmts* (and helper functions *extract* and *varDeclToAssign*) are defined in Fig. 8.

Function parameters are modelled as class parameters (which are implicit fields), while local variables are modelled as explicit fields of the class. This allows access to them as required from the helper methods. For this reason a local variable declaration needs to be treated twice: once by creating a field to model this local variable and assigning it a witness term (**Int** $lv = 0$;) in *extractLocalVars* and once by modelling the initial value for the local variable by assignment (**this.**$lv = x'$.get;) in *extract*.

Treating **while** loops introduces an additional wrinkle: while in C the condition of a while loop can contain side effects, in ABS this is not possible. For this reason the auxiliary statements in the expression wrapper required to calculate the value of the pure expression must be performed twice: once before the **while** loop and once at the end of the loop body before re-evaluating the condition. We re-use the local variables declared in the auxiliary statements by replacing local variable declarations with assignment in *varDeclToAssign*.

4 Experiments

We developed an Eclipse plugin C2ABS which extracts an ABS model from a given C program, following the translation approach described in the previous sections.[13] To validate an extracted model we analyze it with SYCO[14], a systematic tester for ABS concurrent objects. The SYCO kernel includes state-of-the-art partial-order reduction techniques to avoid redundant computations

---

[12] Obviously, a function call can have side effects, by changing the values of global variables, but these will be dealt with in the active object modelling the function call, rather than in the current active object.

[13] C2ABS with example inputs and outputs can be found at: https://www.informatik.tu-darmstadt.de/se/se_research/se_projects/fsen_2019.en.jsp.

[14] http://costa.fdi.ucm.es/syco/clients/web/.

$$extractFunctions : Decl_c{}^* \rightarrow ClassDecl_a{}^*$$

$$\epsilon \mapsto \epsilon$$

$$decl\ decls \mapsto \begin{cases} extractFunction(decl)\ extractFunctions(decls) & \text{, if } decl \in FuncDef_c \\ extractFunctions(decls) & \text{, otherwise} \end{cases}$$

$$extractFunction : FuncDef_c \rightarrow ClassDecl_a$$

```
int f( int p₁ , ..., int pₙ ){ stmts return e ; }
```
$$\mapsto$$
```
class C_f( Global global , Int p₁,..., Int pₙ ) {
    extractLocalVars(stmts)
    Int call () {
        extractStmts(stmts)
        stmts'
        await x' & se'₁ & ... & se'ₙ ;
        Int result = x'.get ;
        return result ;
    }
    ... // required helper methods (see Fig. 6)
}
```

$$extractLocalVars : Stmt_c{}^* \rightarrow FieldDecl_a{}^*$$

$$\epsilon \mapsto \epsilon$$

$$;\ stmts \mapsto extractLocalVars(stmts)$$

$$\{\ stmts_1\ \}\ stmts_2 \mapsto extractLocalVars(stmts_1\ stmts_2)$$

$$e;\ stmts \mapsto extractLocalVars(stmts)$$

$$\textbf{int}\ lv = e;\ stmts \mapsto \textbf{Int}\ lv = 0;\ extractLocalVars(stmts)$$

$$\textbf{if}\ (e)\ st \mapsto extractLocalVars(st\ stmts)$$

$$\textbf{if}\ (e)\ st_1\ \textbf{else}\ st_2\ stmts \mapsto extractLocalVars(st_1\ st_2\ stmts)$$

$$\textbf{while}\ (e)\ st\ stmts \mapsto extractLocalVars(st\ stmts)$$

Fig. 7. The functions *extractFunctions*, *extractFunction* and *extractLocalVars*

during testing [3]. Two runs of an ABS program with the same main method are redundant relative to each other when any possible difference in the scheduling of tasks cannot possibly lead to a data race. Obviously, this is an undecidable property. SYCO safely under-approximates redundant computations.

Table 1 contains C programs that contain expressions with unspecified evaluation order. The programs two-unspec, Schrödinger and one-to-fib are based on an idea by Derek Jones[15], where the C standard allows two-unspec to return

---

[15] http://shape-of-code.coding-guidelines.com/2011/06/18/fibonacci-and-jit-compilers/.

$$extractStmts : Stmt_c{}^* \rightarrow Stmt_a{}^*$$

$$\epsilon \mapsto \epsilon$$

$$st\ stmts \mapsto extract(st)\ extractStmts(stmts)$$

$$extract : Stmt_c \rightarrow Stmt_a{}^*$$

$$;\ \mapsto \epsilon$$

$$\{\ stmts\ \} \mapsto extractStmts(stmts)$$

$$e; \mapsto stmts'\ \textbf{await}\ x'\ \&\ se'_1\ \&\ \ldots\ \&\ se'_n;$$

$$\textbf{int}\ lv = e; \mapsto stmts'\ \textbf{await}\ x'\ \&\ se'_1\ \&\ \ldots\ \&\ se'_n;\ \textbf{this}.lv = x'.\textbf{get};$$

$$\textbf{if}\ (e)\ st \mapsto stmts'\ \textbf{await}\ x'\ \&\ se'_1\ \&\ \ldots\ \&\ se'_n;\ \textbf{Int}\ x = x'.\textbf{get};$$

$$\textbf{if}\ (x\ != 0)\ \{\ extract(st)\ \}$$

$$\textbf{if}\ (e)\ st_1\ \textbf{else}\ st_2 \mapsto stmts'\ \textbf{await}\ x'\ \&\ se'_1\ \&\ \ldots\ \&\ se'_n;\ \textbf{Int}\ x = x'.\textbf{get};$$

$$\textbf{if}\ (x\ != 0)\ \{\ extract(st_1)\ \}\ \textbf{else}\ \{\ extract(st_2)\ \}$$

$$\textbf{while}\ (e)\ st \mapsto stmts'\ \textbf{await}\ x'\ \&\ se'_1\ \&\ \ldots\ \&\ se'_n;\ \textbf{Int}\ x = x'.\textbf{get};$$

$$\textbf{while}\ (x\ != 0)\ \{$$

$$extract(st)$$

$$varDeclToAssign(stmts')$$

$$\textbf{await}\ x'\ \&\ se'_1\ \&\ \ldots\ \&\ se'_n;\ x = x'.\textbf{get};$$

$$\}$$

$$varDeclToAssign : VarDecl_a{}^* \rightarrow Assign_a{}^*$$

$$\epsilon \mapsto \epsilon$$

$$T\ x = e;\ stmts \mapsto x = e;\ varDeclToAssign(stmts)$$

Fig. 8. The functions $extractStmts$, $extract$ and $varDeclToAssign$

either 1 or 2, Schrödinger tests if two calls to two-unspec are equal and one-to-fib(n) returns a value between 1 and the n-th Fibonacci number. Too many false positives are often a problem with static code checkers, so no-reliance is a test case which does not rely on unspecified evaluation order, calculating the same result despite *different* execution paths. Finally, assign-chain returns (x = y = z = 5) + f(), where f returns the sum x + y + z, to test unspecified evaluation order of side effects.

We compared the result of model extraction with C2ABS followed by analysis with SYCO to program analysis using Cerberus[16], a tool for developing a semantic model for a substantial fragment of C [11]. It takes a similar approach than we do by cross-compiling C into a Lisp dialect and performing analysis on that program. Table 1 contains the number of explored states during analysis and the total time spent for the SYCO web interface. The Cerberus web

---

[16] https://cerberus.cl.cam.ac.uk/.

interface has a 45 second timeout and does not give exact run times. We also show the different possible results for the programs and the number of execution paths deemed different by the tools. In the case of SYCO, it shows only those executions that lead to a different configuration after partial order reduction [1].

Table 1. Model validation with SYCO compared to program analysis with Cerberus

Program	Extraction w/C2ABS, validation w/SYCO				Cerberus (45s timeout)	
	Explored states	Time (ms)	Results	Executions	Results	Executions
two-unspec	42	19	1, 2	2	1, 2	7
Schrödinger	148	190	0, 1	4	0, 1	98
one-to-fib(3)	58	35	1, 2	2	1, 2	7
one-to-fib(4)	382	972	1, 2, 3	12	timeout	
no-reliance	104	120	0	2	0	2
Listing 1.1	208	570	−1, 0	5	−1, 0	9
assign-chain	4609	12838	11, 13, 14, 15, 16, 17, 18, 20	480	11, 13, 16, 20	42

While Cerberus times out after 45 seconds for one-to-fib(4), SYCO manages to completely validate the model extracted by C2ABS in less than a second. SYCO recognizes that there are only 4 different paths in the Schrödinger model, while Cerberus claims 98. But most interesting are the different results for assignment-chain: here the difference seems to be that Cerberus assumes the order of the side effects is set (first assign z, then y, then x) and only allows the evaluation of f() to interleave. However, this does not match the C standard which clearly states that the evaluation order of side effects is unspecified. Our model faithfully reflects this, allowing the side effects and function call to occur in any order, resulting in additional possible results.

In addition to the C programs where SYCO could fully analyze the extracted model, we considered programs where the extracted model caused SYCO to time out after 45 seconds when attempting to analyze all possible execution paths. The one-to-fib function for inputs greater than 4 is such a case, as well as a nested **for** loop example with 10,000 inner iterations. Partial validation of these larger models was possible, by enabling constraints in SYCO to only consider certain paths, and by using a simulation tool that creates an Erlang program from an ABS model and executes that.[17] With these we can partially validate one-to-fib with inputs up to 19 in less than 10 seconds.

5   Related and Future Work

We discussed the Cerberus tool in the previous section. Apart from it, there is not much published work on model extraction. The SPIN model checker contains the model extractor Modex from C to ProMeLA [8]. Unfortunately, we did not manage to get it to work on our examples. MISRA-C is a well-known subset of the C language widely used in the development of safety-critical systems [13].

---

[17] http://samir.fdi.ucm.es:8080/ei/clients/web/.

One of its rules checks whether the value of an expression is the same under any order of evaluation that the standard permits. It stipulates that no unspecified behavior is caused by the order of evaluation of subexpressions. There are several, mostly commercial, static code analyzers equipped with a MISRA-C compliance checker, for example , Astrée [6], Polyspace[18], Axivion Bauhaus Suite [15], and ECLAIR[19]. All of these are based on abstract interpretation [5]. Also, some compilers like Green Hills , IAR , TASKING and TI are equipped with a MISRA-C compliance checker. In contrast to MISRA-C compliance checkers we want to analyze and detect also non-compliant behavior and we give detailed feedback to the developer about differing computations.

In the future we intend to add operators that introduce sequencing (in particular the ternary operator), as well as tracking sequencing information to recognize undefined behavior, such as changing a value multiple times between sequence points. We will also extend the types C2ABS can deal with. ABS has a formally defined semantics [9], while a semantics for C is given by the K framework[20], allowing a formal proof of the correctness of the translation in future. *Common continuation region analysis* [10] allows recognizing and optimizing asynchronous calls which can be performed in parallel. Finding parallelization potential in the ABS model could then be transferred back to the C program.

6   Conclusion

We described how to extract an ABS model from a C program to make the implicit non-deterministic behavior explicit. There exist a number of tools built to analyze ABS models [17], because the language was designed to be analyzable. This will help us extend the ABS toolbox with tools built to localize parallelizable parts of the model and thus give feedback to the C developers. We implemented our model extraction approach and validated the models thus extracted using SYCO. In doing so, we have found differences in results between our modelling of the C standard and that chosen by developers of the related tool Cerberus. We feel confident that our results are correct. Our approach also seems to scale better. Additionally, we found areas where SYCO can be optimized and relayed this to the developers.

Acknowledgments. We would like to thank the SYCO development team for their support, in particular, Samir Genaim and Miky Zamalloa.

References

1. Albert, E., Arenas, P., Gómez-Zamalloa, M.: Actor- and task-selection strategies for pruning redundant state-exploration in testing. In: Ábrahám, E., Palamidessi, C. (eds.) FORTE 2014. LNCS, vol. 8461, pp. 49–65. Springer, Heidelberg (2014). https://doi.org/10.1007/978-3-662-43613-4_4

---

[18] See https://www.mathworks.com/products/polyspace.html.
[19] See http://www.bugseng.com/eclair-0.
[20] See https://github.com/kframework/c-semantics.

2. Albert, E., et al.: Formal modeling of resource management for cloud architectures: an industrial case study using real-time ABS. J. Serv. Oriented Comput. Appl. 8(4), 323–339 (2014)

3. Albert, E., Gómez-Zamalloa, M., Isabel, M.: SYCO: a systematic testing tool for concurrent objects. In: Zaks, A., Hermenegildo, M.V. (eds.) Proceedings 25th International Conference on Compiler Construction, CC, Barcelona, Spain, pp. 269–270. ACM (2016)

4. de Boer, F., et al.: A survey of active object languages. ACM Comput. Surv. 50(5), 76:1–76:39 (2017)., article 76

5. Cousot, P., Cousot, R.: Abstract interpretation: a unified lattice model for static analysis of programs by construction or approximation of fixpoints. Fourth POPL. Los Angeles, pp. 238–252. ACM Press, New York, January (1977)

6. Cousot, P., et al.: The ASTREÉ analyzer. In: Sagiv, M. (ed.) ESOP 2005. LNCS, vol. 3444, pp. 21–30. Springer, Heidelberg (2005). https://doi.org/10.1007/978-3-540-31987-0_3

7. Hähnle, R.: The abstract behavioral specification language: a tutorial introduction. In: Giachino, E., Hähnle, R., de Boer, F.S., Bonsangue, M.M. (eds.) FMCO 2012. LNCS, vol. 7866, pp. 1–37. Springer, Heidelberg (2013). https://doi.org/10.1007/978-3-642-40615-7_1

8. Holzmann, G.J., Smith, M.H.: An automated verification method for distributed systems software based on model extraction. IEEE Trans. Software Eng. 28(4), 364–377 (2002)

9. Johnsen, E.B., Hähnle, R., Schäfer, J., Schlatte, R., Steffen, M.: ABS: a core language for abstract behavioral specification. In: Aichernig, B.K., de Boer, F.S., Bonsangue, M.M. (eds.) FMCO 2010. LNCS, vol. 6957, pp. 142–164. Springer, Heidelberg (2011). https://doi.org/10.1007/978-3-642-25271-6_8

10. Kim, W., Agha, G.A., Panwar, R.B.: Efficient compilation of concurrent call/return communication in actor-based programming languages. In: Proceedings 3rd International Conference High Performance Computing (HiPC). pp. 62–67. December 1996. https://doi.org/10.1109/HIPC.1996.565798

11. Memarian, K., et al.: Into the depths of C: elaborating the de facto standards. In: Krintz, C., Berger, E. (eds.) 37th PLDI, pp. 1–15. ACM (2016)

12. MISRA Consortium: MISRA-C: 2004 – Guidelines for the use of the C language in critical systems (2004)

13. Motor Industry Research Association: MISRA C 2012: Guidelines for the Use of the C Language in Critical Systems (2013)

14. OpenMP Architecture Review Board: OpenMP Application Programming Interface, 4.5 edn. (November 2015). https://www.openmp.org/wp-content/uploads/openmp-4.5.pdf

15. Raza, A., Vogel, G., Plödereder, E.: Bauhaus – a tool suite for program analysis and reverse engineering. In: Pinho, L.M., González Harbour, M. (eds.) Ada-Europe 2006. LNCS, vol. 4006, pp. 71–82. Springer, Heidelberg (2006). https://doi.org/10.1007/11767077_6

16. Sirjani, M., Movaghar, A., Shali, A., de Boer, F.S.: Modeling and verification of reactive systems using Rebeca. Fundam. Inform. 63(4), 385–410 (2004)

17. Wong, P.Y.H., Albert, E., Muschevici, R., Proença, J., Schäfer, J., Schlatte, R.: The ABS tool suite: modelling, executing and analysing distributed adaptable object-oriented systems. STTT 14(5), 567–588 (2012)

Verification of Smart Contract Business Logic
Exploiting a Java Source Code Verifier

Wolfgang Ahrendt[1]([✉]), Richard Bubel[2], Joshua Ellul[3], Gordon J. Pace[3], Raúl Pardo[4], Vincent Rebiscoul[5], and Gerardo Schneider[6]

[1] Chalmers University of Technology, Gothenburg, Sweden
ahrendt@chalmers.se
[2] Technische Universität Darmstadt, Darmstadt, Germany
bubel@cs.tu-darmstadt.de
[3] University of Malta, Msida, Malta
{joshua.ellul,gordon.pace}@um.edu.mt
[4] Inria, Lyon, France
raul.pardo-jimenez@inria.fr
[5] Ècole Normale Supèrieure de Lyon, Lyon, France
vincent.rebiscoul@ens-lyon.fr
[6] University of Gothenburg, Gothenburg, Sweden
gerardo@cse.gu.se

Abstract. Smart contracts have been argued to be a means of building trust between parties by providing a self-executing equivalent of legal contracts. And yet, code does not always perform what it was originally intended to do, which resulted in losses of millions of dollars. Static verification of smart contracts is thus a pressing need. This paper presents an approach to verifying smart contracts written in Solidity by automatically translating Solidity into Java and using KeY, a deductive Java verification tool. In particular, we solve the problem of rolling back the effects of aborted transactions by exploiting KeY's native support of JavaCard transactions. We apply our approach to a smart contract which automates a casino system, and discuss how the approach addresses a number of known shortcomings of smart contract development in Solidity.

1 Introduction

Blockchain is a *distributed ledger* running in a decentralised manner on a network of devices that allows for the exchange of data in a trusted manner. Such *values* may be stored and modified without the need for a centralised trusted authority; trust is established through distributed collaboration following specific protocols. *Cryptocurrencies*, particularly *Bitcoin* [15], was the first proposed application of blockchain. A smart contract platform built on top of blockchain, as proposed and built by Ethereum[1], enables for blockchain to be used for many other applications besides cryptocurrencies.

Smart contracts are software programs that are openly stored on the blockchain (they can be read and used by anyone), and—as everything else on blockchains—are

---

[1] https://www.ethereum.org.

ⓒ IFIP International Federation for Information Processing 2019
Published by Springer Nature Switzerland AG 2019
H. Hojjat and M. Massink (Eds.): FSEN 2019, LNCS 11761, pp. 228–243, 2019.
https://doi.org/10.1007/978-3-030-31517-7_16

1. *The casino owner may deposit or withdraw money from the casino's bank as long as the bank's balance never falls below zero.*
2. *As long as no game is in progress, the owner of the casino may make available a new game by tossing a coin and hiding its outcome. The owner must also set a participation cost of choice for the game.*
3. *Clauses 1 and 2 are constrained in that as long as a game is in progress, the bank balance may never be less than the sum of the participation cost of the game and its win-out.*
4. *The win-out for a game is set to be 80% of the participating cost.*

Fig. 1. Excerpt from a legal contract regulating a coin-tossing casino.

permanent and cannot be altered. Their execution is typically performed by "workers" (commonly known as *miners*) that earn some cryptocurrency in return for their work. A smart contract typically offers means of invoking its functionality so end users can interact with it to transfer data and cryptocurrency to the contract. The contract is effectively the logic to manage these invocations and execute the corresponding instructions that manipulate the local bookkeeping of data (including the cryptocurrency). Underlying a smart contract lies a description, and prescription, of an agreement between different parties in order to automate the regulated exchange of value and information over the internet.

The promise of smart contract technology is to diminish the costs of contracting, enforcing contractual agreements, and making payments, while at the same time ensuring trust and compliance, all in the absence of a central trusted authority. Such executable legal contractual agreements suffer from some drawbacks: (i) it is not easy to ensure that the smart contract complies with the legal contractual obligations that the program is intended to implement; and (ii) it is not easy to ensure the correctness of smart contracts. In this paper we focus only on the latter aspect. Consider the legal contract shown in Fig. 1 regulating how a simple casino should make a coin-tossing game available to players. A smart contract implementing this legal contract would carry out concrete actions to ensure that the legal contract is never violated. For instance, clause 3 requires that while a game is in progress, there is always enough money available to pay in case the player wins. This could be achieved by allowing a game to start only if there is enough money to pay for a win, and then to disallow withdrawals which result in not enough money left to pay. Or more radically by preventing the casino from withdrawing any money during a game. Either way, we should be able to *prove* that our implementation satisfies the invariant required by such clauses.

Smart contracts are programs, and as such they are vulnerable to bugs just as any other software. Errors may have many causes, like out of range numbers, unintuitive language feature semantics, or intricate mismatches between internal bookkeeping (in the local data) and external bookkeeping (in the blockchain), to name a few. Erroneous behaviour may be intended, explicitly provoked by malicious contract creators, or exploited by opportunists. Bugs in smart contracts may result in massive losses in an irreversible way (as blockchain transactions are permanent, and no authority has the power to undo them). Recent multi-million Ethereum bugs[2] have shown that this is indeed an issue researchers and practitioners should take seriously [3].

In this paper we focus on the verification of smart contracts written in Solidity[3], by translating them automatically into Java. By targeting Java, our translation can exploit the similarities between the contract-oriented and the object-oriented paradigms, and make use of existing verification tools. We use the deductive source code verifier KeY [2] to verify the translated program since it is among the most powerful verification tools for object-oriented languages, and specifically, it has native verification support for transactions and their abortion, allowing to model the rolling back of program effects. We apply our approach to a case study consisting of a Casino smart contract.

The paper is organised as follows. Section 2 gives some background on smart contracts and the deductive verification tool KeY. In Sect. 3 we present our Solidity to Java translation. Section 4 is concerned with the verification of the translated Java programs using KeY. Section 5 introduces our case study. We discuss scope and limitations of our approach in Sect. 6, followed by related work and a conclusion.

2   Preliminaries

2.1   Smart Contracts in Solidity

Since smart contracts are deployed on a blockchain (or some other form of distributed ledger technology) which typically enforces immutability of deployed smart contract code and also due to the critical nature of applications they are often employed for, a different mind set to traditional programming is required [6]. Ethereum's virtual machine provides a 'one world computer' abstraction: the Ethereum Virtual Machine (EVM) [16] is an abstract machine that executes transactions atomically whereby a transaction is an action initiated by a smart contract user. The predominant language used to write Ethereum smart contract code is Solidity.

A deployed Ethereum smart contract has an associated unique address, can own Ether (Ethereum's native cryptocurrency), and transfer Ether to other addresses which may be other contracts or user accounts. Being Turing complete, the EVM needs to cater for code which may not terminate or takes an unacceptably long time to execute. To get around this, the EVM implements a notion of *gas*—a cost (in Ether) for the execution of each EVM bytecode instruction. If the amount of gas associated with a particular transaction is not fully paid for, then execution of the smart contract stops and the altered state within the transaction is reverted to the original state as it was upon initiation. This ensures that all transactions terminate, and that computationally expensive functionality is financially prohibitive, avoiding attempts to overload the Ethereum execution engine.

Listing 1.1 shows an excerpt of a Solidity contract[4] we have built to model the casino contract from Fig. 1. In particular, the listing shows the implementation of

---

[2] https://www.theguardian.com/technology/2017/nov/08/cryptocurrency-300m-dollars-stolen-bug-ether.

[3] https://solidity.readthedocs.io.

[4] See https://git.io/fx6cn.

function removeFromPot which allows the casino to withdraw money from the casino's bank when invoked. The logic within the function is simple—it reduces the internal state variable pot which keeps track of how much money lies in the casino's bank (using an unsigned 256 bit integer) and transfers the requested amount using the **transfer** method to the caller of the function—**msg** is a variable representing the message invoking the transaction and **msg.sender** is the transaction initiator's address. It is worth noting that on Ethereum, function calls are atomic (though still reentrant), in that they execute to completion (whether successful or not) before another function call can be invoked.

```
1   contract Casino {
2     private uint256 pot = 0;
3     private address operator;
4     ...
5     function removeFromPot(uint256 value) public byOperator noActiveBet {
6       pot = pot - value;
7       msg.sender.transfer(value);
8     }
9
10    modifier byOperator() {
11      require (msg.sender == operator);
12      _;
13    }
14    ...
15  }
```

Listing 1.1. Solidity code to withdraw money from the casino pot and definition of a modifier to ensure that a function can only be invoked by the owner of the casino.

To ensure that the function can only be invoked by the casino owner and not during an active game, the code uses two modifiers byOperator and noActiveBet, which add in-line checks accordingly. The definition of the byOperator modifier is also shown in Listing 1.1. It modifies any function it is applied to (here it has been applied to removeFromPot) such that it executes the original function code where the placeholder _; is specified. The modifier byOperator will thus ensure that the transaction initiator is indeed the casino operator, using a **require** statement (one type of exception raising convenience function provided which checks if a condition holds, or otherwise raises an exception), and then executes the original function code. Internally, the **require** statement triggers the Solidity command **revert** which raises an exception if the condition does not hold.

It is worth noting that if the **transfer** function fails (for example due to insufficient available funds being available in the contract) then it will also raise an exception and abort the transaction reverting the state (including variable values) back to their original values as at the beginning of the invocation. Solidity also provides a **send** function which, in case of failure, will not raise an exception but returns a boolean success response.

Functions are tagged by annotations indicating their visibility in Solidity—defining from where calls can be made: **private** only from functions within the contract; **internal** from functions within the contract or from deriving contracts; **external** only from external contracts (or using a contract interface transaction rather than a function call); or **public** from anywhere.

2.2 Deductive Verification with KeY

We use the KeY system [2] to verify the Java programs (obtained from the original Solidity contracts) to be correct with respect to their specification. The Java Modeling Language (JML) [12], is used to write class invariants and method specifications.

JML specifications are embedded into Java source code as Java comments. Any comment starting with //@ or /*@ marks the start of a JML specification. Consequently, standard Java tools like compilers, simply ignore JML specifications, while JML aware tools can distinguish Java comments from JML specifications and make use of them.

```
1   public class Account {
2       /*@ public invariant accountNr >= 0 &&
3              (\forall Account a; a != this; a.accountNr != this.accountNr); *@/
4       private /*@ spec_public @*/ int accountNr;
5
6       //@ public invariant balance >= 0;
7       private /*@ spec_public @*/ int balance;
8
9       /*@ public normal_behaviour
10       @ requires amount >= 0 && to != this;
11       @ requires this.balance >= amount;
12       @ assignable this.balance, to.balance;
13       @ ensures this.balance == \old(this.balance) - amount;
14       @ ensures to.balance == \old(to.balance) + amount;
15       @ ensures \result == true;
16       @*/
17       public boolean transfer(Account to, int amount) {...}
18   }
```

Listing 1.2. Java source code annotated with JML specifications.

Listing 1.2 shows a class Account, which implements a bank account. It consists of two integer fields accountNr and balance as well as the method transfer, which takes as arguments the target account (parameter to) and the amount to be transferred.

The class is annotated with two *JML invariants*. JML invariants specify properties of objects that have to be established by the constructor and to be preserved by all methods. They are marked by the keyword **invariant** and followed by the actual property written as boolean typed *JML expression*. JML expressions are a superset of side-effect free Java expressions with additional operators like quantifiers **exists** and **forall**. The first invariant (lines 2–3) states that account numbers are unique, while the second (line 6) restricts the value of field balance to be non-negative.

Lines 9–16 contain transfer's *JML method specification*. The method's preconditions are marked by **requires**, which is followed by a boolean JML expression. If the caller ensures that the preconditions evaluate to true at invocation time, then the method guarantees that (i) it terminates normally, i.e., without throwing an exception (line 9), (ii) in its final state the postcondition (keyword **ensures**) holds (line 13–15) and (iii) that at most the values of the fields listed in the **assignable** clause (line 12) have been changed. Multiple **requires** and **ensures** clauses are conjunctively combined, and many method specifications can be connected using **also**. Complementary to **normal_behavior** there are **exceptional_behavior** specifications stating which exceptions are thrown under which conditions as well as assertions about the post state.

For convenience, JML defines a few defaults. For instance, by default all fields, parameters and return values of reference type are not **null**. Further, there is an implicit pre- and postcondition **\invariant_for(this)** for each method specification stating that the method has to preserve the invariant of the **this** object.

To verify that a Java program satisfies its JML specification, KeY translates Java and JML into a program logic called *Java Dynamic Logic* [2]. The formula is then proven using a sequent calculus and symbolic execution. Symbolic execution is seamlessly integrated as sequent calculus rules. KeY supports modular reasoning by using a method specification to symbolically execute a method invocation statement, instead of inlining the method's body. A program in KeY is thus proven to be correct by verifying one method at a time. The use of method specifications makes the approach modular.

Finally, in the context of the current work, it is important to note that KeY not only supports full sequential Java, but also JavaCard, a Java derivative which features a transaction mechanism including rollback of interrupted transactions [2]. The fact that KeY natively supports transaction verification enables us to deal with rollback, which is the mechanism used by the EVM to deal with failure in transactions.

3 Translation to Java

We describe here our translation of Solidity contracts into Java. First, we describe the challenges in realising a semantics preserving translation from Solidity to Java. Then we explain our translation in detail. Some challenges (e.g., challenge 1) are common to all smart contract languages, whereas others (e.g., challenge 4) are Solidity specific.

1. *Distributed ledger.* Solidity contracts execute on the blockchain where all transactions are recorded and the balance of all contracts is maintained. Functions such as **transfer** use the blockchain to record exchanges of money between contracts. Neither the distributed ledger nor the functions operating over it exist in the Java runtime and are thus to be implemented separately if the specification refers to it.
2. *Message passing.* Solidity contracts may trigger the execution of functions in other contracts through *external calls* using message passing. The message not only triggers the right functionality (by naming the function to be executed), it also carries further information such as the address of the message sender and funds sent with the message. So, simply encoding Solidity function calls as Java method calls does not work as the extra information has to be passed within the method calls.
3. *Revertible transactions.* Handling of messages in smart contracts takes the form of a transaction, and failures throughout its execution result in a rollback, reverting the state to what it was at the beginning of the call. Unless explicitly handled, such failures propagate even when they happen in further function calls within the same contract or external ones. Such failures can occur indirectly due to attempts to transfer unavailable funds, or directly through the **revert** command, possibly encapsulated

within other instructions such as **require**. Java has no built-in notion of such revertible transactions, and their interaction with the underlying ledger further complicates their encoding.

4. *Bounded datatypes.* Although the EVM uses a 256-bit stack, Solidity provides a family of bounded datatypes, such as the unsigned 256-bit integers uint256 and signed 24-bit integers int24, none of which have direct equivalents in Java. These datatypes have over- and underflow semantics, e.g. using a uint256, subtracting 5 from 4 would result in $2^{256} - 1$. These datatypes are common sources of errors and many smart contract vulnerabilities are due to insufficient checks for exceeding bounds, hence, these are to be carefully modelled in the translation.

5. *Function annotations and modifiers.* Solidity allows functions to be tagged by visibility and other built-in annotations, but also with user-defined modifiers. Visibility annotations define access to contract functions, while built-in annotations include **pure** and **view** (indicating that a function will and may not change the contract's state) and **payable** (indicating that messages invoking the function may include transfer of funds with the smart contract as beneficiary together with the message). Furthermore, as discussed earlier, functions can also be annotated by user-defined modifiers, effectively code transformations, which are normally used to include recurring snippets of code into functions. Java only supports visibility modifiers and even these do not have a direct correspondence with their Solidity counterpart—the rest remain to be encoded in the translation.

6. *Fallback function.* The message-passing invocation model used by Solidity allows for the handling of messages invoking functions which are not defined in the contract using a fallback function. A contract tries to match the message function name with the functions defined in the contract to which the message is sent, but if none match, the contract's fallback function is invoked. For instance, if a contract at address addr does not define a function f, then any call to addr.f will result in the invocation of the fallback function at address addr. A common instance of this is that unless a smart contract explicitly defines a **transfer** function (to receive funds), whenever another contract tries to send it funds through addr.**transfer**, the fallback is invoked. This means that, in such a case, unless the fallback function is annotated as payable, the contract cannot receive funds. This message handling mechanism is completely absent in Java, and requires to be explicitly modelled at different points of the translation.

We explain now how our automated translation addresses the above challenges in order to preserve the semantics of the original Solidity contract.

(i) **The distributed ledger's functionality is abstracted as a public Java class.** To be able to model the environment of the smart contract—the blockchain system on which it runs—we abstract it as a public class, Address, providing the functionality of the distributed ledger on which the Solidity contracts operate (challenge 1). Thus, the distributed ledger is modelled as several Address objects that interact using the same functionality as in Solidity's blockchain. The class manages the balance of the corresponding Solidity contract and supports methods to send and transfer modelling what happens at the back of the scenes when the corresponding Solidity functions are invoked. Through this class, the functionality of the `payable` annotation, is also handled, transferring the requested amount from the caller to the callee.

(ii) **Built-in datatypes become public Java classes.** To address challenge 4, the functionality of the Solidity datatypes not available in Java has been replicated in Java interfaces and classes. We end up having multiple classes implementing an interface to support different ways of data handling, e.g., should an over- or underflow trigger an exception (used when we want to verify the absence of over- or underflows), or should it replicate the semantics of Solidity bounded integers (used in the rare cases when the smart contract may use over- and underflow in its functionality). For instance, the interface `Uint256` comes with the `Uint256int` and `Uint256BigInteger` classes to model Solidity's datatype `uint256` (see Sect. 4 for more details). Apart from providing the Solidity operators on these types (e.g. addition and multiplication for integers), the interface is also used to specify generic JML class invariants and method specifications.

We also provide Java implementations that model information about a transaction, a message and a block which are provided by Solidity as global variables accessible from within any function call. This behaviour is replicated by making the transaction, message and block information available as attributes (respectively `tx`, `msg` and `block`) in every contract class and which are updated upon every external function call.

(iii) **Solidity contracts are modelled as Java classes.** Every Solidity contract is translated into a Java class extending the `Address` class in order to have the Ethereum specific features (address where it resides, its balance), includes method definitions to handle **require** throwing an exception to deal with rollback, and includes the state variables of the Solidity contract as class attributes.

(iv) **Contract functions are modelled as methods in the contract class.** In order to translate Solidity function definitions into Java, we must address: (i) annotations; (ii) modifiers; (iii) transaction information and (iv) exception (**revert**) handling. Listing 1.3 shows the Java template generated from a definition of a function f with parameters p_1, p_2, etc., the content of which is explained below. Note that from Solidity function f, two Java functions are created: one also called f, which performs all required checks and then executes the original body of the function; and another function call_f, which is the function to be accessed and which adds the necessary machinery to handle exceptions, transaction information, etc.

Visibility annotations **public**, **private** and **internal** are mapped to Java visibility annotations, but **external** (which allows only external calls to the function) has no corresponding annotation in Java and is omitted. Internal uses of such functions would fail at the compilation stage, thus the translation is no less safe. The annotation **payable** is implemented by using the functionality provided by the Java Ethereum model. The visibility annotation in Listing 1.3 is derived from that used in the Solidity contract.

As for user-defined modifiers, we limit our automated translator to deal with modifiers which just inject code before the function's body. Each such modifier is transformed into a method which just executes the code to be injected, and which is invoked at the beginning of the main function call (see Listing 1.3).

Transaction, message and block information is available in Solidity as global variables whenever a function is called. We address this in the Java translation by encoding them as additional parameters to the call_f function. To handle failing transactions, Java exceptions are used (since catching exceptions is not possible in Solidity yet, there is no contract code in **catch**). Upon catching an exception, we use the JavaCard transaction rollback mechanism (supported by KeY) to undo the effects of the transaction so far (see the JCSystem.* calls appearing in lines 4, 6 and 9 in Listing 1.3).

(v) **Fallback function**. If a Solidity contract has a fallback function defined, then it is translated as described above. If not, we emulate the Solidity compiler and define an empty payable fallback method.

(vi) **Function calls**. Function calls are handled differently depending on whether they are internal or external, as determined at translation time. External calls performed as A.f(); (or using the Solidity **call** mechanism) are translated as calls to A. call_f(..., **msg**, **block**, **tx**) in the corresponding contract class, defaulting to the fallback function if no such function is defined. In contrast, internal calls are simply translated as direct calls to method f(...) in the contract class.

```
1   visibility_annotation return_type call_f(p₁, p₂, ..., Message _msg, Block _block, Transaction
         _tx) {
2       msg = _msg; block = _block; tx = _tx;
3       try {
4           JCSystem.beginTransaction(); // Only for verification purposes
5           return this.f(p₁, p₂, ...);
6           JCSystem.commitTransaction(); // Only for verification purposes
7       } catch (Exception e) {
8           System.out.println(e);
9           JCSystem.abortTransaction(); // Only for verification purposes
10      }
11  }
12
13  visibility_annotation return_type f(p₁, p₂, ...) {
14      this.user_defined_modifier₁();
15      this.user_defined_modifier₂();
16      ...
17      this.payable();
18      // Translated Solidity function code
19  }
```

Listing 1.3. Methods in contract class for each function in Solidity contract.

We implemented our translation in the tool JAVADITY[5]: it takes a Solidity contract and gives a Java file that can be enriched with JML specifications to be verified with KeY.

Example 1. Consider the Solidity function removeFromPot (shown in Listing 1.1). We define, a specification that uses the following three preconditions: (i) only the operator can remove from the pot, (ii) the value to be removed may not exceed the current value of the pot, and (iii) no game may be in progress (the game state must be either idle

---

[5] See https://github.com/rebiscov/Javadity.

or available); and three postconditions: (i) the variable pot is reduced by the amount withdrawn, (ii) the caller's balance is increased by this amount, and (iii) the contract's balance is reduced by the withdrawn amount. Furthermore, only the variable pot and the balances of the caller and the casino smart contract may change as a result of calling this function.

Upon applying the translation defined in this section (which is automatically carried out by JAVADITY), we obtain the Java implementation shown in Listing 1.4. We (manually) enrich the implementation with the JML specification (lines 2–9 in Listing 1.4) corresponding with the requirements above. Lines 2–4 correspond to the preconditions, lines 6–8 correspond to the postconditions and line 5 includes an assignable clause indicating the variables that may be modified during the execution of the function.

4   Verification with KeY

In this section we outline the idea and principal approach for two aspects of the specification and deductive verification of the Java translations of Solidity contracts.

```
1    /*@ private behaviour
2      @ requires operator.eq(msg.sender);
3      @ requires \invariant_for(value) && value.gr(Uint256.ZERO) && value.leq(pot);
4      @ requires state == State.IDLE || state == State.GAME_AVAILABLE;
5      @ assignable pot, msg.sender.balance, this.balance;
6      @ ensures pot.eq(\old(pot.sub(value)));
7      @ ensures msg.sender.balance.eq(\old(msg.sender.balance.sum(value)));
8      @ ensures this.balance.eq(\old(this.balance.sub(value)));
9      @ ...
10     @*/
11    private void removeFromPot(Uint256 value) throws Exception {
12        // Modifiers
13        this.byOperator();
14        this.noActiveBet();
15        // Requires
16        this.require(value.gr(Uint256.ZERO) && value.leq(pot));
17        //Function code
18        this.pot = this.pot.sub(value);
19        msg.sender.transfer(this, value);
20    }
21
22    /*@ ... @*/
23    public void call_removeFromPot(Uint256 value, Message _msg, Block _block, Transaction _tx)
          throws Exception {
24        msg = _msg; block = _block; tx = _tx;
25        try {
26          JCSystem.beginTransaction();
27          this.removeFromPot(value);
28          JCSystem.commitTransaction();
29        } catch (Exception e) {
30          JCSystem.abortTransaction();
31        }
32    }
```

Listing 1.4. Java translation of the removeFromPot function.

Unsigned Integer of 256 Bit Length. As explained in Sect. 3, Solidity's scalar uint256 datatype is mapped to the interface type Uint256 in Java. The interface provides all the arithmetic operations and comparisons needed which we specified accordingly in JML. To specify the interface in an efficient manner, we used JML's ghost fields, i.e., fields that only exist on the specification level and not on the implementation level. The advantage of ghost fields is that they can be declared for interfaces as instance fields to be implicitly present in any implementing class. Using a ghost field allows us to relate the interface type to an abstraction and to use the abstraction in other specifications.

We use a ghost field called _value of the JML type \bigint to model the value as integer. JML's bigint datatype represents the mathematical whole numbers. An additional invariant restricts the range of the ghost field to the range of Solidity's uint256 datatype. The method specifications can then describe their effect with respect to the ghost field _value. Listing 1.5 shows an excerpt of the specification. The expression \dl_MAXUINT256() refers to the maximal value of the uint256 datatype. The specification for the addition (method sum) specifies the result in relation to the ghost field value and takes care of overflow issues.

To allow the reasoning about Uint256 to be efficient and to a large degree automatic, the classes using this interface had to be enabled to treat it more similar to a primitive type than a reference type. To achieve this the immutability of the instances of this type needs to be exploited. This is until now not directly supported by KeY and will be added in a future release as additional contribution of our work.

To clarify the issue and solution, assume a class C has a field f of type Uint256. The invariant of class C will include the boolean expression \invariant_for(this. f) to assert the range restrictions. During verification of each method of class C we have in particular to show that its invariant is preserved. This can become tedious as it involves unpacking the invariant of **this**.f even though the method did not reassign any value to f and thus because of the immutability could not possibly have changed the validity of \invariant_for(**this**.f). Exploiting the knowledge about immutability allows the prover to quickly determine that no operations are able to invalidate the respective invariants. In our proof of concept we simulated this feature by specifying the dependencies of the invariants accordingly via so called **accessible** clauses. Due to the not yet implemented support for immutability in KeY, we are currently not able to prove the correctness of our accessible clauses, but can make use of them when proving.

Support for Solidity's State Rollback. To provide support for the Solidity's rollback in case of exceptions, the translation makes use of JavaCard's transaction mechanism with explicit commit and abort calls. Note again that KeY supports verification of code using revertible JavaCard transactions [2].

In order to model unexpected failures (by external events and not visible by program semantics), we generalise the JML specifications of the methods such that they allow normal as well as exceptional termination. For these methods a wrapper method call_m (..) is created (see Sect. 3) which wraps the call to m(..) using JavaCard transactions. For the JML specification of the wrapper method, we need to distinguish between the commit and abort case. For this we use a boolean ghost field (specification only field) that is true if the abort case has been triggered and false otherwise.

```
1   public interface Uint256 {
2   /*@ private instance invariant _value >= 0 && _value <= \dl_MAXUINT256();
3       @ private final instance ghost \bigint _value; @*/
4
5   /*@ private normal_behavior
6       @ requires \invariant_for(value);
7       @ ensures \result._value == (this._value+value._value > \dl_MAXUINT256() ?
8       @   ((\bigint)-1)*\dl_MAXUINT256() - 1 : (\bigint) 0) + this._value + value._value;
9       @ ensures \invariant_for(\result);
10      @ accessible _value, value._value;
11      @ assignable \strictly_nothing;
12      @ ...
13      @*/
14  Uint256 sum(Uint256 value) throws Exception;
15  }
```

Listing 1.5. Excerpt from the Uint256 interface specification.

JavaCard's transaction mechanism is API based. JCSystem.beginTransaction () starts a transaction and any code until a JCSystem.commitTransaction() or JCSystem.aboutTransaction() is symbolically executed on a copy of the original heap. In case of a commit the copy replaces the original heap; otherwise, the copy is discarded and the original heap is used instead, thus rolling back the changes in case of an abort.

5   Case Study: Casino Contract

As a case study, we use a Solidity contract modelling a casino whose legal contract is given in Fig. 1. The casino manages a pot represented as a uint256 value representing the amount of ether that can be won in a game consisting of a coin toss: A player places a bet on the outcome, transfers her stake to the contract and records the amount. If the prediction of the player is correct, the pot is transferred to her wallet, otherwise the money the player has bet is added to the pot.

The Solidity contract is translated to a Java program by our tool, and annotated with JML specifications, which describe the full functional behaviour of the contract[6]. In particular, an invariant which states that the balance of the contract is equal to the amount in the pot if no bet is currently placed; otherwise, the contract's balance equals the sum of the ether in the pot and the player's wager.

We verified that a representative selection of methods (i.e. all supported features occur) satisfy their contract and preserve the stated invariant. In particular, we verified for the methods call_closeCasino and call_removeFromPot that they behave correctly w.r.t. the rollback semantics in case of exceptions. For instance, the proof of call_removeFromPot required around 22,000 rule applications of which 207 were interactive. The most critical rule applications were target unpacking of parts of the class invariant. The rationale is to only unpack those parts whose property is required to prove a property, e.g., if the fields occurring in a conjunct of an invariant have been changed by the method and the conjunct has to be shown to be reestablished. For the

---

[6] See https://github.com/raulpardo/casino-contract-java-solidity.

unchanged parts, dependency contracts are used which exploit the fact that if a formula does not depend on changed parts of the heap then it cannot be invalidated.

The verification effort is rather straightforward. It requires some tedious but trivial interactions due to the `Uint256` datatype being modelled as interface. The necessary rule interactions are less than 1.5% of all rule applications. Thereof the vast majority of interactive rule applications consist of unpacking of class invariants. This could be easily automated by enforcing the unpacking of invariants before method contracts are used. A small minority require proving or making use of framing properties, which can be easily avoided if KeY were to make use of the fact that instances implementing the `Uint256` interface are immutable, and by tweaking the proof search strategies taking advantage of the specifics of the Solidity translation.

6   Limitations and Challenges

One of the most difficult issues to be handled by our approach is the undefined evaluation order of nested expressions in Solidity. This means the semantics of contracts with nested expressions is dependent on the compiler being used (similar to the situation in C). There are several alternatives to address this issue in our approach: (i) forbid nested expressions to be used in a Solidity contract, and to reject such contracts early on; (ii) provide compiler specific calculus rules to be chosen prior to a verification attempt, at the cost of rendering the verification result compiler specific; (iii) split the proof into one subproof for each possible evaluation order when encountering a nested expression. As all possible orders are considered, a successful verification would be meaningful independent of the used compiler. However, this can lead to rather large (number of) proofs in the presence of nested expressions; (iv) and when reaching a nested expression during symbolic execution, prove that the result is independent of the evaluation order and continue with the uniquely determined result. In our current experiment we used the first alternative, but we plan to adopt alternative (iii) or (iv) in the future.

One of the major challenges which static verification of smart contracts faces is that of modelling the blockchain environment within which the smart contract is executed. For instance, in Solidity, one may access the current block number, timestamp of the block, and other parameters which may only be known at runtime. Our approach is to make no assumption on these values, and thus proofs must go through with the values being completely non-deterministic. In this manner, we ensure soundness but we may lose completeness when an algorithm may have been designed to use implicit constraints on these values e.g. that block numbers are strictly increasing. From our experience, few smart contracts make such assumptions, and when one wants to verify a property of such a smart contract, one can still add such assumptions explicitly.

Many of the bugs and security flaws of Solidity are due to specific decisions taken when designing the language. In the white paper [7, Chapter 4.4] Everts and Muller provide a comprehensive overview of these issues. In what follows we summarise some of these issues and explain to which extent and how we deal with them.

One class of issues is rooted in the design choice concerning the semantics of certain programming constructs in Solidity. Some examples of this are: (i) a differing semantics whether division is on literals (and precomputed by the compiler) or involves variables (evaluated at runtime), (ii) difference in the treatment of method calls depending on using an implicit or explicit **this**, i.e., the statements/expressions **this**.m() and m() may result in different behaviour, and (iii) usage of copy-by-reference and copy-by-value looks the same on the source code level. All of these issues are or can be easily supported by our approach at the translation level by choosing the correct Java implementation of the used Solidity construct. This is indeed possible as these differences, although invisible or surprising to the user, can be identified unambiguously by static analysis and taken care of accordingly.

Another issue is how a programming language decides to deal with integer overflow (and underflow). Solidity joins C's and Java's approach by silently overflowing. This easily leads to mistakes, as programmers often use natural or whole numbers as internal mental models. Our approach models overflow and underflow semantics faithfully and proves a program correct only if the overflow was intended and/or does not invalidate the property to be proven. KeY for Java provides also a second sound (but incomplete) approach to the same problem by enforcing to prove that no overflow happens.

7   Related Work

Although the need for formal verification, particularly compile-time static analysis techniques, for smart contracts has been highlighted various times e.g. [3,7], actual work in the domain is still sparse. Most work on static analysis techniques for smart contracts falls in one of two categories—either Lint-like syntactic analysis of code to find potential vulnerabilities like Solcheck (https://git.io/fxXeu) and Solium (https://git.io/fxXec), or semantics-based static analysis specialised to identify commonly encountered problems with smart contracts (e.g. gas leaks, reentrancy problems).

Of the latter type, one finds approaches designed for different types of vulnerabilities. Fröwis et al. [8] address smart contract control-flow mutability which is typically not desirable. OYENTE [13] is a tool which can perform reentrancy detection and other analysis using symbolic execution. Mythril [14] uses concolic analysis, taint analysis and control-flow analysis for identifying security vulnerability, while SmartCheck (https://tool.smartdec.net) uses both Lint-like and semantic analysis to identify various vulnerabilities. Bhargavan et al. [5] transform Solidity into F* on which they perform analysis to identify vulnerable patterns. The other approaches perform their analysis at the EVM bytecode level, mainly because the control-flow analysis used typically does not use the program structure. This enables the analysis of any smart contract deployed on the Ethereum blockchain. It is worth noting that the semantics of Solidity are only informally described in the language documentation, and effectively pragmatically decided based on what the compiler does. In contrast, there are published formal semantics for EVM bytecode either through direct formalisation or via translation in [9–11].

Both these types of static analysis approaches have been shown to readily scale up to large smart contracts, the former because the complexity of syntactic analysis is of the order of the size of the source code, while the latter typically use overapproximations to ensure tractability. However, the downside is that neither of these approaches allow reasoning about the functional aspect of the smart contract under scrutiny, i.e. what the contract is actually trying to achieve. There is little published work towards achieving specification-specific static analysis for business logic verification of smart contracts.

Bai et al. [4] perform model checking using SPIN but perform the analysis on a model of the smart contract rather than directly on the code. Similarly, Abdellatif et al. [1] build a model not only of the smart contracts but also the underlying blockchain and miners using timed automata to enable verification. In both cases there lies a substantial gap between the actual smart contract and the model, raising questions of the faithfulness of the model with respect to the concrete code. Our approach suffers also from this issue due to the translation from Solidity to Java. However, our model is much more granular (no loss of precision), and thus the gap between our Java model and the original is much narrower.

8   Conclusions

We have presented a translation-based verifier of smart contracts using the deductive verification tool KeY. Our approach is one of the first to go beyond verifying standard sanity checks (e.g. *there are no integer over- and underflows*) and enable verification of business-logic and thus contract-specific specifications (e.g. *when a player guesses a number, the casino contract will pay her 1.8 times the bet they placed*). We implemented the translation in a tool and illustrated its use on a simple casino smart contract.

Although our results indicate that our approach is promising, our contribution uncovered new unexpected questions and challenges. The first question is how the approach fares with real-life contracts. What is promising is that the size and complexity of smart contracts is trivial compared to typical software systems and matches well with our case study. They typically run into some hundreds lines of code, and use loops sparingly due to gas concerns. This may indicate that typical smart contracts are within reach of automated verification techniques. We are currently applying our approach to a number of real-world use cases (some with known bugs) to evaluate better this claim.

Currently we depend solely on hand-waving argumentation that the semantics of Solidity and our translation match, which is a concern. However, we have to emphasise that there is no established (or otherwise) formal semantics of Solidity, with the language manual and the compiler acting as arbiters as to how constructs actually work. Until now, the only semantics available are at the EVM assembly level, making a proof of correctness of the translation impossible at present. However, translating between two structured high level formalisms—Solidity and JavaCard—we believe that the leap of faith is across a much narrower gap than using a semantics at a lower level of abstraction, and the fact that both languages have a native transaction (rollback) mechanism strengthens this point. Still, a proof of semantics-preservation is highly desirable. We are also currently investigating how to build a verification tool handling Solidity programs directly rather than through a translation.

References

1. Abdellatif, T., Brousmiche, K.: Formal verification of smart contracts based on users and blockchain behaviors models. In: NTMS 2018, pp. 1–5 (2018)

2. Ahrendt, W., Beckert, B., Bubel, R., Hähnle, R., Schmitt, P.H., Ulbrich, M. (eds.): Deductive Software Verification - The KeY Book. LNCS, vol. 10001. Springer, New York (2016). https://doi.org/10.1007/978-3-319-49812-6

3. Atzei, N., Bartoletti, M., Cimoli, T.: A survey of attacks on Ethereum smart contracts (SoK). In: Maffei, M., Ryan, M. (eds.) POST 2017. LNCS, vol. 10204, pp. 164–186. Springer, Heidelberg (2017). https://doi.org/10.1007/978-3-662-54455-6_8

4. Bai, X., Cheng, Z., Duan, Z., Hu, K.: Formal modeling and verification of smart contracts. In: ICSCA 2018, pp. 322–326 (2018)

5. Bhargavan, K., et al.: Formal verification of smart contracts: Short paper. In: PLAS 2016, ACM (2016)

6. Delmolino, K., Arnett, M., Kosba, A., Miller, A., Shi, E.: Step by step towards creating a safe smart contract: lessons and insights from a cryptocurrency lab. In: Clark, J., Meiklejohn, S., Ryan, P.Y.A., Wallach, D., Brenner, M., Rohloff, K. (eds.) FC 2016. LNCS, vol. 9604, pp. 79–94. Springer, Heidelberg (2016). https://doi.org/10.1007/978-3-662-53357-4_6

7. Everts, M., Muller, F.: Will that smart contract really do what you expect it to do? White paper (2018)

8. Fröwis, M., Böhme, R.: In code we trust? – measuring the control flow immutability of all smart contracts deployed on Ethereum. In: Garcia-Alfaro, J., Navarro-Arribas, G., Hartenstein, H., Herrera-Joancomartí, J. (eds.) ESORICS/DPM/CBT 2017. LNCS, vol. 10436, pp. 357–372. Springer, Cham (2017). https://doi.org/10.1007/978-3-319-67816-0_20

9. Grishchenko, I., Maffei, M., Schneidewind, C.: A semantic framework for the security analysis of Ethereum smart contracts. In: Bauer, L., Küsters, R. (eds.) POST 2018. LNCS, vol. 10804, pp. 243–269. Springer, Cham (2018). https://doi.org/10.1007/978-3-319-89722-6_10

10. Hildenbrandt, E., et al.: KEVM: a complete semantics of the Ethereum virtual machine. White paper (2017)

11. Hirai, Y.: Defining the Ethereum virtual machine for interactive theorem provers. In: Brenner, M., et al. (eds.) FC 2017. LNCS, vol. 10323, pp. 520–535. Springer, Cham (2017). https://doi.org/10.1007/978-3-319-70278-0_33

12. Leavens, G.T., Baker, A.L., Ruby, C.: Preliminary design of JML: a behavioral interface specification language for Java. ACM SIGSOFT Softw. Eng. Notes **31**(3), 1–38 (2006)

13. Luu, L., Chu, D., Olickel, H., Saxena, P., Hobor, A.: Making smart contracts smarter. In: CCS 2016, pp. 254–269 (2016)

14. Mueller, B.: Smashing Ethereum smart contracts for fun and real profit. In: HITB SECCONF Amsterdam (2018)

15. Nakamoto, S.: Bitcoin: a peer-to-peer electronic cash system. White Paper (2009). https://bitcoin.org/bitcoin.pdf

16. Wood, G.: Ethereum: a secure decentralised generalised transaction ledger. Ethereum Project Yellow Paper 151, pp. 1–32 (2014)

An Approach to Generate Effective Fault Localization Methods for Programs

Babak Bagheri, Mohammad Rezaalipour, and Mojtaba Vahidi-Asl[⊠]

Faculty of Computer Science and Engineering,
Shahid Beheshti University G. C., Tehran, Iran
mo_vahidi@sbu.ac.ir

Abstract. Software Debugging is a tedious and costly task in software development life-cycle. Thus, various automated fault localization approaches have been proposed to address this problem, among which, spectrum-based fault localization has attracted a lot of attention. Using various formulas, known as ranking metrics, spectrum-based fault localization techniques assign scores to the entities of programs (e.g., statements) based on their suspiciousness of being the root cause of failures. Despite the obvious advantages of spectrum-based fault localization techniques, such as being lightweight, they cannot effectively locate faults in every program owing to the fact that they do not consider the characteristics of the programs. We believe that program characteristics can be helpful at finding the right ranking metrics for programs, and they can assist at combining several existing ones to produce a customized ranking metric specific to a given program.

In this paper, we have proposed an approach which combines 40 different ranking metrics to generate a new ranking metric specific to a given program. Employing mutation testing operators, the proposed approach retrieves information from the program and then, using different preferential voting systems, it combines various ranking metrics based on the collected information. We have evaluated our approach on 154 faulty versions from eight different programs of Space and Siemens test suite and compare it with nine state-of-the-art ranking metrics. The experimental results indicate that the ranking metrics generated by our approach is superior with respect to evaluation metrics such as the *Exam* score and *TOP-N*.

Keywords: Software fault localization ·
Spectrum-based fault localization · Mutation testing · Ranking metric ·
Preferential voting system

1 Introduction

Manual debugging is a difficult task that consumes a lot of resources in software development process [21]. It is reported that up to 80% of the total software

© IFIP International Federation for Information Processing 2019
Published by Springer Nature Switzerland AG 2019
H. Hojjat and M. Massink (Eds.): FSEN 2019, LNCS 11761, pp. 244–259, 2019.
https://doi.org/10.1007/978-3-030-31517-7_17

development budget might be consumed by debugging tasks [20]. To address this problem, a wide variety of *Automated Fault Localization* (AFL) techniques have been established in the literature to assist developers at locating the root causes of failures [23]. There are several approaches to automated fault localization such as slicing-based [12,22,27], machine-learning-based [14,26,30], and spectrum-based fault localization [1,6,10,19,28]. The *Spectrum-based Fault Localization* (SFL) approach has been shown to be competitive compared to the rest [16]. Also, SFL is a lightweight approach, and it can be applied to large-scale programs [29].

SFL techniques execute a given program with an existing set of passing and failing test cases. Then, leveraging *program spectra* [23] (i.e. program execution traces of test cases), and employing a *ranking metric* [26], the *suspiciousness scores* of *program entities* are computed. Program entities are source code elements with any granularity such as statements, methods, and basic blocks. Suspiciousness scores indicate the likelihood of each program entity to be faulty, and ranking metrics assign higher suspiciousness scores to entities covered by more failing tests and fewer passing ones. After the computation of suspiciousness scores, program entities are sorted according to their suspiciousness scores and handed to developers or *automated program repair* techniques [13]. Finally, the source code is examined from the most suspicious entity to the least suspicious one with the purpose of diagnosing the root causes of failures.

Several SFL techniques such as *Ochiai* [1] exist in the literature, each of which performs effectively on specific programs while not ranking entities of other programs, appropriately [28]. In other words, for most programs, current techniques assign higher suspiciousness scores to program entities that are not related to the fault at hand [12]. Our intuition is that this issue can be addressed if program characteristics are considered while suspiciousness scores are computed, which is also mentioned by Wong et al. [23]. The semantics and structures of programs are two examples of program characteristics. We believe that program characteristics can lead us toward finding right SFL techniques (among the existing ones) for any given program. Also, we hypothesize it can assist us at combining various existing ranking metrics (i.e., SFL techniques) to produce more effective ranking metrics, explicitly customized for a given program.

In this paper, we present an approach that combines various ranking metrics to generate an effective one for a given program. In this approach, first, using *mutation testing* [9], several mutants are produced for the given program which are then executed by an existing test suite. Then, runtime data such as program spectra generated for the mutants are collected which are employed as a representation of program characteristics. Afterward, these runtime data are utilized to compute the effectiveness of 40 state-of-the-art ranking metrics. In the end, considering the effectiveness calculated for these ranking metrics and employing *preferential voting systems* [2,4,11,18], the 40 ranking metrics are combined to generate a new ranking metric. We evaluate our approach using 154 faulty versions of the Siemens suite and the Space program and compare it with nine state-of-the-art SFL techniques. According to the experimental results, the ranking metrics produced by our approach always perform more effective compared to the nine comparative ranking metrics, regarding well-known evaluation metrics such as the *Exam* score and *TOP-N*.

The remainder of this paper is structured as follows: Sect. 2 reviews preliminary materials and related work; Sect. 3 presents the proposed approach of this paper; Sect. 4 provides the experimental results and discussions; Sect. 5 concludes this work.

2   Background and Related Work

In the following, Sect. 2.1 provides a brief description of the preliminary materials related to our work, and Sect. 2.2 reviews some of the state-of-the-art automated fault localization techniques.

2.1   Preliminaries

Spectrum-Based Fault Localization. The goal of Spectrum-based Fault Localization (SFL) techniques is to locate faulty program entities such as statements, methods, and basic blocks. SFL techniques take as input a faulty program and two sets of test cases. One of these sets contains failing test cases while the other set has passing ones. Afterward, it collects program execution traces of the test cases, referred to as program spectra [23], by instrumenting and executing the given program, using the failing and passing test cases. Each program spectrum reports information regarding program entities that are executed by a test case. Various tools can record program spectra. For instance, in our experiments, we use *Gcov* [8] to instrument programs and retrieve runtime data. Based on program spectra, several statistics are computed for each program entity e_j such as $N_{CF}(e_j)$, $N_{CS}(e_j)$, $N_{UF}(e_j)$, and $N_{US}(e_j)$, which are the number of failing and passing (successful) test cases covering e_j, and the number of failing and passing test cases not covering e_j, respectively. Using these statistics, and employing a ranking metric [26] such as Ochiai [1], which is shown in Eq. (1), SFL techniques compute the suspiciousness score of every program entity. After computing the suspiciousness scores, the program entities are sorted and handed to developers or automated program repair techniques [13] to assist them in their debugging task.

$$Score_{Ochiai}(e_j) = \frac{N_{CF}(e_j)}{\sqrt{(N_{CF}(e_j) + N_{UF}(e_j)) \times (N_{CF}(e_j) + N_{CS}(e_j))}} \quad (1)$$

Mutation Testing. As a testing technique, mutation testing [9] is used to measure the effectiveness of test suites regarding their ability to detect faults in programs. This technique produces several mutants p_i $(1 < i < m)$ for a program p by seeding it with m faults. Faults are seeded by employing *mutation operators*, which perform syntactical modifications to programs, such as replacing a relational operator by another one. Then, the mutants are executed against the whole test suite. If the result or behavior of a mutant p_i is different compared to p, p_i is said to be killed. The higher the number of killed mutants, the more effective the test suite is. Besides being the most successful metric to measure test suite effectiveness [3], mutation testing can be used for other purposes, as well. For example, state-of-the-art automated program repair techniques such as *ELEXIR* [17] apply various mutation operators for patch generation. In this paper, we use mutation testing to measure fault localizing capability of SFL techniques for a given program. We generate several mutants for the program at hand and then, compute the effectiveness of SFL techniques at finding the faults in these mutants.

Preferential Voting System. *Ranked voting* refers to special electoral systems in which voters can vote for more than one candidate and sort them in their ballots in order of their preferences. This type of ballot, referred to as *ranked ballot*, contains more information compared to those that only mention one candidate. Therefore, they must be processed and aggregated using certain methods specific to them called preferential voting systems. There are various preferential voting systems in the literature each of which is subject to criteria such as *monotonicity* which states that when a candidate is the winner of the election, changing a ballot in favor of this candidate must still keep it as the winner of the election. Reviewing these criteria and the advantages of different preferential voting systems are beyond the scope of this paper, and we encourage interested readers to refer to [5] for further details. For this research, we choose four preferential voting systems *Instant Run-Off Voting* [4], *Kemeny-Young* [11], *Condorcet* [2], and *Schulze* [18] because of their popularity among researchers. We use these systems to aggregate ranking ballots produced by different mutants which act as voters that prioritize various SFL techniques (ranking metrics) in their ballots.

2.2 Automated Fault Localization Techniques

There are hundreds of studies about Automated Fault Localization (AFL) techniques [23]. Program slicing-based AFL techniques obtain a *slice* for a given program by collecting its executable statements that might have an impact on the value of a specified variable. Xuan and Monperrus [27] proposed a method called *test case purification* which utilizes program slicing to reduce failing test cases with several assertions into several test cases with only one assertion. They also indicated that employing test case purification improves the fault detection capability of spectrum-based fault localization techniques. Mao et al. [12] proposed a novel approach which first employs program slicing to identify program entities that affect the given program output, and then, it uses a spectrum based fault localization technique to rank the remaining entities with respect to their suspiciousness. Wang et al. [22] presented a debugging framework called *DrDebug* that enables users to debug multi-threaded programs while focusing on a specific slice.

Machine learning, a field of artificial intelligence, has been used in various studies on different software engineering tasks such as automated program

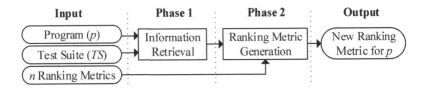

Fig. 1. Overall structure of the proposed approach

repair [17] It has also been used in automated fault localization. Xuan and Monperrus [26] employed machine learning to present a fault localization technique that estimates the suspiciousness of program entities by automatically combining 25 ranking metrics. Zhang and Zhang [30] employed a Markov logic network to compute the suspiciousness of program statements. Nath and Domingos [14] presented a probabilistic-based fault localization technique that finds faults according to the bug patterns it learns. This technique has the capability of employing the output of spectrum-based fault localization techniques as features, and can be trained on a set of faulty programs.

Spectrum-based fault localization is probably the most studied approach in the field, which is thoroughly reviewed in [19]. The first ranking metric, Tarantula, was proposed by Jones et al. [10] which is based on the idea that program entities covered by more failing and fewer passing test cases are the most suspicious ones of being the root causes of failures. Dallmeier et al. [6] proposed Ample as a plug-in for the Java IDE Eclipse to locate faults in object-oriented programs. Abreu et al. [1] studied three widely used ranking metrics Tarantula, Ample, and Ochiai and reported that Ochiai outperforms the other two techniques. Yoo et al. [28] studied different ranking metrics and realized that some of them are equivalent and do not dominate each other. They also concluded that there is not a ranking metric that outperforms all the other ranking metrics for every program.

The proposed approach of this paper is not based on program slicing and does not employ machine learning. Our approach combines several existing SFL techniques using preferential voting systems and mutation testing. In this regard, it is different from the studies mentioned above.

3 Proposed Approach

This section presents the proposed approach of this paper, by which an effective ranking metric is produced for a given program. As illustrated in Fig. 1, the proposed approach receives three different inputs: (1) a program p, for which a new ranking metric is produced; (2) a test suite TS; (3) n existing ranking metrics. Following two phases, the proposed approach generates a new ranking metric for p by combining the n given ranking metrics.

At the first phase, various mutation operators are applied to p to generate m mutants for it. Then, the mutants are executed by every test case in TS, and the

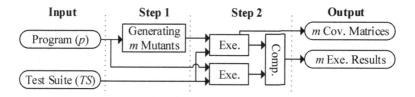

Fig. 2. Details of phase 1

execution results are collected and passed to the second phase (see more details in Sect. 3.1). At the second phase, for each mutant, the effectiveness of every n ranking metric is computed, employing the output of the first phase. Then, these ranking metrics are combined based on their effectiveness so that a new ranking metric is generated that is more effective for p, compared to each of the n given ranking metrics, individually (see more details in Sect. 3.2).

3.1 Phase 1: Information Retrieval

The proposed approach generates ranking metrics specific to a given program. To this end, the characteristics of the given program must be retrieved and taken into consideration. The purpose of this phase is to collect this information, employing mutation testing. As illustrated in Fig. 2, this phase comprises two steps.

Step 1: Mutant Generation. At this step, m mutants are generated for the given program p, subject to three criteria: (1) the test suite TS must be capable of killing them all; (2) the mutants must be free of any infinite loops; (3) executing the mutants on TS must not result in any crashes or runtime errors. Those mutants that do not satisfy the criteria, mentioned above, are thrown away, and new mutants are generated to replace them. The following mutation operators are randomly used to seed a fault in a randomly selected statement:

- modifying a character or numerical literal
- changing a relational operator (e.g., >)
- changing a logical operator (e.g., &&)
- replacing a function call by another one with the same signature
- replacing a variable by another variable of the same type
- inserting a statement
- replacing a predicate with *TRUE* or *FALSE*.

Step 2: Execution. At this step, each mutant, produced at the previous step, is executed by every test case in TS. As a result, for each mutant, a matrix is produced known as program spectra for that mutant, and we refer to it as the *coverage matrix*. The output produced after executing each mutant using TS is also collected. By comparing a mutant's output with the output produced for p, the execution results for that mutant is obtained. For instance, Fig. 3 shows an example of a coverage matrix collected for a mutant, along with its execution results. Column one shows the five test cases within the test suite. Column two through eight illustrate the coverage matrix, where 0s and 1s indicate that program entity e_i is covered and not covered, respectively, while executed by test case t_i. Column nine contains the execution results for the mutant, where 0s and 1s indicate that test case t_i is failed and passed, respectively.

	e_1	e_2	e_3	e_4	e_5	e_6	e_7	r
t_1	1	1	1	1	0	1	0	0
t_2	0	0	1	0	1	1	1	0
t_3	1	0	1	1	1	1	1	0
t_4	1	0	0	1	1	1	0	1
t_5	1	1	1	0	1	0	1	1

Fig. 3. Example of a coverage matrix and execution results produced for a mutant.

3.2   Phase 2: Ranking Metric Generation

According to Fig. 4, phase 2 comprises three different steps. Following these steps, the n given ranking metrics are combined to produce a new ranking metric for p.

Step 1: Generating Ranked Ballots. At this step, for each of the m mutants, the effectiveness of the n ranking metrics are computed, using the coverage matrices and execution results produced at the previous phase. By doing so, m ranked ballots are produced, each of which contains the n ranking metrics listed according to their effectiveness at locating the fault within the corresponding mutant. Table 1 illustrates an example of 45 ranked ballots produced for a program, while $m = 45$, and $n = 5$. Column 2 and 4 show the ranked ballots, and column 1 and 3 indicate the number of instances of each ballot. For example, according to this table, for five different mutants, the sequence "$T_1 > T_2 > T_3 > T_4 > T_5$" has been produced as the ranked ballot. This ballot states that T_1 and T_5 are the most and the least effective ranking metrics at locating the faults within these five mutants.

Step 2: Selecting Ranking Metrics. At this step, the ranked ballots produced at the previous step are aggregated into an ordered list of ranking metrics, using one of the two preferential voting systems *Instant Run-Off Voting* [4] and *Kemeny-Young* [11]. For instance, applying Instant Run-Off Voting to Table 1 produces "$T_2 > T_3 > T_1 > T_4 > T_5$", and using Kemeny-Young results in "$T_4 > T_3 > T_1 > T_5 > T_2$". Then, as the output of this step, k best ranking metrics are selected among the resulting list, which is referred to as B. For example, for $k = 4$, using Instant Run-Off Voting and Kemeny-Young results in $B = [T_1, T_2, T_3, T_4]$ and $B = [T_1, T_3, T_4, T_5]$, respectively.

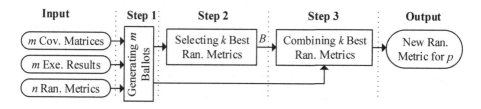

Fig. 4. Details of phase 2

Table 1. Example of ranked ballots produced at step 1 of phase 2

No. of mutants	Ranked ballot	No. of mutants	Ranked ballot
5	$T_1 > T_2 > T_3 > T_4 > T_5$	7	$T_2 > T_1 > T_4 > T_3 > T_5$
5	$T_1 > T_5 > T_4 > T_2 > T_3$	2	$T_2 > T_3 > T_1 > T_5 > T_4$
8	$T_3 > T_4 > T_5 > T_1 > T_2$	7	$T_5 > T_2 > T_4 > T_3 > T_1$
3	$T_2 > T_1 > T_3 > T_4 > T_5$	8	$T_4 > T_3 > T_1 > T_5 > T_2$

Step 3: Combining Ranking Metrics. As illustrated in Fig. 4, this step receives B, which contains the k best ranking metrics selected at the second step. It also gets the ranked ballots produced at the first step. Then, using Eq. (2), a new ranking metric is generated, which is the output of the proposed approach.

$$NewScore(e_j) = \sum_{i=1}^{k} w_{B_i} \times NormScore_{B_i}(e_j) \qquad (2)$$

In Eq. (2), e_j represents program entities in p, for which suspiciousness scores are computed; the term w_{B_i} is the weight computed for ranking metric B_i according to its effectiveness at locating faults in p; the term $NormScore_{B_i}(e_j)$ is the normalized suspiciousness score computed by ranking metric B_i for e_j, employing the *feature scaling* method presented in Eq. (3).

$$NormScore_T(e_j) = \frac{Score_T(e_j) - min_T}{max_T - min_T} \qquad (3)$$

Equation (3) standardizes the range of suspiciousness scores that a given ranking metric (T) computes by scaling them in the range $[0, 1]$. The term $Score_T(e_j)$ is the suspiciousness score computed by T for program entity e_j; the terms min_T and max_T are respectively the minimum and maximum suspiciousness scores computed by T for all of the program entities in p.

The terms w_{B_i} ($1 < i < k$) in Eq. 2 are determined by employing one of the two preferential voting systems *Condorcet* [2] and *Schulze* [18], and using the ranked ballots produced at the first step. In case of using Condorcet, first, Condorcet's pairwise matrix of the given ranked ballots is produced which indicates the number of times each ranking metric has been more effective compared to the rest of them. Figure 5a shows an example of a pairwise matrix computed for the ballots in Table 1. Afterward, the terms w_{B_i} $(1 < i < k)$ are calculated using Eq. (4), where M is Condorcet's pairwise matrix. For instance, considering Fig. 5a as the pairwise matrix, w_{B_1}, w_{B_2}, w_{B_3}, and w_{B_4} are $\frac{68}{270} = 0.251$, $\frac{72}{270} = 0.266$, $\frac{59}{270} = 0.218$, and $\frac{71}{270} = 0.262$, respectively.

$$w_{B_i} = \frac{1}{\sum_{i=1}^{k} \sum_{j=1, i \neq j}^{k} M[i,j]} \sum_{j=1, j \neq i}^{k} M[i,j] \qquad (4)$$

		Against			
		B_1	B_2	B_3	B_4	Total
For	B_1	-	26	20	22	68
	B_2	19	-	29	24	72
	B_3	25	16	-	18	59
	B_4	23	21	27	-	71
						270

(a)

		Against			
		B_1	B_2	B_3	B_4	Total
For	B_1	-	26	26	24	76
	B_2	25	-	29	24	78
	B_3	25	25	-	24	74
	B_4	25	25	27	-	77
						305

(b)

Fig. 5. Example of a pairwise and strength matrix produced for the lists in Table 1. (a) Pairwise matrix; (b) Strength matrix.

In case of using Schulze, first, Schulze's strength matrix is computed for the given ranked ballots. This matrix illustrates the strengths of the strongest paths for each pair of ranking metrics. In other words, it indicates how effective a ranking metric has performed compared to the other ranking metrics (for further details on strongest paths refer to [18]). Then, the weights are computed employing Eq. (4), where M is Schulze's strength matrix. Figure 5b indicates an example of a strength matrix calculated for the lists in Table 1. Using this matrix, w_{B_1}, w_{B_2}, w_{B_3}, and w_{B_4} are $\frac{76}{305} = 0.249$, $\frac{78}{305} = 0.255$, $\frac{74}{305} = 0.242$, and $\frac{77}{305} = 0.252$, respectively.

4 Experiments

In this section, we present the evaluation of the proposed approach. Section 4.1 reviews the experiment setup; Sect. 4.2 provides the results of the experiments; Sect. 4.3 presents the discussion; Sect. 4.4 explains the threats to the validity of the experimental results.

4.1 Experiment Setup

Subject Programs. The proposed approach is evaluated on eight popular programs, the Siemens suite along with the Space program, provided by *Software-artifact Infrastructure Repository* (SIR) [7], which has been employed by various fault localization studies. Table 2 illustrates the details of these programs.

The first row shows each program's size. Row two indicates the number of faulty versions we have used in our experiments, each of which contains a single bug. Row three shows the size of each program's test suite, and row four illustrates the number of mutants generated for the programs, which is the parameter m of the proposed approach. During the experiments, we made sure that the generated mutants were different from their corresponding faulty versions by analyzing them, manually.

Table 2. Subject programs.

	Print tokens	Print tokens 2	Replace	Schedule	Schedule 2	Tcas	Tot info	Space	Total
LOC	478	399	512	292	301	141	440	6218	**8781**
No. of faulty versions	5	10	31	9	9	36	19	35	**154**
No. of test cases	4130	4115	5542	2650	2710	1608	1051	13858	
No. of mutants (m)	143	127	203	118	126	96	183	483	

Evaluation Metrics. To evaluate the effectiveness of the proposed approach, we used three metrics of evaluation, which are defined as follows:

1. Exam: The *Exam* score [23] indicates the percentage of code that needs to be inspected to locate the fault within a program. This metric is used to compare AFL techniques on a single program while in our experiments, we had 154 faulty versions of eight different programs (see Table 2). Therefore, for any ranking metric T, we computed T's *Exam* score on every faulty version, and then, reported the mean of these 154 resulting scores as the *Exam* score of T. A lower value of this metric indicates higher effectiveness.

2. Proportion of Located Faults: This evaluation metric indicates the percentage of faults located while a specific percentage of program entities are inspected. To compute this metric for a ranking metric T, the top 10% of the program entities in each faulty version were inspected, and the percentage of located faults was reported. A higher value of this metric indicates higher effectiveness.

3. TOP-N: This metric is similar to the previous one with the only difference that in this metric, instead of a specific percentage of program entities, a certain number of them are inspected. Considering the fact that regardless of the size of programs, developers usually inspect a few of the top-ranked program entities presented by AFL techniques [15], this metric is important in practice. In our experiments, to compute this metric for a ranking metric T, top ten program entities in each faulty version were examined, and the number of located faults were reported as T's *TOP-10* score. Note that a higher value of this metric indicates higher effectiveness.

Configuration and Implementation. We utilized the 40 state-of-the-art ranking metrics presented in Table 3 as the third input to the proposed approach, and thus, in our experiments, n was always 40. As stated in Sect. 3, for the task of selecting k best ranking metrics, the proposed approach can use one of the two methods *Instant Run-Off Voting* and *Kemeny-Young*, and to perform the task of combining these ranking metrics, it may employ *Condorcet* or *Schulze*. As a result, four different instances of the proposed approach was implemented, each of which utilizes one of the two possible preferential voting systems for these two tasks. These four instances are: "Instant Run-Off Voting + Condorcet", "Instant Run-Off Voting + Schulze," "Kemeny-Young + Condorcet," and "Kemeny-Young + Schulze," which we refer to as IRV-C, IRV-S, KY-C, and KY-S, respectively.

Table 3. Ranking metrics used in the experiments.

#	Name	#	Name	#	Name	#	Name
1	Braun-Banquet [23]	11	Ample [6]	21	Hamming [23]	31	Sorensen-Dice [23]
2	Baroni-Urbani & Buser [23]	12	Phi (Geometric Mean) [23]	22	Hamann [23]	32	Tarantula [10]
3	Mountford [23]	13	Arithmetic Mean [23]	23	Sokal [23]	33	Naish2 [24]
4	Fossum [23]	14	Cohen [23]	24	Scott [23]	34	Ochiai [1]
5	Pearson [23]	15	Fleiss [23]	25	Rogot1 [23]	35	Wong [24]
6	Gower [23]	16	Zoltar [23]	26	Kulczynski [23]	36	GP13 [25]
7	Michael [23]	17	Harmonic Mean [23]	27	Anderberg [23]	37	GP02 [25]
8	Pierce [23]	18	Rogot2 [23]	28	Dice [23]	38	GP03 [25]
9	Dennis [23]	19	Simple Matching [23]	29	Goodman [23]	39	GP19 [25]
10	Tarwid [23]	20	Rogers & Tanimoto [23]	30	Jaccard [23]	40	Russel & Rao [24]

All of the four instances of the proposed approach were implemented in C++, and the experiments were conducted on a virtual machine with Intel Core i5 CPU at 1.60 GHz, 2 GBs of RAM, and the 64-bit version of Ubuntu 16.04. To instrument code and retrieve runtime data, we employed *Gcov* [8], the GNU coverage testing tool that considers code lines as program entities.

4.2   Results

In this section we present the results of comparing the four instances of the proposed approach namely KY-S, IRV-S, KY-C, and IRV-C with nine state-of-the-art ranking metrics *Naish2* [24], *Zoltar* [23], *GP13* [25], *Ochia* [1], *Tarantula* [10], *Jaccard* [23], *GP03* [25], *GP02* [25], and *Wong* [24]. Figure 6a shows the results of the effectiveness comparison with respect to the first evaluation metric presented in Sect. 4.1. According to the results, the four instances of the proposed approach perform better than the rest of the ranking metrics. Also, KY-S shows better effectiveness compared to the other three instances of the proposed approach. Furthermore, the results indicate that fault localization effectiveness can be increased by up to 62% using KY-S.

Figure 6b compares the effectiveness of the proposed approach with other ranking metrics with respect to the second evaluation metric presented in Sect. 4.1. The purpose of this experiment is to evaluate the proposed approach while only a small portion of program entities (in our case 10% of them) are examined, which is an important perspective since developers tend not to examine every program entity presented by AFL techniques. Based on the results, the proposed approach has the best effectiveness compared to other ranking metrics, and again, KY-S performs better than the other three instances of the proposed approach. To further investigate the effectiveness of the proposed approach, we also compared KY-S, and KY-C with Naish2, Ochiai, and GP13 while the portion of inspected program entities varied from 20% to 50%, and the results are illustrated in Fig. 6c. As can be seen, no matter how many program entities are inspected, KY-S is always superior.

Figure 6d shows the results of comparing the proposed approach with other ranking metrics, regarding the third evaluation metric presented in Sect. 4.1, which indicates the number of located faults by each ranking metric while only ten program entities are inspected. According to the results, KY-S is superior compared to the other ranking metrics.

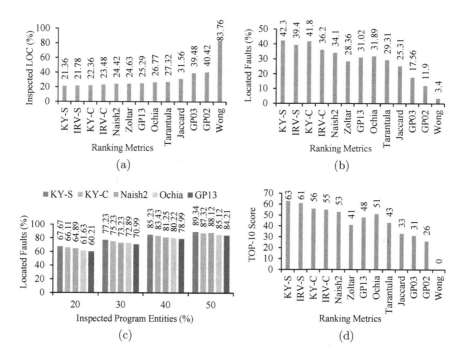

Fig. 6. Experimental results. (a) *Exam* scores; (b) proportion of located faults; (c) proportion of faults located with respect to inspected program entities; (d) *TOP-10* scores.

4.3   Discussions

According to the experimental results presented in Sect. 4.2, the preferential voting system used at step 3 in phase 2, which combines the best ranking metrics, has a significant impact on the effectiveness of the generated ranking metric. Considering the experimental results, employing the Schulze method results in ranking metrics that are more effective than those produced by the Condorcet method. We believe that this advantage is rooted in the ability of Schulze in considering the transitive relation between the ranking metrics in ranked ballots produced at step 1 in phase 2. In other words, compared to Condorcet, the Schulze method can more appropriately determine the effectiveness of different ranking metrics based on given ranked ballots.

Another important factor for generating an effective ranking metric is the preferential voting system employed at step 2 in phase 2, which selects k best ranking metrics among n. To investigate the impact of this factor, we removed this step by setting k to n, and then, repeated the experiments. By doing so, the *Exam* score of KY-S growed from 21.36% to 31.54% (which demonstrates a decline in its effectiveness), and also the effectiveness of KY-S with respect to the second and the third evaluation metrics presented in Sect. 4.1 decreased from 42.3% to 16.8%, and from 63 bugs to 28 bugs, respectively. The parameter k also has a significant influence on the effectiveness of the proposed approach. To investigate the impact of this parameter, we repeated the experiments by setting k as 5, 20, and 40. The results of this experiment is illustrated in Table 4, according to which KY-S has the best effectiveness for $k = 5$.

Table 4. Sensitivity analysis of the parameter k for KY-S.

	$k = 5$	$k = 20$	$k = 40$
Exam score (%)	21.36	29.46	31.45
Proportion of faults located (%)	42.3	24.3	16.8

4.4   Threats to Validity

The most critical threat to the validity of our experimental results is whether they generalize to other programs. We have evaluated the proposed approach using the Siemens suite which comprises relatively small programs. However, these programs have been employed by many researchers in the field, and also, we tried to mitigate this issue by using 35 faulty versions of the Space program which are quite larger compared to the items in the Siemens suite.

In addition, the type of mutants generated at step 1 in phase 1, and the number of ranking metrics selected at step 2 in phase 2 (the parameter k) can also affect the experimental results, and thus, they are considered as other threats to the validity of our results.

5 Conclusions

In this paper, we presented an approach to generate SFL ranking metrics for programs by combining various existing ranking metrics. We implemented four instances of the proposed approach based on the preferential voting systems used for two different tasks within the approach. All four instances of the proposed approach were evaluated using the Siemens suite and the Space program, and they were compared with nine state-of-the-art ranking metrics. According to the results, using Kemeny-Young for selecting the best ranking metrics and employing Schulze to combine them leads to better ranking metrics compared to the other three instances of the proposed approach. Also, all four instances of the proposed approach generate ranking metrics that are more effective than the baselines with respect to the evaluation metrics such as the *Exam* score and *TOP-N*.

In this work, we used four different preferential voting systems while there are many other such systems that we plan to investigate their impact on our approach. Also, to reduce the threat to the validity of our results, we are going to evaluate our approach on Object-oriented, real-world, and large-sized programs, as well. Since each subject program used in our experiments had only one bug, we are going to evaluate our approach on programs with multiple bugs, as well.

References

1. Abreu, R., Zoeteweij, P., Van Gemund, A.J.: An evaluation of similarity coefficients for software fault localization. In: Proceedings of the 12th Pacific Rim International Symposium on Dependable Computing, pp. 39–46 (2006). https://doi.org/10.1109/PRDC.2006.18
2. Amy, D.J.: Behind the Ballot Box: A Citizen's Guide to Voting Systems. Greenwood Publishing Group (2000)
3. Andrews, J.H., Briand, L.C., Labiche, Y.: Is mutation an appropriate tool for testing experiments? (software testing). In: Proceedings of the 27th International Conference on Software Engineering, pp. 402–411 (2005). https://doi.org/10.1109/ICSE.2005.1553583
4. Cary, D.: Estimating the margin of victory for instant-runoff voting. In: Website Proceedings of the Conference on Electronic Voting Technology/Workshop on Trustworthy Elections (2011)
5. Cranor, L.F.: Declared-strategy voting: an instrument for group decision-making. Ph.D. thesis, Washington University (1996)
6. Dallmeier, V., Lindig, C., Zeller, A.: Lightweight bug localization with ample. In: Proceedings of the 6th International Symposium on Automated Analysis-driven Debugging, pp. 99–104 (2005). https://doi.org/10.1145/1085130.1085143
7. Do, H., Elbaum, S., Rothermel, G.: Supporting controlled experimentation with testing techniques: an infrastructure and its potential impact. Empir. Softw. Eng. **10**(4), 405–435 (2005). https://doi.org/10.1007/s10664-005-3861-2
8. Gough, B., Stallman, R.M.: An Introduction to GCC for the GNU Compilers gcc and g++. Network Theory Ltd. (2004)

9. Jia, Y., Harman, M.: An analysis and survey of the development of mutation testing. IEEE Trans. Softw. Eng. **37**(5), 649–678 (2011). https://doi.org/10.1109/TSE.2010.62

10. Jones, J.A., Harrold, M.J., Stasko, J.: Visualization of test information to assist fault localization. In: Proceedings of the 24th International Conference on Software Engineering, pp. 467–477 (2002). https://doi.org/10.1145/581396.581397

11. Kemeny, J.G.: Mathematics without numbers. Daedalus **88**(4), 577–591 (1959). https://www.mitpressjournals.org/loi/daed

12. Mao, X., Lei, Y., Dai, Z., Qi, Y., Wang, C.: Slice-based statistical fault localization. J. Syst. Softw. **89**, 51–62 (2014). https://doi.org/10.1016/j.jss.2013.08.031

13. Monperrus, M.: Automatic software repair: a bibliography. ACM Comput. Surv. **51**(1), 17:1–17:24 (2018). https://doi.org/10.1145/3105906

14. Nath, A., Domingos, P.: Learning tractable probabilistic models for fault localization. In: Proceedings of the 13th AAAI Conference on Artificial Intelligence, pp. 1294–1301 (2016)

15. Parnin, C., Orso, A.: Are automated debugging techniques actually helping programmers? In: Proceedings of the International Symposium on Software Testing and Analysis, pp. 199–209 (2011). https://doi.org/10.1145/2001420.2001445

16. Pearson, S., et al.: Evaluating and improving fault localization. In: Proceedings of the 39th International Conference on Software Engineering, pp. 609–620 (2017). https://doi.org/10.1109/ICSE.2017.62

17. Saha, R.K., Lyu, Y., Yoshida, H., Prasad, M.R.: Elixir: effective object-oriented program repair. In: Proceedings of the 32nd IEEE/ACM International Conference on Automated Software Engineering, pp. 648–659 (2017). https://doi.org/10.1109/ASE.2017.8115675

18. Schulze, M.: A new monotonic, clone-independent, reversal symmetric, and condorcet-consistent single-winner election method. Soc. Choice Welf. **36**(2), 267–303 (2011). https://doi.org/10.1007/s00355-010-0475-4

19. de Souza, H.A., Chaim, M.L., Kon, F.: Spectrum-based software fault localization: a survey of techniques, advances, and challenges (2016). http://arxiv.org/abs/1607.04347

20. Tassey, G.: The economic impacts of inadequate infrastructure for software testing. Technical report 7007.011, National Institute of Standards and Technology (2002). https://www.nist.gov/document/report02-3pdf

21. Thung, F., Wang, S., Lo, D., Jiang, L.: An empirical study of bugs in machine learning systems. In: Proceedings of the 23rd International Symposium on Software Reliability Engineering, pp. 271–280 (2012). https://doi.org/10.1109/ISSRE.2012.22

22. Wang, Y., Patil, H., Pereira, C., Lueck, G., Gupta, R., Neamtiu, I.: Drdebug: Deterministic replay based cyclic debugging with dynamic slicing. In: Proceedings of the Annual IEEE/ACM International Symposium on Code Generation and Optimization, pp. 98:98–98:108 (2014). https://doi.org/10.1145/2544137.2544152

23. Wong, W.E., Gao, R., Li, Y., Abreu, R., Wotawa, F.: A survey on software fault localization. IEEE Trans. Softw. Eng. **42**(8), 707–740 (2016). https://doi.org/10.1109/TSE.2016.2521368

24. Xie, X., Chen, T.Y., Kuo, F.C., Xu, B.: A theoretical analysis of the risk evaluation formulas for spectrum-based fault localization. ACM Trans. Softw. Eng. Methodol. **22**(4), 31:1–31:40 (2013). https://doi.org/10.1145/2522920.2522924

25. Xie, X., Kuo, F.-C., Chen, T.Y., Yoo, S., Harman, M.: Provably optimal and human-competitive results in SBSE for spectrum based fault localisation. In: Ruhe, G., Zhang, Y. (eds.) SSBSE 2013. LNCS, vol. 8084, pp. 224–238. Springer, Heidelberg (2013). https://doi.org/10.1007/978-3-642-39742-4_17
26. Xuan, J., Monperrus, M.: Learning to combine multiple ranking metrics for fault localization. In: Proceedings of the IEEE International Conference on Software Maintenance and Evolution, pp. 191–200 (2014). https://doi.org/10.1109/ICSME.2014.41
27. Xuan, J., Monperrus, M.: Test case purification for improving fault localization. In: Proceedings of the 22nd ACM SIGSOFT International Symposium on Foundations of Software Engineering, pp. 52–63 (2014). https://doi.org/10.1145/2635868.2635906
28. Yoo, S., Xie, X., Kuo, F.C., Chen, T.Y., Harman, M.: No pot of gold at the end of program spectrum rainbow: greatest risk evaluation formula does not exist. Technical report Research Note RN/14/14, University College London (2014). http://www.cs.ucl.ac.uk/fileadmin/UCL-CS/research/Research_Notes/rn-14-14_03.pdf
29. Zhang, M., Li, X., Zhang, L., Khurshid, S.: Boosting spectrum-based fault localization using PageRank. In: Proceedings of the 26th ACM SIGSOFT International Symposium on Software Testing and Analysis, pp. 261–272 (2017). https://doi.org/10.1145/3092703.3092731
30. Zhang, S., Zhang, C.: Software bug localization with Markov logic. In: Companion Proceedings of the 36th International Conference on Software Engineering, pp. 424–427 (2014). https://doi.org/10.1145/2591062.2591099

Correction to: Verifying System-Wide Properties of Industrial Component-Based Software

Thomas Neele, Marijn Rol, and Jan Friso Groote

Correction to:
Chapter "Verifying System-Wide Properties of Industrial Component-Based Software" in: H. Hojjat and M. Massink (Eds.): *Fundamentals of Software Engineering*, LNCS 11761, https://doi.org/10.1007/978-3-030-31517-7_11

In Definition 2 of the originally published version, the first equation and the second paragraph were missing and the block of 5 equations was not aligned correctly. This has been corrected.

The updated version of this chapter can be found at
https://doi.org/10.1007/978-3-030-31517-7_11

Author Index

Printed in the United States
By Bookmasters